Encyclopaedia of Indian Theatre - 3

KALIDASA

Encyclopaedia of Indian Theatre - 3

KALIDASA

Biswajit Sinha

Raj Publications
Delhi - 110009 (INDIA)

KALIDASA

First Published in 2002

ISBN 81-86208-18-6 (Series)
ISBN 81-86208-22-4

Published by : **Poonam Goel**
Raj Publications
R-115/2, Model Town - III,
Delhi - 110009
Tel. : 011-7143321
E Mail: rajpub@now-india.net.in

Laser Typesetting by : Aarati Computers, Delhi-110 009

Printed at : Chawla Offset Printers, Delhi-110 052

PRINTED IN INDIA

Contents

Preface

To quickly reconnoitre Indian Theatre in English, we have so far a single reference tool 'The Cambridge Guide to Asian Theatre.' This too covers about twenty countries of Asia and Oceania. To me, in all previous international sources 'World Theatre' meant 'Euro-American Theatre'. Therefore the above mentioned attempt is undeniably a very significant contribution in the direction to know what's what of Asia and Pacific theatre, the nations otherwise always relegated to the backwater collectively as the Third World. The Cambridge's slim volume devotees fifty three pages on India. Enough to have from the foreign soil. Nevertheless both for buffs and students-researchers, there is a real need for an independent encyclopaedia or similar guide to understand Indian Theatre in its depth and breath, the land whose theatrical tradition flourising from the days of 'Veda' is so diverse and powerful. This old heritage of humanity is in no way to be studied as a shadow of Western or Asian Theatre. The corpus is huge and to prepare a single source book in the realm exhaustively and meticulously is not an easy task. Realising the magnitude of the efforts, time and materials that involve, instead of bringing out an all encompassing volume, under the Series 'Encyclopaedia of Indian Theatre', came out my first volume on 'Bhasa', followed by second one that dealtwith thirteen great masters of Sanskrit drama.

Present volume (Series Three) is a definite guide to *Kalidasa*, the author of *Shakuntala* (*The Recovered Ring*), hailed as one of the masterpieces of World drama. Here is presented all pertinent informations about this classical playwright in the form of a comprehensive information package furnishing the date, time, legends surrounding the life of the author, an insight into his three great plays with synopsis, list of dramatis personae, time-analysis, plot and critical views. A pain staking chronicle of various productions of Kalidasa drama from the last half of the 19th century upto the end of the last millenium, enacted in India and abroad in original as well as in different Indian and foreign vernaculars are documented, enriched with still-visuals of the productions, portraits of the eminent directors and translators, sketches of costumes etc. Even Kalidasa epics in dramatic versions find inclusion in this work. In keeping with the time, i.e. in multimedia milieu and fusion of art genres, life and writings of Kalidasa as depicted in visual arts and Cinema is also added, Comprehensive bibliography of his work, both text and renderations are put together with ofcourse enumeration of bio-critical notices.

All the three independent volumes published so far under this series are biographical in nature.

I Yearn to bringout one more similar and few theme based theatre encyclopaedia's before embarking on either an all encompassing or fully interlinked reference tools on Theatre gestating in my mind in the form of "Visva Natya Kosha".

– Biswajit Sinha

PART- ONE

Introduction

In the reckoning of both East and West, Kalidasa is the greatest of Sanskrit poets. But this greatest dramatist and poet never hankered after popularity and remains tantalizingly silent about himself in all his work, whether plays and poems. Even one does not know precisely about his parent, age, locality or even date. M.R. Kale, therefore, rightly writes that we find on allusion, no incident mentioned, that may directly shed any light either on is personal history or any remarkable event of his life. In the words of Hazlitt 'he was the least of an egoist that it was possible to be'. His poetical productions alone stand on his surpassing poetic excellence. And we must content ourselves with gathering what little information we can about a poet of such world-wide repute from external sources, and a few incidents found here and there in his works, which may be supposed to have a distant bearing upon the history of his life.

Agnimitra, who was the hero of the drama 'Malavikagnimitra' was not a well known monarch to deserve special notice by Kalidasa. He belonged to the second century before Christ and his capital was Vidisa. Kalidasa's selection of this episode and his reference to Vidisa as the famous capital of a king in Meghaduta suggest that Kalidasa was a contemporary of Agnimitra. It is clear that Kalidasa flourished after Agnimitra (B.C.) and before A.D. 634 the date of the famous Aihole inscription which refers to Kalidasa as a great poet.

Another theory is called 'Gupta Theory' that tells us that as because the title Vikramaditya was assumed by Chandragupta after having defeated the Sakas in 395 A.D., Kalidasa must have lived in the period of Chandra Gupta II of Ujjaini (who ruled up to about A.D. 413).

The change in the name of the hero of 'Vikramorvasiyam' from Pururavas to Vikrama lends support to the view that Kalidasa belonged to the court of king Vikramaditya of Ujjayini. This evidence is regarded as positive in assigning Kalidasa to the first century B.C. Sir William Joines, Peterson, S.P. Pandit and M.R. Kale, etc. shares this view.

Fergueson is the exponent of 'Korur Theory' that states that the founder of the Vikrama era was Harsa Vikramaditya of Ujjaini, who defeated the Sakas in the battle of Korur in 544 A.D. and in commemoration of his victory, he not only started an era of his own but antedated it by 600 years in order to make it look ancient and respectable. But this theory has been exploded by the recent discovery of Mandosar inscription dated 472 A.D. Some of the above inscriptions are clearly an imitation of Kalidasa's Meghduta and Ritusamhara.

Another theory that Kalidasa used the word 'Yavana' in Raghuvamsa and the Yavana's are none other than Mahomedans who first came to India in the 7th century A.D. and therefore, Kalidasa must have flourished sometime there after. But it is now universally accepted that the word 'Yavana' was used in connection with the Greeks (Ionians) also.

M. Hippolyte Eauche hold the opinion that Kalidasa lived at the time of the Posthumous child of king Agnivarna, the last dynasty of the Raghu's described in the XIXth canto of Raghvamsa. This theory that the dramatist lived as early as 8th century B.C. comes from the idea that Kalidasa brought his description of the King from the Raghu family upto King Agnivarna's child, therefore he must have been a contemporary of Agnivarna. This theory has not earn much support from the scholars. The date of Kalidasa is therefore a subject of controversy. According to K.M. Pannikar, the playwright flourished during the reign of king Agnimitra (second century B.C.). According to Professors Lassen and Weber : second century A.D.; Max Muller and Dr. Bhandarkar put him in the sixth century. As said before Keith, Block, Pandit Ramavatara Sharma and Kokileswar Sastri etc. prefer the fourth century.

The age-long tradition, supported by internal and external evidence, associates the name of Kalidasa with that of the epoch making King Vikramaditya of Ujjayini - the founder of the Samvat era (57 B.C.). It is believed that Kalidasa was one of the 'nine jewels' (navaratna) of a certain king who had the epithet Vikramaditya. Thus it is presumed that Kalidasa received the royal patronage of

Chandragupta II and Kumaragupta I (415 - 455), and thus saw ancient Indian courtly culture at its Zenith, which is duly reflected in his poems and dramas. A critic has rightly observed that the art of naming a literary work on the model of the names of patrons finds an analogy with the naming of Spenser's Faery Queen, the title where of is supposed to allude to Queen Elizabeth, for, in the first three books of this work 'the shadowy Faery Queen sometimes represents the glory of God and sometimes Elizabeth, who was naturally flattered by the parallel.

If we collate the views of different scholars, Kalidasa may be placed between the second century B.C. and the fourth century A.D.

Kalidasa speaks very little of himself and thus, his native place. With profound interest and admiration, he describes the city of Ujjayini. He sings in praise of her beauty, the dread shrine of Shiva, Mahakala, of her rich gardens and lotus-lakes etc. All this makes us to believe that he must have been a native of that city.

Legend also, indentifies Kalidasa with Matrigupta, king of Kashmir, in north - west India.

We do not know much of him, but legend tells us that Kalidasa was not a born poet, but a born idiot. He was the son of a Brahmin who lost his parents in his childhood and was brought up by a shepherd. The king of his country had a beautiful daughter. The king's minister played a cruel joke on him and brought about a marriage between Kalidasa and the princess. But soon after the marriage, the cat of the ignorance of the bridegroom came out of the bug. The wise princess advised her husband to propitiate the Goddess Kali. He did so and was blessed by Kali. On returning home his wife enquired 'Is these any improvement in your speech? This query was answered by him in terms of his three great epics, viz, the Kumarasambhava, the Meghaduta and the Raghuvamsha. The Kumarasambhava begins with the work *'asti'* (in the line *astyuttarasyam dishi 'devatatma'*), the Meghduta opens with the word *'kascit'* (in the line *'kaschit kantaviraha - gurana'*) etc. Thus, he was an illiterate shepherd boy who was initiated into the art of poetic creation by the deity Kali. The name 'Kalidasa' implies that he was a devotee of Kali.

Another anecdote has it that Kālidasa considered that the princess was responsible for his good fortune and hence looked upon her as his guru and mother. The princess enraged at this cursed him that the woman whom he would love, would murder him. It is said that Kalidasa while in his sojourn to Ceylon to meet his friend King Kumardasa, stayed with a dancing girl and eventually fell in love. Kumaradasa, was also a poet. He wrote on the wall of a courtesan's room the beginning of a verse. "Kalidasa added the following :- "*Bale tava mukhambojat kathamindivaradvayam*". To secure the prize for herself, the dancing girl killed him and buried him and herself took the credit. Even today Kalidasa's last resting place is pointed out to travellers in Ceylon. But the king could detect the deception, for he was well acquainted with Kalidasa's art.

Kalidasa had self confidence. At one place he writes "It you have hearts which can melt in pity, do not set aside this canto of mine".

Again we see that his sense of assurance is not inconsistent with humility. He begins his Raghuvamsa with a confession of his rashness in undertaking the work. Where is the race originating from the Sun and where is my talent limited in scope? Through infatuation, I am desirous of crossing with a raft the ocean that is difficult to cross.

Kalidasa seems to have widely travelled, at least in Northern India. It is pertinent to mention here that Dr. Bhau Daji once commented that he is the only poet who describes a living saffron - flower, of the plant which grows in Kashmir. His graphic description of the Himalayan scenes looks very much like that of one who was an eye-witness.

Ryder says "Kalidasa moved among the jarring sects with sympathy for all, fanaticism for none". This is evident in his works, for if the Kumarasambhava is distinctly Shivaistic, the Raghuvamsa is no less distinctly Vishnuite in tendency; while Vedantic monism or Samkhya dualism, or the active devotion of Yoga engaged his regard. He was truly eclectic in his religion and philosophy.

Numerous legend that surrounds him clearly shows that unlike Bhavabhuti and some other poets, he was extremely popular in the land of his birth.

Ruben observes that as early as 473 the author of an inscription imitated Kalidạsa's verse; thus he must already have been famous at that time. He was mentioned as a famous poet in an inscription of 634, the author of which was especially impressed by "the line of Raghu". Kalidasa's works were transcribed again and again and thus spread gradually all over India. This shows how well loved they were, but had also the disadvantage that the texts became more and more inaccurate with each transcription.

In his book 'the age of Kalidasa', Sri Aurobindo comments "Kalidasa himself seems to have been a man gifted with all the learning of his age, rich aristocratic, moving wholly in high society, familiar with and fond of life in the most luxurious metropolis of his time, passionately attached to the Arts, acquainted with the Sciences, deep in law and learning, versed in the formalised philosophies. His business was like Shakespeare's to sing of the immediate past in terms of present. At the same time he occasionally informed the present with the hints of the future, like Shakespeare also he seems not to have cared deeply for religion. In creed he was Vedantist and in ceremony a Shaivait. In morals also he seems himself to have been destitute of the finer elements of morality.

The American poet Ryder appreciated Kalidasa as such "We know that Kalidasa was a great poet because the world has not been able to leave him alone".

It has aptly been stated that Kalidasa's beauties and merits are tarnished by any translation, but few who can rend him in the original would doubt that, both as poet and dramatist, he was one of the great men of the world.

Though a poet of the first rank, a critic states, Kalidasa's dramatic genius can hardly be minimised. His greatness as artist does, infact, rest much upon his rare creative genius which proved excellently capable of producing both poetry and drama which are to a great extent, respectively subjective and objective in nature. As a dramatist Kalidasa shows a gradual development in his art. Among his plays; Malavikagnimitra and Vikramorvasiyam, are definitely inferior to the last and the best, Abhijnana Sakuntala in charm and appeal. His fine diction and beautiful versification, the various dramatic devices used in his plays, and above all the stamp of originality on them, especially on the Abhijnana Sakuntala, are such factors as are never surpassed and rarely equalled. His genius reaches it zenith in Abhijnana Sakuntala, the appeal of which is universal even now. His other plays, however, have a popular appeal and show to a great degree skill as a successful dramatist.

Biswanath Bhattacharya aptly says the fact that Kalidasa is the greatest of the Sanskrit poets that helped him as a dramatist as well. The fine poetic elements of his play succeeds wonderfully in charming his audience and leading them to the delectable realisation of the inaffable joy which literature produces. So we can say that the real appeal of his dramas lies in the effective fusion of poetry and drama.

Malavikagnimitra appears to be first play composed by the dramatist as is apparent from the ways in which he has in the prologue tried to plead on behalf of the nava kavya (new poetry). The principle story of love and his wearing of sub-episodes are an imaginative creation of the poet. Kalidasa creates in this play a type of court comedy of royal love, in which harem jealousies and court intrigues mingle to raise romantic situations of love, amusing scenes of confrontation and a merry, light - hearted air which are thoroughly enjoyable.

One can not speak of a regional recension of the Malavikagnimitra. There is no special problem regarding it text. All the available manuscripts, be it of

Bhandarkar. Oriental Research Institute, Poona; Sanskrit College, Calcutta; the Raghunath Temple Library, Jammu; or the Tanjore Maharaja Serfoji Saraswati Mahal Library, Tanjore; each one of these represent, on the whole, one and the same recension, and All - India one. They may be in different scripts, such as the Devanagari and Bengali scripts and there are, of course, variant readings of a very large number of words, scattered throughout the text, as the foot-notes show, but unlike Abhijnana - Sakuntalam or Vikramorvasiyam, there is no such thing as more than one recension of the Malavikagnimitra.

What is remarkable about Malavikagnimitra is the this is the only play of Kalidasa in which the dramatic action occupies a period of about a week. This comfortness prove amply the great skill of the playwright.

About Malavikagnimitra, some critics opine that the unreality of the plot and the fact that the action is entirely manipulated by the Vidushaka reduce the interest of the play. It is, however, a pleasant comedy in so far as that type of Natika is concerned.

A scholar writes that his Malavikagnimitra is an amusing play wherein Kalidasa's skill in creating dramatic situations is beyong doubt. The quarrel of the dance masters leads to an amusing tension with the sensitivity of the older master Ganadasa, Dharini's desperate efforts to stop further developments, and the Vidushaka's hilarious provocations. Vidushaka Gautama proves to be a superb actor too in his pretence of snake - bite and a resourceful schemer. Malavika's dance performance and the Ashok - dohada scene have the charm of art, the lyrical element of love and poetry to produce an appropriate emotional impact. Kalidasa's fine dialogue, occasional poetry and the pervading wit and humour add to the play's entertaining value. It should not be surprising that the play created a model which succeeding dramatist like Sri Harshavardhana or Rajasekhara could not help imitating. From the point of view of humour, Malvikagnimitra is the best work of Kalidasa. In the words of Gayatri Verma, it is a mild satire about the follies and frailties of mankind. Some critic believe it to be a veiled satire on some royal family of his time, if not on Agnimitra himself. It is really a light hearted comedy of court life where the hero is perfectly carefree, feels lightly the royal responsibilities, uses his full ingenuity to achieve the love of his new beloved. While the war is going on, he is busy with amorous sports with his companion - the jester. The most interesting thing of this drama is that the whole play revolves upon the jester. He is more important figure even than the royal hero. So the comic spirit is from the beginning to the end. It is the jester who brings about the dancing test, so that the king may have a glimpse of his beloved Malavika. When the king was caught red handled in the pleasure garden, with his darling, it is the jester only who suggested a way out. When Malavika was confined in an under ground cellar, again he comes to her rescue and arranges a tryst of the lovers. Truly he is called '*Kamatantrasaciva*'.

Henry W. Wells says that in all probability 'Malavikagnimitra' was written for some special occasion at court during the spring festival. It is sophisticated entertainment, studiously light, airy, witty, and in no sense profound. As frequently observed, its effectiveness depends almost as much upon the dancing in its earlier scenes and the singing in its later as upon its glittering poetry or its slender plot, which combines the charms of Twelfth Night and A Midsummer - Night's Dream. The overheard conversations in the g arden remind a Westerner of comic opera, as in the central scenes of Cosi fan tutti, or the last act, of Figaro. We observe the ladies of court, or perhaps it would better be said of the harem at their recreation, enjoying swings or ball - playing, or the plucking and arranging of spring flowers. The slight plot is deliberately repellent to prosaic credibility. An almost tinkling gaiety, as in rococo dance, prevails through most of its scenes. The Jester plays a leading role; the girls are merely love - sick; and no one views the amarous woes of the king over seriously. The prevailing mood resembles that of an idyllic pastoral painting by Lancret, though, again Kalidasa enjoys the advantage of a singularly ripe culture.

On Malavikagnimitra, there are commentaries by Kataya Vema, Nilakantha, Viraraghava, Mrtyunjaya Nissanka, Tarkavacaspati, Srikantha, Parikshit Kunjunni Raja.

His second play 'Vikramorvasiyam' depicts in five acts the romantic tales of a mortal for a nymph, of which the earliest version is available in a hymn of eighteen stanzas in the tenth book of the Rigveda (95). This popular folk tale was adapted by Kalidasa into play that is much superior than his Malavikagnimitra, in terms of conception and execution of the drama.

To quote K.V.K. Sundaram "Bharata Muni's curse of Urvashi is the central feature of the play, but instead of taking a severe and savage form as in the Pauranas, it is humanised and transformed by Kalidasa's art into a tale of intense and true love. Since, forgetting her divinity, allegiance, and affiliations, Urvashi's mind turns at a crucial moment to a mortal because of the common human failing called love, it is but natural for the celestial dance - master to expect her from heaven. In the play, however Pururavas is not elevated to the level of a divinity and placed in the audience; nor is Urvashi said to have messed up all her abhinay (taught her by Bharata). Being with him in her innermost mind, she slips up on a single word. Instead of saying "Purushottama" - another name for Vishnu gives utterance to what is in her mind, "Pururavas".

References to the love of king Pururavas for Urvashi, the famous danceuse of Heaven can be found in the Rigveda X. 95 Puranas, Katha Sarit Sagara - (III 3) and Satapatha Brahmana, (V., 1-2). But the exact source of this play (Trotaka in five acts) of Kalidasa is difficult to ascertain. Biswanath Bhattacharya has rightly observed that Kalidasa has taken the kernel of the plot from any or all of these books, but has given altogether a new form to his play. He has charged, so to say, the 'la belle dame sans merci' of the Vedas and Puranas into a loving and loveable heroine. Even though the story may be weak, the characterisation of the poet is remarkable magnificent. Pururavas, Urvasi and the jealous queen, Ausinari are not mere shadows of Agnimitra, Malavika and Iravati or Dharini of his first play. Even the Vidusaka of this play differs from Malavikagnimitra. Here in the Vidusaka speaks always of his appetite and thereby causes laughter. This characteristic of the Vidusaka, it is to be noted, owes its origin to Kalidasa.

Kalidasa transformed the legend into a story of immortal love, endowing it with human emotions and motives G.K. Bhat notes that the play might does not attempt to change to supernatural into credibly natural or give it symbolic interpretation, but juxtaposes the supernatural against the natural. With Urvashi's visits to the earth the story moves continuously from heaven to earth and back again, savouring of the celestrial marvels and the compulsive realism of the earth. Kalidasa, however, leaves out the absurd elements of the legend and saves it from fantasy. Bhat further observes that is Act IV where Pururavas his wanders about in the forest in search of Urvashı, asking every bird and animal, cloud and river, mountain, earth creeper, about her whereabouts. He sings and dances. Even a number of Apabharamsha verses are sung off the stage. This scene is regarded as spurvious or a later addition is to ignore the demands of the stage techniques. Prolong pathos, repetitive inquiries, one character moving alone on the stage for more than half an hour are tiring for the actor and boring to the spectators. Drama is not along narrative or descriptive poem which can be read with chosen intervals or breaks. With a true dramatic instict Kalidasa turns this long - drawn pathetic scene into a musical ballet, and he makes a dexterous use of Praksit suitable for music as well as the lonesome state of the hero.

Another scholar also opines that the poetry of this famous soliloquy attains richness scarcely formed in any other scene of Sanskrit Drama. It strikes the very core and soul of Kalidasa's humane and poetic vision. Repugnant to prosaic reason, the soliloquy is a triumph of aesthetic intuition eloquent with the overtones of the dominant philosophy and religion of the East... The central scene in Vikramaorvasiyam is indelibly stamped with the signature of the Orient. Moreover, it reaches an exalted height of creative imagination.

R.S. Tiwari feels that 'Vikramorvasiyam' which is decidedly built on sambhoga shringara rasa has many features with Abhijana Shakuntalam. For instance, in both the plays the main protagonist is an emperior of men and friend to the gods. Each experiences the two phases of Vipralambha and achieves a blissful romantic union at the end of each phase. Furthermore, the love - union is aided and blessed by heavenly powers in Abhijana as well as Vikramaorvasiyam. In either of these plays, the protagonist is shown to experience the thrills of joy. One can find the similarity in poetic style too. But inspite of these strikingly similar features, both the plays are distinct for various reasons. One is a more standard form of nataka and other a trotaka. The different is also evident in their structural component.

Vikramorvasiyam, as Henry W. Wells put it, maya best be appreciated as a simplified version of Shakuntala, with both loss and gain in this comprehensive transition. In its formal aspects Shakuntala is the more romantic, Vikramorvasiyam the more classical, even through the characters in Shakuntala are more of the earth, in Vikramorvasiyam, more of the heavens. The latter is briefer and much closer to a pure or lyric poetry. The vivacity of threatrical action has been reduced but the basic force of the conception remains powerful. The lesser play rises to a climax in Act four. As in Shakuntala, the beginning is on a relatively modest plane, but here the force of the poetry does not mount towards a magnificent final. In this play the final act takes on more the aspect of a stageleau, or ritualized festival, than of a climax in drama. Father, mother and child are united and promised felicity together for the span of mortal life. The child is crowned heir to the kingdom; the celestial nymph told that on the occasion of her husband's death, still well removed in years, she will return to her place in heaven. The charm of the scene lies in its simplicity; if resembles the finale of Rama's Later history somewhat as chamber music resembles the symphony. S.K. Dey also holds the same opinion that though melodramatic in places and weak in its denoucement, the drama reaches lyrical heights in the description of the king's ardent but hopeless passion. There is hardly anything else remarkable in the drama but for this lyric passion of great intensity, which, however, makes it unique. Kalidasa seems to have concentrated more on characterize than on plot-construction as he has done in the Malavikagnimitra. The play standout, as stated before, Act IV where Agnimitra, the hero distracted by seperations gives vent to his feelings in short, pathetic lyrics. The unity of time is fully maintained in Vikramorvasiyam also. The dramatist introduced one or the other Intermediate scenes to indicate the passage of time and consequently the play that covers as period of about 12 & 1/2 years has got an integrated dramatic form. In Vikramorvasiyam, there are in all 75 stanzas in its fourth act of which 19 are in Maharashtri Prakrit dialect, 11 in Apabhramsha dialect, and 45 in Sanskrit. There has been controversy regarding some portions of the text. Since some manuscripts contained only the Sanskrit verses, doubt arose regarding the verses and songs in dialect. Were these stanzas composes by Kalidasa or being interpolated? It is important to mention here the opinion of H.D. Velankar who feels that the dramatist himself penned all the 30 verses and songs in dialect. The plot of the play is skilfully constructed. In every act the readers feel that they are on the verge of a catastrophe, but the playwright averts them very dramatically and therefore, what at first sight, looks a simple love story opens up so many complications which are still very natural 'Vikramorvasiyam' is in two recentions, in North India and South India. The Northern recension represented by Bengali and Nagari Manuscripts, and the Southern recension represented by most of the South Indian manuscripts. The former is commented upon by Ranganatha, who wrote his 'Vikramorvasiyam prakasika' in 1712 (Ca 1656 or 1790 A.D.) according as we take it to be the Samvat or the Shaka era, while the latter by Katayavema, the Minister of the Reddi Prince Kumaragiri of Kondavidu, and call his commentary after the name of his King and patron. In the Northern recension the play is called 'Vikramorvasi', and is spoken as a 'Trotaka'.

In the Southern recension, however, it is called 'Vikramorvasiya' and is designed as a 'Nataka'. C.R. Devadhar states that the Northern recensions shows a marked tendency towards amplyfying the matter contained in the Southern recension. This is the case especially with several prose passages with appear in a terse form in the Southern recension, while in the Northern we find them swollen and amplified by means of the addition of words whch scarcely improve the sense. In regard to metrical portions the Northern recension shows considerable deviations from the southern recension. Thus in the Northern recension we find four stanzas in excess of page appearing in the Southern recension. These are in :-

I (2.6)

I (5-4)

IV (29.5)

V (24)

Besides these four stray verses we find in the Northern recension in Act IV, thirty one stanzas in Maharashtri and Apabhramsha (six in Maharashtri, and twenty five in Apabhramsha) in various metres, as also directions in prose as to the way in which they are to be sung to the accompaniment of music and dance. In the Southern recension, however, we have nothing corresponding to these. Few noteworthy commentaries on Vikramorvasiyam are by : Katya Vema, Ranganatha, (Abhayacarana, Ramamaya) Taranatha, M.R. Kale.

Kavyeshu natakam ramyam tatra ramiya Sakuntala :- Their goes the saying that "The drama is the most enjoyable of all the literary forms, and of all the dramas the Shakuntala is the most enjoyable. Abhinanasakuntalam belongs to the nataka variety of drama and contains seven acts. Based on the legend of Sakuntala in the Adiparva of the Mahabharata, 'Abhijnana - Sakuntalam' is the most finished of Kalidasa's dramatic compositions as indicated by almost universal feeling of genuine admiration which it has always evoked. This magnum opus 'Abhijnanasakuntala' was probably written towards the end of his career. The last verse of the play, which is a prayer to Siva for release from rebirth, perhaps indicates this. Kalidasa made this dull narrative into a fine specimen of dramtaic art with a lot of innovations. While transforming the epic story into a drama, Kalidasa made some changes in it. The entire episode of the curse and the ring is fabricated by the playwright which is not even remotely mentioned in the Mahabharata. M.L. Varadpande rightly observes that this has given Kalidasa an opportunity to give a charming twist to the Mahabharata story and take the story still further. What is the source of Kalidasa's ring episode? According to S.N. Majumdar Shastri, Kalidasa is indebted to the Greek historian Herodotus (484 - 431 B.C.) who has narrated a near similar story in connection with Polycrates (B.C. 532), the king of Samos, one of the principal Islands of the Aegean sea off the coast of India.

One explanation is that he might have borrowed the idea from the Ramayana where Hanuman is show taking Rama's ring as a mark of recognition to Sita who was captivated and kept in the Ashoka grove by the Ravana, demon king of Ceylon.

One also refers to the Buddhist birth - story of the Kattahari Jataka as the source of Kalidasa's ring episode. The idea of the king's ring is very much there in the Jataka tale. Even the opening scene where Shakuntala is shown watering the trees alongwith her two friends, seems to have been inspired by the girl picking up fire wood in the garden while singing. In the original Mahabharata, there is no such scene. Again in Jataka, the idea of a miracle happening in the king's court is also there. However, in Kalidasa play, the miracle happens in the form of an apsara taking away Shakuntala to heaven after she is rejected by the king.

Another deviation from the epic and the Jataka story is that the ladies bring their sons to the court, but in the play of Kalidasa the son is born after this incident.

Some scholars hold the view that Kalidasa did not borrow the 'ring' episode from any source, but it is his own creation that gave the Mahabharata story a dramatic turn and helped Kalidasa to stretch the plot of the play further beyond Dushyanta's court. Kalidasa even delected the episode of Shakuntala extracting promise from her royal lover that their son will be the next king and also to remove the blemish of the king of not accepting Shakuntala on her arrival, he innovated the 'curse and ring' episode and thus made his hero and heroine of the play, the model of perfection. In this superb dramatic piece, the playwright has shown how love, polluted by the rashness of youth, became purified by a process of suffering and austerity, like gold purified by fire, and hence their reunion in the hermitage of Maricha was a matter of deeper conjugal love, where it did not depend on the outward glamour of physical beauty, and where even the rustic attire of the beloved undergoing austerities would not be a deterrent. The Abhijnana - Sakuntala of Kalidasa, which represents the perfection of his art is not based on the mere banality of a court - intrigue but gives us a picture of love, at first youthful and heedless, but soon purified by suffering and gaining in depth and beauty by tribulation of the spirit contrasted with the Malati - Madhava and Vikramorvasiya, the suffering of the hero and the heroine in this drama is far more human, far more real, for love here is no longer an explosive emotion, ending in a frame of mind akin to madess, but a deep and steadfast feeling for rather a developing emotional experience, ending in an abiding spiritual enrichment.

One may praise the critical acumen of A.A. Mcdonell for his comment on Kalidasa: 'The richness of creative fancy he display in these, and his skill in the expression of tender feeling, assign him a high place among the dramatists of the world. The harmony of the poetic sentiment is nowhere disturbed by anything violent or terrifying. Every passion is softened without being enfeebled. The ardour of love never goes beyond aesthetic bounds; it never maddens to wild jealousy or hate. The torements of sorrow are toned down to a profound and touching melancholy. It was here at last that the Indian genius found the law of moderation in poetry, which it hardly knew elsewhere and thus produced work of enduring beauty. Hence it was that Sakuntala exercised so great a fascination on the calm intellect of Goethe, who at the same time was so strongly repelled by the extravagances of Hindu mythological art'. Kalidasa was celebrated only as a supreme poet of beauty and enjoyment. It is only Rabindranath who took his readers to the inmost soul of his poetry, making manifest that it was the great poetry of a great poet, the Mahakavi.

In 'Prachin Sahitya' (Ancient Literature) are compiled some of Rabindranath's critical appreciations of some great works of Sanskrit literature. The compilation contains two pieces named respectively, 'Kumara Sambhava and Shakuntala' and 'Shakuntala'. In the latter Rabindranath devotees a part to a discourse on what he calls the external similarity and the intrinsic difference between the Tempest and its heroine, Miranda, and Abhijnana - Sakuntalam and its heroine Sakuntala.

Rabindranath Tagore

Rabindranath Tagore, in his devoted essay, therefore tried to bring out, "the inner meaning" of the play by describing it as an allegory in which the fibers of physical passion are toughened by pain and separation into a deep, domestic, semi spiritual love. The play is, of course, concerned chiefly with exploring the range of sringara rasa, but Tagore's zealously argued point is illuminating in another way : it reminds us and that needs constant reminding that Kalidasa, in writing Shakuntala was also summing up, unconsciously, an entire drama, a code of human values. Atul Chandra Gupta observes: ...... The first flush of joyous delight and desire in young love has been painted by Kalidasa in intensely beautiful poetry, both in Sakuntala and in Kumarasambhavam. But he has gone on to show in both that this béauty is ephemeral and is not to be, trusted. For full consummation this love requires the penance of pain and a second and maturer love, as it were, between the lovers. This second love on the real fulfillment of the first Kalidasa has painted both in Sakuntala and Kumarasambhavam. In Rabindranath's words : 'Kalidasa has not refused to recognise the hurricane strength of this first love which smashes every barrier in its way, but has not exhausted the tribute of his poetry in celebration of its victory'. Rabindranath took this saying of Goethe as the text for his discourse and intensely fragile, perfecting itself into the second love, unbreakable as steel, and captivating in its innate beauty, not requiring any elaborate device of poetry. According to Rabindranath, Goethe's verse points to this apotheoses of love, which Rabindranath's criticism shows as the inner core both of Sakuntala and of Kumarasambhavam : an apotheoses by which the divine does not cease to be human, for then he would become the subject not of poetry not of theology. The human develops into the devine and yet remains human.

Characterisation of Kalidasa deserves high appreciation. Nowhere his characters appear as the spokesmen of the dramatist. on the contrary, all his characters exhibit individuality of their own. The greatest proof of this success is the fact that the drama of Kalidasa has superseded its original in the Mahabharata in sheer beauty and charm. Dusyanta, as presented by Kalidasa, has become the real Dusyanta after being shorn off the hard - heartedness which stains the character of his original in the Epic.... He presents Kavya not while performing a Yajna ceremony, nor even engaged in teaching or penance but as a loving father with a noble character, thus making him also universally appealing.

T.G. Mainkar has observed that in the play, the forest girl of the epic is transformed into a child of nature with rare grace and delicacy, Kalidasa presents Sakuntala as child of nature, innocence incarnate. The nature plays a pivotal role in the play. While Kanva (Kashyapa) was the foster father of Sakuntala, nature was her foster mother. Her love for Sakuntala was natural, but her presence was as ethereal as that of the deceased mother of Christabel in Coleridge's celebrated poem of the same name, writes a literary critic. He presents the king as a dignified monach with decorum, humility and a regard for all that is sacred. He has no heir and this makes his love for the woodland girl more acceptable than Agnimitra's love.

C.R. Devadhar points out that in the play the dramatist has added to the meagre number of characters in the Mahabharata tale very largely from the grove, the city and the heavenly regions. It is remarkable that with great insight Kalidasa gives but little part to the conventional Vidusaka in this play than in the others; he has absolutely very little place in so serious a play.

In the first three acts, the erotic (Sringara) rasa dominates followed by pathetic (Karuna) in next three acts, and the quiescent (Savita) in the last act. But as the play progress, one may notice the other mutually - connected rasas. That appears and disappears.

In the introductory pages of the text brought out by Haridas Granthamala Series given us a clear account of the rasas employed by Kalidasa. Abhijnana is a nataka based on the shringara rasa. Its agni rasa (main aesthetic emotion) is shringara and its subsidiary rasas are the humorous, the terrible and the filial. A number of subsidiary Bhavas, too, are experienced in the play. Because of the greater speed in it of Vipralambha shringara, some hold it be the main rasa. This, however, appears to be incorrect. A nataka in Sanskrit does not end in sorrow; it always implies a joyous ending. Moreover Act II anndn VII of Sakuntala are built on Sambhoga Shringara. Vipralambha naturally precedes (the union) in natakas of Shringara rasa. The Sambhoga which is found dominant at the Conclusion of the drama should be identified as its principal rasa... At the end of Act VII the promise of permanent union of the hero and the heroine registers the final dramatic impact on the mid of the spectators. Hence, this should be accepted as a nataka of Sambhoga Shringara. A critic interprets the play within the requirements of Hindu metaphysical theory, suggesting that it has a circular development of theme beginning with santa (the peaceful hermitage in Act I), developing into sringara (love seen as rajas, the quality of passion seeking fulfillment, in Acts II - III), moving further into karma (repudiation, seen as tamas, the quality of dark, tragic passion in Act IV - VI, and finally santa once more (in the reunion scene, the quality of sattva in Act VII).

There are various local versions of the drama of "Sakuntala", for the innumerable handwritings in which this popular work was written can be classified according to origin and writing style into four groups - a Kashmiri, a Central Indian (in Nagari alphabet), a Bengali and a South Indian. The Bengali version contains the largest number of verses, the principal feature of the Central Indian version is the considerable abbreviation of the love scene in Act III, the South Indian version is said to contain some falsifications. It is important that in the case of the great popular epics one comes upon very similar local handwriting groups. A closer investigation of such conditions may reveal that the local versions can actually be called national, for as the Bengali and Punjabi nations etc. developed during the last thousand years, the languages along with their written forms have also developed into national languages, and these honourable old tests were handed down in the old language - in Sanskrit and in the Prakrits - but nevertheless in the local i.e. national versions.

The first text of the Sakuntala to be published was the Bengali. Pischel supported this recension in his papers and brought out a critical edition of it. First edition, Keil 1877. The second edition appeared in the Harvard Oriental Series, 16, 1922 with Capeller's Preface. Buhler brought to light the Kashmiri text in his Detailed Report on the search for manuscripts in Kashmir (1877, PPL XXV-C), and this Kashmiri text was reproduced in Roman script by Burkhard in 1884. The Devanagari version was edited by Bohtlingk in 1846 (Bonn), then by Monier - Williams in 1853. The second edition appeared in 1876 (Oxford), after consulting more manuscripts, and then by P.N. Patankar in 1902. Its second edition appeared from Poona. Patankar gave what he called the purer Devanagari text. It is the Devanagari text which is commented upon by the well-known scholar Raghavabhatta. The South Indian text, which is close to the previous, is familiar to us in editions with the gross of abhirama, Katayavema and others. A well known Indian edition which discusses in detail all the controversial passages in the different recensions is the one by S.R. Ray. Its 6th edition appear in 1908 from Calcutta. This is necessarily an eclectic edition.

Based on Maithili manuscripts, the Mithila Institute, Darbhanga brought out a new edition under the editorship of Ramanath Jha, with the commentaries of Sankara and Narahari in 1957. Its claim to be a fifth recension (Maithili recension) is not justified by fact and the text belongs to the Bengali. Kashmiri family Devadhar observes that in the erotic passages in Act III in the Bengali recensions are out of taste and mar the delicacy of the love - scene and as Weber points out, some of the Devanagari readings are distinctly better, and some of the Bengali stanzas are mere repetitions of others found in both the versions. So, sometimes priority is being given to the Devanagari text. However, nothing conclusive can be said regard to which of these recensions gives Kalidas's text correctly, in short we can say that usually two recensions are taken into account, the longer one being the Bengali, with 221 stanzas with the commentaries of Sankara and Chandrasekhara and the Devanagari with 194 stanzas with Raghavabhatta's commentary, the Kashmiri gives an introductory scene to act VII, but is no more than a combined version of these two, while the South Indian with the commentary of Katayavema closely follows the Devanagari.

Mukund Madhav Sharma says that longer Bengali recension is characterised by the preponderance of erotic elements. Hence, the shorter Devanagari recension is recognised as the genuine one. Latin and English renderings of the

Bengali recension by Sir William Jones done in 1788 immediately made Shakuntala an object of admiration for western scholars like Goethe and Herder Subsequent translations of Shakuntala into various languages of the world make a legion.

Shakuntala has a very special place in Western appreciation of Sanskrit literature. It was one of the first Sanskrit works ever to be translated into English - in 1789, only five years after Charles Wilkin's pioneering translation of the Bhagavad Gita. The translation was by the brilliant orientalist Sir William Jones. When the book was published, it caused a great stir. It went into five edition within twenty years, and was in turn translated into other European languages - into German in 1791, and Schuyler in his 'Bibliography of the Sanskrit drama', appeared in 1906 recorded twelve translations of 'Abhijnanasakuntalam' into English, six into French, eighteen into German, two into Dutch, two into Swedish, two into Danish, one into Icelandic, four into Italian, one into Spanish, three into Russian, one into Polish, one into Hungarian and one into Bohemian and several translations into various Indian languages.

In his introduction to the play, Jones describes how after his arrival in Bengal (as a judge of the Supreme Court) he investigated reports of a type of book called natac (i.e. nataka), supposedly consisting of historical records. But on enquiry he was assured by Brahmins that these works in fact abounded with fables, and 'consisted of conversations in prose and verse, held before ancient Rajas in their public assemblies, on an infinite variety of subjects, and in various dialects of India'. Jones was still at a loss, until 'a very sensible Brahman' told him that the English presented similar compositions at Calcutta in the cold season under the name of 'plays'. Equally surprised and delighted, Jones ascertained that the most universally esteemed play was Sakuntala, and set about studying it with the aid of a pandit. He made a word - for - word translation, and then 'disengaged it from the stiffness of a foreign idiom'. The result is a very fine example of muscular eighteenth - century English, though sadly too full of misunderstandings of the original to be more than historical interest today.

When he asked which Sanskrit play was most admired Jones had quoted to him a verse which said :

Of literary forms drama is the most pleasing,

And of dramas 'Sakuntala',

And in 'Sakuntala' the Fourth Act,

And in that Act four verses.

Johann Volfgang Goethe (1749-1832)

Goethe says Shakuntala blends together the young year's blossoms and the fruits of its decline, that it combines heaven and earth in one. Tagore remarks that the Shakuntala according to Goethe. "Contains the history of a development - the development of flower into fruit, of earth into heaven, of matter into spirit". The drama was meant for translating the whole subject from one world to another - to elevate love from the sphere of physical beauty to the eternal heaven of moral beauty. One sudden gust of youthful impulse had in a moment given her up to Dusyanta, but that was not the true the full winning of her; the best means of winning is by devotion, by Tapasya. Therefore, the poet has made the two lovers undergo a long and austere tapasya that they may gain each other truly, eternally".

In this drama Kalidasa has extinguished the volacanic fire of tumultuous passion by means of the tears of the penitent heart.

Georg Forster, produced his German prose translation of Jones' English version of "Shakuntala" in 1791. The work had a considerable impact on German middle class society. Forster sent a copy to Goethe, who was so enthusiastic about the drama that he sang its praises in two couplets :

If in one word of blooms of early and fruits of riper years,

Of excitement and enchantment should tell,

Of fulfillment and content, of heaven and Earth;

Then will I but say "Sakuntala" and have said all.

Goethe had the lines printed in the "Deutsche Monatsschrift" (German monthly Journal) as early as 1791, and in the following year Herder, who was also living in Weimar at that time, set them at the head of his article "On the Eastern Drama". He mentioned Shakuntala again in 1798 : "since Shakuntala is unfortunately still the only example of her (India's) perfected culture, one lingers with pleasure over it. We must have more Sakuntala's in the near future, for they are the finest contributions to the cultural history of the peoples". And yet several years later old Goethe wrote Chezy the French editor of the Sanskrit text of the Sakuntala :-

"When for the first time I became aware of this work of unfathomable depth, I was filled with great enthusiasm and it attracted me in such a manner that even at the time when I had hardly finished its reading, it goaded me towards the impossible undertaking of adapting it, even approachingly, for the German theatre.... I am still carrying the ineffaceable impression that this book made in me so early. Here the poet seems to be at the height of his talents in representing of the natural order, of the finest mode of life, of the purest moral endeavour, of the most worthy sovereign and of the most sober divine meditation, still he remains in such a manner the lord and master of his creation. The fact that he has worked upon common and comical contrasts, must be considered as the necessary connecting link of the entire organisation.

Schiller too wrote to W.V. Humboldt, "that there is no poetical presentation of woman hood or of more beautiful a life in the whole of Greek antiquity, that might reach the Sakuntala even from a distance".

Ruben in his 'Kalidasa; the human meaning of his work' mentions about the publication of Heinrich Heine's posthumous works of 1869 that brought to light that.

Hiene had noticed something very important about German drama. In the chapter entitled, 'Thoughts and Ideas' he wrote : Goethe made use of Sakuntala at the beginning of Faust; here he means that Goethe conceived the idea of the, "Vorspiel auf dem Theater" in Faust from prologue to "Sakuntala". Ruben further writes in "Sakuntala" an actor appears first on the stage and speaks a prayer to

Siva, for Indian drama is deeply rooted in the religious ceremony which used to fill several hours of the day and night. Then the stage director comes on, calls the leading actress and informs her that Kalidasa's drama "Sakuntala", is to be performed before a cultured audience, so that the actors must do their utmost.

"Madam, I tell you plainly that I value our theatrical talent only in so far as an enlightened audience derives pleasure from it. But I am filled with doubts of my own powers, however great my efforts". The stage director then calls on the leading actress to sing a strophe in praise of the prevailing summer season, and the play can beigin.

Goethe's prologue takes the following course : the director comes out on the stage with the theatre poet and the comedian and asks both for their help. He is embarrassed, for his public is frighteningly well read. The poet refuses at first to hear anything of the people and thinks only of posterity. The comedian will hear nothing of posterity and wants only to amuse contemporaries. The director wants to produce an impressive spectacle.

"Plunge into the fullness of life", the comedian advises the poet; "everybody lives it, but few know it. And wherever you seize upon it, it is interesting". The poet speaks of "the urge towards truth and the joy of deceiving". The three thus discourse on the deepest problems of art in witty dialogue, quite unlike Kalidasa, who has only followed the old Indian custom in composing a short prologue which introduces the audience to the poet and the title of the play, since there were no theatre programmes. He takes this opportunity to flatter his audience, which was not composed of a crowd of people looking for entertainment, night after night, in professional theatres, as they were accustomed to do in Goethe's Weimar, but of a small group of gentlemen, nobles and Brahmans, higher officials, perhaps a few wealthy merchants, who gathered on some festive occasion in a comparatively small theatre or hall at the king;s court to be entertained. The mass of the people did not even understannd the language of the play - Sanskrit. Thus the two prologues are very different, indicating two different kinds of society, each with different expectations of the theatre. But we have to thank the Indian poet for inspiring Goethe to this gem of his art.

There are several commentaries on Abhijnanashakuntalam, some of these are by : Raghava, Katayavema, Srinivasa, Ghanasyama, Abhirama (Krisnanatha Pancanana, Chandrasekhara, Narayana, Ramabhadra, Sankara) Premacandra, D.V. Pant, Vidyasagara, Venkatacarya, Sri Krisnanatha, Bala govinda, Daksinavartanatha, Ramavarman and Rama Pisharoti and five anonyomous.

Besides three dramas, his undisputed literary output comprises of two 'Mahakavyas, is secondary epics or long pomes; the Raghuvamsha (Dynasty of Raghu) and the Kumarasambhava (Birth of Kumara, i.e. Karttikeya); two 'Khandakavyas', is shorter poems : the Meghaduta (cloud - messenger) and the Ritusamhara (Cluster of seasons).

Raghuvamsa, an epic poem of nineteen cantos describing the lives of the kings of the solar race; Kumarasambhava, also an epic poem of seventeen cantos concerned withthe marriage of Siva and Parvati and the birth of Kumara, the lord of war; Meghaduta, a poem of 111 stanzas describes the message of a Yaksa to his wife, to be conveyed through a cloud; Ritu - samhara is a descriptive account of the six seasons.

Many a love poem like Ghatakarpara, Puspabanavilasa and Nalodaya (the Yamaka Kavya in four cantos based on the Mahabharata episode of Nala and Damayanti) and many a devotional stotra such as 'Symaladandaka are ascribed to Kalidasa by a very unreliable tradition.

Kalidasa is the great, the supreme poet of the senses, of aesthetic beauty, of sensuous emotion. His main achievement is to have taken every poetic element, all great poetical forms, and subdued them to a harmony of artistic perfection set in the key of sensuous beauty. In continuous gift seizing an object and creating it to the eye he has no rival in literature. A strong visualizing faculty such as the greatest poets have in their most inspired descriptive movements, was with Kalidasa an abiding and unfailing power, and the concrete presentation which this definitene of vision demanded, suffused with an intimate and sovran feeling for all sensuous beauty of colour and form, constitutes the characteristic Kalidasa's manner. He is besides a consummate artist, profound in conception and suave in execution, a master of sound and language who has moulded for himself out of the infinite possibilities of the Sanskrit tongue a verse and diction which are absolutely the grandest, most puissant and most full voiced of any human speech, a language of the Gods. The great commentator Mallinatha commented "The beauty of Kalidasa's kavya has been understood by only three persons - the creator Brahma, the goddess of speech Saraswati and Kalidasa himself. How an humble person like me delve deeply in the beauty of his kavya". Kalidasa has received encomiums from writers and critics al over the world for the richness of his aesthetic sensibility, intensity of lyrical emotion, communion with nature, and his reconciling the earth and heaven, sensually and spiritually, fate and free will etc. in a vision of cosmic harmony, which happens to be the very cream of Indian culture.

1

Plays of Kalidasa

1. MALAVIKAGNIMITRA

Synopsis :-

Probably this is Kalidasa's earliest play, a comedy of harem intrigue that deals with the love of king of Agnimitra, the king Vidisha for Malavika, the younger sister of the king of Malava,, who took shelter in the palace of Agnimitra himself in guise of a girl student of one of the two royal dance - teachers named Ganadasa and Haradatta. From a painting portraying the harem inmates, the King Agnimitra learns about Malavika an unkknown beautiful girl who has taken refuge in the royal harem and is very proficient in the field of music and dance. The King is captivated by her exquisite beauty and desires to see her. Gautama, the jester of the king makes a plan. It is due to his ingenuity, skill and ability that enables Agnimitra to meet Malavika. The two dance teachers are shown challenging each other's superiority in the art of dancing. The king is approached for a verdict at the instigation of the jester. As Ganadasa is queen Dharini's man, the king refuses to act as a judge for fear of being called partial and Kausiki, a Buddhist nun, as an arbitrator.

Kausiki suggests that the test should be based not of their knowledge of the art of dancing of the two contestants but rather of their ability to impart the knowledge to their pupils. Thus a test is being held.

Agnimitra gets an opportunity to observe Malavika's dancing skill and beauty from close quarters and he fells in love with her. After this incident, Agnimitra again requests his jester friend to arrange a meeting with Malavika

Queen Dharini had a favourite golden Asoka tree which had not blossomed. Cleverly the jester makes Dharini fall from a swing and hurt her foot. Eventually Dharini deputes Malavika to the 'Pramodavana' to fulfill her longing (for flowers) of the Ashoka. According to the custom, Malavika was to kick the tree gently with her left foot and if it blossomed in five nights, Dharini promises to grant her wish.

The love-sick King enters the Pramodavana with Gautama at the invitation of another queen Iravati for swing riding. Gautama informs the king that he has taken into confidence Bakulvalika, friend of Malavika who has promised help.

Here Malavika is seen with Bakulvalika, who decorates Malavika's foot with royal ornaments to make her ready for the ritual in order to make the Asoka tree blossom within the stipulated period.

Interestingly Iravati has also reached the spot. Both the pairs, King and Gautama, the jester on the one hand and Iravati and her maid on the other, watch this from two different hiding places.

Bakulavalika inflames Malavika's love for Agnimitra. The King can not resist himself and appears on scene to express his feeling. But Iravati who was witnessing King's overtures of love also comes out. The king tries to appease her, but she leaves in terrible anger and goes to complain Dharini, the senior queen. As a consequence, Malavika and her companion maid are confined in the cellar of Samudragriha. Now Gautama makes another plan to set Malavika and her companion free. To secure their release Gautama will have to show the queen's ring to the female prison guard. So he pretends that he was bitten by a serpent while picking flowers to visit the ailing Dharini. The royal physician was asked to say that a mantra - rite would be necessary to remove the poison, for which he wanted an effigy of a serpent.

To save herself from the inevitable curse (as a result of an indirect cause of a Brahmin's death) Dharini readily gives her signet ring which bears the mark of a serpent.

Within five days of the dohaba, the golden Ashoka tree puts forth blossoms in abundance. The queen makes up her mind that the suitable present she has promised Malavika is her own husband. The news comes that king's mighty forces has bent his enemy down. In the garden where the queen was to make the presentation, the chamberlain brings two young maids from Vidarbha forming part of the rich tribute sent by the country's defeated king. The queen turns to

Malavika to select one of them as her music assistant. Seeing Malavika, the maids cry out and it is revealed that Malavika is none other than Madhavasena's sister, the Vidarbha princes and Parivrajika was the sister of Madhavasena's minister. Both had escaped during the war, but caught by maranders, but escaped again and separately found refuge in Agnimitra's harem. With this revelation, Dharini personally offers Malavika's hand to Agnimitra and the play ends with a happy note.

Dramatic personae

AGNIMITRA	King of Vidisha
VAHATAKA	A minister
GAUTAMA	The king's jester and companion
HARADATTA	Dance master, protege of the king
GANADASA	Dance master, protege of the queen
MAUDGALYA	Chamberlain of the inner apartments
SARASIKA	A hunch-back, attendant of the queen
DHARINI	Queen of Vidisha
IRAVATI	King's second wife
MALAVIKA	Princess of Vidarbha
PANDITAKAUSHIKI	Buddhist nun
BAKULAVALIKA	The queen's maid
KAUMUDIKA	Another maid of the queen
SAMAHITIKA	A maid servant of Panditakaushiki
MADHUKARIKA	A gardener
NIPUNIKA	Iravati's maid
NAGARIKA	Another maid of Iravati's
JAYASENA	An attendant
JYOTSNIKA	A maid from Vidarbha
RAJANIKA	Another maid from Vidarbha.

Scene and Time of Action

The action takes place in Vidisha in different parts of the king's palace.

The time of the play is a few years before 150 B.C.

Time Analysis

Act I & II	...	Part of one day
		(Interval, hardly more than a day)
Act III	...	Part of one day
		(Interval, slight, if any)
Act IV	...	Part of one day
Act V	...	The next day

PLOT

Prologue : After the invocation, the stage manager tells his assistant that the spectators has asked them to present the play entitled 'Malavikagnimitra' at that spring festival. But the assistant in utter surprise, enquires how the spectators could neglect the works of such great authors like Bhasa, Saumilla and Kaviputra. The assistant further adds that how can the spectators feel any respect for a budding modern poet a Kalidasa?

The stage manager answers that he is misled and says that :

Not all is good that bears an ancient name,

Nor need we every modern poem blame.

Wise men approve the good, or new or old;

The foolish critic follows where he is told.

By saying this he bids him make haste and assist him to carry out the task entrusted to them by the spectators.

Act One :-

After the usual prologue, the maid Bakulavalika enters with another maid Kaumudika. They tells us that Agnimitra, the king in Vidisha had been in the palace picture galery where he saw a new painting of Queen Dharini with her retinue. One of these maids named Malavika is so graceful that the king has developed a great longing for her. But he is prevented by the jealous queen from viewing the original. At this moment, the dancing master Ganadasa emerges. He informs Bakulavalika that Malavika is an intelligent and proficient discipline and from Bakulavalika, on enquiring he comes to know that Malavika has been sent as a present to Queen Dharini by Vira Sena a general commandry, in command of a border fortress, also the queen's brother of inferior caste.

After this prelude, the main act commences with the King's entrance. He listens to a letter sent by the king of Vidarbha. The latter had kept in captivity a prince Madhavasena, his sister, princess and cousins of Agnimitra and in response to Agnimitra's demand to the rival monarch to set them free, he replies that the princess has escaped, but the prince shall be liberated only on the condition that he set at liberty his brother - in - law, the Maurya minister. The infurious Agnimitra at once sends his troops to fight against the Vidarbha king under the command of Virasena.

To divert King's mind, the jester Gauṭama tells him that he has worked out a scheme for bringing Malavika in front of the King. He has stirred an envious rivalry between the two dancing masters.

These masters soon emerges, each abusing the other vigorously and claiming their supremacy in their domain of arts. Finally it is decided that each shall exhibit his best disciple before the King. Queen Dharini, and the learned Buddhist nun, Kaushiki. The nun, who is in the secret of the King's desire, is made mistress of ceremonies and the Queen's jealous is overborne.

Act Two :-

The scene shifts to the concert hall of the palace. The nun Kausiki declares that Ganadasa should present his student first. Malavika appears on the stage. She is being introduced and then begins her dance and also sings a song where she expresses her love for the king. The King in turn captivated by her unparalled beauty even than the painting.

The jester very cleverly manages to detain her some time by indulging in a discussion as to her skills and tells that he has found a serious flow in her performance.

Finally, when she is allowed to leave, both she and the King are deeply in love. The court poet proclaims the noon hour and the performance of the other dancing master is postponed. In this act, we are first acquainted with the dancing skills of the two masters. Yet Ganadasa has an edge over his rival on account of the some strikingly admirable qualities of his student, Malavika. The king is now languising because of love with her but in order to spare the feelings of Dharini, he makes no use of his power to behold the object of his desire.

Act Three :-

Venue of this act is the palace garden called 'Pramadavana' In the prelude, from the short deliberations of the two maids, we are also told that a favourite Ashoka - tree is late in blossoming. As the myth goes that if touched by the foot of a damsel in splendid garb, such trees can be burst into blossom.

Main scene begins with the maids departure. The King enters with his jester friend. The former describes him of his love lorn conditions. The jester listens to him and then asks him to possess his soul in patience because as a matter of fact he has confirmed an expedient for the ensuring. The end that he wished to attain. He further reminds the King of his consent to meet the young Queen Iravati in the garden and swing with her.

At this moment arrives Malavika, who was deputed by Dharini to touch the Ashoka - tree with her foot to make the tree blossom, for the Queen herself is injured due to Gautama's carelessness. She has had a fall from a swing and thus, unable to perform the ceremony herself. Both the King and his jester conceals themselves behind a thicket to have a glimpse of Malavika.

The maid Bakulavalika follows to adorn Malavika for the ceremony. The latter engages her in conversation about the King.

Incidently a third pair emerges in the scene. Queen Iravati, somewhat flushed with wine comes with her maid Nipunika. To spy upon the young girls, they also hide themselves.

Here both the King and the jester are aware of the two girls, as well the queen and her maid. But these two pairs are absolutely unaware of the presence of the other. Therefore, Malavika freely expresses her longing for the King and Bakulavalika tells her how the King is madly in love for her.

As the scene progresses, the King comes out to express his desire for Malavika.

Suddenly Queen Iravati, who is envious, badly rebukes the King and immediately sends the two girls away. In vain, the king tries to appease the angry Queen by telling that any man may be caught in such a predicament. The Queen utters words of jealousy and leaves him in frustration to inform Dharini of the whole episode.

Act Four :-

The jester informs Agnimitra that Queen Dharini has kept Malavika and her friend in the cellar and has given strict instructions to the door keeper that they shall be let out only on the presentation of her own signet - ring bearing the mark of a serpent. But he tells the King that he has contrived a plan to release them. At his instances, the King goes to meet the Queen to inquire how she is doing, when the jester rushes into their presence. He pretends as if he has been bitten by a cobra and shows his thumb marked with two scratches of the teeth. He begs the King to take care of his ill fated mother. The Queen who witnesses all these, become sympathetic and atonce parts with her serpent - ring, supposed to have a magical effect on such snake bite that heals the wound. Subsequently the jester uses the ring to procure the freedom of Malavika and her friend. He then leads the them to the summer - house, where Malavika meets her lover Agnimitra. This is followed by a love scene that is once again interrupted by Queen Iravati. But luckily the King is saved this time from further embarassment, when the news comes that his little daughter named Vasulaksmi has been terribly frightened by a monkey and will be comforted only by the father. The act closes with the proclamation that even before the fire nights have elapsed from the time of the ceremony performed by Malavika, the Ashoka - tree has fully blossomed.

Act Five :-

Now the queen Dharini herself wishes that the king should meet her lady love Malavika under the Asoka tree which is now covered all over with blossoms. The maids brings the happy news that the avenging army of the king have defeated the Vidarbha king. The king and the jester now goes to the garden where they find the queen and her retinues that includes Malavika waiting for their arrival.

At this juncture, the chamberlain brings the message from the minister the present sent by the king of Vidarbha comprises two maids having remarkable qualities, who could not be introduced so far because of their fatigue as a result of long journey.

Now they are brought before the group gathered under the tree. These two maids surprise everyone, when they fall on their faces before Malavika with the exclamation, 'our princess'. The king learns that Malavika was the younger sister of Prince Madhavasena and now the Buddhist nun tells how her brother Sumati, the councellor of the captive prince had saved her and Malavika from the clutches of Vidarbha king and had started for Agnimitra's court. But they were attacked by robbers on the way, her brother was killed and she herself got separated from

Malavika and became nun. Then she made her way to Agnimitra's court and here, she found Malavika, again. She adds that she did not divulge the matter because of a prophecy that Malavika would have to endure for one year only the position of maid before she becomes a king's bride. Meanwhile, another happy news comes that his son by Dharini called Vasumitra, who was appointed as the defender of the sacrificial horse let loose by Puspamitra,his grand father, has won a victory over a force of Greek Cavalary and inviting the Court (through the letter of Puspamitra) to be present at the sacrifice which was to follow the victory. The joyous queen Dharini sends an attendant to ladies of the harem to carry the message of her son's triumph and at the same time, to communicate Iravati of the promise she had made to Malavika when she deputed her to perform the ceremony of fertilizing the Asoka tree.

But the jealous queen gives her consent, in somewhat ungraciously, now offers Malavika to the king. The play ends with the happy note that the king may ever retain his queen's regard and that his citizen may never meet any calamity as long as Agnimitra is the king.

2. VIKRAMORVASIYAM

Synopsis :-

The play is considered a Trotaka, as it depicts the love between Pururavas, a mortal king and Urvasi, a semi-divine nymph of exquisite beauty who. This daring king saves the heroine who belongs to the race of the apsaras (Celestial Dancers) while she was being abducted by the demon Kesi and gratitude results in fascination of the Urvasi for the king, who reciprocates with great ardour. From the heavens Urvasi comes down to the earth to meet her lover on some moonlinights. Indra, realizing her affection, permits her to live with her mortal lover till she bears him a son.

While travelling int he Gandhamadana Hills, an angry Urvasi enters a curse, but still retained her inner consciousness and thus witnessing kings single - minded love for her. The grief-stricken king starts searching Urvasi, madly inquiring after her from the birds and beasts. This lamentations continues till he finds a stone called Samgamaniya that leads to their happy reunion Urvasi reappears as soon as Pururavas embraces the creeper.

The plays closes with Indra's withdrawal of the condition that Urvasi should go back to the heavens on seeing the face of her son.

Dramatis Personae

PURUŔAVAS	Son of Buddha, grands on of the moon, the first king of the lunar dynasty with his capital at Pratishthana.
CHARIOTEER	King of the Gandnharvas, musicians of heaven.
CHITRARATHAH	The clown and the king's friend, a Brah man
MANAVAKAH	
GALAVAH	Disciples of Bharata Muni
PALLAVAH	
LATAVYAH	Chamberlain in the king's palace
AYUH	Son of Urvashi and Pururavas
NARADAH	A divine sage, son of Brahma
URVASHI	A celestial nymph
CHITRALEKHA	
SAHAJANYA	Urvashi's companions
RAMBHA	
MENAKA	
AUSHINARI	The queen
SATYAVATI	An ascetic woman
	Doorkeeper, bards, maids, etc.

Scene of Action

Act I	...	Hemakuta Hill in the Himalayas.
Act II	...	The king's palace in Pratishthanah at the confluence of the Ganga and the Yamuna.
Act III	...	The same
Act IV	...	Gandha-madana Hill in the Himalayas.
Act V	...	The king's palace.

Time of Action

Pre-historic, when Pururavas, the first king of the lunar dynasty ruled on this earth.

Time Analysis

The action covers a period of about 12-1/2 years.

Act I	...	Part of one day (Interval - one or two weeks)
Act II	...	Mid-day of one day
Act III	...	The same afternoon and evening (Interval - twelve years)
Act IV	...	Indefinite but condensed into a single day of the rainy season.
Act V	...	Part of one day, probably the next.

The Plot :-

In the prologue, there is a pathetic cries of nymphs for immediate help, which is explained by the stage-manager and thus the main story begins.

Urvasi on her return from the Kailasa mountain to attend on Lord Kubera has been captured by the demons.

Act One :-

In the first act, the nymphs rushes in and meets the king who comes in his chariot driven first by the charioter.

Pururavas is returning from his usual worship of the sun. The agitated companions of Urvasi seek his help, where upon he gives chase to the demon Keshi who has gone towards the north - east.

The nymphs keeps waiting on the top of Hemakuta Hill and the charioter droves the horses first towards that direction. Eventually Pururavas rescues Urvashi and Chitralekha from his hands. To show how Pururavas win her love by his heroism, the act is prolonged by the dramatist they falls in love at first sight. The king returns unhurt and Urvashi is brought back to her companions. They embraces each other excitedly. At this moment, enters Chitrarath, the king of Gandharvas, who at the instruction of Lord Indra has come with his army to rescue and bring Urvasi back.

But he learns from his scouts that Pururavas has saved Urvasi. He requests Pururavas to come along and restore Urvasi to Indra. But Pururavas excuses himself saying that it is not an opportune time for him to call on Indra.

Act Two :-

In this act, we see that repercussion on the life and attitude of the king of his meeting with the nymph. Aushinari, the queen with the help of her maid Nipunika comes to know about his secret love for the celestial nymph. They succeed due to the clumsy carelessness of the inevitable jester. The jester enters and we come to know that he is waiting for the king who is to come from court. He goes up to the Devacchhanduka mansion and waits for him. Here he meets the queen's maid Nipunika. After a brief deliberation she reveals his masters secret to her and tells that he is trying to divert his friend from his mirage. After sometimes, the king arrives and both of them goes to the Madhavi bower and sits on the blue marble dais. The king is pinning for Urvasi. The jester requests the king to take off his mind from Urvasi and enjoy the graceful creepers or the bees that humming round the blossoms that are greeting the majesty. The king tells him that neither the creepers nor the graceful bending trees can divert his mind and his eyes are dazed by the vision of divine damsel. He tells his jester friend to think out a way for winning her love.

This moment, Urvasi and her companion Chitralekha comes by the aerial car. For sometimes they hovers in the air and enjoy the beauty of the capital city of the king and then descend in the pleasure garden which looks like a part of Nandana Vana and look for the king.

Infact Urvasi comes down to the king's palace to see for herself the king's love-lorn condition.

They hear his lamination and realising how harshly the king thinks of her, Urvasi who is not in a position to approach the king, Urvasi drops a letter (written on birch leaf) before him unseen confirming her own love for him. At first jester assuming it to be a snake skin, gets frightened. But after discovering that to be a brich leaf with a writing on it, tells jokingly that Urvashi might have dropped this love letter for the king.

His guess appears true and the king reads it out. The king admits that he can no more bear the separation of his lady love and seeks union. He handover the letter to the jester, as his moist fingers may spoit it. Chitralekha makes herself visible and then comes Urvasi who is also love - struck, but finds her beloved's plight as worse as hers.

While both of them are feasting on the presence of each other, from the off stage, a 'Divine Message' is heard. All listenns to it. Urvasi is recalled to heaven to play an important role in a drama staged by Bharata. Urvasi feels dejected and departs with her companion.

Meanwhile the addle - pated down carelessly droppes the missive of love, all in excitement. He goes about searching. To distract his eyes, the king asks him to bring that birch leaf letter. But jester tells in distress that the letter is lost.

At king's instances, the jester goes about searching. In the mean time, enters Aushinari with her attendants. As ill luck would have it, the letter written by Urvasi is picked up by the queen Aushinari's maid. The queen asks her to read it out and the rumour of the love affairs of king and the nymph is confirmed.

The queen waxes wild and leaves in a huff despite the king's protestations and his sue for pardon.

Act Three :-

The Viskambhaka is placed in the beginning of the third act wherein two disciples named Galava and Pallava of Bharata, the preceptor of drama, acquaints the audience with the fact that while playing in the drama, Laksmi-svayamvara, in the court of Heaven, Urvasi forgot her own part and spoke out the name of Pururavas as her choice husband instead of the name of Visnu which she ought to speak as Laksmi. The Bharata cursed her that since she failed in what the Guru taught her, Urvasi forfeit her right to be in heaven. They further tells that Indra sent Urvasi, out of his appreciation of Pururavas, his ally in war to the world in order to satisfy both the longing lovers, till she was with child by him. While speaking of this story, both the disciples forget that it is already Guru's time for ablutions, so they departs to attend on him.

In the main act, the chamberlain enters and brings then message of queen to the king. The queen desires to be in her husband's company on the palace roof and watch for the conjunction of Rohini and the Moon. Pururavas enquires from his jester friend reason behind her invitaion. The jester takes the king to the palace roof. Wherein the latter again expresses his desire for Urvasi. In an aerial car,Urvasi comes along with Chitralekha to see her beloved. But unfortunately seen the queen with her attendants carrying offerings. The king learns from Nipunika that queen's vrat is called 'Priyanuprasadanam' which is designed to win the favour of the husband lover.

Aushinari takes the vow before the heavenly couple Rohini and Mrigalanchhana that whomsoever the king may seek, or whoever him may seek, for union in mutual love, for her the queen shall entertain no ill feeling.

Queen is weighed down by the enormity of her crime in abusing her husband. Thus as an ideal Hindu wife, she gives him freedom to indulge his vagaries. She leaves with her attendant maids; there by making ground for Pururavas to meet Urvasi. He takes her in his embrace.

Act Four :-

Before the main scene, the two nymphs Chitralekha and Sahajanya, appears. However, entrance is preceded by 'Akshiptika', a song that is set through this musical pattern, and is sung offstage with instrumental accompaniment, prescribed by Bharata in his 'Natya Shastra'. Through their conversation, we are told that puting his minister in charge of state affairs, the king accompanies Urvasi on the high reaches of Mount Kailas. While dallying with the king, on the banks of the Mandakini, the king happens to see Udayavati, a Vidyadhara girl engaged in building sand - castles for fun. Thinking that Pururavas is gazing at the girl, Urvasi gets enraged.

Angry at her husband for this trivial cause, Urvasi leaves her mortal lover in a spasm of jealousy and enters the grove of Kumara, the divine war lord, which is forbidden to women.

Once Kumara took a vow of eternal celibacy and went to Gandha - Madana Hill for meditation and a rule that any female who entered his finest would be metamorphosed into a creeper. So, Urvasi is cursed to be transformed into a Jasmine creeper. Now begins the pathetic pursuit of the king after his invisible beloved. He enters in a mad fenzy with eyes fixed on the sky.

He keeps asking birds (chakors), the swans, the tusker, the fragrant cave (the favourite haunt of the celestial nymphs), the black deer about his sweat heart. But all his efforts go futile until he notices some bright red thing that shines from the crevice between the rocks.

The gems fall into Pururavas hands at the instance of a divine sage, who from behind the stage asks him to take it, as it is through the power of this gem called 'Sangmaniya' meaning 'Reunion' created from the red of mother Gauri's feet that he would regain his lady-love. The king looks round in all directions and sees the sage in deerskin. Pururavas takes the advice as blessings and accordingly picks up the gem. Shortly he comes near slender creeper and embraces it.

Under the influence of the gem, Urvasi is at once brought back to herself. Seeing her the king swoons and falls. When he regains his consciousness Urvasi informs him that it was due to the curse of Kumara that she became a creeper and regained her own form due to magic stone.

Pururavas shows her the gem and places it on her forehead. Happily they enter the city of Pratishthana to enjoy each other's company.

Act Five :-

In the prelude, the jester announces the return of the king from, the Kailasa regions. Back to the town he has resumed his rule and the subjects are happy. But pity he has no son.

He further tells us that the king after having his holy dip at the place where Ganga and Yamuna mingle has entered his tent along with the ladies. So the jester expresses his willingness to enjoy his share of flowers and sandal paste. Suddenly a female voice behind the scene breaks the news that a vulture has pounced upon the gem and carried it away. The bird might have took it for a piece of meat. The jester reminds us that this is the crest jewel that brought about the union of lovers. He leaves the stage.

Main scene open with kings entry with his charioter, chamberlain, the guard Rechaka and attendants. The king looks for his bow and Yarani attendant brings it, but by that time the carrioneater had flown beyond his arrow's reach. The king in anger asks the chamberlaifn to proclaim to the subjects that the vulture must be traced at any cost. But after sometimes, the chamberlain arrives with the jewel and an arrow.

All are astonished, as no one know whose arrow was this. As the chamberlains eyesight was poor, the king himself reads out what was inscribed on it "arrow of Ayus, son of Aila by Urvasi".

The king is amazed for he knows nothing of Ayus' birth and concealment by Urvasi.

Satyavati, an ascetic woman from Chyavana's hermitage with a gallant boy to return him to his mother since he has violated the rules of the hermitage by shooting a bird, at the instance of the sage Chyavana. The truth is revealed that Ayus is the son of Urvasi and Pururavas. The prince was in the custody of this ascetic woman. The holy sage Chyavana himself taught him the art of archery and all the rites and ceremonies prescribed for princess were dully performed in the hermitage. The woman, however cannot tell the king as to with what object in her mind that Urvasi left the child in her charge, immediately after his birth. At her instigation, the prince goes to the king and touches his feet. The king rejoices over his son and seats him on the foot stool.

At this juncture, enter Urvasi and the chamberlain. She is surprised to find Pururavas fondly patting his son's hair. Satyavati now hands over the prince to her in the presence of the king, after releaving of her duties. After her departure, Urvasi admits the fact of concealment, and weeps to think of their separation, as Indra permitted her to be with the king, but set a time limit. She tells Pururavas that she was only permitted to remain with him until he had seen his son.

The lovers are lamenting the perversity of fate. The king falls unconscious, wakes, laments over his fate.

Urvasi, however, doesn't fall unconscious like the king, she only reproaches him softly that she does not return happily to heaven after accomplishing her task on earth and bearing a son. It is time to soar away to heaven. Pururavas does not accept her reproaches, but neither does he offer any objection to her renewed dependence on the king of the gods. He is ready to abdicate in favour of the boy. He thinks of placing Ayus on the throne. He resolves to take to sack - cloth and ashes and retire to the forest in grief.

He orders his council of ministers to prepare everything for princes coronation. Chamberlain leaves sorrowfully. All look downs cast. At this time Narada, the heavenly musician appears. Urvasi brings the arghya (water, etc.) to the king for the reception of this divine guest. Pururavas takes the arghya from her hands and pours it. The couple bow to him. The king asks him to occupy the seat and grace it. He sits down and all other take their seats.

Now, Narada tells them the message of good tidings. In grateful recollection of the aid received in the destruction of demons by the army of Pururavas, and also a new war between gods and demons threatens, Pururavas's arms will be needed, he may not at this moment lay down his arms. In reward, he may have the company of Urvasi for life. Narada instructs Rambha, the celestrial nymph to bring down the things collected by Indra himself for the investiture of Ayus as crown prince. Narada anoints Ayus as heir to the throne. Rambha greets Urvasi and share this good fortune. Urvasi takes the prince by his hand and leads him to his "older mother", the queen and the king also wishes to accompany them.

At the end, the king expresses his deep sense of gratitude as he is being greatly favoured my Lord Indra.

The play ends with the usual Bharatavakya.

3. ABHIJNANASAKUNTALAM

Synopsis :-

Based on Mahabharata epic, the play depicts the love and lives of Sakuntala, the forest girl and king Dushyanta. As a diversion from his heavy royal duties at Hastinapur, the strong - armed king, Dushyanta is on a hunting expedition and enters a thick wood with his troops and his chariots. While pursuing a deer, he sees the hermitage of sage Kanva, situated on the bank of the sacred river Malini. He lays aside the insignia of royalty and goes alone. Here he meets Sakuntala with her companions Priyamvada and Anasuya, watering the garden plants. He reveals himself as the king's agent and from Sakuntala learns that the sage is away and falls in love with her at first sight, who was radiant in her beauty. He wondners how was she born Kanva's daughter, later Sakuntala explains how she is the child of a sage Visvamitra and a divine apsara (nymph) Menaka, deserted at birth, cared for by birds 'Sakuntas', found and reared by high - souled Kanva, who gave her the name "Shakuntala".

The king now pines for her love and sends his jester friend and his retinue back to the palace to participate in ritual there. Fortunately, at this juncture comes the request of the sages of the forest to clear the hermitage of the menance of demons. Dushyanta extends his stay in the hermitage.

Sakuntala, the heroine of the play, is also deeply in love with the king. But in her attempt to hide her feelings and secret suffering, her love sickness increase beyond a limit. Taking advantage of the situation, her two maids manages to wrings a confession from her and becomes her agents to bring about a union of the lover. Sakuntala is made to write a love - letter on a lotus leaf and the king, who witnesses their talk secretly from behind, now comes out into the open. Dushyanta proposes her and clears the doubts of her companions and promises son to be born out of their wed lock would be king's heir. Eventually a secret marriage is conducted by them, without waiting for her foster father' return. The king goes back to his capital, giving his bride a ring and asks her to follow him at the earliest.

At this moment, the dread sage Durvasa, known and feared for his uncontrollable angers, calls Sakuntala, who is completely lost in the thoughts about Dushyanta and her future life in the royal palace. Durvasa seeks her hospitality, but wrapped up in her lover, Sakuntala does not hear him and neglects her duties toward him. He atonce flies into a rage and curses her that the man for whom she heeds him not, will forget her, when she meet him next.

Sage Kanva comes to the hermitage. As Sakuntala was ashamed, she could not come to meet her father. But blessed, austere Kanva had divine discernment. He realizes everything with celestial vision that Sakuntala is pregnant and carrying Dushyanta's child in her womb. He approves of the marriage that was held without ceremony. Seeing her approaching maternity. Kanva arranges to send Sakuntala to her husband's home.

Kanva's disciples Sarngarava, Saradvata and Sakkuntala's foster - mother Gautami accompanies her. Sakuntala bids farewell to her father, friends and leaves the parental roof. One the way, she stops to bath in the holy river and her ring falls off. On reaching the palace, Sakuntala is horrified to find that king does not remember her and deceives her.

The king receives the party politely, but as Durvasa's curse has made him forget everything about his love affairs in the hermitage, he outrightly rejects Sakuntala as his married wife.

The hermit - girl is half fainted from shame and grief, but still stands stiff as if pillar. In despair she talks of all the things they did together and of the things of which they talked. Finally she decides to show him the ring as proof but to her utter dismay she finds that the ring is missing. She is repudiated and her misery is beyond repair. She accepts her defect and her fate and in frustration decides to leave the palace. Her mother, the celestrial nymph Menaka carries her daughter away to the heavens.

Much later a fisherman who had recovered the king's ring from the belly of a fish he had caught in the river, goes to a market - palace to sell it. He is apprehended by the police as the ring bear the king's signature. He is accused of the theft and finally the matter is referred to the king for disposal. Seeing the ring the king's memory returns, the curse is completed and he loses all interest in his kingly duties. When the king is almost lost his hope of reunion, the good fortune falls upon him. At the instance of Indra, the king of the gods, the goes to the heaven to save the gods from attacks of demons the brood of Kalanemi. He succeeds in his venture and the pleased god sees to it that Dushyanta visits the hermitage of Marica - midway between heaven and earth, in his way back to the earth.

Here he comes upon an unruly child playing with a lion's cub. The king exclaims "What fire is in the child".

His heart goes out to him and then as he stretches his hand, the marks of imperial birth are revealed and soon learns that he had a heavenly nymph for mother who was abondoned by her cruel husband. The king is amazed, but when is being told by the guardian - maid that none other than father or mother who can touch the magic amulet. With impunity, he realises that why the amulet did not become a snake and bite him, his son's identity is revealed.

The maid runs to report the matter to Sakuntala. Sakuntala appears on the scene to greet her husband. The king apologises to her, but embodiment of understanding wife, who forgives her husband, Sakuntala blames only herfate. The sage Marica explains how Durvasa's curse had made Dushyanta forget Sakuntala and the days he passed in the hermitage. The king is united with his wife and son and happily leaves for the kingdom.

Dramatis Personae

DUSHYANTAH	King of India
HIS CHARIOTEER	
MADHAVYAH	The king's jester and companion
SENAPATHI	The army chief
KANVAH KASHYAPAH	Chief of the hermitage
SHARNGARAVAH	Hermit of the hermitage
SHARADVATHA	Hermit of the hermitage
RAIVATAKAH	Warder
KARABHAKAH	A messenger
VATAYANAH	Chamberlain
SOMARATAH	The king's priest
NAGARIKAH	The superintendent of the city
JANUKAH SUCHAKAH	Gaurds of the city
MATALIH	Indra's charioteer Fisherman
SARVADAMANAH	The king's son or Bharata
MARICHAH	The divine procreator of gods and men

GALAVAH	His disciple
SHAKUNTALA	Foster - daughter of Kanvah
PRIYAMVADA /ANASUYA	Her companions
GAUTAMI	The matron of the hermitage
ADITIH	The divine consort of Marichah
VETRAVATI	A female warder
SANUMATI	A celestial nymph
MADHUKARIK PARABHRITIKA	A Garden attendants
CHATURIKNA	A maid - servent

Scene of Action and Time Analysis

Act I	...	Forenoon of a mid-summer day, first in the forest adjoining Kanva Rishi's hermit age and then in its precincts.
Act II	...	The next morning, in the forest camp of the king.
Act III	...	A few days later, afternoon, within the grounds of the hermitage and in a shady bower near the hill stream Malini.
The prelude to Act IV	...	A few more days later, forenoon, in the hermitage grounds.
Act IV	...	Five or six months later, morning, in and in the vicinity of the hermitage.
Act V	...	Two or three days later, forenoon, in the king's palace in Hastinapuram.
The prelude to Act VI	...	A few weeks later, in the city near the palace.
Act VI	...	About five years later in the palace.
Act VII	...	Some weeks later, first in mid air and then in the hermitage of the divine Maricha and Aditi.

The whole action of the 'Sakuntala' is spread over a period of about six years.

Plot :

Act One :-

Once the Benedictory Stanza (Nandi) invoking Shiva is over, the stage manager enters with a Nati (actress) and informs the assembly that a new play called 'Sakuntala Recognised' would be staged in a short while.

Here Kalidasa shows his sense of artistic modesty in not mentioning anything else but the name of his patron, Vikramaditya, the play and the play wright. He briskly introduces king Dushyanta, the hero in just few sentences for the main act to commence.

The play opens with king Dushyanta of the Lunar race in his full hunting garb, with a bow and arrow in his hands and charioteer by his side.While the king is about to shoot his arrow at an antelope pursued by him, voice behind the scenes interrupts him. At kings's instance, the charioteer stops the chariot. Enter a hermit with two other ascetic. He raises his hand and tells that the animal belongs tot he ashrama, of Kulpati Kanva, and the sanctity of the place must not be violated by its slaughter. The king refrains from killinng by withdrawing his arrow.

In turn he is blessed by the hermits that he would beget an emperior son. Now the ascetics set out to collect dry twigs for the sacrificial fire. But before leaving, they invite the king to receive such hospitalities as the Ashrama could offer. They further tells that on the banks of the Malini, there is the hermitage of their chief. He is away her on a pilgrimage to Somatirtham to mitigate an adverse trend in her daughter Sakauntala's star. So the latter is there, who could mosturely look after the guest's comfort. The king accepts the invitation, and asks him charioteer to wait outside. He himself enters the woods of the ascetic in modest garb and hands over his bow and ornaments to the charioteer. The king instruct him that by the time he returns from the hermitage, his horses may be watched and rubbed down. After the departure of the charioteer, the king enters. There he finds the damsels of exquisite love liness watering the young plants. He gazes at them appreciatively. He at once falls in love with Sakuntala who is one of them, and other two being her comrades - Anasnunya and Priyamvada.

Here the king hears Priyamvada and Anasuya joking with Sakuntala who is troubled by a naughty bee and ask her to seek the help of hte king. At this suitable point, the king who was hither to concealed in the background goest forth and addresses them.

From the conversation between Sakuntla's friends nand the king, it is revealed that Dusyanta was in every way worthy of her, and her friends too feel that if father Kanva were present he would do honour to the guest and offer him the one possession he prized most. Dusyanta's doubts regarding her birth are stilled when urged by him. The maidens narrate to him the tate of Sakuntala's birth and how she was the daughter of Visvamitra and Menaka and is being reared not for hte religious life but marriage with someone worthy of her. Sakuntala in feigned and gen rises to leave when Priyamvada stops her saying she had promised her the watering of two trees and she could not leave before she had paid her debt; at which the king most gallantly gives her the ring to redeem her debt (This is the fatal ring which failed Sakuntala just at the critical moment, and whose recovery restored the king's memory).

Dushyanta, thus, discovered her to be of Kshtriya parenntage, and, therefore a suitable bride for him. He, however, does not disclose his identity to them, but intends for the present to remain incognito. At this juncture, a voice behind the scenes breaks, the news that elephant frightened by the chariots, running amok and causing damage, and all listen and are somewhat disturbed. The king assures that the hermitage would ifn no way harmed. And at that the company breaks up. Sakuntala, on her part, is struck by the visitor's grace and charm, trees to delay on one pretext or another, leaves with her companions. The king, head over ears in love, admits that he is no longer interested to go back to town.

He would encamp somewhere near the hermits wood for he cannot draw his mind away from Sakuntala.

Act Two :-

It shows how Dusyanta in a love - lorn state and pines for Sakuntala's love, which allow him no rest at night and deprives him of all his zest for the pleasures of hunting. The commander's praise of hunting does not much appeal to him. He directs him to stop the hunt as they are in the precints of a sacred grove and asks him to order his followers not to disturb hermitage.

When the army chief departs, the king sits with his jester friends. Here he narrates his feelings to his companion and the priviledged court - jester who is very unsympathetic. The latter tries in his own way to soothe and divert his royal master's mind. But the king was alluding to that gem of the hermitage Sakuntala.

The king asks him to findout some means by which he can manage to stay in the vicinity of the hermitage without arousing comment or suspicion. He even tells the jester that could he think of some excuse for visiting the hermitage again?

Quite unexpectedly, at this point, arrives two young ascetics to request the king to stay and look after the safety of their sacrificial rites, which were being disturbed by evil demons , in the absence of their superior, the great sage Kanva.

Dusyanta at once accept the invitation and instructs the door keeper to ask the charioteer to bring round the chariot with his bow. The hermits leave and in a short while, the door - keeper enters again to inform that the chariot is ready, but the palace messanger Karabhaka has arrived.

Karabhaka brings the message that within four days, the Queen - mother's fast would come to an end, and the occasion deserves to be graced by her son, thereby, requesting the king's presence at the festival. This gives him the opportunity to send off the jester to perform the son's role and be near his royal mother. Dusyanta dismisses all his retinue. In order to prevent a scandal, he takes the jester by his hand and assures him that his affair of Sakuntala was all a joke and he is going to the hermitage out of regard for the hermits only.

Act Three :-

From the interlude we are informed through an acolyte that the maid Priyamavada is taking herbal paste and fresh lotus leaves for Sakuntala, the life - breath of their chief preceptor, revered Kanva. She is suffering much from exposure to the sun and those are to cool her body which is burning hot. So, the acolyle also expresses his desire to offer a pot of water hallowed at the sacrifice to the Gautami, who in turn, give it to the ailing Sakuntala. Thus the audience is told that Sakuntala, too, is now attacked by the malady of love.

After the departure of the acolyte, enter the king in a love sick state. The hermits have completed their rites and permitted him to rest. But he wonders how can he find diversion for his love - racked mind? He walks about and notices a flower bower where Sakuntala is lying with her two maids ministering unto her cooling remedies.

Sakuntala confesses her passion for Dushyanta. She admits that the moment her eyes beheld the good king, guardian angel of the sacred grove - she long for him. She requests her friends to seek some way by which she may find the king's favour. Otherwise threatens that they will soon be pouring the last oblation over her. The king takes advantage of the opportunity to make a formal declaration of his suit.

The king assures them of his deep devotion for Sakuntala. But Sakuntala jealously remarks that her companions should not tax great king's courtesy. He is perhaps pining to return to his beloved ones in the palace. Upon which comes the confession of his passionate love for her.

Anasuya remarks that they have heard that kings are prodigal of their love to many.

The king appeases them that inspite of many a wife in the palace courts, henceforth Sakuntala shall be the chief glory of his throne.

Both Priyamvada and Anasuya are now relieved. They make excuse and leave and the lovers are left to themselves. But the playwright does not allow love to go beyond aesthetic bounds.

The scene is ended by the arrival of Gautami who comes to take away Sakuntala to the cottage. The disconsolate king who is left alone, decides to stay in the same bower where his beloved spent a rupturous day. But at this juncture a voice in the air declares that the evil spirits are flying round the altars, where the evening sacrifice has just begun. The king departs atonce to keep he demons away from the sacrificial affairs.

Act Four :-

This act opens with Anasuya and Priyamvada, who are gathering flowers for the offering. The maidens tell us that the king has left after his secret Gandharava form of marriage with Sakuntala. He has promised to send a suitable guard to take his bride to rightful place, Dushyanta's palace.

Anasuya expresses her fears that surrounded by the bright ladies with their courtly ways, the king may not remember Sakuntala or the hermitage. Priyamvada, however, assures her that persons so noble are not changeable. She adds that what troubles her on the other hand is to know what father Kanva will say when he hears of this occurrence.

At this moment, a voice behind the scenes says "Look, o I am here". : Though Sakuntala is present in the hermitage, Anasuya exclaims that it sounds like a guest announcing himself. Priyamveda finds that this is none other than the dread Durvasa.

In her sadness Sakuntala has forgotten to receive properly the wrathful ascetic. Sakuntala fails to offer proper hospitality to the choleric sage and has offended someone entitled to respect. Durvasa who is so easily angered curses her with the words "He, of who thou thinking neglecting to receive me properly as guest, - he won't remember you even when reminded / of you."

But when Priyamvada pleads Sakuntala's absent - mindedness. But Durvasa replies that his words cannot be denied their effect. But now, Durvasa who earlier cursed Sakuntala, to be forgotten by her lover graciously may grants that he may re-collect at the sight of a ring, which the king gave her in token of their union.

The maidens decide to tell no one of the incident; for poor Sakuntala ought not to be troubled, because her gentle nature may not be able to bear this shock. Here, the prelude ends.

In the main act, Anasuya tells us that father Kanva has returned to the hermitage and is scared to reveal him the recent happenings, i.e., Sakuntala's marriage and her pregnancy.

But her companion Priyamvada breaks the news that a heavenly voice from the sacred fire informed Kanva of the secret marriage and of Sakuntala's approaching maternity.

She joyfully tells her that they have to prepare to send off Sakuntala to her lawful husband. Kanva decides to send Sharngarava and the others to escort Sakuntala.

A scene of intense pathos begins that vividly describes her departure from he penance - grove where she had resided so long, and where every plant, creeper and animal was bounded to her by ties of affection.

The aged hermit unwillingly parts with his beloved foster - daughter. But who can tear the fond parent from his beloved child. But before she bids farewell, Kanva gives her advice on the duties of a wife and a daughter-in-law. Sakuntala is desolated to leave him, her friends, and all that she has loved at the hermitage.

The friends are already filled with apprehensions and tell her to show the ring in case the king is slow to recognise her.

Their doubts makes Sakuntala tremble. But both of them promptly answer that in their fond concern they imagined the worst.

Finally she bids farewell to the forest - world and leaves with her journey companions.

Act Five :-

From the ideal world of hermitage, this act takes us to the Dushyanta's capital, at the royal court.

We hear a woman's voice singing in an impassioned strain; it is a taunt to the king for his forgetting of Hamsapadika, on account of queen Vasumati. The song causes a strange disturbance in Dushyanta's soul, who is listening to soft music off stage.

The king asks the jesters to see her and somehow or other mollify her. The hermits escorting Sakuntala arrive at the royal palace. The chamberlain announce that some hermits have come from forest bearing a message from the sage Kanva there are also some women with them makes him more anxious and distressed.

Dushyanta, however, orders his chamberlain to admit the party into his royal presence, little suspecting their mission.

After an exchange of greetings, Sarngava, the chief of the sages that accompanied Sakuntala, congratulates the king of his marriage and invites him to accept his wife as the Queen. Kanva's message, far from pleasing him, strikes him as a bolt from the blue.

Thus, under the malign influence of the curse, the king does not recognise Sakuntala, his secretly married wife. He denies all knowledge of the affair and can not receive her. He does not recognize her when her veil is removed by Gautami. Even Sakuntala fails to rouse his curse -swept memory. As a last resort, she wants to show him his ring, which Dushyanta had given her at parting and which would have been a sure token. But by a most fatal chance, the ring had slipped off her fingers while she was washing her hands. She looks at Gautami in despair. She goes to relate an incident of their all too brief love life in the jasmine bower. All this seems to him totally false and fabricated.

This is followed by Sakuntala's final outburst calling him an ignoble man who judges others by perfidy of his own mind, well hidden by the cloak of virtue he wears.

But the king can not admit her story of this secret love. Sakuntala covers her face with her veil and burst into tears.

Sarangarava roundly abuses both Sakuntala and Dushyanta. Sarangarava's behement condemnation of the king's conduct leads to nothing.

Sharadvata tells the king that Sakuntala is his wife. It is upto him to reject her or the take her. The man's authority over his wife is absolute.

The sages insist on leaving Sakuntala refusing her the right to go back with them in the forest world, since her duty is by her husband's side, even if she is to live as a slave maid.

The king now seeks his priest's advice, who shows his willingness to give her shelter till the babe is born. He informs that wise men have foretold that the king's first-born son will be an emperor. If the sage's daughter gives birth to a child bearing imperial marks on its hands Dushyanta can joyfully take her into his palace, if not she should be sent back to her father.

Sakuntala rushes out from Dushyanta's with the words "*Bhagavati Vasundhare, dehi me vivaram* - Oh, Goddess Earth break open and give me shelter." Outside, while she is bemoaning her fate, a miracle occurs. The wonder struck priest narrates the happenings to the king.

Dushyanta learns that when Kanva's pupils turned and walked away, a celestial lady decended from the heaven and took Sakuntala away leaving the king filled with wonder. Dushyanta tells the warder that he is very much disturbed and ask her to lead the way to the bed chamber.

Act Six :-

Enter the city superintendent and two guards bringing a fisherman with his hands tied behind. From the prelude, it is reported that policemen have arrested a fisherman accused of theft of a royal ring found inside a fish which he has caught.

It is Dushyanta's ring which Sakuntala had dropped earlier while bathing en route to the king's palace.

The fisherman is brought before the king for being properly dealt with. The city superintendent asks his men to keep close guard over the fisherman at the city gate and he himself goes to his majesty to tell him how he got it, obtain his orders and come back. The fisherman is, however, let off by Dushyanta, who at the right of that token of recognition, is freed from the influence of sage Durvasa's curse. The king even favours him by giving him money, half of which the poor man offers to the Superintendent that makes them friends and the friendship is attested by a cup of wine.

The main act opens with Sanumati, the celestial nymph who comes by aerial car to witness on behalf of her friend Menaka to find out for her daughter's sake the reason why the palace gardens show no festive signs, when the spring has already arrived. She makes herself invisible and witness two maids attending the palace grounds.

Parabhritika nad Madhukarika, are found to be entranced by the mango tree in full bloom. So this is the season for traditional rite of offering flowers to the god of love with song and dance.

The chamberlain suddenly enter to interrupt them announcing that the king has forbidden the observance of the spring festival in the palace ever since he regained his memory.

From the chamberlain, it is learnt that the sight of the ring has reminded the king of his marriage with Sakuntala and ever since, the grief and repentence has overcome him.

He has recognised the wrong unwillingly done and is in extreme depression at loss of his beloved wife.

Meanwhile, the king enters the garden with the jester to whom he pours out his heart. The king seeks to divert his mind in the company of his jester - friend.

Dushyanta recalls how just before parting from her in the hermitage he slipped his signet ring on Sakuntala's finger and told her "Repeat each day one letter of my name engraved on this ring. When you have said them all the messenger I shall send to bring you to my house will be with you."

The king is sure that the ring must have slipped from her finger and fallen in Ganga's stream at Shachi Ghat when poor Sakuntala was offering her prayer and the ring got into the stomach of the carp.

Enter Chaturika hurriedly, with painting board in her hand. Dushyanta seeks to console himself with a portrait he had himself drawn of his love.

Chaturika arrives to report that the queen Vasumati is coming to see him. At king's instance, the jester lifts the painting and leaves running.

Meanwhile the warder comes with a ministers letter. On his enquiring whether the queen is on the way or not? He learns that the sensible queen has given precedence to affairs of state and has left to enable the king to pursue his work. The king now reads out the report of the case which the minister has referred to him for decision.

Dhanamitra, a sea faring merchant has perished in a shipwreck. He died sonless, and his immense property becomes by law forfeited to the king.

The king replies that as Dhanamitra had great riches, he must have several wives. Let inquiry be made. There may be a wife who is with child.

He is being informed that one of his wives - the daughter of a merchant from Saketa is soon to become a mother. The king gives decision that the unborn child has the right to his father's property and thus, shall receive the inheritance.

His decision regarding hte right of inheritance is proclaimed before the subjects and the latter rejoices over Dushyanta's edict.

This episode only deepens the king's regret by reminding of his childlessness. When on the headman's death the family is left without support because of a break in the lineage, all its wealth passes to a stranger. So too when he die, the glory of Puru's race will vanish like seed sown at the wrong time.

Chaturika instructs the warder to go to the cloud palace and fetch Arya Madhavya to cheer him up. But the king is deeply in distress and subsequently faints away.

At this moment, invisible Sanumati who was witnessing everything (owing to her connection with Sakuntala's mother) rises in the air and vanishes to cheer Menaka's daughter with an account of what she had seen and heard.

From his despair, the king is awakened by the screams of the jester roughly handled by Matali, Indra's charioteer.

Hearing the voice behind the scenes, the king takes his bow and arrow from the Yavani and angrily moves towards the terrace to save the unknown person. But he does not find anyone. Meanwhile Matali appears after releasing the screaming jester.

Matali explains that he has come to take the king, as Indra needs his aid in quelling the demons - the brood of Kalanemi, whom the gods find it difficult to subdue. So, Matali had to act this way to bring the king back to the realisation that there are duties superior to private feeling the brave man sometimes needs to be provoked to show the spirit he has in him.

Dushyanta shakes off his dejection and leaves in Indra's car to proceed on his mission - to the heavenly regions, as Lord Indra's order cann not be transgressed.

Act Seven :-

In a divine car, the victorious king is travelling with Matali after his successful expedition. From a talk, we are informed that the king was received with extraordinary honour by Indra. In presence of the gods, Indra made Dushyanta share his seat garlanded with the flowers of paradise. The grand farewell that was given to him was beyond the wildest dreams of the king. But Matali justifies that his highness deserved all of this from the chief of gods. After traversing a short distance, they reach Hemakuta, where dwells in the place of supreme bliss the seer Maricha and Aditi, the divine progenitors of gods and men whom the king wanted to salute reverently. So the car descends and when they are in the hermitage of holy Maricha, Matali stops the chariot.

As Maricha is in hard penance, the king decides to wait while Matali departs to announce Dushyanta's arrival to the sage. Here the king, meets a unruly boy pulling up young lion from its mother to the terror of two attendants.

The first matron tells the boy not to tease the animals. Dushyanta's heart goes to out to this gallant boy, the very image of himself. Dushyanta experiences a strange emotion, as if the boy were his own son.

The second matron warns the boy that the lioness would attack him, but the fearless boy laughs and makes faces at the cub. The first matron tells him that if he let the lion cub go, she shall give him a nice toy, the boy stretches his hand, the marks of imperial birth are revealed.

They request the king to intervene and to free the lion from his clutches, he comes into close contact with the boy, but feels a pang as he thinks of his childlessness.

He also comes to know that the child is not a hermit's son. The matrons are surprised at the 'speaking likeness' between him and the child.

On enquiry, they tell him that the child belonged to Puru's line, that he had a celestial nymph for mother who was cruelly abandoned by her heartless husband. This becomes a second ground for hope.

The second matron comes with a clay peacock and say to him "Is not the Sakuntala lovely"? The child begins to look around for his mother Sakuntala and asks "where is she?"

So he mistook the word and dotes on his mother. The king who suspected the truth, that most likely the boy is his own son, however feels that the identity of name may just be a mirage leading him to further disappointment.

At this moment, the first matron notices the amulet is missing from the boy's wrist. But the king assures them that not to be disturbed. While hitting the lion cub, the amulet must have dropped. Dushyanta stops to pick it up, but both the attendant prevent him as baring the child and its parents, no one can pick it up, once it falls on the ground.

To their utter surprise, picks up the amulet. The king enquires what happens if one attempts?

First matron narrates that after this boy's birth, at the very first rite, the devine sage Maricha gave him this amulet, naming it "Invincible". If any other person touches it, it would turn into a serpent and kill him. Now the boy desires to see his mother. The king tells him that they shall go together to gladden her mother's heart. The boy says that his father is Dushyanta, not he. To his amazement he becomes sure that this is his own son.

Sakuntala appears to him in the dress of an ascetic. They looks at each other. They boy runs towards his mother and informs that this stranger calls him son and has embraced him.

Mutual explanations follow. King feels sorry for his ill treatment and falls at her feet.

Sakuntala blames only her fate which had been fixed for her by some former transgression of hers.

When Sakuntala notices the signet ring, the king tries to convince her that it was this ring that his memory revived. Sakuntala says that she does not trust it any more. Meanwhile comes the sage Maricha who explains the whole episode of the curse and how it clouded Dushyanta's memory and of its equally inexplicable revival. Maricha crowns their happiness by making it clear to Sakuntala that her husband was not responsible for the delusion. The pair is reconciled. Maricha blesses the couple and sends them off together with their son, in that same car of Indra to their capital. The play comes to an end with the customary Bharatavakyas:

May monarchs of the world stive for the common weal!

May the heavenly muse inspire the learned and the wise!

May the self-created, omnipotent blue-red god release me from re-births!

The play, therefore ends, as it commences, with a prayer to Lord Shiva.

2

Plays in Performance

(I) MALAVIKAGNIMITRA IN PERFORMANCE

A scene from 'Malavikagnimitra' of Kalidasa.

In ancient India, plays were presented either in Temples or in Palaces of either the ruling Princess or the Nobility. P.V. Raja Mannar rightly points out that there were no regular daily dramatic performance as now. A special event, e.g. a religious festival, or a celebration concerning the Ruler or a Nobleman provided the occassion for the presentation of a drama. Malavikagnimitra of Kalidasa was performed at the Vasantotsava (the spring festival).

In modern period, the Malavikagmitra was staged at Pathuriaghata (at Tagore's residence) in 1859 (Calcutta Review, 1873, Page 259).

However the journal '*Somprakash*' on 2 July 1860 wrotes that the play was enacted in the early 1860 and not in 1859 as told by Shri Kishorichand Mitra. The drama was staged for the second time on 7 July 1860. On 23 July in '*Somprakash*', a spectator wrote in appreciation of this production.

Raja Jatindra Mohan Tagore, the great patron of Bengali stage. The Bengali version of the 'Malavikagnimitra' of Kalidasa was staged in the year 1865 in his residence.

At the residence of Late Gopinath Tagore, at Pathuriaghata (the then residence of Raja Jatindra Mohan Tagore), Malavikagnimitra of Kalidasa was presented in Bengali in the year 1865 [1271], but the exact date is not known. Some actors from the caste of Ratnavali [that was signed in 1859 at Paikpara] was invited to take part in it. Ramnarayan Pandit rendered this classic in Bengali and handed over the script to Maharaja Jatindara Mohan Tagore. For the first time, Raja Saurindra Mohan Tagore took part in it and played 'Kanchuki'.

After the show, Raja Pratap Chandra Singh personally came to congratulate Mohendranath Mukhopadhyay in the green room and said "Mohendra Babu you are the second best Vidhusaka I have seen".

After the success of Malayalam rendering of Sakuntalam, A.R. Rajaraja Varma went on to translate Malavikagnimitra that appeared in 1916. In the forword to Malavikagnimitra he states : "To my mind which had to wander about in the inaccessible and pathless forest of grammer, what a great relief it is to rest a while in the beautiful garden park of drama! The craze for that pleasure can not be contained and it is on account of this craze that I have translated Malavikagnimitra successfully or not."

In the summer of 1916, this play was staged by the 'Kalavilasam' drama troupe and the response of the public was splended.

'Literarisches Zentralblatt' wrote on 17 March 1917 that the "Der konig and die Tanzerin", the German version of Malvikagnimitra rendered by Lion von Feuchtwanger that closely adheres to the original, in its first performance in the Munchener Kammerspielen on March 5, 1917 had a sympathetic success.

The Students of the Baroda College performed Kalidasa's Malavikagnimitra in Sanskrit at the Seventh Oriental Conference that was held at Baroda from 27th to 30th December 1933.

In the Thirteenth Session of the 'All India Oriental Conference' which was held at Nagpur from 19th to 21st October, 1946, under the auspices of the Nagpur University, Kalidasa's play 'Malavikagnimitra was produced in Sanskrit'.

Madame Menaka, the choreographer of 'Malavikagnimitra' in Kathak style

In the first half of this century, Madame Menaka initiated a new kind of choreography in her dance - drama. In Kalidasa's 'Malavikagnimitra' she introduced Kathak technique for dramatic purposes. She also relied on Kathakali and Manipuri idioms. The ballet was a resounding success in which Ramanarayan, Damayanti Joshi and nother participated with this great dancer.

G. Venkatachalam in his book 'Dance in India' has stated that "… her first Rasleela" ballet, which was impressive and moved with tempo and swing which one missed in her latter attempts. The ambitious one was her interpretition of Kalidasa's Malavikagnimitra', in which she used both the Kathaka and Kathakali technique. The history is silent about the date of its presentation. We have no documentary evidences, but dance historian say that it was performed in the third or fourth decade of the present century.

A scene from the dance drama 'Malavikagnimitra'

The Sanskrit drama group 'Sanskrita Ranga' which was founded by V. Raghavan had performed the 'Malavikagnimitra' of Kalidasa in the Summer Drama Festival of the Information and Broadcasting Ministry in Delhi. At the Annual Conference of the Madras Music Academy, infact, all the three plays of Kalidasa was staged by Sanskrit a Ranga that created quite a record in respect of audiance and enthusiasm.

Malavikagnimitra was staged in 1956 at the Hall of Columns, Moscow in 1956 during 'Kalidasa Festival held in Russia.

An exhibition of eastern drama was held in the Brander Mathews Dramatic Museum of the Low Library in Columbia University, New York. Alongwith the photographs of all the Sanskrit productions of the Madras Samskrita Ranga on show, a tape - record of the Sanskrit Ranga's full production of Malavikagnimitra was played in that exhibition.

Govind Dharmadhikari and Suman Dharmadhikari produced the Hindi version of 'Vikramorvasiyam', 'Malavikagnimitra', 'Shakuntalam'. They also presented 'Mahakavi Kalidasa' and 'Asad ka ek din' at 'Bharatiya Rangmanch, Ujjain on the occassion of 'Kalidasa Jayanti'.

In 1964, Mrinalini Sarabhai of the Darpana Academy presented 'Malavikagnimitra' in dance-drama form in the year 1964.

Bhagavati Sharma directed 'Mahavikagnimitra' of Kalidasa in 1972 at Kalidasa Festival in Ujjain.

Dr. Premlata Sharma had directed 'Malavikagnimitra' of Kalidasa in the prestigious Kalidasa Festival at Ujjain.

Shri Ram Bharatiya Kala Kendra and Kathak Kendra presented Kalidasa's Sanskrit play 'Malavikagnimitra' in their Festival of Ballets in 1975. It was Choreographed and music rendered by Birju Maharaj. The script for the ballet was penned by Naresh Mehta.

At the Summer Theatre Festival of the Rangamandal of Bhopal, Kalidasa's 'Malavikagnimitra' was chosen and the classic was rendered into Hindi by Madan Soni and directed by Alakhnandan. The festival started 30th April, and lasted till 2nd June 1982.

Rangmandal Bhopal repeated Kalidasa's Malavikagnimitra in Bundelkhandi dialect at the 25th Akhil Bharatiya Kalidas Samaroha that was held at Ujjain from 27th November to 5th December 1982.

South Zone Theatre Festival was held in Vijayawada from 8-13 October 1990. This festival was organised by the Sangeet Natak Akademi, New Delhi in collaboration with the South Zone Cultural Centre, Thanjavur and the Municipal Corporation of Vijayawada. On 12 October 1990, Kalidasa's 'Malavikagnimitra' was presented in Kannada by the Ranga Vibhagha Raja Rajeshwari Education Society, Manchikeri, Karnataka under the direction of B.R. Venkataramana Aithal.

(II) VIKRAMORVASIYAM IN PERFORMANCE

In the revival of classical drama, the contribution of Babu Kaliprasanna Sinha of Jorasankho, Calcuttā is indisputably immense. On 24th November 1857, [Agrahayan 1264] he staged Kalidasa's 'Vikramorvasiyam' in Bengali, in it he himself acted and the production was hailed a big success.

This was the second venture of 'Vidyotsahini Theatre' The cast comprised of eminent personalities such as Kaliprasanna Sinha (Pururaba), Bihari Lal Chatterji of Bengal Theatre and, Woomesh Chandra Banerji; the first President of the Indian National Congress.

'*Calcuta Review*' had mentioned about the production in the year 1873. '*Hindu Patriot*' also published a review of the play on 13 December 1857. On 25 November 1857, '*Samvad Prabhakar*' wrote in praise of the production.

'Vikramorvasiyam' in Marathi translation by Govind Ballal Deval was Kirloskar Natak Mandli's first play that was produced in the year 1889. Bhaurao Kolhatkar had produced this play.

In Poland, Kalidasa's Vikramorvasiyam was staged by Tadeusz Pawlikowski [an adaption of Erazm Dluski] entitled 'Urwasi'. It was staged at Lwow, the Polish Theatre on February 25, 1902 [European Premier - 1890 at Munich].

Greatly inspired by Padmanabha Narayana Dev, Sri Gopinath Nanda ventured into his rendering of Kalidasa's play 'Vikramorvasiyam' into Oriya. The work was dedicated to Srinivasa Dev, the Prince of Manjusha and appeared in 1908. This drama was staged in Padmanabha Rangalaya of Orissa.

Vikramorvasiyam of Kalidasa was rendered into Oriya by the Prince of Subarnapur Raja Birmitrodaya Simhadev. This was his third rendering of an ancient classic. It was brough out from Sambalpur in 1910 and later staged in Orissa.

One of the Rana generals, Dambar Samser, was much impressed by the theatre he saw in Calcutta and founded The Royal Imperial Opera House at Kathmandu in 1893. In the year 1925, Kalidasa's 'Vikramorvasiya'; Nepali rendering of Kesar Samser was performed at this Royal Imperial Opera House, Nepal.

'Andhra Bhasabhimani Samajam' which was formed on 31st April 1899 and functioned upto 1925 had staged Vedam Venkataraya Sastry's Telugu rendering of Vikramorvasiyam (published in 1921) wonderfully several times in 1922. Earlier it produced Kalidasa's Shakuntalam, but never staged his Malavikagnimitra.

At Kalidas Jayanti celebration (1958) at Ujjain, all the three plays of Kalidasa was enacted in its original language. The festival was sponsored by the Madhya Pradesh Kala Parishad. This Kalidasa Samaroh is now a regular annual feature. The Vikramorvasiyam was performed by the Artist Combined of Gwalior.

Sanskrita Ranga of Madras staged Kalidasa's Vikramorvasiyam in Sanskrit at the 34th Conference of the Music Academy Madras. Faubion Bowers wrote in 'Theatre Arts' (New York Magazine) in April 1961 under the heading 'India: a passage to progress' "This was only one of the several productions that Raghavan has mounted, but it was the only one I saw. It was done thoughtfully, and was intellectually of the glory that was India's theatrical art a timely reminder, somehow that growth in the future can be accompanied by a revival of the past."

1974 witnessed Shanta Gandhi's production of Vikramorvasiym in the natyadharmi style presented in Vikrishta theatre specially designed by Govardhan Panchal. In Kalidasa festival at Ujjain, Shanta Gandhi, an authority on ancient Indian drama staged Kalidasa's 'Vikramorvasiyam'.

Prof. V. Venkatachalam had produced 'Vikramorvasiyam' in Sanskrit at "Kalidasa Jayanti" that started in the third decade at Simhapuri, Ujjain. At Bharatiya Rangmanch, Ujjain Shri Govind Dharmadhikari and Suman Dharmadhikari presentned the Hindi version of Vikramorvasiyam on the occasion of Kalidasa Jayanti.

At Ujjain, the Veteran stage director K.N. Pannikker presented the Fourth Act of Kalidasa's Vikramorvasiyam in Kutiyattam style in the 25th Akhil Bharatiya Kalidasa Samaroha in 1982. The solo actor Shri S. Gopalkrishna received instant acclamation from the distinguished audiences for his superb acting. Shri Kumar was equally appreciated for his melodious voice.

'Vikramorvasiyam dhavaninat yarupantaram' by Rama Kant Shukla, is a Sanskrit adaptation in the form of Radio play of the Vikramorvasiyam of Kalidasa. The play was broadcast from the Delhi station of the All India Radio on 1st March 1983.

"Vikramorvasiyam" presented by National School of Drama in New Delhi in Nov. 1997 is an interesting study in exploration of Sanskrit Drama. Romesh Chander writes that Kalidasa's "Vikramorvashiyam" enacted by II Year students of the National School of Drama in New Delhi under B.V. Karanath's direction, is one of the best productionns from the pedagogical point of view in recent years.

It introduces drama students to own classical tradition in theatre As Karanath says "since there is no definite living tradition of Sanskrit theatre that is available to theatre workers today, the director has to use his own style which of course cannot be objectively called the style of Sanskrit play production because it is bound to differ from individual to individual."

Karanth had admirably shown the students the immense possibilities open to them of exploring Sanskrit drama. Then again, it was thoughful of him to invite the best available talent in this part of the country to design his set, lighting and costumes.

From the master designer Bansi Kaul, students learnt how acting areas can be created by simple ramps and platforms to fit in with the director's overall plans, movement and simultaneous action in different areas as for instance when Urvashi comes down from the heavens to meet Pururava with whom she has fallen in love and listens to his wife talking on the Priyanuprasadan vow to pave the way for a smooth union between Urvashi and Pururava. Then again, Bansis creation of a forest with just long drapes, beautifully lit by Ashok Bhagat, in itself must have been a rare learning experience for the students. And of course, Dolly A. Tiwari's choice of fabrics, her eye for design for the various characters in heaven and those on earth was no doubt an aesthetic learning experience.

Yet another plus point of the production, both for the students and the audience, is Karanth's music,. Since "Vikramorvashiyam" is more like a fantasy, Karanth's music too is complementary to "imaginative space and time."

The same year B.V. Karanth, directed 'Vikramorvashiyam' of Kalidasa in Hindi version, rendered by Dr. (Smt.) Induja A wasthi. The play was presented at the 'Kalidasa Festival' Ujjain.

Some scenes from 'Vikramorvashiyam', presented by students of the National School of Drama in New Delhi (1997), directed by B.V. Karanth.

Under the direction of Rita Ganguli, the second year students of National School of Drama presented 'Abhishaap', a play based on Sanskrit classic in the first week of De cember 1998. The literary composition of Kalidasa & Meghdutam, Shakuntalam and Vikramorvasiyam into one d ramatic piece was done by Suman Kumar. The set was designed by Ram Gopal Gajaj and Ashok Sagar Bhagat. The costumes by Kriti V. Sharma and lights by Ashok Sagar Bhagat.

Costume Design of Kalidasa's Vikramorvashiyam

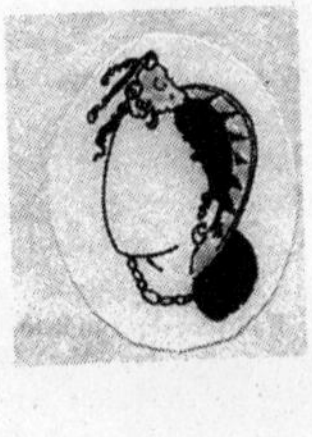

(III) ABHIJNANA SAKUNTALAM IN PERFORMANCE

(Abhijnana Sakuntalam in Kutiyattam) *One of the most ancient and popular of Kerala's entertainments in Kutiyattam. It has pan - Indian importance for in this we have the Sanskrit dramas staged. Here the particular act of the particular drama is enacted. Chakyar's act the chosen act of the chosen drama, because to produce a whole play require the better part of several months. It is pertinent to put it on record that like Bhasa's Carudattam, Sakuntala of Kalidasa are among about a dozen other works from which acts were presented but which were eventually dropped from their repertoire.*

Franz Schuber (1797 - 1828) began a Sakuntala opera as early as 1820. Libretto was by John Philip Neumann, but it was never finished and is not preserved.

In France, the first attempt to stage Kalidasa's Abhijnana Sakuntalam was the ballet pantomime in two acts entitled 'Sakuntala', adapted by Theophile Grautier. The play, intended as "a history of love and the fight against the magic" was staged against the gigantic scenery in Paris Opera House.

Theophile Gautier's Ballet - Pantomime of Sacountala, Paris Opera House, 1858.

Considering the dimensions of the theaters involved and the number of the performances given, the success of Gautier's ballet with its eighty performances, earning 185,000 francs in receipts, was quite extraordinary.

Theophile Gautier's Sacountala ballet, the first form under which the Parisian public saw Kalidasa drama performed had its debut in July 1858. Its plot and characterisation diverge considerably from the original. The ballet consists of two acts and nine scenes, rather than the seven of Kalidasa's play. Gautier learned from earlier experience with Paquerette and Gemma, that a ballet should not extend beyond two hours. Therefore, his primary task was to reduce Kalidasa's work to two decors.

The setting of the First Act was an elaborately designed hermitage. Only the hunt and love scenes of the original are retained. Romance develops very quickly. The coup de foudre passion seems almost to parody Kalidasa's subtle depiction of love's awakening. The king does not linger in the hermitage, nor does he marry and impregnate the heroine. With these significant omissions, Gautier dismisses the central conflict in the play, (i.e., that of the cruelty of Dusyanta's repudiation of his pregnant wife).

The Second Act, set amid a sumptuous decor, continues to diverge from the original plot line. It is as though Gautier abandons the story in order to practice his descriptive skills. Not only is Sacountala rejected by the king, but his jealous wife sends her to be tortured and executed. Before the sentence is carried out, a fisherman returns the ring and the king regains his memory. The flames into which Sacountala has been cast are transformed into flowers.

Although many of the ballet's distortions are due to the change in genre from language to dance and mime, others could only have been inspired by Gautier's manipulation of imagery. Along with the simplification of plot, there is a tendency to enhance the visual trappings of the play for "poetic" effect. In this sense, Sacountala conforms to Gautier's general criteria for ballet : Un ballet demandedeclatantens decorations, des fetes somputeuses, des costumes galants et magnifiques; le monde de la feerie est le milieu ou se developpe le plus facilement une action de ballet.

Kalidasa's subtle drama was thus reduced to pictorial images. That Gautier strove primarily to abandon fidelity and heighten imagery and to add, whether in the decor or the dance sequences, sensual and decorative elements, is suggested in a review of the ballet that he himself wrote. His intention was to evoke the "vigoureux parfum, [les] languers pamees et [les] reculements" of Kalidasa's verse in dance. His choice of composer was not fortuitous.Ernest Reyer, who had composed dances depicting Arab desert life, was expected to bring Sacountala his "profound sense of oriental melodies, i.e., strange timbres, imperious rhythms, bizarre cadences, and songs of savage grace. The production was fantastic : the cast consisted of three hundred and fifty members (brahmans, hermits, Negroes, courtesans, jugglers, bayaderas, priestesses, nymphs, goddesses, and genies) and eight often recalcitrant horses. The general effect of the staging, decor, exotic imagery and music, combined with the belief in the plot's "literary" merits, assured the ballet's success. One year after its premier, Fauche published his translation of the Sakuntala. In the introduction to his rendition, Fauche prophisized a future success for Gautier's ballet, which was not to be.

Karl von Perfall (1824 - 1907) composed along with the librettist Teichert, opera 'Shakuntala' for a Munich debut in 1854. As may be judged from its two performance, it was not a big success.

Residence of Babu Ashutosh Deb where 'Sakuntala' was staged in 1857

In the year 1857, Babu Ashutosh Deb ushered a new era by organising the play 'Sakuntala' in Bengali. He took 'Simla Palace' as its venue with a chosen few public. Though critics observed that the play failed to arouse interest as most of the actors were not equipped enough to handle the classical drama, but Sylvain, Levi once commented that the attempt created a spirit of emulation. An aristocratic home of Calcutta, in 1857 set up a theatre called Ashutosh Deb's Theatre in the home of Ashutosh Deb popularly known as "Satu Babu" with the intension of staging Bengali plays. The Kalidasa's 'Sakuntala' was enacted in Bengali translation by Nanda Kumar Roy was performed on 30 January 1857 and the show was repeated on 22 February and 23 July 1857.

Considering its importance and the enthusiasm the production created in its first run, the 5 Feb. 1857 issue of '*Hindu Patriot*', a well known newspaper commended the effort and paid compliments to the descendants of Satu Babu. His grandson Sarat Chandra Ghose who did the role of Sakuntala received wider applause both by the masses as well as critics.

A review of the play also appeared on 9 February 1857 in '*Sambad Prabhakar*'.

The second show was performed at Satubabu's residence on 22 February [12 Phalgum] Sunday, 1857.

In its third show, only three acts were enacted.

On 9 Feb. 1857, '*Samachar Chandrika*' and in 26 Feb. 1857 '*Sambad Pravakar*' praised him for bringing 'Sakuntala' alive on stage. The cast of this successful production was as under :-

Dushyanta	...	Priyamadhav Mullick
Shakuntala	...	Sarat Chandra Ghose
Durbasa	...	Ananda Prasad Mukherjee
Priyambada	...	Bhuban Ghose
Anusuya	...	Abinash Chandra Ghose.

The cost of costume designs and jewellary exceeded over ten thousand rupees. It was again staged at the Paikpara residence of Raja Pratap Narayan Sinha and Iswarchandra Sinha. The dramatis personae were:-

Sakuntala	...	Sharatbabu

Dusyanta	...	Priyamadhav Mullik
Durvasa	...	Ananda Mukhopadhyay
Anusuya	...	Abinashchandra Ghosh
Sage	...	Mahendranath Mukhopadhyay
(Stage-Manager	...	O.C. Dutt.)

In mid 19th century, the craze for theatres began to spread among the middle class Bengali youths with the series by successful performances in the houses of the Calcutta's leading aristrocrats. In spite of their limited resources, a number of good productions came up. Here mention could be made of Kalidasa's classic 'Sakuntala' at the house of the Mukherjees of Janai at Ahiritola in 1859 under the managership of Shri Jayram Basak. The actors were trained by Sri Abhaychandra Gupta. The cast comprised of :-

Dusyanta	...	Atulchandra Mukhopadhya
Jester	...	Aghornath Pandit
Kanva	...	Hemchandra Mukhopadhyay
Sangarav	...	Mahendranath Gupta
Sharadvat	...	Nilkantha Bandyopadhyay
Kanchuki	...	Kalinath Bandyopadhyay
Sarathi	...	Mahadev Ghosal
Shakuntala	...	Abinashchandra Mukhopadhyay
Anusuya	...	Hemchandra Bandyopadhyay
Priyamvada	...	Gopalchandra Datta
Menaka	...	Purnachandra Mukhopadhyay

The production was witnessed by many distinguished personalities of the time such as Babu Kaliprasanna Sinha, Sharatchandra Ghosh, Iswarchanda Gupta, Dwarkanath Vidyabhusan, Gaurishankar Bhattacharya and the Magistrates from Hoogly and Shrirampur. The review of the play appeared in '*Prabhakar*' and '*Bhaskar*'.

Dharmadas Sur, a well-known stage-designer of the eighteenth century, has mentioned in his autobiography about the staging of 'Sakuntala' in Bengali at the instance Shri Kalikrishna Pramanik, (who was also the financer of the production) in middle of the last century (but prior to 1869).

The Elphinstone Society of the Elphinstone College in Bombay performed Kalidasa's Abhijnana Sakuntalam in English in 1867 and in Sanskrit in 1870.

Alfred Freiherr von Wolzogen's Sakuntala written in 1869, exemplifies the way in which Kalidasa's drama was reduced to an adventure tale. In this stage adaptaion, the king's impetuous love is put on trial. He himself is subjected to a series of intrigues and ordeals. In confrontations with Kanwa and Gautami, the king must prove himself immune to the seductions of the world. Eventually, he is reunited with Sakuntala, but only after the heroine has died and been resuscitated. In this version, the king is made to perform many deeds of valor and honour, which distinguish him from his counterpart in the nataka. As in Gautier's ballet, Sakuntala is not impregnated in this version.

A curious episode is appended to the plot. The king initiates a long discussion with his wife onthe virtues of the life of duty and involvement in worldly affairs as opposed to the life of asceticism. When he believes that Sakuntala has died, the king renounces his kingdom and retires to the hermitage. Once revived, Sakuntala forces him to return to his kingdom and rule. The king;s desire to reject the world is presented as less a product of his will than of Indian cultural attitudes and values. Moreover, this theme of the tension between conflicting life aims (i.e., world-renunciation versus active living in the world) is incorporated in other adaptations where a character's passivity is both philosophically rationalized and built into the narrative. These emendations prefigure a larger problem with which the adapter had to contend.

When king Ludwig decided to mount a production of the Sakuntala, he found this adaptation to be free for his tastes and Ruckert's translation to be too literal. He commissioned Karl Von Heigel to rework the play for production in 1877.

Jagannadha Vilasini Sabha at Vizianagaram was started by Vijayarama Gajapati Maharaj in 1874. Popularly known as 'Butchi Sastry Company', the theatrical group was also known as the 'Sanskrit Academy' as it produced only Sanskrit plays such as Abhijnana Sakuntalam of Kalidasa.

The Indian (Late Great National) Theatre of Calcutta staged 'Kanakapadma', an adaptation of Kalidasa's Abhijnana Sakuntalam in Bengal by

Haralal Ray on 25 September 1875. The versatile Bengali actor Amritlal Basu appeared as 'Dushyanta'.

Nandakumar Ray's Bengali version of Kalidasa's classic 'Sakuntala' was first produced by the Bengal Theatre [at 9, Beadon Street, Calcuta] on 18 January 1878. For the first time the Viceroy witnessed a play in an indigenous Theatre House on 21 January 1878 (Monday). The '*Indian Daily News*' wrote :- "BENGAL THEATRE" :- An entertainment in aid of the Society for the Prevention of Cruelty to Animals was given at this place of Amusement on Friday evening last. His Excellency the Viceroy, accompanied by Lady Lytton, Sir Richard Temple and Staff, arrived shortly after half past nine, when the band immediately performed the National Anthem. We used the word 'performed' advisedly, as the strains were as measured as so many doses of strychnine. We have no doubt the Viceregal party enjoyed the fun immediately, but having 'very private engagement' elsewhere, were reluctantly compelled to retire after the first act.

The drama selected for the Occasion was "Sakuntala, or, the Lost Ring". We will not attempt to describe the intricate plot of the famous play, nor indeed is it necessary, as all lovers of high art must be well acquainted with its labyrinthine mysteries. Suffice it to say that the parts of the King and the Jester were sustained by Baboos S.C. Ghose and W.C. Roy with all that dash so observable on the native stage and that Sreematy Narayani as Sakoontala, the foster daughter, was everything that could be wished. This young lady, together with her attendants, Priambada and Anusuya, favoured the audience with some excellent singing, with the usual neuralgic effects. The house was crowded in every part, and the performance appeared to be heartily appreciated. The exterior of the building was prettily decorated wth well-arranged flowers and the legitimate amount of red cloth. There was some well-executed scenery, judged from a native point of view; and if the perspective in one or two of the 'drops' was rather adrift, it was decidedly unison with the representation generally. The orchestra played several airs, and was as hurdy-gurdyish as the most devoted Bengalee could desire.

The '*Indian Mirror*' commented : "Lord and Lady Lytton visited the Bengal Theatre on Friday last. We are not going to say anything against the management of this Institutuon. But considering that the theatre has drawn to itself the prostitutes of Calcutta, who are known to ply their dirty trade openly to public, and that the practice of employing them as actresses is one that is utterly repugnant to Hindu feeling, Lord Lytton might have paused before taking a step so ill calculated to promote the ends of morality. The presence of the Head of Government before sons of gentlemen acting with the prostitutes, offered an encouragement to that sort of thing which it must be very hard to resist. We fear that Lord Lytton was mis-informed and ill-advised in the matter. Only the other day Lord Northbrook's Government tried to suppress one of the Native theatres for its gross immorality, (Quoted in t he *Indian Daily News* of 22nd January, 1878).

The 'Oriental Dramatic Company' was founded during 1879-80 at Madras by Gomatham C.V. Sreenivasacharyulu who was not only its President, but the main actor of the troupe. He was bestowed with the title 'Indian Garrick' for his memorabloe role of the 'Dushyanta' in Sakuntalam. The actor who laid great stress on sattvika abhinaya became the Director of the Sanskrit Academy when he moved to Vizianagaram.

'Andhra Bhashabhimani Samajam' was founded by an outstanding scholar and Telugu playwright called Vedam Venkataray Sastry. The group produced Kalidasa's callsic 'Sakuntalam' and its main attraction was Kandadai Srinivasan, who gave a brilliant performance in the role of Dushyanta.

In January 1880, a version of 'Sakuntala' was staged in Baroda by Indian actors. Harold Littledale who after witnessing the production vividly documented the grandeurs of this production in the *Macmillan's Magazine* of May 1880.

Balwant Pandurang alias Annasaheb Kirloskar who is revered as the Father of modern Marathi drama earned his reputation with the premiere of his Marathi version of Shakuntala presented on 31st October 1880 at the Anandodbhav Theatre in Pune. Only four acts were staged but it came to be recognized as a major landmark as the first Marathi music play as we know the form today. But according to K.B. Marathe, a reseach scholar from Belgaum, furnished enough evidence to suggest that the first four acts of the Marathi version 'Sangeet Shakuntal' had been staged by an organisation in Belgaum some years before the 1880 first night in Pune. Nevertheless, in praise of Marathi Shakuntal, Tilak had once commented ".... This was something not only to be applauded, but a thing with which every Maharashtrian ought to be applauded, but a thing which every Maharashtrian ought to associate himself not merely for the sake of amusement but, more, for the revival of ancient Indian Culture."

Annnasaheb Kirloskar

In the words of Vasant Shantaram Desai "Shakuntal" was an adaptation of the work ofa genius by a genius. Kirloskar remained faithful to the script of Kalidas, but not merely to the script. He had assimilated the charm of Shakuntala and mastered the appropriate diction which could render that charm into Marathi through a suitable expression. He retained the 'Nati-Sutradhar' dialogue, replaced the shlokas with appropriate songs; and thus the Marathi 'Shakuntal' was combination of prose and songs and was the first of the Sangeet (musical) plays which founded a tradition that was to dominate the Marathi stage for nearly half a century."

An art historian documented that a new phase in stage music began with Annasaheb Kirloskar's Sangeeta Sakuntala and the style remained in vogue for nearly twenty-five years.

The sutradhara's singing style (which had its origins in the kirtankara tradition) made for a certain degree of monotony. Besides the sutradhara's music hardly blended with the acting styles of the other actors. Perhaps directors would have liked these actors to resort to music and thus add some verve to a performance. But there was a dearth of actor-singers and the sole responsibility for music had to be entrusted to the sutradhara mainly to avoid the possibility of a performance being marred through indifferent singing by other actors. The situation remained unchanged from the days of Vishnudas Bhave till 1880, when Annasaheb Kirloskar arrived on the theatre scene.

Two scenes from 'Sangeet Shakuntal', Kirloskar Sangeet Mandali 1880, featuring Moroba Wagholikar, Annasaheb Kirloskar and Shakarrao Mazumdar

In Annasaheb Kirloskar's biography there is a reference to the inspiration he derived from Wajid Ali Shah's production of Inder Sabha in which accomplished musicians and dancers of the Lucknow court paticipated to make the performance a success. Annasaheb Kirloskar was also acquainted with the musical tradition of Karnataka where several actor - singers used to take part in Sangeeta Parijataka and other plays. In Maharashtra, efforts in this direction had to be abandoned in the previous decades mainly because good actor-singers were not available in sufficient numbers. But Annasaheb Kirloskar who could count on the support of two good actor-singers, Balkoba Natekar and Moroba Wagholikar, initiated a change in the conventional pattern. A little later he was fortunate enough to enlist in his troupe an exceptionally talented actor-singer, Bhaurao Kolhatkar. As a result, the Kirloskar Sangeeta Mandali's dominance in the sphere of stage music continued for twenty five years.

Balkoba Natekar was a proficient singer. Moroba Wagholikar (owing to his kirtankara background) had a powerful voice; he had also spent some years with a lavani troupe, imbibing that style of music. Annasaheb's own connections with Karnataka prompted him to include some attractive melodies based on the Karnatic style in the music of Sangeeta Sakuntala. But these were transformed on the stage to blend with the general Haridasi kirtana style of singing and almost nothing was left of the Karnatic mode of presentation.

A characteristic feature of the music of this play was the prominence it gave to words. The tana-s, khatka-s, murki-s were not patterned on notes but intended to stress poetic essence and word arrangement. This was insisted upon at the time of rehearsals on the suggestion of connoisseurs like Kerunana Chatre. Balkoba Natekar, being primarily a musician, tended to emphasize the note-structure, which provoked criticism from the press. As stated, Sakuntala's Music was superb where Kirloskar made use of the popular ragas of Hindustani and Karnatic music and also the 'Lavani' and other homely tunes of Maharashtra for the songs. The indigenous instruments such as table and tanpura were played from the wings and were only audible but invisible to the masses. There were more than hundred songs and as a result, the full performance of Sakuntala which commenced at about 10 pm., used to last till the early hours of the morning.

As Shankerrao Majumdar who played the central female role 'Sakuntala' was not a singer, there was, thus not a single song for him. However, when Bhaurao Kolhatkar joined the Kirloskar company, he began to play the role of Sakuntala and the songs were composed for the role by Govind Ballal Deval.

The dramatis personae comprised of very talented team of singers and actors such as :-

Sakuntala	...	Shankerrao Majumdar/Bhaurao Kolhatkar
Dushyanta	...	Moroba Wagholikar
Sutradhar and Sharangrav	...	Annasaheb Kirloskar
Kanva	...	Balkoba Natekar

Bhaurao Kolhatkar

In Marathi theatre world, Bhaurao Kolhatkar occupies a permanent place for his eminence as a singer. He associated himself with Kirloskar Natak Mandali and appeared for the first time as heroine in Annasaheb's 'Sangeet Sakuntala'. This Marathi version was premiered on 31st October 1880. Then, was in the year 1905, i.e., after the untimely demise of Bhaurao, the role of 'Sakuntala' went to Narayan Rao Sripad Rajhans alias Balgandharava who was the first recipient of Sangeet Natak Academy Award for Drama.

Narayanrao Rajhans alias, Natsamrat 'Balgandharva'

Felix Weingartner's Sakuntala opera was performed at the Hoftheatre in Weimar on March 23, 1884. The libretto emphasizes the love story : love transforms the king from a callow hunter into a sensitive lover of all life. Moonlit love scenes stretch over two hundred and twenty measures. Kanwa imposes a trial separation upon the guilty lovers. However, it is the king's wife, neglected and rejected, who curses the king. Throughout this version, the king fights off the effects of this curse. He goes off in search of Sakuntala only to learn that she has died. The king decides to become a hermit, but is reunited with his revived bride. As in Wolzogen's adaptation, ascetic renunciation is presented as an alternative to a broken heart. Action scenes are added to the plot and the character of the king develops from a vain Lothario into a penitent husband. Weingartner wrote both the music and the libretto.

The tendency to transform the Sakuntala into a melodrama reaches its furthest extension in Ludwig Philipp Scharwenka's operatic version (1885). Relative fidelity to the original is found in those scenes that are the most dramatic (the repudiation, assumption, and fisherman episodes,) although these are considerably heightened. Scharwenka adds to the plot several long battle scenes with demons, missions in the service of Siva, and a seven-year-long search by the king for his repudiated bride. This opera had its debut on March 9, 1886.

In his '*Divyopadesa*', Prithvinarayana decreed that no dancer and musician from India should be encouraged in Nepal. He wanted the artists and musicians of the valley to the patronised. How far this policy affected the growth of drama in Nepal is a question which finds no easy answer. However; the luxurious palace of Bir Samser Rana was filled with dancers and musicians from India since he came to power in 1855. In his palace, Hindi and Urdu plays were regularly staged. He is said to have encouraged Motiram Bhatta, an astute translator to render. Kalidasa's Abhijnana Sakuntal into Nepali, though the drama was staged in 1887 its manuscript has not yet been traced.

Sakuntalam is not only great poetry, but great drama too. Kerala Varma's Bhasa Sakuntalam first published ifn 1882 though couched in Sanskritised Manipravala style made a tremendous appeal on the Kerala stage also.

It was received with a thrill not only by literary men but also by actors who got interested in staging it. Kerala Verma felt great satisfication when he saw that the drama was staged in various parts of Kerala by different drama companies coming forward for the purpose. The staging of the drama in different parts of Kerala proved to be a great cultural event that brought people great enjoyment as this drama was entirely different from the Kutiyattam and Kathakali which the people were used to in those day.

Shri Vedam Venkataraya Sastry (21/12/1853 - 18/6/1929) was a dominent figure in the Telugu literary field for over a half a century beginning from the last quarter of the nineteenth century and ending with the first of the twentieth. This literary giant, became a by word for Sanskrit and in 1886, he was appointed as Sanskrit Pandit at the Madras Christian College where he served till 1910. An important factor in the life of Sri V enkataraya Sastry was his dramatic activity as a literary past time. He was not only a playwright but a stage director as well. In the eighties of the 19th century it was his practice to see that every year his students at college enacted the Sanskrit Drama in its original prescribed for that year. Thus he saw Abhijnana Sakuntalam of Kalidasa; Bhababhuti's Uttararamacharitam, Harsha's Naganandam and Priyadarsika and the like enacted year after year.

Even outside the educational limits, associations of Sanskrit lovers enacted these dramas in its original form Dramatic Association called 'Andhra Bhasabhimani

Samajam' was formed on 31st April 1899 to enact the Telugu play of Venkataraya Sastry. The eminent scholars like Sri Poondla Ramakrishnayya, Gunapati Yenadi Reddi and a list of others associated themselves with this organisation. The Samajam felt that Vedam Venkataraya Sastry was the dramatist and the other Telugu playwrights were no where. The group attracted enlightened graduates poets, writers and many of the old students of Sri Sastry who happened to settle down at Nellore. Sri Sastry was made the President of the Samajam and under his direction it enacted his Telugu rendering of Sakuntala (published in 1896). The Samajam functioned upto 1925.

In the twentieth century when Bengali drama was flourishing, some energetic Nepali youth staged various plays in Darjeeling. For e.g. James Dunne's Sakuntala in (1911).

Kunjabihari Basu's Bengali adaptation of 'Sakuntala' was staged by Bengal Theatre on 23 & 30 November, 7, 14 and December 1889. The show was repeated on 4th January and 7th January 1890. Queen Victoria's eldest son Prince Albert Victor was present at Gader Maath, at the fete on the maidan, Calcutta on 7th January. Bengal Theatre received the title 'Royal' for their brilliant performance Eventually on 11 January 1890, the group was renamed as 'Royal Bengal Theatre'. On 11 February 1890, the journal '*Anusandhan*' also wrote in praise of the production.

Statesman wrote on 11th January 1890 that Sakuntala was performed with immense success on Tuesday last at the fete on the Maidan before, T.E. The Viceroy and the Marchioness Lansdowne, H.R.H. Prince Albert Victor and other distinguished personages. The play was again performed on 11, 18, 25 January 1890, 1,9, 15, 22 February 1890; 23 andn 30 March 1890; 17 May 1890; 15, 28, June 1890; 12 and 27 July 1890; on 9th August 1890 at Candle-Light [source : Statesman] 23rd August 1890; 7 September 1890; 26 October 1890; 8 Nov. 1890; 6, 20 and 27 December 1890. On 20 December's show Raja of Rangpur Sir Gobindalal Ray was the chief guest.

On 11 January 1891; 14, 28 February 1891; 21 & 27 March 1891; 11 April 1891; 21 May 1891; 17 June 1891; 4 & 12 July 1891; 2 August 1891; 20 September 1891; 21 October 1891; 1 November 1891; 5 & 25 December 1891; 1 & 27 January 1892; 20 March 1892; 24 April 1892; 28 August 1892; 8 October 1892; 6 & 27 November 1892.

The play was again produced on 4 December 1892, a day earlier, i.e. on 3rd December 1892. '*The Statesman*' wrote: Last performance before re-appearing upon a thouroughly repaired stage.

The show was repeated on 25 December 1892; 8 & 17 January 1893; 23 April 1893; 10 May 1893; 24 June 1893; 10 September 1893; 3 March 1893; 17 March 1894; 12 May 1894; 24 December 1894 on the X'mas eve [source : 23rd December 1824]; 21 April 1895, 1 June 1895; 1 September 1895; 6 & 19 October 1895; 15 December 1895; 30 December 1896; 20 March 1897; 22 May 1897; 7, 14 & 21 November 1897; 29 January 1898; 13 March 1898. The play was again repeated on 3rd September 1898 and the chief dramatis personae were :

Dushyanta ... Shri Mathuranath Chattopadhyay

Fisherman ... Shri Nripendrachandra Basu alias Nepa Bose.

The show was again resumed on 11 September 1898; 26 November 1898; 17 December 1898; 27 August 1899; 21 January 25 August 1900; 2 & 25 December 1900.

In 1895, the symbolist director Luge-Poe directed Andre Ferdinand Herold's translation of L'Anneau de Sakuntal at the Theatre de l'Oeuvre. L'Anneau de Sakuntala debuted at the Comedie Parisienue on Dec. 10, 1895; the decór was by Paul Ransosn (La Revue de l'Oeuvre, Nov. 1927) and the music by Pierre de Breville (Henri Albert, Mercure de France, Jan. 1896). It is interesting to note that Rucand's adaptation of Sudraka's Mricchakatika, with the title Le Chariot d'enfant. For several reasons, Sudraka's play enjoyed a mediocre reception: the text was poorly translated, Barrucand significantly altered the play to fit his anarchistic politics, and the audience was shocked by the actor's nudity. L'Anneau de Sakuntala, on the other hand, was received sympathetically.

In his production, Lugne-Poe employed Indian dramatic practices familiar to him through his reading of Sylvain Levi's Theatre indien (1890). To Lugne-Poe's way of thinking, the Sakuntala presented a dramatic system not in conflict with the aesthetics of the Symbolist school. At a time when traditional theatrical techniques were spurned by the naturalists, Indian dramatic conventions, as presented by Levi and recreated by Lugne-Poe, could be construed as reinstating artificiality in the theater. The lack of psychological realism found in Indian theater, as well as its indifference to real life further contributed to the perception that it shared many characteristics with the Symbolists. Both accentuated the role of visual, poetic, and contemplative descriptions of nature. The simplified decor of Indian drama, with little or no props, was identical to that being presented at hte Oeuvre. Even Levi's formulation of Indian dramatic method seemed to correspond to the declamatory style taught by Lugne-Poe. In this adaptation of the Sakuntala, the audience experienced "un espece de candeur lascive." Lugne-Poe himself played the role of Kalidasa's theater director and L'Anneau de Sakuntala was one of the few uncontested successes in the Oeuvre's short existence. This production both challenged the classical norm, championed by critics such as Brunetiere, and corroborated the innovative method of the Symbolists.

In the later half of the nineteenth century, some noteworthy plays were performed in Dacca by the then leading groups these are Abhijnana Sakuntalam,, Nildarpan, Bilvamangal, Sitar banabas and Indra sabha.

Prince of Subarnapur, Orissa, Birmitrodaya Simhadev rendered his second work 'Abhijnana Sakuntalam' in Orissa in the year 1900. It was successfully staged in Sonpur.

Ferdinand Humnel's Sakuntala ballet (Lib. M.Moller) performed in Berlin on April 29, 1903 at the Schauspiel Haus.

A lost Sakuntala opera is by Balduin Zimmermann (Lib. H. Schmilinski) performed in Erfurt in March 1905.

Coehrne's work entitled a 'melodrama' was based on Monier William's English translation of Sakuntala adapted by Alice Morgan Wright. It was performed once for the graduation ceremonies of Smith College in 1905.

The Recovered Ring (Sakuntala of Kalidasa) drew the attention of writers in the West to the beauties of Sanskrit literaly with the publication of William Jones English rendering from Calcutta in 1790.

The first realized stage adaptation of 'Sakuntala' in English took place in 1857. The next attempt to adapt it to the s tage was undertaken by A. Wolzogen in 1869. In 1899 the play was staged for the second time, in London, at an open air performance in Regent's Park by the Elizabethan Stage Society; it was followed by performances in 1912 and 1913.

Franco Alfano, La Leggenda di Sakuntala (Milan : Riccordi, 1921). The opera had its debut in Bologna on October 12, 1921 and was performed most recently in 1982 at the Wexford Festival. The text of La Leggenda di Sakuntala was destroyed in the Allied bombing of Italy, but was reconstructed by Alfano after the war.

Alfano altered the original very title. If anything, he added to the characterizations by exploiting for dramatic purposes the child and the charming scenes involving the hermit girls, the bee scene, the King's spying on Sakuntala, and Hamsapadika's song. Deletions in the plot are few the most significant of which occurs at the end of the opera. Sakuntala is not reunited with the king. The son, however, is brought to Dusyanta by a heavenly Lost the opera ends this manner.

The Sakuntala inspired yet another Symbolist production. In 1914, Alexander Tairov opened the Kamerny Theatre in Moscow with a production of Kalidasa's play. It was based on a translation by the Symbolist poet Balmont; the decor was designed by the Symbolist paitner Kuznetsov. Tairov's theory of the theater lay between the Stanislavsky School of Realism and Meyerhold's method of symbolism. According to his lifelong companion, Alisa Koonen, who played the role of the heroine in this production, the choice of Sakuntala was not accidental. This adaptation presented a protest against the banality and lower middle - class taste that reigned in the Russian theater. It has also been suggested that, in choosing a Sanskrit play, Tairov sought to refine and develop his own theatrical concepts.

In the months proceeding the premiere, Tairov had studied Indian costumes, masks and Levi's book while in Paris. By adapting principles of Indian set design, Tairov sought to present his own ideal : a stage design in which nothing hindered either the actor or the portrayal of emotion. The trend then current in Moscow production design, the art movement of Mir iskusstava (the World of Art), was characterized by grandiose and extravagantly painted backdrops, overshadowing the actor. Tairov and Kuznetsov rejected Mir iskusstava's dramatic preferences. The action of this Sakuntala was performed before simple colored curtains depicting the rasa of the given scene. As in other staged versions of the play, Tairov also emended the plot. Having deleted those scenes which alluded to morality, he retained only those which forwarded the action (love scenes, the curse, leavetaking and repudiation).

With his production of the Sakuntala, Tairov also experimented with other problems of production design (gesture, pantomime, and costume). Many scenes were dialogue-free, and stylization was used to enhance the tableau effect. The actors were semi-nude. In keeping with Bharata's information, their bodies were painted according to their character. Tairov had adapted the colour scheme to suit Western sensibilities. The actors moved in a half-dancing fashion of pantomime and stylized gestures ostensibly reminiscent of Sanskrit dance. The Sakuntala and Indian dramatic practice could thus be used to confirm the value of Symbolist aesthetic theories. Kalidasa's play presented Tairov with a propitious model upon which his theories could be developed.

Jan Ciechowicz writes that the strongest link with the Polish experiments of Jerzy Grotowski (1960) was the premiere performance of 'Sakauntala' by the Little Theatre of Aleksander Tairov (1914). Shakuntala became for Tairov a splendid material for the polemics with the naturalistic theatre, and transposed onto the stage in the rhythmical theatrical way constituted the mystery credo of the stage manager.

Rajaraja Varma published his own Malayalam version of Sakuntalam under the title 'Malayala Sakuntalam' in 1912. This was a simpler version of the classic for the benefit of the less scholarly reader. But this translation also was well received both on and off the stage. The play was performed at Mavelikkara in 1915, it was so much of a sucess that A.R. Rajaraja Varma promised to give 'Kalavilasam' drama troupe of Trivandrum a new play every year.

Indian Broadcasting Company (IBC) was formed in the year 1927. The company was allowed to open its Radio Station on 15th July and on 23rd July, its first centre was founded at Bombay. On 23rd July, the Associated Press of India commented "Broadcasting throw's open sluice Gates of Education. The then Secretary of India exclaimed... I ask you however, to visualise the day, the sceptic might suppose when in very village of the country side there will be men, women and children and those not only of the well-to-do classes listening through the mediums of their own vernacular to the true story of world and to the expression of quickening thoughts and ideas, which but could never reach them." During that period mostly historical and religious plays were broascasted but some plays on social reformation were also produced. On 15 August 1930, Ray Bahadur Bholanath Bandnyopadhyay's Bengali play entitled 'Sakuntala' was broadcasted by them. The play was inspired from Kalidasa's magnum opus Sanskrit drama.

D.D. Deolalikar was an eminent painter who received his art education from the J.J. School of Art. The Principal of the Indore School of Art (1929), he later became Professor Emeritus (Honorary) at the Gwalior School of Art. Honoured with the title 'Rajaratna' by the Indore Durbar, this great teacher and artist once choreographed a dance-drama in Sanskrit based on Sakuntala.

For the Art Theatre, Calcutta presented Bengali version of Shakuntala by Aparesh Chandra Mukherjee on 30 October 1930. A highly successful venture, its scenic design was created by Paresh Basu. Durgadas Basu appeared as Dusyanta, while Sushila (Jr.) was Shakuntala.

Other cast was :-

Kanva ... Tinkari Chakravarti

Vidushak ... Tulsi Charan Banerji

Goutama ... Kusum Kumari

The play was staged at 'Star Theatre'.

Antonin Modharelli (Lib. Jul. Hart) performed 'Sakuntala' opera in Augsburg in December 1930. M.Krishnamachariar in his book 'History of classical Sanskrit literature 1937 mentions that Sakuntala was recently staged at Melbourne from a translation made by Lawbonce Bunyon and the adaptation of the music is thus described:-"The overture opens with the King's lovesinging theme, given first in the low register of the orchestra. This is continued by the higher strings and wood wind to a climax, with a first hint of the curse motive. A bridge passage for strings and wood wind leads to Sakuntala's love singing theme played by the violin; this works up to a repeat of the same given in the higher octave by the flutes and oboes. A tremolo passage for strings, with a further hint of the curse motive, is followed by the development of the King's theme working to a full climax of both the King's and Sakuntala's themes leading straight to the curse motive at full orchestral strength. A quiet passage for strings rading with a cadenza for the oboe is followed by the golden peak theme given by the flute in its highest register. The overture foreshadows thte entire development of the drama : the sublimation of the earthly unstable love to the universally significant reunion at the mystic's retreat in the Himalaya Mountains. The incidents of the drama are limited in the use of the curse and other motives. Before and during part four, an off - shoot of the Golden Peak theme will be heard, suggestive of the nymphs, who sing their farewell to Sakuntala."

Andhra Association formed in 1936 at Calcutta performed its first play 'Sakuntala' in Telugu in 1937. Fourth act of the 'Sakuntala' was staged in Sanskrit at the Twelfth Oriental Conference held at Benaras from 31st December 1943 to 2nd January 1944.

Sakuntala, Act III. Prithvi Theatres, Bombay, 1944. Prithviraj Kapoor as King Dusyanta

Shri Prithvi Raj Kapoor

On 15 January 1944, Prithviraj Kapoor established his own Prithvi Theatres. In the same year, This group from Bombay produced its maiden play 'Sakuntala' in Hindi.

It was staged along Western realistic lines, with live trees and plans and a hut constructed in careful detail, followed the influence of British Theatre. Prithviraj Kapoor did the role of Dushyanta, while the Shakuntala was played by Uzra Butt (Segal).

Uzra was a well known dancer and actress who worked with Prithviraj Kapoor for several years as a leading lady in Prithvi Theatre. Basically she was a dancer. Khwaja Ahmad Abbas was directing a play called Zubeida which was about a Muslim family from U.P. he could not find a girl who could speak Urdu fluently and Uzra was chosen for the play and when Prithviraj saw her on-stage, she was impressed enough to cast her in Sakuntala. Initially, he just told this dancer to read the script and attend rehearsals, but pay special attention to the role of Sakuntala.

Today Uzra recalls "I told my husband Hamid and he just laughed and said" You? Sakuntala? Don't be funny. When there are leading ladies like Vanmala and Swarnalata, why should Prithviraj take you? But I was very excited and I learnt up the whole role of Sakuntala by heart. One day at a rehearsal, Prithviraj asked me to do a scene. I put down the script he said that I could keep the script with me but I did not need the script because I already knew the whole role. Everyone was stunned. This impressed Prithviraj and he gave me the role of Sakuntala.

But Uzra was very nervous; Hamid told her that every time Prithviraj, who played Dushyant, came near her, she perceptibly froze into an iceberg! But Uzra worked with Prithviraj for 14 years.

To Zohra Segal, who witnessed performances of Prithvi Theatre's 'Sakuntala' comments about her sister Uzra who was starring in it. She said "In Prithvi Theatre I met Shri Prithviraj Kapoor, the founder - director and leading actor of Prithvi Theatres. I was greatly impressed by his personality, Though I did not think much of the play, and found the sets atrocious, the overall effect being dated and laboured. The only redeeming feature to my mind was Uzra's dignified grace and beauty which stoodout amongst her companions" Joan L. Erdman with Zohra Segal also mentions in the book "*The Art and adventures of Zohra Segal*" that the first performance of Shakuntala was held on March 9, 1945 which resulted in a financial loss of nearly a lakh of rupees, but to celebrate this first show Prithvi paid a bonus of two month's salary to the entire cast and management from his own resources. All his earnings from film contracts were put into the theatre."

After the performance of 'Sakuntala' in Bombay, the troupe took the play on a tour of some neighbouring tours, creating an unprecedented sensation wherever they went.

Uzra Butt (Segal)

In Simhapuri at Ujjain, 'Kalidasa Jayanti' that started in the third decade of this century is presently a national event. In the festival, intially only local talents were exploited. Here mention could be made of Prof. V. Venkatachalam who had directed 'Vikramorvasiyam' and 'Sakuntalam' in Sanskrit.

Smt. and Shri Kanetkar Shastri, presented the fourth Act of 'Sakuntalam' in its original for the first time at the "Mahakavi Kalidasa Samaroha" held at Maharajawada Higher Secondary School.

In 1945, Reece Clifford Lawson gave a description of ballet performancne of Sakuntala given at the Embassy Theatre. (*Source : Journal 'Indian Art and Letters' Vol. XIX, No. 2, 1945; Pp. 91-92*).

The Fifteenth Session of the 'All India Oriental Conference' was held in Bombay under the auspices of the University of Bombay and the Bombay Branch of the Royal Asiatic Society, from 5th to 7th November 1949. On the occasion the 'Abhijnana Sakuntalam' of Kalidasa was staged in Sanskrit.

Star Theatre produced Kalidasa's 'Sakuntala in Bengali on 12 July 1951'. The play was adapted by Mahedra Gupta. The cast was :-

Dushyanta	...	Mahendra Gupta
Kanva	...	Santosh Das
Madhyaba	...	Ajit Banerjee
Sakuntala	...	Purnima
Anusuya	...	Ferozabala
Priyambada	...	Ketakī Dutt
Bawadebata	...	Indubala

First National Drama Festival - 1954

The Sangeet Natak Academy adopted a resolution in March 1954 to celebrate a National Drama Festival in Delhi. The Natya Sangh was vested with the responsibility to organise this festival. Thus, the First National Drama Festival was organised by The Sangeet Natak Academy, New Delhi from November 22, 1954. In all, 22 plays on varying themes, mythological, historical and social, in different languages were staged during the Festival. These were witnessed by thousands of spectators and eminent men of the theatre world. The then President of India, Dr. Rajendra Prasad inaugurated the Festival. The opening and the termination of the Festival symbolically highlighted the diversity and range of modern theatre activity in India as it befittingly opened with an Indian classic 'Sakuntala of Kalidasa, performed by the Brahman Sabha, Bombay under the the direction of Daji Bhatvadekar.

At that time, there was no single theatre in Delhi which was good enough for a stage. An open-air stage was an impossibility due to the severe winter. The Sapru House Hall, at Barakhamba Road (Mandi House) which was used for the first time for the Radio Sangeet Sammelan in October, 1954, was chosen for the First Indian Drama Festival at National level.

A critic writes that in Delhi, probably the audience had no idea that a play entirely in Sanskrit could be presented on the stage. Faultless prounciation and appropriate histrionics were the strong points of the play. Though the language of the play was Sanskrit, yet the response of the audience was spontaneouns. Proper laughter and the applause provoked in various corners of the multi-lingual audience, were themselves sure signs of the success of the play. The Prime Minister, Pandit Jawaharlal Nehru, sat for five hours to witness this play from the beginning to the end. He also expressed his appreciation of the troupe.

Shri Bhargavaram Vithal, alias Mama Warerkar, a veteran Marathi playwright, novelist and drama-critic presented his personal gold medal to the troupe that staged this immortal play in its original.

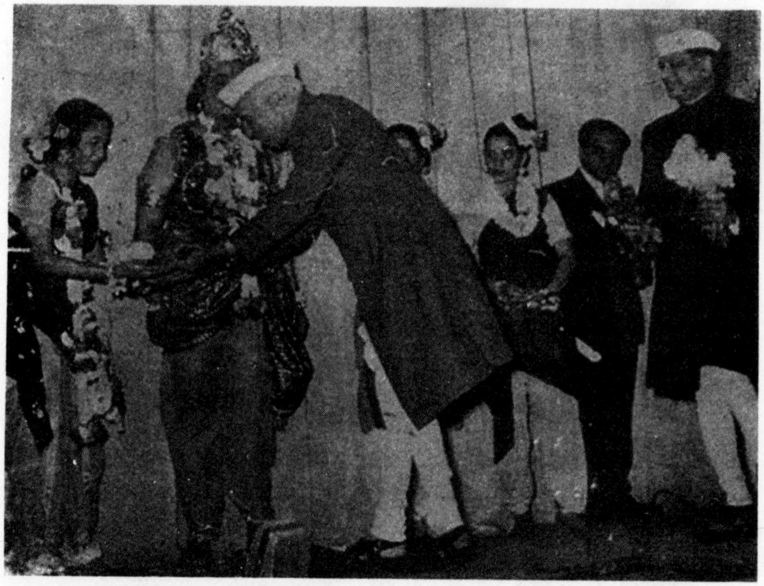

The artists, who took part in 'Sakuntala', being presented to the Prime Minister, Shri Nehru

Brahman Sabha's presentation of Kalidasa's Sakuntala in the National Drama Festival did indeed reveal the unravished beauty of Kalidasa's master piece. In the presentation Sanskrit shlokas were sung and two new songs had also been composed. The drama was beautifully produced, but it left unresolved problems of staging Sanskrit play in modern times.

In 1956 'Kalidasa Festival' was organised at the Hall of Columns, Moscow. The programmes include third Act of 'Abhijnana Sakuntalam'; recitation of verses from Meghdutam and 'Malavikagnimitra'. For the first time, Soviet Government released a postal stamp in the honour of this great dramatic genius.

Sergei Esenin mentions in our indigenous journal 'Natya' (Autumn International Number, 1958) that in the Pushkin Theatre in Moscow, was running the play of Kalidasa, the magnum opus 'Abhijnana Sakuntalam' was staged that kept the Soviet theatre - goes spell bound.

Chinese Youth Centre, Peking staged Kalidasa's classic 'Sakuntala' in 1957. After six months of rigorous rehearshal, when finally the play was put up by the Chinese actors, the drama received immense popularity.

A scene from Act II of Shakuntala

Sakuntala, Act III. Chinese Youth Theatre, Peking, 1957. King Dusyanta with Sakuntala in the garden. The trees, flowers and deer are stylized scenic elements not called for in traditional Sanskrit practice.

In 1957, the Karl Marx Stadt Theatre produced Kalidasa's Sakuntala but were not satisfied with their first production. So in their second presentation they took the assistance of an Indian adviser. Srimati Snehlata Sanyal, well-known in Delhi and Punjab for her pioneer work in theatrical ventures like Hir Ranjha, got the assignment to advice them on the settings, costumes and basic interpretations after this immortal Sanskrit play.

Kalidasa Jayanti Celebrations - 1958

Kalidasa Jayanti Celebrations held at Ujjain - The city with which the poet's name is closely associated in literature and legend - were sponsored by the Kalidasa Samaroha Samiti and organised by The Madhya Pradesh Kala Parishad. The Sangeet Natak Academy, New Delhi nominated Dr. V. Raghavan on its behalf to serve on the Samiti set up by the Madhya Pradesh Government and gave financial assistance to the Kalidas Samaroha. Besides symposium, All-India Kalidasa Art Exhibition (20 November 1958), the week long celebrations were marked by performances gives by various toupes in the Natya Samaroha. This Samaroha proved to be a veritable Feast of tributes paid to the poet in the form of dance, drama and music. Apart from dance - dramas from his epic poetry, the festival comprised of renderings in original Sanskrit (including Prakrit in the case of Sakuntala) of all the three dramas, viz, Abhijnana Sakuntalam, Malavikagnimitra and Vikramorvasiyam. These dramas were performed by the Sanskrit College, Calcutta, the Madras Natya Sangh, Madras and the Artists Combined of Gwalior, respectively.

Hindi version of 'Sakuntalam' was staged at Bharatiya Rangmanch, Ujjain under the direction of Shri Govind Dharmadhikari and Suman Dharmadhikari, on the occasion of 'Kalidasa Jayanti'.

Kalidasa's Sakuntala was staged in the Netherlands in the summer of 1958 as part of the Holland Festival. The play was translated by the well-known poet, Bert Voeten into Dutch from English and German translations of the Sanskrit original.

According to a spokesman of the Indian Embassy at The Hague, "the successful actor producer and director Cees Laseur achieved yet another mile-stone in the history of dramatic art in the Netherlands when he presented Kalidasa's Sakuntala at a gala performance during the Holland Festival. The decor and costumes were excellent and contributed to a large extent to the admirable atmosphere that was created. Westerners, who might find it difficult to fully comprehend the simplicity of the play, were vividly affected by the poetic genius of adaptation. The credit, however, goes also to Nicolaas Wijnberg for translating in actual effect the spirit of Kalidasa on the Dutch stage.

Contributing to all this was Indian music adapted to Western ears by Jurriaan Andriessen which completed the picture.

The Dutch Press on July 1 acclaimed the performance of the Indian play Sakuntala as a "climax of the Holland Festival". Queen Juliana, the Indian Ambassador, Shri John A. Thivy, Shrimati Thivy and several Dutch Cabinet Ministers attended the performance.

Cees Laseur, Producer and Director of Dutch version of Shakuntala

Narendra Sharma directed 'Shakuntala' of Kalidasa for Hindustani Theatre, New Delhi in 1959-60. The Hindustani Theatre was organized specifically to stage classical Sanskrit dramas in modern vernacular translation. Sakuntala was an early production utilizing mime, song, and dance in a nonrealistic style. No settings, other than the single background, were used.

The Hindustani Theatre's 1959-60 production of Sakuntala (Act V) : Sakuntala pleads with King Dusyanta to recognize her, but he rejects her

For the first time Wroclaw Laboratory Theatre of Grotowski produced Kalidasa's Sakuntala in November 1960. This Polish presentation of the ancient Indian play was the result of on extensive theatre research and experimentation, be it the yoga exercise (a psycho-physiological discipline), sphere of gesture or some elements of actor's training from Kathakali art form or the rigorous practical acting be it yoga (Body gesture) or imparting education to actor's. Byrski writes "This choice of the classical Indian drama as one of the first plays in the repertoire would indicate deeper reasons and broader plans. So it was. For one of the foremost purposes of Grotowski seems to have been the liberation of actors out of an overwhelming tyranny of dramatic texts, i.e., literatures which have been serving obediently in the Euro-American theatre.

Grotowski was not so much looking for a drama as for a score which could be executed by the troupe free to choose its own maner of orchestration i.e. free to choose its means of artistic expression. Sakuntala in a way seems to be a kind of score - as all classical Sanskrit drama - even in its original intention...

On December 13, 1960 Polish premiere of Sakuntala took place in Opole, at the Theatre of 13 Rows. It is worth while to mention that the staging was preceded by a radio drama broadcast by the Cracow Broadcast Station of the Polish Radio.

Play : Sakuntala [In Polish]

Group : The Labouratory Theatre

Dramatis Personae :-

Sakuntala ... Rena Mirecka

Dushyanta ... Zygmunt Malik

With A Jaholkowski, Barbara Barska, Ewa Lubowiecka, Andrezej Bielski, Adam Kurczyna. Thus, the Sakuntala was staged in Polish under the able direction of Jerzy Grotowski at Opole, The Theatre of 13 Rows in December 13, 1960 [European Premier - 1957 at London].

Grotowski - the Polish director of Sakuntala in 1960.

Dushyanta and Vidushaka in Wroclaw Laboratory Theatre production (1960).

'Sutradhara' and 'Nati' in Grotowski's Polish version of 'Sakuntala'

'Sakuntala, Priyamvada and Anasuya' in the production of Theatre Laboratory, Wroclaw; directed by Grotowski.

In 1960, Kelucharan Mahapatra, Odissi Guru, enriched Odissi repertoire through contemporary poems (Pala Sangeet) such as 'Kuntala Sakuntala' 'Nayane Sunayana Re' etc.

At the Annual Conference of the Madras Music Academy, all the three plays of Kalidasa was staged by Sanskrita Ranga that created quite a record in respect of audience and enthusiasm.

Sakuntnala of Kalidasa was staged in Sanskrit by Sanskrit Ranga, Madras in the All-India Kalidasa Festival, Ujjain and bagged an award and the same production was witnessed by an audience of two thousands. The review of the play appeared in the Hindu of January 14, 1962 where Prof. R. Srinivasan observed : ofcourse the fourth act of play which is considered the finest gem in the whole Sanskrit literature, produced the greatest impression; several of us in the audience found tears running down our cheeks automatically. The essence of Indian outlook on life, the meaning of sainthood, the grandeur and beauty of life in ancient asramas, was all depicted with great effect.

Russiun version of 'Sakuntala' was produced on 1 January 1964 at Riga. Inspired from Kalidasa, it was basically based on a book by Theophile Gautier, choreographed by Lucien Petipa. Lucien himself took the role of Dushyanta and Amalia Farraris, the Italian ballerina, that of Sakuntala.

Shri N.K. Sivasankaran of Rabindra Bharati University; and Kathak dancer Maya Rao assisted the ballet master in producing 'Sakuntala' in Riga.

Ebrahim Alkazi; directed 'Abhijnanashakuntalam' for the National School of Drama (1964)

The National School of Drama and Asian Theatre Institute produced Kalidasa's Abhijnana Sakuntalam on 5th, 8th and 10th January 1964 on the occasion of XXVI International Congress of Orientalists meeting in Delhi.

In the South, the production of dance - dramas by the Kalakshetram started with Srimati Rukmani Devi Arundale's presentation of the dance - drama 'Kutrala Kuravanji'. The succes that attended this effort paved the way to the production of more dance - drama such as Abhijnana Sakuntalam and Kumarasambhavam of Kalidasa.

In 1971, Mrinalini Sarabhai presented 'Sakuntala' in her dance idiom. At a press conference someone asked her "why do you choose to dance Sakuntala?" And her replay was "I never choose a subject, it chooses me". She started "In all the choreographic works I have created, the subject has always become something of an obsession that becomes entangled with my mind and strives continuously for liberation. While this thought within the center of my mind years for recognition, my peace of mind is continually threatened for it is like an imprisoned soul within a cage that is me. Thus it continues, night and day, and creation becomes torture, anguish."

She further said that she was not reading it nor had she thought of it in recent years. But childhood memories are impregnated within the deepest recesses of one's being. The curse of Durvasa suddenly haunted her like a lean spectre, out of the shadow of the past into the present crises of her life. Was there a destiny for each one of us, or were our everyday actions our destiny, with us making our future every day?

Unknowingly, thoughtlessly we go through life. Our great ancestors told us to be careful of our actions, to be careful with each word we spoke, for as the Upanshads say, words go forth like arrows and boomerang upon ourselves, not always blessed like the crow seeking shelter from Rama.

Why was the innocent Sakuntala so maltreated by everyone around her? What had she done? Why was she cursed so vehemently by an irate saint?

In her own words "Within the limited sphere of the stage, I had to give to these situations dynamic actior. Through the ways of the dance, the meaning was to be turned into the poetry of dance. I chose Kathakali as dramatic message."

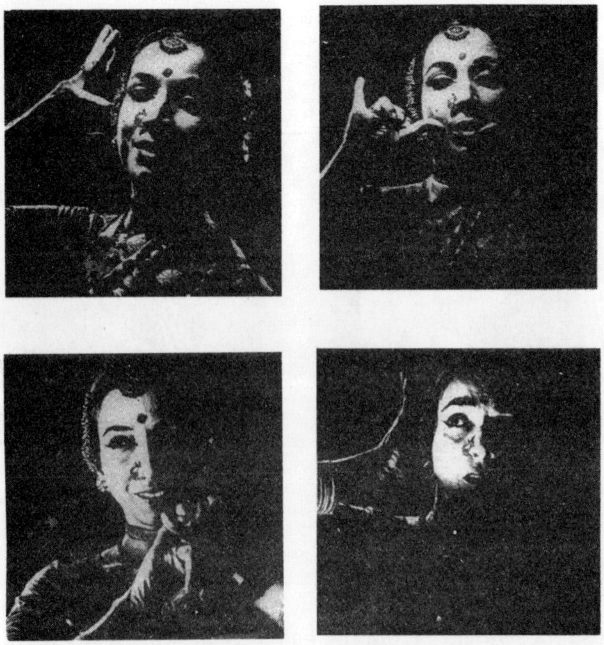

A contemporary interpretation of the classic Sakuntalam in Kathakali idiom

She expressed her feelings in the article "Issues in Indian dance" where she said : Ideas flow from many sources an incident, a memory, a scene, a story all give rise to thought that stirs the imagination. Kalidasa's Sakuntala was a drama that had been familiar from childhood to me. The rishi whom Sakuntala did not welcome immersed as she was in the thoughts of her beloved, became in this interpretation the Destiny that predicts our lives the small turning points that change the couse of human plans. Is it coincidence or some force that acts and creates a wholly unexpected situation? Philosophy tells us that we are all players on the stage of life. In Durvasa's curse production, each player was present throughout, on the stage. Within each incident Durvasa's curse shadowed the drama, the disquieting factor that ran through the entire play. Episodes came to life as they took place moving from one scene to the other till the confrontation of Sakuntala with Dushyanta who does not recognize her. She searches for her ring, the gift of the king and then in anger asks, 'If your signet ring is not with me, where is it? An interpretation that was relevant at that moment in time. It led to discussions of many problems of Values and attitudes, amongst students studying Kalidasa's dramas..."

The curse of Durvasa : a sequence from the ballet 'Sakuntalam' by Mrinalini Sarabhai'

Another scene from the ballet 'Sakuntalam' by Mrinalini Sarabhai

Rabindrabharati University (West Bengal) has given several productions of dance - dramas. It has performed Kalidasa's Sakuntala and Kumarsambhava in dance - drama form.

The Polish version of Sakuntala (Shakuntala) was again staged on 21 January 1972 under the direction of Jowita Pienkiewicz.

Sakuntala [In Polish]

Direction ... Jowita Pienkiewicz

Scenography ... Michal Jedrzejewsk

T.V. Direction ... Cezary Logiewski

Dramatis Personae

Sakuntala ... Jadwiga Skupnik

Dushyanta ... Andrez Hrydzewicz

[**Premiere : January 21st, 1972; TV Theatre Wroclaw**.]

Dhaneshwar Patnaik directed his own Oriya version of 'Sakuntala' in September 1975 under the banner of "Annapurna 'B' Group", a renowned theatre organisation of Cuttuck. The play was based both on the Sanskrit classic and the Mahabharata epic. Eminent actor Artabandhu stood out for his role of 'Dushyanta' in the play.

Originally composed in Gujarati and later translated into Sanskrit by the author himself, Gajendrashankar Lalshankar Pandya's 'Sakuntalnrtyanatika' is based on Kalidasa's classic. The Gujarati version was enacted thrice and Sanskrit rendering (appeared in print in August 1975) too was put on boards in Ahmedabad successfully.

In Kalidasa Festival, B.V. Karanth in association with Adyarangacharya presented 'Abhijnana Sakuntalam' in 1976.

During the summer of 1979 The Theatre Arts Department in Co-operation with the Music and Dance Departments at the University of California at Los Angeles presented the first production in the Los Angeles of Kalidasa's Sakuntala as a part of its Asian Performing Arts Summer Institute and Festival. The Sakuntala production was the last of six Asian performance events which, along with the numerous classes taught by guest artists, focused on the music, dance, and theatre of India, Bali and Java.

The basic concept which guided all aspect of the production from preliminary planning through performance was capturing the essence of Sanskrit Theatre - integration of dance, music, and acting by using convenions, techniques, and designs based on extant Kerala performancne traditions, specially Kathakali dance - drama and Kutiyattam Sanskrit temple drama.

Stage for the production of 'Sakuntala' at the University of California in tune with Kerala performance tradition

Kavi Raz rehearses his role in Dushyanta with M.P. Sankaran Namboodiri for the University of California for production of the Sanskrit classic

M.P. Sankaran Namboodiri, the great Kathakali exponent was invited to join the UCLA faculty for the summer programme to teach a class in Kathakali and to assist in the production of Sakuntala. Dura Michl - Temple, one of the promising young playwrights with a gift for poetic language, was invited to begin work on adaptation. Nazir Jairazbhoy ethnomusicologist at UCLA, advised on music, leading to the selection of Peter Manuel and Gordon Thompson, both accomplished musicians on the sitar and tabla respectively, to compose and arrange music. Phillip B. Zarrilli, the director of the production used a script which was poetic, which differentiated between the high imagery of the language of the court, the expressions of love between Dushyanta and Sakuntala and the more colloquial language of the Vidusaka (Madhavya) and the low-life scene with the constable, chief of police and fisherman. He preferred a new version so that south Indian conventions could be used.

The Structure of the Performance of the University of California

Kathakali

Kelikayyu : 1st announce-ment with drums Prelude:

1. Suddamaddalam : 2nd announcement with drums and lighting of the oil lamp
2. Todayam : "Pure dance" behind the curtain (Often omitted today)
3. Vandana slokas or prayers sung
4. Purapattu : another "pure dance", the ideal being one performed by the major characters of the heroic class in the play which follows
5. Melapadam : singing of part of Gitagovinda, with elaborate drumming

Play Proper Begins

Final Prayer and Closing

Dance

Kutiyattam

First Day

Preliminaries(Kuttupurapattu)

Adornment of Stage Worshiping of Instruments

Invocation

Nandi Ceremoney Benendication

Sprinking of Holy Water

Nandi Verse Recited

Invocation

Kruaccvuttuka - special dance

Sthapana : Introduction of Main Character

Second Day

Nirvacana : Introduction of the Act to be presented with Sutradhara or Stage Manager

Third & Fourth Days

Purusartha : Aims of Life Expounded by Vidusaka

Fifth - Seventh Days

Performance of Act Begins

Sakuntala

Preliminaries

Introductory Music "pure music " Lighting of Oil Lamps by State Attendants Benediction to the Audience

"Sari" Dance by Sakuntala, Anansuya and Priyamvada

Prologue :

Stage Manager, Actress and Vidusaka (Madhavya)

Play Proper Begins

Act I

Act II

Act III

Act IV

Intermission with "pure music"

Act V

Act VI

Act VII

Benediction in Sanskrit to the Audience

The music ensemble at the University of California, Los Angeles for the production of 'Sakuntalam'

All the essential elements of the preliminaries of Kathakali and Kutiyattam was taken into consideration. The introductory music lasted approximately fifteen to twenty minutes begining prior to the scheduled "curtain time" for the opening of the play. As the audience began to enter the theatre, then they were met by the playing of this introductory music. Offerings had been placed in the lobby, as well as on stage next to the two traditional Kerala oil lamps.

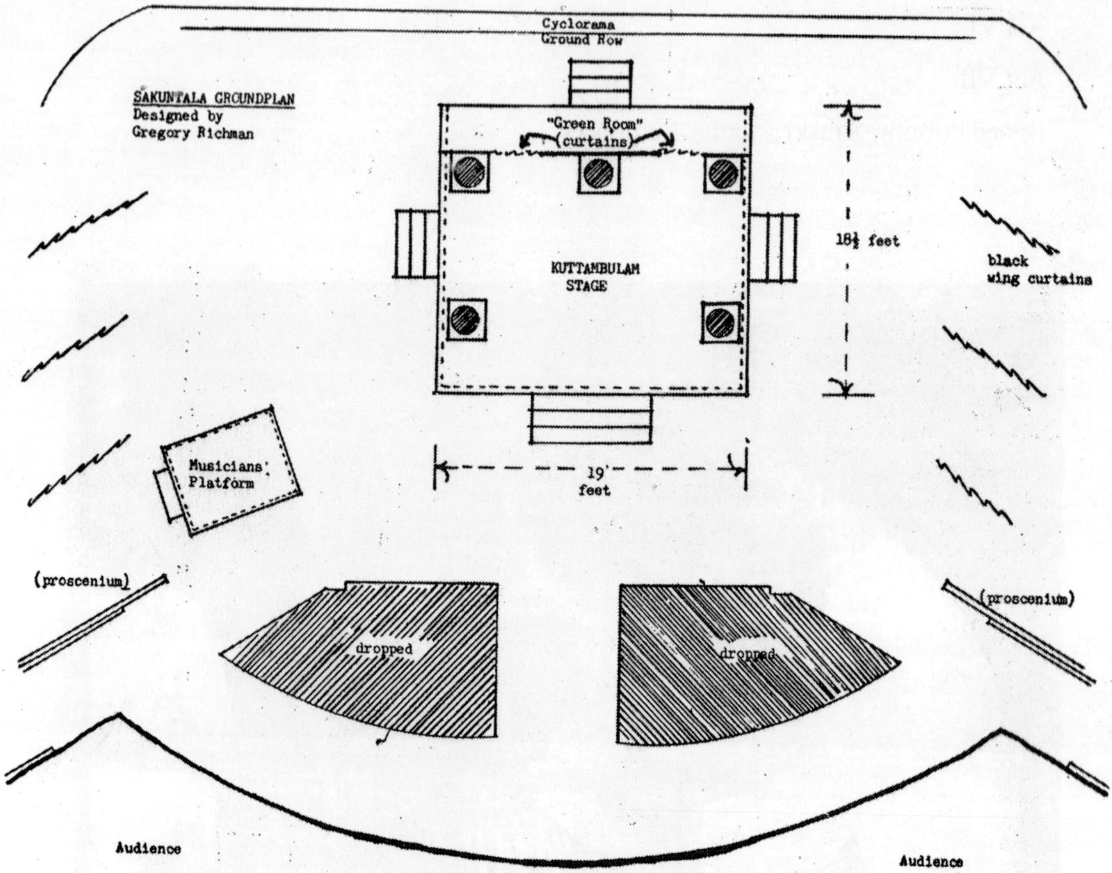

Stage design, Gregory Richman

In keeping with the use of South Indian staging conventions Gregory Richman's set design was modeiled on the Kutiyattam Kuttambulam stage of Kerala. Interestingly, two simple square stools were used as the only set pieces throughout the performance, also in keeping with Kerala staging conventions. They were placed as needed by two stage attendants who would enter and exit as necessary to place or remove a stool. The stool served as a seat, a bed, a chariot in the course of the production.

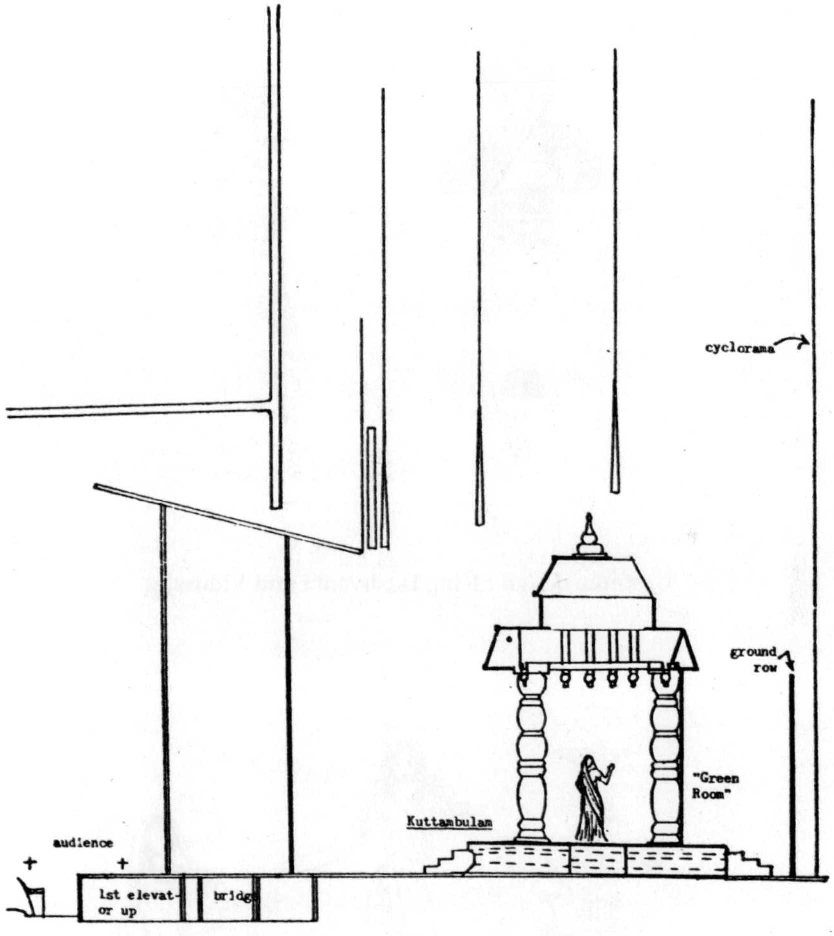

Cross-Section Stage design by G. Richman.

The two stage attendants also held the traditional multi-coloured Kathakali or Kutiuyattam curtain. Many of the major entrances and exits were accomplished with the curtain, including the opening of the play with Dushyanta riding in the chariot driven by his charioteer, the revealing of the dancers for the "Sari" dance, the tiranokku or "curtain look" by the demons on their entrance and Sanumati's entrance and exit.

Costume design : King Dushyanta and Vidusaka

Costume design : Demon, Aditi, Sakuntala

The only stage properties constructed for the production were bows and arrows, swords and the offerings presented to Sakuntala before her departure from the Hermitage. As with the stage design, the costume designs by Joy Densmore were based upon South Indian models, Kathakali annd Kutiyattam. The Vidushaka's costume and make-up were exact copies of the Kutiyattam Vidusaka, while the Demon's make-up costumes were close replicas of the Kathakali hunters.

Though it was not possible to attempt a full scale re-creation of either Kathakali techniques nor Kutiyattam Vocalization with regard to acting style. The production had to be content with selecting places to emphasize the stylization of hand and facial gestures, and integrate this use of styled technique into over all style of the production.

On August 2, 1979, the production of Sakuntala opened and ran for five performances. Approximately 1,500 people saw the production which had taken nine months to plan and prepare, wth an involvement of a cast of thirty-three, a production body of fourteen, and countless man-hours in the various construction shops. In UCLA's office of Instructional Developed commissioned the production of a complete videotape by its professional crews, now in distribution for educational purposes.

A scene from American version of 'Sakuntala'; directed by Phillip B. Zarrilli

Dushyanta describes the beautiful Sakuntala in American version (1979)

Madhavya makes fun of Dushyanta in Phillip B. Zarrilli's production 'Sakuntala'

Sakuntala's entrance with Priyamvada and Anasuya in University of California's production 'Sakuntala' in English

Comic scene with Fisherman in English version of 'Sakuntala' at Los Angeles

Dushyanta mourns the loss of Sakuntala to Madavya while the 'invisible' Sanumati looks on in Production 'Sakuntala'; directed by Phillip B. Zarrilli

With a German cast, Vijaya Mehta directed Sakuntala (1980) in Germany at the instance of renowned German theatre director Fritz Bennewitz. She staged Kalidasa's Sakuntala at Leipzig Theatre, Germany. In her production of Sakuntala, she sought the collaboration of Kathak exponent Rohini Bhate for dance movements. In this case one also saw the use of dance in the nandi, the prologue, according to the conventions of traditional theatre with a Sutradhara and Nati, and after their exit the enactment of the play proper with dance movement at appropriate junctures, which fitted very well. Vijaya Mehta's productions tried to associated itself with the clalssical traditions in Indian music, for e.g. in Sakuntala reminded one of the Dhrupad - Dhamar tradition.

Vijaya Mehta

German actor Gottfried Richter as Dushyanta in Kalidasa's Sakuntala directed by Vijaya Mehta in German Leipzig Theatre, (1980)

Abhijnana Shakuntala (Kalidasa) - Marathi Dir. Vijay Mehta

The great doyen of Maharashtrian set designers, D.G. Godse had a highly creative approach to set designing and lighting. He did a lot of work for the distinguished producer Vijaya Mehta. Dnyaneshwar Nadkarni observes : “It is enough to mention the sets and costumes he designed for her Natyasastra - inspired productions of Mudrarakshasa and Sakuntala. The entire setup cnceived by Bharata as ideal for presenting a Sanskrit play was imaginatively duplicated on stage by the brilliant designer. The forestage, the entrances and exits, the platforms - all these were brought alive, as it were, after being in disuse for centuries.

Godse and Mehta regularly went to the German Democratic Republic and played the same function in German language productions of Mudrarakshasa and Sakuntala as they did in the local pilot productions. We have, of course, no idea of how these productions were lit in the G.D.R. but how fascinating those blonde actors and actresses look, makeup and costumed as Rakshasa or Sakauntala or Dushyanta. The indigenous character of the scenography here easily crosses the seas and reflects every detail of the original decor. It is the deep creative impulse in both versions which, I think, is responsible for this convincing demolition of national barriers."

A Video-copy of a performance of Shakuntala, in German, directed by Smt. Vijaya Mehta, is available at Sangeet Natak Akademi Archive, housed in Rabindra Bhawan, New Delhi. Vijay Mehta's 'Abhijnana Sakuntalam' was also staged in Kalidasa Festival at Ujjain.

To commemorate the 25th anniversary of All India Kalidas Festival which is celebrated every year, The Govt. of Madhya Pradesh celebrated its silver Jubilee from 27 Nov. to Dec. 1982 at Ujjain. The function began with the production of 'Abhijnana Sakuntalam' in Sanskrit and Prakrit by Kalidas Akademi, Ujjain. A team of celebrated scholars annd artists were invited by Prabhat Kumar Bhattacharya that included Sir Shrinivasa Rath, Kamleshdatta Tripathi, Omprakash Sharma, Rajkumud etc. The play was performed on Vikristamadhyam manch and the actors followed both the folk and realistic style. The same play was also enacted in Bengali as well as in Kuddiyattam style of South India. The latter production that was directed by Shri K.N. Pannikkar curtailed some major scenes.

Sahana Sangeet Shikshayatan (Gadia), West-Bengal a wellknown cultural troupe completed its 120 years on 27 January 1983. A souvenir brought on the occassion mentions about the staging of dance - drama 'Shakuntala' from its repertoir.

The 'Goa Hindu Association' of Mumbai had staged 'Sakuntala' of Kalidasa in 1985.

In the rural area of North - West Karnataka, there is an unknown village called Heggoddu in the Shimoga district of the state in the year 1949, Ninasam came into being as an amateur dramatic society and it was K.V. Subbanna, the modest visionary who has been the guiding spirit of the group that has grown into a full pledged Theatre Institute'. Ninasam focuses on theatre work, implemented through the training of fifteen students a year at the Institute and concretized through the productions of Ninasam Tirugata, an itinerant Repertory Company that has performed in all nineteen districts of Karnnataka Between October 1985 to April 1988, Tirugata has performed 430 shows of eleven productions from Shakespear's Macbeth, Brecht's Three penry Opera, Gorky's The Lower Depths to our indigenous classic Mrcchakatika of Sudraka.

K.V. Subbanna, the recipient of Magsaysay Award for his theatre and cultural movement in rural Karnataka, wrote and directed Loka Shakuntala (an adaptation of Kalidasa's classic into Kannada). It was first produced in the Yakshagana style in Delhi. Oflate, Tirugata which has enacted Subbanna's most controversial "rewrite" Lokashakuntala', is nothing less that an attempt to redefine the social context of Kalidasa's classic from the point of view of the "Common man". In the words of Rustom Bharucha, "What happens to a man-woman relationship in an imperialist structure? How do the worlds of the ashram 'and the court, the city and the woods, depend on each other for definition and reinforcement of existing modes of power"? To what extent is Dushyanta's problematic forgetting and remembrance of Shakuntala conditioned by his own institutionalized role as monarch? Inevitably, to confront these "crude" questions (the kind Brecht would have liked), Subbanna had to "rewrite" the play by elaborating on the minor characters like the hunters and the fisherman. He also added two incidents depicting Dushyanta's love-affair with a hunter girl and a performance of Yajna by his subjects, who pray to the gods to bless their king with a child. Shakuntala's rejection at the court was edited so that it appeared as if she had been granted an official hearing, nothing more significantly it was enacted in a formal, Sanskrit, which contradicted the colloquial idiom of the rest of the play, inspired by the rough lyricisim of Yakshagana.

Though 'Lokashakuntala' has been criticized for its "populism", a charge that is often raised against Tirugata's work in general, I think the very impulse to "rewrite" a sacrosant text is refereshing. Shakuntala is enriched, to my mind, through questioning rather than deference. Instead of perpetuating the assumptions of "purity" and "authenticity" underlying proscenium-bound spectacles of "traditional theatre", invented by our most prominent contemporary directors, Subbanna rejects any false veneration of the past. He is not reluctant to assert the discontinuities in our tradition, which are so often glossed over or subsumed within categories of "timelessness" and "eternal truth".

In 1990, Rangamandal, Bhopal produced Kalidasa's Abhijñāna Śākuntalam', where the director Sankhya Ibotombi applied Manipuri dance and scenography with unforgettable lyricism.

Rangamandal's production of Abhijñanaśākuntalam in 1990 directed by Sankhya Ibotombi

A scene from the Manipuri ballet "Shakuntala"

In the year 1990-91, Darpana Academy of Performing Arts, Ahmedabad produced a puppet play based on the story of 'Shakuntala' by Kalidasa.

To suppliment and enrich the teaching programme a number of play-reading enactment sessions were organised followed by discussion with experts by the National School of Drama in the year 1991-92. Kalidasa's Abhijnana Shakuntalam featured in this programme.

On July 3, 1994, Kshtij Natya Sansntha of Delhi staged Kalidasa's Sanskrit classic 'Shakuntala' in Shrawan Kumar Goswami's Nagpuri adaptation at Jawahar Nawodaya School Auditorium, Loharada, Bihar prepared during a workshop with tribal performers, the play was designed by Vipin Kumar and directed by Bharti Sharma.

Under the 'Study Tours' scheme of the National School of Drama, every year a batch of students is taken on tour to some region. They observe and study the traditional theatre forms of the region and acquire basic skills in the traditional arts of the region. Under this scheme the second year students went to Imphal, Manipur on 11 December, 1995 to work under the direction of S. Ebotombi.

Nandini Ramani is the daughter of Late Dr. V. Raghavan, the energetic Secretary of the prestigious Music Academy and the founder of the Sanskrita Ranga, that came into existence to enable the staging of Sanskrit dramas and the Sanskrit College at Mylapore. In 1996, Nandini presented Kalidasa's classic Abhijnana Shakuntalam in Chennai at Narada Gana Sabha. This ancient play was well staged and received both critical and mass acclaim for many reasons. Actors were well-trained and spoke Sanskrit with utmost ease as if they were speaking in their mother tongue.

There was no promting either. Everyone did his/her role very effectively and communicatively. Subbudu observes 'The sets were simple, suggestive and elegant... The musical scores were unobtrusive and blended harmoniously with the various sequences'.

A scene from the 'Shakuntalam' staged in Madras : Dushyanta proposing to Shakuntala

In recent times, Bengali version of 'Sakuntala' by Aparesh Chandra Mukhopadhyay was produced by 'Theatre Centre', Calcutta. The play was experimented in an extended open arena under natural environment. It was directed by Debraj Ray and the music was rendered by Shri Jnanprakash Ghosh, an authority on Indian Classical Music. The main dramatis personae were Debraj Ray as Dushyanta and Smt. Anuradha Ray as Sakuntala.

In 44th Art Festival mounted by Kalashetra Foundation at Bharata Kalashetra Auditorium the repertoire of Rukmini Devi's Kalashetra presented Kalidasa's Abhijnana Sakuntalam in dance-drama form. Critic Leela Venkataraman writes. 'In attempting a theatre/dance mix posed greater challanges for Rukmini Devi'. Elocuting in the old classical modern Sanskrit and also dancing to the verses of Kalidasa can be tricky combination. For accomplishing this without letting narration drag, the production needed more of the type of prowess of a Balagopalan who, as the eternal funster in the Vidushaka's role, was brilliant. Having filled the role for all of 27 years, he seems to have developed an uncanny feel for timing annd power of every natural gesture. The dramatic intensity in his enactment was certainly out of the oridinary, every little gait measured in theatrical impact and drawing enthusiastic applause. This vivid movements made the Sanskrit language communicable to one and all. As Sarangadeva, he quickly changed track to became a different character. His ability in projecting the voice in the dialogue portions, was an object lesson to other actors. The other veteran performer was Janardhanan who in the character roles as rishi Kanva and the Chief guard Syla, exhibited his versatility. The fisherman's scene with Janardhanan and with Thomas as Dasa and Kapil and Hari Padman as the two Policemen (who even moulded in Kalidasa's version strike one as being totally contemporary in character) was enacted with finesse. Narendran in looks, voice and clarity of Sanskrit diction not to speak of the dance expertise, made an ideal Dushyanta. Even with the sylvan stage setting creating an ideal 'Tapovasam' and the carefully worked out costumes, the impact of the production could have been greatly enhanced by a differennt choice for the crucial role of Sakuntala... Sonali and Mutangi as Anusuya and Priyamvada did their parts with enthusiasm. Little Prithvija as the deer was delightful - Particularly in the fond looks thrown backwards at Sakuntala while making an exit. The fish tattoo on the arm of Dasa, the fisherman was another aesthetic touch. The music was sung by Sai Sankar was effective. The supporting musicians who otherwise performed well, sometimes made false starts with ripples on the flute and the violin. The stage decor deserves kudos..."

On July 21, 1996, Ruchika presented Shovana Narayan in Maithilisharan Gupta's love epic 'Sakuntala' designed and directed by Arun Kuckreja, at Triveni Chamber Theatre, New Delhi. This was Arun Kuckreja's multimedia presentation of Gupta's magnum opus. It was soliloquised by the well-known Kathak dancer Shovana Narayan with additives like Raja Ravi Verma's paintings on the Sakuntala theme projected on a large screen in some of the sequences and music from Music Today's series, "The Elements". The 2 1/4 hour production, presented in Delhi by Sahitya Akademi, was a beautiful fusion of dance, histrionics and music.

Maithilisharan Gupta's "Sakuntala is in 12 chapters and Kuckreja's production design encompasses the entire epic with Shovana dancing to her recitation of the lines in the ambience created by different compositions selected from the The "Elements" album. There is, for instance, Zakir Husain's "Shawasuchhashwas" (The beginning) and Brahmand (The Final Frontier). For the second chapter "Upkarma", the mood is set with pieces from Vanraj Bhatia's composition.

Hari Prasad Chaurasia's compositions and Pandit Jasraj's voice create the atmosphere for the third chapter, "Janma Aur Balyakaal". At some other places we have snatches from compositions by Bhaskar Chandavarkar and Shiv Kumar Sharma with slide projections of Ravi Verma's paintings depicting Shakuntala's birth, her parentage, her letter to Dushyanta, her child Bharat at her breast, and Durvasa's curse along with two or three other paintings. Critic Romesh Chander observes: Most of the time Shovana danced without the music and only to the rhythm of Maithilisharan's poetry. A difficult task indeed, but her movement, mudras and facial expression were a beautiful projection of the verses. Both in Hindi and Urdu recitation of poetry central lines are often repeated to create a dramatic effect or to under line the meanings of the couplet or subtly suggest a different meaning through voice inflection. Shovana effectively used the technique not only in her recitation but more so through her abhinay and vistar with each recitation. As theatrical device it was both innovative and visually beautiful.

Shovana's interpretation or the beautiful vistar in the last scene when the poet asks whether the golden days will ever come back and Shovana's faith and hope in the younger generation will be long remembered and also so will be the marriage of dance with theatre in Ruchika's "Sakuntala".

The noted director B.M.V. Karanth once commented : I am frightened of Kalidasa. He is too subtle and too poetic for his play we need actors who are subtle and poetic, actors of very fine nuance. I do not feel that school's students are ready for Kalidas as yet. This he said in 1981 with his conversation with ENACT about National School of Drama. About fifteen years later in 1995, second student of the same school presented 'Tridhara', a blending of Sanskrit classics under Rita Ganguly's direction.

As a part of theatre training in the National School of Drama, every year, the students in the second year, are introduced to Sanskrit classics - as text, and in performance. The various training inputs like study and analysis of a few selected Sanskrit plays, principles of Natyashastra, Indian aesthetics, understanding of Sanskrit theatre architecture, stylised acting, earning from witnessing traditional dance / theatre performance etc. culminate in a public performance of a Sanskrit play production by students under the guidance of a teacher / director. In 1995, The second year students presented 'Tridhara' : a performance of three Sanskrit plays - Kalidasa's Abhijnanashakuntalam in Sanskrit, Bodhayana's Bhagavadajjukiyam and Vishakhadatta's Mudrarakshasa's in Hindi under the direction of Rita Ganguly, a senior faculty member of NSD and a well known classical singer also trained in several classical dance traditions. Abhijnana Sakuntalam was presented in Sanskrit with the assistance of Dr. Baldev Anand Sagar who trained the students in Sanskrit speech.

Held from 17-22 November, 1995, the five hour long performance in the specially erected Vikrisht Madhyam auditorium was aesthetically visualised and designed incorporating meticulously the various aspects of Sanskrit play production like stylised acting, music spatial design etc. Thus, an effort was made for the first time to capture the spirit and ambience of Sanskrit stage through a detailed study and research of various texts like Vastushastra, Shilpashastra and Manasara - Shastra in consultations with scholars, architects, designers and technicians was an electrifying and brilliant piece of theatre. Despite the fact that the entire production lasted around five hours, people were excited and enthused by it and some even saw it more than once.

Unfortunately, when Sanskrit has almost vanished into oblivion in India. So it comes as a surprise when a foreign country insists on having an Indian classical play staged on its soil and that too in classical Sanskrit. The country in question is Sri Lanka and the play that was staged for the first time in Sri Lanka is Kalidasa's Sakuntalam in the year 1997. The play was directed by Rita Ganguly, this classic was produced by the final year students of the National School of Drama. But it's not been an easy task. The entire cast of 21 had to under go months of rigorous training in recitation and pronunciation of under the able guidance of Dr. Sagar. The ardous job of making students recite dialogues was really difficult given their varied backgrounds. Before selecting the play Rita too had to do intensive research on the subject. Not only the costumes but even the sets had to be designed keeping the Kalidas period in mind. There was no elaborate hairdos snor costumes that stand out a mile. The colours of the costumes were natural and all the jewellery was made from wooden beads in different colours and shapes. Another notable feature was the music. Rita Ganguly had introduced Dhruv geet, music described in Natyashastra in the play. The director of the play says, "An attempt has been made to meet the requirements as per the specifications of the Natyashastra. Right from designing the stage to music and costumes details have been taken into account so that play comes alive on the stage. It was a prestigious event and was able to rise to the expectations of the Sri Lankas.

Second year students of National School of Drama presented Abhishaap, a play based on Sanskrit classics in the first week of December 1998. Taking three works of Kalidasa - Meghdootam, Sakuntalam and Vikramorvashiyam - writer

Suman Kumar and director Rita Ganguly have melded them into one connected piece. Using Meghdootam as the frame binding the three, the action segues into Sakuntalam and Vikramorvashiyam.

Final Year Students of NSD in 'Sakuntalam' (1997)

The production chose to contemporise Meghdutam by palcing it within a military situation and making the Yaksha and army officer. Pining for his beloved, he sends the Megh or cloud to her with message, exhorting Megh all the while not to rain before reaching her. Not even for Sakuntala or Urvashi, thereby tying the other two plays into the action.

Aesthetically, the design of the production was very pleasing and the technical aspects (Lights : Ashok Sagar Bhagat; Sets; Ram Gopal Bajaj, Ashok Sagar

Bhagat; Costumes : Kriti V. Sharma) melded well together to form a cohesive whole. The music (Rita Ganguly) and the choreography were outstanding.

Scene from the NSD second year production. Abhishaap (1998)

3

Epics in Performance

Ritusamhara being just a descriptive peom has little of drama in it and has not been drama in it and hasnot been explotied for purpose of transforming it into a play but only in dance-drama form. However, dramatists, choreographers and creative writers have sought to present his other poems such as Kumarasambhavam, Meghadutam and Raghuvamsam in pure drama idiom and also the original epics itself in dance-drama style from time to time.

Kumarasambhavam in Dance-Drama

Kalidasa's epic 'Kumarsambhava' was dramatised into Bengali by Shri Haribhusan Bhattacharya. The play was produced by National Theatre, Calcutta on 12 September 1885 for the first time. Sukumari Datta played the role of 'Rati'. The special mention should be made of Dharmadas Sur's skillful application of Mechanical Diorama in an important scene.

An advertisement of the show appeared in print ['*The Statesman*' dated 12th September 1885] : National Theatre/Saturday, The 12th September 1885, At 9 pm/First Grand Opening of that popular piece/Kumarasambhava/the celebrated work of our immortal Kalidas, nobly/dramatised in Bengali by an able hand. The show was repeated on 19 and 26 September 1885; 7,22 and 29 November 1885; 6 and 24 December 1885.

The Emerald Theatre [at Beadon Street, Calcutta] under took this production in a refreshed manner for first time on 25 March 1888 and followed by 1,14 and 28 April 1888; 26 May 1888; 4 July 1888; 1 and 15 August 1888, 1 September 1888.

Famous choreographer and dance-director from Bengal is Atinlal. Under the banner of 'Bharatiya Shilpi Parishad' estd. (1948) he produced Kumarsambhava of Kalidasa.

The Bhartiya Kala Kendra, Delhi, put up a performance of dance-drama based on Kumar Sambhava of Kalidasa for the first time in Kalidas Jayanti Celebrations held at Ujjain-sposnored by the Kalidasa Samaroha Samiti and organised by the Madhya Bharat Kala Parishad in the month of November 1958. It won first prize in the festival and was later produced in several cities of USSR. Choreographed by Birju Maharaj, the music was composed by senior Dagar Brothers. Its set and costumes was done by Naina Devi.

The Indira Kala Sangeet Vishvavidyalaya also made the same experiment by writing an opera based on this great epic and presented it in this Natya Samaroha.

Rukmini Devi Arundale-a highly placed Brahmin and wife of President of International Theosophical Society, Dr. George Arundale, established Kalakshetra. Her reperatoire includes Kumar Sambhava of Kalidasa.

Kumarasambhavam in Theartical Performance

Madanadahanam is a Sanskrit musical Natika in two scenes on the theme of the Siva's burning of Kama, based on Kumarasambhava of Kalidasa. It was first staged in the Sanskrit Seminar of the Wilson College, Bombay, it was later broadcast by the Bombay Station of the All India Radio. The broadcast lasted half an hour.

Kumarasambhavam natakam by Srijiva Nyayatirtha of Bhatpara, West Bengal is an original Sanskrit drama in five acts depicting the theme of the Kumarasambhava At the instance of Prof. Ramranjan Mukhopadhyay, the then Professor of Sanskrit, Jadavpur University, Calcutta the playwright wrote this drama for the presentation at the Annual Kalidasa Samaroha at Ujjain.

Tapahphalam is a short Sanskrit play that hightlights an incident in Kalidasa's classic, the Kumarasambhava. This radio play is more in nature of a dialogue or a trialogue. It has a lot of action in it. The play was broadcast from the Bangalore Station of the All India Radio.

Parvatiparamesvariyam of Vanamala Bhawalkar is a Sanskrit drama in three scenes adapted from the Kumarasambhava of Kalidasa. That it is stageworthy is proved by two of its successful performances, one at Ujjain on Nov. 2, 1968 and the other at Bhopal on Nov. 4, 1968.

Meghadutam in Dance-Drama

Kalidasa Rangam Ujjain and Dr. Purudadhich presented in dance drama form the 'Meghadutam' of Kalidasa.

In the fortees, wellknown danseuse Sadhana Bose created history with her dance-drama 'Bhukh' based on Bengal famine. To quote Mohan Khokar. "It was a new trend in ballet composition". She had established 'Calcutta Art Players' and her noteworthy dance-dramas include 'Meghadutam' of Kalidasa, Vidyut-parva and Savitri Rajnati etc.

Mrinalini Sarabhai, the recipient of 'Deshikottam' title had also performed Meghadutam of Kalidasa in dance-drama.

Recitation of verses from 'Meghadutam' was organised at the Hall of Columns, Moscow in 1956 at 'Kalidasa Festival' held in Russia.

Manjulika Rai Chaudhuri staged Kalidasa's Meghdut in dance - drama form for the group 'Anamika' of Calcutta.

Meghadutam in Theatrical Performance

Natyarupam Meghadutam is a Sanskrit drama adapted from Kalidasa's Meghaduta. An interesting effort to retell the immortal classic that was broadcast from the Bombay Station of the All India Radio on 6th July, 1965.

Meghadutottaram of S.B. Velankar, based on the Meghaduta of Kalidasa is an original Sanskrit play that was staged in Jabalpur on December 8, 1967. The performance was repeated several times, At Bhopal, it was staged on March 31, 1968 under the auspices of Surabharati. Apart from Bombay which has witnessed many of its performances, it has been staged at Kurukshetra, Jammu, Delhi, Nagpur, Pune, Nasik and so on.

An eminent scholar and playwright Roma Chanduri had a troupe of her own which had staged most of her plays, that include **'Meghameduramediniyam'** (published in 1971), a play in nine scenes attempts at prosiding the purvabhaga and the Uttarabhaga the addition at the beginning and the end to the Meghaduta and to give these as also the theme of the older work a dramatic garb.

In 1973, 'Meghaduta' of Kalidasa was presented at the Kalidasa Festival, Ujjain

S.B. Velankar's original Sanskrit drama **'Meghadutanvitam'** (1991), a musical drama in three acts, based on the Meghadutam of Kalidasa unfolds the theme much in the same way as does his innovative play, **'Meghadutottaram'**, a nine literary piece **'Megadutanvitam'**.

Mohan Upreti composed the music and directed Nagarjun's Hindi translation of Kalidasa's Meghdoot in Sahitya Kala Parishad, Delhi's Theatre festival held in 1993.

'**Abhishaap**' is a play in Hindi based on three works of Kalidasa, namely Meghdutam (epic) and two plays Sakuntalam and Vikramorvasiyam. Written by Suman Kumar, the play was directed by Rita Ganguli for the second year students of National School of Drama and it was staged in the first week of December 1998. Meghdutam was employed as the frame binding the three.

Raghuvamsam in Theatrical Performance

Srijiva Nyayatirtha of Bhatpara, West Bengal wrote a play **'Raghuvaṁśam'** (1963) in six acts that seeks to describe the main points in the narrative of the Raghuvamsa. This play was written for the purpose of being produced at the Kalidasa Festival, an annual feature at Ujjain at the instance of the Principal of the Govt. Sanskrit College, Calcutta. This innovative play was well-received by the audience.

Vishvanath Keshava Chatre Shastri's **Nandinivarapradinam** is a drama in Sanskrit adopted from the Dilipa and lion episode of the second canto of the Raghuvamsa of Kalidasa. It was broadcast from the Bombay station of the All India Radio on 14th August, 1966.

The Bangalore Station of the All India Radio has successfully boradcast the play '**Sitatyagah**' of K.T. Pardurangi. A play that followed the incident of the exile of Sita as shown in the Raghuvamsa of Kalidasa and Uttararamacaritam of Bhavabhuti.

Riju Samhar in Thertical Performance

Lalit Kala Kendra, Gwalior staged 'Ritu Samhara' of Kalidasa in November 1958 at Kalidasa Jayanti celebrations held at Ujjain - sponsered by the Kalidasa Samaroha Samiti and organised by the Madhya Pradesh Bharat Kala Parishad. However, Kalidasa Rangam, Ujjain and Dr. Purudadhich presented it in dance drama form.

4

Inventory of Epics in Drama Form and Other Genres

Kumarsambhavam

Anonymous. Hrdaya aur rudra-Kasi : [s.n.], [n.d.] A Play in Hindi adapted from 'Kumarasambhava'.

Bharata Pisharoty, E.P. Kamadahanam. *Samskrtamanjari* (Sanskrit Academy) Delhi; Jan-March 1992; Vol. II, No. 1. One act play in Sanskrit reproduces the story of Canto III of the Kumarasambhava as related to the burining of Kama with only few innovations.

Bhawalkar, Vanamala. Parvatiparamesvariyam - Sagar : Sanskrit Parishad, University of Sagar, 1966.

The playwright has appended at the beginning, a list of the melodies, the Ragas, in which the stanzas are to be sung with an indication of the marking of the time, Talas.

A drama in three secnes based on the Kumarasambhava of Kalidasa.

Chudamani, Girishchandra. Parvatiparinaya - Calcutta : [s.n.], 1870.

Bengali play based on the Kumarasambhava of Kalidasa.

Goswami, Durgadas. Kumarasambhava Parvati Paramesvarayossamvadah. *Pranava-Parijata*. Sept.-Oct. 1963, Vol. VI, No. 1. pp-6-7.

Play adapted from Kumarasambhava.

Iyer, E.S. Sundaram. Uma parinaya - Tiruchi : [s.n.], 1952. Kumarasambhava of

Kalidasa adapted into a play. Mentioned in the 'Bibliography of stageable plays in Indian languages/ed. by C.C. Mehta' (Vol. 1, 1963), P-163.

Jha, Anand. Punahsangamaḥ. *In* Kalidasiyoparupakanam Samuccayah - Darbhanga : Kameshwar Singh Sanskrit. University, 1963. Vol. 1, No. 2. pp 3-13. Sanskrit play in five scenes based on the Kumarasambhava of Kalidasa.

Kher, Ramesh. Madanadahanam. *In* Kalidasiyoparupakanam Samuccayah Darbhanga : Kameshwar Singh Sanskrit University, 1963. Vol. 1, No. 1, pp 32-37. A musical Natika in two scenes on the theme of the Siva burning of Kama, based on Kumarasambhava of Kalidasa.

Maharaj, R.S. Madanadahanam. *KUS*. Vol. 1, No. 2. pp 49-56. Play based on Kama-dahana of Kumarasambhava.

Pandurangi, K.T. Topahphalam - Dharwar : [s.n.], 1959. Play adapted from Kumarasambhava (canto V) of Kalidasa.

Raghavan, V. Kamasuddhi - [s.l.], 1946. An interpretation of the message of Kumarasambhava. The play is mentioned in the 'Bibliography of stageable plays in Indian languages/ed. by C.C. Mehta' (Vol. 1, 1963). Play was staged and produced in All India Radio, Madras.

Ramaswami Sastrigal, K.S. Rativijayam - The author, 1923. Play inspired from the story of Rati as described in Kumarasambhava of Kalidasa.

Rishi Mahanadahanam. *In* Kalidasiyoparupakanam Samuccayah - Darbhanga : Kameshwar Singh Sanskrit University, 1963. Deals with the theme of Kama in three Pravesakas or scenes, drawn from the Kumarasambhava of Kilidasa.

Shukla, Nalini. Parvatipascarya. Kanpur. In Manuscript. This is the Kama burning episode in the form of a small play in five scenes which only depicts Parvati practising hard penance to win Siva over to herself, adapted from Kumarasambhava of Kalidasa.

Saijiva Nyayatirtha. Kumarasahbhavam. *Paranava-parijata;* 1965 [Saka Year 1886]; Vol. VIII, Nos. 1-4; pp 43-51. A play in six acts that dramatizes the theme of the Kumarasambhava in Sanskrit.

Meghdutam

Bharadwaj, Shiva Prasad. Meghadutam. *Visvasamskrtam* (Hoshiarpur) March & June 1985; Vol. XXII, Nos. 1 & 2. An adaptation of Meghaduta in the form of Sanskrit opera in five scenes.

Chaudhuri, Roma. Meghameduramediniyam - Calcutta: Pracyavani, 1992. An original Sanskrit play in nine scenes aims at providing the Purvabhaga and the Uttarabhaga, the addition at the begining and at the end to the Meghduta and to give these as also the theme of the loder work a dramatic grab. Thus, an adaptation of Meghadutam, on the background of the curse of Yaksa in dramatic form.

The play was staged on 29-3-1972, New Delhi at International Sanskrit Conference, 1972.

Nityanand, Smrtitirtha. Meghadutam. *Pranava Parijata,* 1962.

<u>**Contents**</u> : Part I, Jan.-Feb. 1962, Vol. IV, No. 5 pp 145-153.

Part II, Mar.-Apr. 1962. Vol. IV, No. 7.pp 186-195.

Part III, Apr.-May 1962, Vol. IV, No. 8.pp 210-218.

Five act Sanskrit drama based on Kalidasa's poem and with artistry it depicts the parts of the separation of Yakṣa and the Yaksi which cover the whole play.

Pant, Sumitranandan. Meghaduta. An adaptation to musical drama based on the Meghaduta.

Raghavan, V. Asadhasya prathamadivase. *Sanskrit Ranga,* 1959-60, Vol. II. pp 57.59.

A Dramatic theme of the Meghduta in Sanskrit. Review appeared in *Sanskrit Pratibha* April 1961, Vol. III, No.1.p.145.

Rao, Balantarapu Rajnikant. Meghasandesam. An adaptation in Telugu of Kalidasa's Meghaduta in dramatic form Mentioned in the Bibliography of stagable plays in Indian languages; ed. by C.C. Mehta.

Shastri, Vishvanath Keshava Chatre. Natyarupam Meghdutam Amṛtalata (Paradi, Balsad) Feb. 1966; Vol. II, No.4. Sanskrit play adpted from Meghdutam of Kalidasa.

Singh Indermohan. Yaksaśāpah. *Visvasaṁskṛtam* (Hoshiarpur)' Sept. 1993 Vol. XXX, No.3. A play based on the Meghadutam of Kalidasa aims at supplying the Purvabhaga, the addition in the begining, to the Meghaduta.

Velankar, S.B. Asadhasya parthamadivase. *In* Tat Tvam Asi - Bhopal : Surabharati, 1972. This Sanskrit playlet is in a way complimentary to the Meghaduta of Kalidasa. This piece visually presents the journey as described by the Yaksa for benefit of Megha to undertake his mission and in keeping with the spirit of the original poem.

______Meghaduottaram - Bhopal : Surabharati, 1968.

Work carries a translation of the Sanskrit drama into English and Hindi. The play is the Uttarabhaga, the addition at the end, of the Meghaduta of Kalidasa. But dramatist clarifies that it supplies the preface as well as the denouement to the Meghaduta the former in act I & the latter in acts II & III.

______Meghadutanvitam - Bombay : Devavanee Mandiram, 1991. A musical ballet that has three acts based on the Meghadutam of Kalidasa. It unfold the theme much in the same way as does his 'Meghadutottaram' except for the fact that it has a new character called Rasana who acts as a maid to the Yakṣ aputri, the wife of the Yakṣa.

Rahuvaṁsam

Chaudhuri, Jatindra Bimal. Svapnaraghuvaṁsam. Calcutta.

A play inspired from 'Raghuvamsam' of Kalidasa in manuscript form; broadcasted by All India Radio, Calcutta in Dec. 1956 and staged on 2nd January 1957.

Mentioned in the 'Bibliography of stageable plays in Indian languages/ed. by C.C. Mehta' (Vol. 1, 1963).

Dwivedi Vasudeva. Kautsasya Gurudaksina - Varanasi : Sarvabhauma Sanskrit Prachara Karyala, 1954.

An one act play in Sanskrit, the plot is taken from the Raghavaṁsa's fifth act. The story pertains to sage Varatantu and his pupil Kautsa.

Majalgaonkar, Achyut Tatyarao Bobade. Sitatyagah - *In* Samuccayah - Darbhanga: Kameshwar Singh Sanskrit University, 1963. pp 105-107.

This play is based on the works of Kalidasa (Raghuvamsa), Valmiki, Bhavabhuti & others that depict the episode of Sita's exile.

Mishra, Gangesh. Gurudaksinanatakam - Delhi : Bhartiya Vidya Prakashan, 1990.

Sanskrit play in seven acts that retell the Kautsa - Raghu episode of the fifth canto of the Raghuvamsa of Kalidasa.

Mishra, Narayan. Indumatiparinayah. *In* Kalidasiyoparupakanam Samuccayah - Darbhanga : Kameshwar Singh Sanskrit University, 1963; pp 67-78.

A play in three lengthy scenes that dipicts the episode of the svayamvara of

Indumati in Kalidasa's work 'Raghuvamsa'.

Mishra, Yaduvamsha. Gurudaksina. *In* Kalidasiyoparupakanam. Samuccayah - Darbhanga : Kameshwar Singh Sanskrit University, 1963, pp 60-63.

Sanskrit drama in four scenes wherein is related in three scenes the Kautsa - Raghu episode as described by Kalidasa in his Raghuvamsa.

Pandurangi, K.P. Sitatyagah. Bangalore.

In manuscript. A radio play in Sanskrit that depicts the scenes of the exile of Sita. The playwright has followed these incident as given in the Raghuvamsa of Kalidasa and Uttararmacaritam of Bhavabhuti.

Mentioned in the 'Bibliography of stageable play in Indian languages/ed. by C.C. Mehta' (Vol. 1, 1963).

Rangacharya, Shrinivasa. Gurudaksina.

A dramatic production of the Raghu and Kautsa theme of the Raghuvamsa.

Mentioned in the 'Bibliography of stageable plays in Indian languages/ed. by C.C. Mehta' (Vol. 1, 1963).

Sharma, Ogeti Parikshit Sharma. Gurudakshina. *In* Pariksinnatikacakram : [collection of twenty seven plays]. Poona : The author, 1983.

A Sanskrit drama in nine scenes that retell the story of Raghuvamsa in play form.

Shastri, Vishvanath Keshava Chatre. Nandinivarapradanam *Amrtalata* (Paradi, Balsad); 1965; Vol. 1, No. 4. Sanskrit play based on the second canto of the Raghuvamsam of Kalidasa.

Shukla, Chandrika Prasad. Viravadanyam. *In* Kalidasiyoparupakanam Samuccayah - Darbhanga: Kameshwar Singh Sanskrit University, 1963. pp 17-28. Four acts drama in Sanskrit that deals with the story of Raghu's munificence, as described by Kalidasa in the third canto of the Raghuvamsa; based on the Dilipa and Raghu characters of the Raghuvamsa. The playwright makes use of original quotations of Kalidasa.

Srijiva Nyayatirtha Raghuvamsam. *Pranava Parijata* (Calcutta) 1963 (Saka year 1884)

Contents : Part I Jan-Feb 1963; Vol. V, No.5. pp 99-112 Part II (Feb-March 1963; Vol. V, No.6 pp 122-132.

A drama (inspired from Raghuvamsa) in six acts.

5

Life of Kalidasa in Performance

I Kabi Kalidas (Bengali)

Minerva Theatre, Calcutta presented Jaladhar Chatterji's 'Kabi Kalidas', a play in Bengali on 19 July 1941. The cast was:

KALIDAS	......	*Dhiren Das*
BHOJRAJ	......	*Bhanu Chatterjee*
VIKRAMARKA	......	*Amal Banerjee*
VISHNU SHARMA	......	*Sibkali Chatterji*
GUNOMANI	......	*Nirodasundari*
BHARATI	......	*Uma Mukherjee*
SATYABATI	......	*Aparna Das*

II Asadha Ka Ek Dina (Hindi)

A landmark in Hindi drama, Asadha Ka Ek Dina (one day in the Ashadha month) was written by Mohan Rakesh in 1958. It depicts the life of the great Sanskrit poet Kalidasa and his love for a simple village girl before and after he rose to eminence. The theme develops out of both internal and external conflicts which begin on a day in Asadha, and end, on a day in Ashadha. In between the long interval of time, Kalidasa and Mallika (his love and source of inspiration) are both subjected to suffering. This lends intensity to the conflict and the play ends in romantic agony. The effective use of dramatic irony, evocative imagery, economy of words the theatrical poetry of its language makes 'Ashadh Ka Ek Dina', an outstanding contribution to the contemporary Indian dramatic literature.

Mohan Rakesh

In 1960, Calcutta's & Hindi troupe 'Anamika' staged 'Asadha Ka Ek Dina' under the direction of Shyamanand Jalan

In the year 1962-63, Asadha Ke Ek Din was staged under the direction of E Alkaji. It was National School of Drama's [School Production]. It was also presented at the XXVI International Congress of Orientalist's meeting in New Delhi.

Scene from NSD production of Mohan Rakesh's Asadha Ka Ek Din'

Mohan Maharish; the director of 'Asadha Ka Ek Dina'.

Asadha Ka Eka Dina

Asadha Ka Eka Dina by Mohan Rakesh had an interesting set in this production by Mohan Maharisi at Jaipur. The stage setting had been reduced to a bareminimum and two elliptical forms on the stage floor lend a typical quality as well as suggest the split personality of characters whichformed the backbone of Mohan Rakesh's later play.

In July 1980, 'Asadha Ka Ek Dina' was staged by the students of National School of Drama. The play was directed by Kirti Jain. The first years students presented it on 15 October, 1980.

In Patiala, Ram Gopal Bajaj did 'Asadha Ka Ek Dina' which produced very good response from the Punjabi audience [ENACT. April-June 1981].

Ram Gopal Bajaj, directed 'Asad Ka Ek Dina'

In 1981, Amal Allana staged 'Asadha Ka Ek Dina' in Delhi. J.N. Kaushal had righly said wherever she takes up an old play, much produced, Amal Allana has always something new to offer. Her Aashad Ka Ek Dina was also like wise. She directed Kalidasa of all the glamour and aura of a demi-dod which is the Indian way of treating by-gone heroes and writers. She made him just a villager with some poetic brilliance. Her Vilom was also behaved like a normal human being, who is ruthless, jealous and does not feel shy of man-handing his wife to vent his hatred against someone. Amal's Mallika sheilds Kalidas against Vilom in the first act like a bird shielding her offspring. She is all out for Kalidas against Vilom in the first act like a bird shielding her offspring. She is all out for Kalidasa though she does not have her doubts regarding her future-she seems to agree with Vilom when he asks Kalidasa regarding Mallika's future after his departure for Ujjaini. Amal achieves this with striking pictorial compositions. She is able to focus attention on the characters at appropriate moments like zooming in on her object.

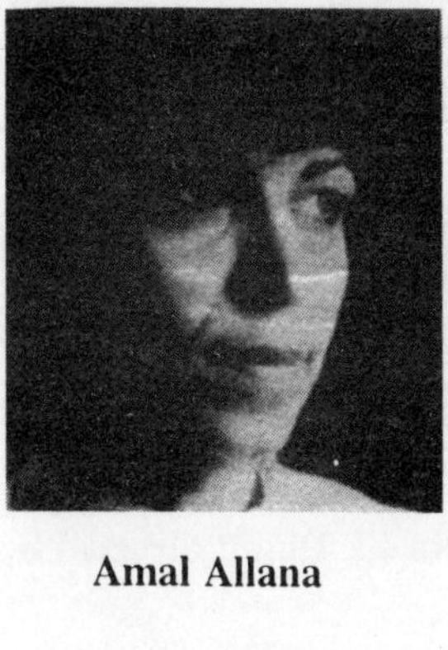

Amal Allana

Mona Chawla brough out the emotional aspect of Mallika who initially has her doubts but ultimately surrenders to the circumstances with great clarity. Abha Sood's Ambika was an equal match to her. Banwari Taneja was probably the finest Vilom one has seen. Sudhir Kulkarni's Matul was a delightful character study. Ravi Jhankal's Kalidasa was insipid. He did not gain stature even in the third act. Kaushal wonders that Rakesh' Kalidasa is a weak character but why actors fail to bring out this weakness?

Mohan Rakesh' Aashad Ka Ek Dina was interpreted in Maniputi dance idiom by second year students of the National School of Drama at the Aiwan-e-Ghalib auditorum, Mata Sundari Marg.

Sanakhaya Ebotombi has provided the music design and direction for the production which while visually attractive, tends to drag at places. However, considering that the students had to meet the demands of a largely unfamiliar cultural mode, their performance was creditable. The production was the outcome of the NSD Theatre workshop in Imphal held from December 14 to January14, 1990?

The dance-drama enacted in three acts was well served by the music rendered live by the five-man orchestra. the costumes, particularly of the female artistes, were attractive the student's playing Mallika and Kalidasa, Jaya Seal and Ashraf-ul-Haque respectively excelled. This then is Mohan Rakesh in language and plot. But the overall framework is Manipuri dance, and therefore an unusual dance drama.

A scene from 'Aashad Ka Ek Dina'; directed by Sanakhaya Ebotombi

To commemorate 20th death anniversary of Mohan rakesh, the National School of Drama Repertory Company organised 'Mohan Rakesh Natya Samaroha which opened with a performance of Aashad Ka Ek Dina on 3 December 1992. It was directed by Ram Gopal Bajaj and the festival concluded with Kirti Jain's production 'Lehron Ke Raj hans' Shri Bhaskar Chandravarkar scored the music. Shri Ashok Sagar Bhagat designed the lights while Dolly Ahluwalia designed the costumes for these plays. The set of Ashad Ka Ek Dina was designed by Bansi Kaul based on as earlier design by Meena Williams.The festival created a lot of interest among the theatre lovers of Delhi with the halls running to full houses forcing the school to arrange matinee performances. The schedule of performances was as follows:

3-5 December 1992, 4 to 10, 21-31 January 1993.

National School of Drama's Repertory Company visited Mauritius during November-December 1993 on the occasion of the 4th International Hindi Sammelan. The Company was invited to perform Mohan Rakesh's Aashad Ka Ek Dina, Lehron Ke Rajhans and Adhe Adhure. The three-play festival opened with Lehron Ke Rajhans on 6 December followed by a repeat performance of it on 7 December Adhe Adhure was performed on 9 and 10 December (two performances of the same day) and Aashad Ka Ek Dina on 12 December. There was repeat performances of Aashd Ka Ek Dina (8 performances) in New Delhi in the same year.

Mr. Cassam Uteem, President of the Republic of Mauritius greeting the artist after the performance

Excerpts from the 'Aashad Ka Ek Dina' was presented by the 'Roopantar Theatre Training Centre of Gorakhpur' in May 1998 at their 'Dikshanta Samaroha' the dramatis personae included Hemlata Sahi, Isha Gaur and Shailesh Shrivastava.

'Aashad Ka Ek Dina' based on the life-story of Kalidasa was produced by Shri Govind Dharmadhikari and Suman Dhamadhikari at Bharatiya Rangmanch, Ujjain, on the occasion of 'Kalidasa Jayanti'.

III. Mahakavi Kalidasa (Hindi)

On the occasion of 'Kalidasa Jayanti 'Mahakavi Kalidas' a Hindi drama depicting the life of Kalidasa was performed at 'Bharatiya Rangmanch, Ujjain under the direction of Govind Dharmadhikari and Suman Dharmadhikari.

IV. Mahakavi Kalidasa (Telugu)

Mahakavi Kalidasa by A Hanumantha Rao is a full length play in Telugu on the life of Kalidasa; staged in September 1996 on the occasion of drama festival organised by Samskara Bharati at Rabindra Bharati, Hyderabad,

V. Prakriti Purush Kalidasa

Dr. Prabhat Bhattacharya directed 'Prakriti Purush Kalidasa', written by Dr. Shivmangal Singh for the Madhav Mahavidyalaya. The drama was staged at Kalidasa festival, Ujjain.

6

Inventory of Kalidasa's Life in Drama and Other Genres

Anonymous Kalidasa: Pimpal ani Ramayana [s.l.]: [s.n.] A Marathi satire on the life of Kalidasa.

Anonymous. Kalidasa prahasana-nataka. - Madras: [s.n.], 1983 Work is mentioned in the 'A bibliography of Sanskrit drama/by Schuyler' and 'Catalogus Catalogorum/by T. Aufrecht'.

Bakshi, Padumalal Pannalal. Meghaduta men Kalidasa ka atmacarita. *Sarasvati*; Dec. 1920, Vol. XXI, Pt. 2, No. 6. Pp 289-292. Essay.

Bandyopadhyay, Saradindu Kalidas/by Saradindu Bandyopadhyay. Calcutta : Gurudas Cattopadhyay & Sons, 1943.
158 p; 18 cm
Bengali drama on Kalidasa.

Saradindu Bandyopadhyay

Bhatt, Udayshankar. Kalidasa/by Udayshankar Bhatt. Delhi : Raj Kamal Prakashan, 1950. A Hindi drama on the theme of Kalidasa.

Bhattacharya, B.K. Kavikalidasam. *Indian Literature* 1969; Vol. XII, No. 4 P 97 Review by V. Raghavan appeared in *Sanskrit Pratibha;* 1969; Vol. VIII, No. 1 p 97. A play on the life of the poet.

Bhattacharya, Birendra Kumar Kavi Kalidasam. Calcutta, [s.n.], [1968-69]. A Sanskrit play on the life of Kalidasa.

Bisi, Pramathanath. Bichitra samlap.

Written by one of the eminent writers of Bengal, the book is an imaginary novel in the form of converstations between celebritiesin life and literature, ancient and modern and ends with a conversation between Kalidasa and Rabindranath. In it Kalidasa expresses his deep gratitude to Rabindranath and explains that for all his fame he is celebrated only as a supreme poet of beauty and enjoyment. It is only Rabindranath who has taken his readers to the inmost soul of his poetry, making manifest that it was the great poetry of a great poet; the Mahakavi. And he had to wait fifteen centuries for a critic of the genius of Rabindranath.

Chaturvedi, Chancharik. Kalidasa ke naam patra *Sar* June 1963; Vol. L XIV, Part. 1, No. 6; Pp 524-529 In Hindi A satire in letter-writting form describing the modern society addressed to Kalidasa.

Cinasesagiriravu, Malakapalli, Kalidasa / by Malakapalli Cinasesagiriravu. - 4th ed. - Kakinada: Andhra Jatiya Granthamandali, 1928.

133 p; 18 cm.

Telugu story of Kalidasa's life.

Divekar, Hari Ramachandra. Kalidasamahotsaham. *Sanskrita Pratibha* (New Delhi); 1965 Vol. V, No. 2; Pp 141-201. It is a Sanskrit farce (in five acts) par excellence on the trend of studies and researches on now-a-days on Kalidasa. The conversation between Kalidasa and Narada is the bridge under which flows the entire theme. The aim of the play is to know the state of Indian culture, anything but forgotten for long, by the people in the absence of the Britishers with the great poet in heaven.

Dwivedi, Jayashankar. Kalidas ki Atmakatha-1 *Tri; Sep.* 1958; Vol. III, No. 12; Pp 23-40.

Kalidas ki atmakatha-II. *Tri;* Jan 1960; Vol. V, No. 4; 119-128.

Kalidas ki Atmakatha III *Tri;* Oct. 1961; Vol. VII, No. 1.

Written (as if an autobiography) on the basis of the works of Kalidasa.

Dwivedi, Mahavir Prasad. Kalidasa ki vaivahik kavita. *Sar*; Vol. VI. No. 6; Pp. 223-227.

A fiction based on the married life of Kalidasa.

Gadanayaka, Radhamohana. Kalidasa/by Radhamohana Gadanayaka.-Angul : the author, 1940. vi, 120 p; 18 cm. Oriya drama on the life of the Sanskrit poet Kalidasa.

Gupta, Virendra Kumar. Mahakavi Kalidasa. Delhi : [s.n.], 1971.

In Hindi. Life-sketches of Kalidasa is drawn in prose style for children.

Hanumantaravu, Avatapalli. Kalidasa caritra/by Avatapalli Hanumantaravu.-Masulipatam : The author, 1927 iv, 132 p; 20.5 cm Telugu drama on Kalidasa.

Hasyakalanidhi, tr. Kalidasa lambodara prahasanam/Hasyakalanidhi [pseud] Pondicherry : Kama Granthalaya 1922. 78 p; 21 cm.

Jha, Jivanath. Kalidasa gauravam. *KUS* [Darbhanga]; 1963; Pp. 81-86 Sanskrit play based on the life of the Kalidasa; as described in the legend.

Jiva, Nyayatirtha. Mahakavi Kalidasam. *Pranava Parijata,* Oct-Nov. 1963; Vol. VI, No. 2.

Contents : Acts I-II; No. 3. Pp 75-88 Acts II-IV; No. 4. P 117-127 Act V; No. 8 (1964). Pp 256-258 Sanskrit drama in five acts.

Kṛsnamurtisastri, Sripada. Kalidasa vilasamu/by Sripada Krsnamurtisastri.-Madras : [s.n.], 1889. iv, 86, [2] p; 18 cm Poem in Telugu on Kalidasa.

Laksminarasimhamu, Cilakamarti. Kalidasa caritra/by Cilakamarti Laksminarasimhamu - Rajahmundry : T.V. Ramanayya & Bros., 1925 X, 172 p; 21 cm. Telugu fiction on Kalidasa.

Laksminarasimhasastri, Calla, Kalidasa Kathamanjari/by Calla Laksminarasimhasastri.-Masulipatam: Aryananda Press, 1918. 2 Vols.; 21 cm Fiction in Telugu on Kalidasa's life.

Mahalinga, Sastri. Srikalidasacaritasangrahah. *Manjusa.* May 1950; Vol. IV, No. 9. Pp.-269-280 Drama in Sanskrit on the theme of Kalidasa.

Mishra, Abhiraja Rajendra. Vidyottama.-Delhi: Eastern Book Linkers, 1992.

A Sanskrit play in four acts with a delicate blend of history and imagination that depicts the life of Kalidasa and the playwright opines that Kalidasa was born in the Kapisthala village (Kavitha) of the Modern Garhwal (Pauri) district.

Mangurlkar, Arving. Kalidasa: eka lalitacarca: *Navabharata* (Marathi). March, 1957; Vol. X, No. 6. Pp. 40-50.

Play on the life of Kalidasa with profuse quotations of Kalidasa.

Mukhopadhyay, Prabhat Kumar. Kalidaservivaha *In* Prabhat Granthavali Vol. II Life of Kalidasa in Bengali (Prose form).

Prabhat Kumar Mukhopadhyaya, the author of 'Kalidaser Vivaha' in Bengali

Narayana Sastri. Kalidasiyamantimamaitihyam. *San. Bh.;* Vol. II, No. 3; Pp. 183-186 & Vol. III, No. 1; Pp 6-10. A fiction in Sanskrit on Kalidasa's life.

Pathak, Subhanath 'Natha'. Kalidasapani karanam In. *KUS.*-Darbhanga: [s.n.], 1963. Pp.99-101.

Sanskrit play on the early life of Kalidasa that depicts him as a fooll who got married to a princess.

Pathak, Vaneshvar. Kalidasah/by Vaneshvar Pathak, *In* Kalidasasamarohavasare nibaddhanam Kalidasiyoparupakanam sumuccayah (KUS) ed. by Umesh Mishra.-Darghanga: [s.n.], 1963.

Vol. 1. No. 2. Pp. 41-46.

One act play in Sanskrit on the legend that Kalidas was a fool who married to princess.

Ramanarayana Kavulu. Kalidasa caritramu/by Ramanarayana Kavulu. 3rd ed.-Vijayawada: Kandula Govindam, 1928.

vi, 96 p; 18 cm.

Story in Telugu on the life of Kalidasa.

Shah, N.N. Mahakavi Kalidas ni prasadi.-Ahmedabad: [s.n.], 1932 In Gujarati Life of Kalidasa in Prose style.

Sharma, Hemcandra. Kalidas/by Hemcandra Sarma.-Golaghat: Purnacandra Gosvami, 1951 V, 79 p; 19 cm.

Sharma, Thakurdatta. Kalidas ki kahani-Jodhpur; [s.n.] Story of Kalidasa in Hindi for children.

Sharma, Venkataramanya. Kalidasa caritam.-Madras: [s.n.], 1983.

In Telugu prose, the life of Kalidasa is narrated.

Srinivasaravu, Kolacalam. Kalidasa natakamu/by Kolacalam Srinivasaravu.-Bellary: Kolacalam Satrughnaravu, 1925. 87 p; 23 cm Drama on the life of Kalidasa in Telugu.

Vandematram. Kalidasa koun tha? *Vikrama* (Hindi); Dec. 1942; Vol. 1, No. 3; Pp 27-29 A story based on Kalidasa.

Varnekar, Shridhar Bhaskar. Kalidasarahasyam/by Sridhara Bhaskara Varnekara; tr. into Hindi by Kamala Srivarnekara.-Nagpur: Vagishwari Prakashan Sanstha, 1958.

Velankar, B. Kalidasa caritam.-Bombay: [s.n.], 1961. Review appeared in *Sanskrit Pratibha,* April 1961; Vol. III, No. 1. P 144. Five acts play on the life of Kalidasa.

Venkataramanujasarma, Cilakapati, Kalidasa caritra prakaranamu/by Cilakapati Venkataramanujasarma.-Madras: [s.n.], 1908.

184 p; 18 cm.

Ten acts drama on the life of Kalidasa in Telugu.

7

Life and Works of Kalidasa Through Cinema

I Sakuntala (Tamil)

Kalidasa made the Mahabharata story of Shakuntala into an immoratal play that has been staged in India and abroad in various forms be it pantomine ballet, classical dance idioms or theatre. The classic has been made and remade into films also. Here special mention could be made of a Tamil film 'produced in 1940 with M.S. Subbulakshmi as the heroine.

M.S. Subbulakshmi as 'Sakuntala' in the Tamil film (1940)

II Sakuntala (Hindi)

A Hindi film was make under the same title and veteran director V. Shantaram himself acted in the film and took the lead role 'Dushyanta. His actress wife Sandhya was the heroine of this new experimentation.

Sandhya as 'Sakuntala' in V. Shantaram's Hindi film of the same title

Shakuntala with King Dushyanta

Shakuntala with the young Bharata

III Kavi Kalidasa

In the fiftees, a Hindi film was made under the title 'Kavi Kalidasa'. The film was directed by S.M. Tripathy who also scored the music. The lyrics was written by Bharat Vyas. The film was based on the life and times of Kavi Kalidas, one of the greatest litterateur of India. He was desired by the royalty, worshiped by playmates, nurtured by nature. Kalidas, devoid of parental affection, was slack at school and dubbed as an artless fool, except by a little girl Pushpavali. Their devotion to each other was matchless. Pushpavali clinged on to him when he was thrown out of his house by his step-mother. At Kashi, he worked as a woodcutter and she did household chores. By subduing his opponent in an arms contest, he won the hand of princess Vidyottama. The Princess turned him out of her chamber for his naive and foolish attitude. Pushpavali saved him from taking his own life. In an Ujjain ashram Kalidas learnt to write poetry. His first work of verse "Seasonal transformation verses" was Ritusanghar. Subsequently his concentration resulted in literary masterpieces. When Princess Vidyottama got him seperated from Pushpavali and maltreated both, that inspired him to write Meghdoot, Kalidas' most celebrated work. At the instance of the king, Kalidas was finally reunited with his beloved.....

Bharat Bhooshan played the title role. Others: Nirupa Roy, Anita Guha, Sapru, Niranjan Sharma, Baby Raja, Mridula, Ratnamala, Indira, etc.

Bharat Bhusan, the hero of the Hindi film 'Kavi Kalidasa'

IV Mahakavi Kalidasa

K.K. Rao's Telugu feature film 'Mahakavi Kalidasa' won him the National Award in the language concerned for the year 1960.

V Sakuntala

Bhupen Hazarika's Assamese film 'Sakuntala' bagged the National Film Award in the language concerned in 1961.

VII Komal Gandhar (1960-61)

The filmmaker Ritvik Ghatak was deeply rooted in Indian tradition. In his film Komal Gandhar he kept harking back to Kalidasa. Komal Gandhar explores the tragic dimensions of partition, but his admirer gets confused by seemingly unconnected reference points and intrusion of literary and theatrical ideas and usages.

Kironmoy Raha observes that without a coherent narrative structure, the film appears on the surface to recount the tribulations of the new theatre movement in Bengal with its ideological and factional quarrels. It interpolates at the same time overt references to characters in ancient Sanskrit literature to underline the need to integrate tradition with contemporary existence. On it again is imposed the visual and emotional anguish of partition. In this film Ghatak has shown Bhrigu's theatre troupe performing Kalidasa's Abhijanan Sakuntalam. The character Bhrigu himself playing the role of Dusyanta.

Rustom Bharucha in his article 'Theatre, cinema, Ghatak' writes "... theatre becomes an element in Ghatak's struggle that he refuses to suppress or erase in his search for an uncompromising, if resolvently imperfect cinema. At once mythic and interruptive, grounded in ordinariness and transcendent in being, theatre provides many point of references. In Komal Gandhar, it becames a matter of life and death. Not only is it the subject of the film, the source of 'Creative unity' in struggle, it is the metaphor of Ghatak's most observed concern with the Partition, which is contextualised in the film within the inter-group rivalries of two theatre companies. All this is familiar in the oeuvre of Ghatak's film but what never fails to stun is the impact of separation within the site of theatre. I am thinking here, unforgettably, of that moment in Komal Gandhar when Shakuntala has been disrupted by the contemporary asuras on stage, and the curtain of the New Empire Theatre rises like a guillotine to reveal an emply auditorium into which Bhrigu-as-Dushyanta stumbles in confusion while Anasuya-as-Shakuntala watchless helplessly on state. This, for me, as a theatre person writing about cinema, is a reckoning, a moment of death, the deepest betrayal in which there is no one to see you act and that you are left with is your artifice glinting in the house lights. Ghatak's empathy in this moment for Kalidasa's disillusioned protagonists is deeply felt. For all its irony, it is the empathy of a distanced theatre worker..."

VII Gajagamini (1999)

Gajagamini is an artistic film, a milestone in Indian cinema, directed by M.F. Hussain, the veteran painter turned film maker. It is his debut film, a combination of three things, visual happenings, singing words and moving images. This film is to be viewed in that manner. Well-known Hindi actress Madhuri Dixit has essayed four characters in Gajagamini. The title has nothing to do with her walk. "I am playing four different roles in the film. One is of Kalidasa's Sakuntala, the other is of a blind street singer, the third is of Monica Mathur, a character inspired by Monica Lewinsky, and the fourth is that of the woman of the millennium." One of her roles in Gajagamini is almost similar. She plays Madhuri Dixit, the actress who has Kamdev expressing his sexual desires for her, while Leonardo Da Vinci expresses his platonic love for her. Inder Kumar is Kamdev, while Naseeruddin Shah plays Vinci. "It's an experimental film with a series of roles which are interwoven. There are characters picked at random from various spheres and made to talk with each other. Like there is a conversation between C.V. Raman and Kalidasa.

M.F. Hussain and Madhuri Dixit; the latter played 'Sakuntala' in the film 'Gajagamini'

VIII. Sakuntala

Doordarshan has produced the tale of Shakuntala for children under the series 'Amar Chitra Kathāy' in Hindi on 11 December 1999.

The episoded was directed by Shri Rohit Kausik.

8

Kalidasa Drama Through Visual Arts

Sakuntala in Sunga Sculpture :- Rising into prominence, the Sungas replaced the Mauryas in the North in 184 B.C. The purlieux of Magadha as the pivotal point of the Mauryan empire touched Malwa in Central India. It was in the first quarter of the first century B.C. that the Satvahanas, a rising dynasty, became prominent as a political power to be reckoned with in South-Eastern Maharashtra. The sway of their role extended from Andhra Pradesh upto Malwa in Central India. New creative forces got unleashed in the domain of art, which earned active patronage, both from the Mauryan dynasty and Satavahanas. Scholar B. Chhabra in his article "Sakuntala in Sunga Sculpture" appeared in the Journal Natya (New Delhi) 1964; Vol. VIII, No. 1 has tried to identify a damaged state plaque with the scene of the IIIrd Act of the Abhijnanasakuntala and thinks that Kalidasa might have flourished in the 2nd in 3rd Century B.C. Theme is evidently borrowed from Kalidasa. It derives its theme from III Act of Sakuntala viz. "Kim Śitalaih klamavimardibhirardravatam."

M.L. Varadpande in his book 'Mahabharata in performance' 'has informed that a very interesting terracotta medallion was found in the excavation of the Bhita mound near Allahabad with a scene of Shakuntala story inscribed on it. The drawing of this scene is published in the Archaeological Report of 1911-12. The dominant figure on the medallion is that of a king mounted on a chariot drawn by four horses. The running dear near the chariot indicates that the king is pursuing the animal with an intention to kill it. A person with outstretched hands is seen standing before the chariot resisting its further progress. In the first act of the play Shakuntala, the sage Vaikhanasa stops the king Dusyanta on hunting expedition in the same way. In thebackground Kanva's hermitage is shown. The girl is shown standing under a tree, probably watering it. Another one is kneeling by the side of a pond plucking a lotus bud. The girls standing is Shakuntala. The scholars feel that this scene is inspired by Kalidasa's play.

Orissa-Cave Reliefs :- The culptured panels and friezes adorning the facades and walls of the caves existing in the two hills of Udayagiri and Khandagiri in the vicinity of Bhuvaneshwara (Orissa) have Jainist motivations. The caves were excavated in the period of Kharavela, king of Kalinga. In Khandagiri the Ranigumpha cave is the finest specimen of adornments with detailed sculptures and friezes. This two-storeyed cave has also some independent sculptures, which show a distinctive style of modelling and execution. The stories of Dushyanta and Sakuntala and Udayana and Vasavadatta havebeen depicted on the wall surfaces of the upper storey of the above - said cave.

Scholar C. Shivaramamurti in his brochure on "Sculpture inspired by Kalidasa (1942) tried to illuminate many a text from Kalidasa's works by sketches of sculptured and painted figures in many rock-cut temples and caves. But the sculptured reproduced in this treatise are only instances of an unintentional parallelism rather than that they represent a deliberate design to reproduce Kalidasa's ideas in rock and stone.

Raja Ravi Varma (1848 - 1906)

Raja Ravi Varma (1848 - 1906) was great artist of the nineteenth century. His paintings emerged as the first important signifiers of 'modernity' and 'nationality' in the Indian art scene towards the end of the century. Tapati Guha Thakurata, a fellow in History at the Centre for Studies in Social Science, at Calcutta, observes : soon after the success of his female figure (his forte) studies in the 1870's, emerged his first new-classical painting 'Sakuntala Patralekhan' that became the prize winning exhibit of the Madras Display of 1876. Ravi Varma's choice, henceforth, of themes from ancient mythology and Sanskrit literature, would reinforce the key constructs of classicism and tradition in contemporary orientalist and nationalist thought. He located the 'classicism and tradition in contemporary orientalist and nationalist thought. He located the 'classics' a certain corpus of lyrics and romantic themes in keeping with the new aesthetics of 'high art'... In Kerala, Ravi Varma's direction of work, significantly, coincided with the rise of a new genre of Sanskrit - style mahakavyas and epic dramas in Malayalam literature, and a new spurt of translations of the Sanskrit classics. In fact his painting of the Sakuntala picture in 1876 followed closely on a famous translation of Abhijnanasakuntalam by a member of the same Travancorean aristocracy, Kerala Varma (known as 'Kerala Kalidasa') who stood at the head of these new literary trends. With these literary ingredients before him, the artist dipped into his reservoir of visual imagery (some readily available), others consciously searched out in conceiving his Pauranic composition.... Ravi Varma had ventured forth on an all-India tour in search of typical, pan-Indian motifs and costumes for his paintings. From his 'Bharat-darshan' we come to know that he even witnessed theatrical performance of Kirloskar Company's Sakuntala for the authenticity of his pictoral project."

Balendranath Tagore in his essays has commented upon the rich reservoir of pictoral imagery in ancient Sanskrit literature, particularly in the works of Kalidasa. The 'picturesque' language of Kalidasa the vivid 'word pictures' evoked in the passages of Raghuvamsha or Abhijnana - Sakuntala - seemed to be wanting to be translated into pictorial form. In fulfilling this mission, in giving the 'right' visual form to these classical literary subjects and imagery, was seen to lie the unique success and significance of Ravi Varma in modern India.

As said before, by 1876, Ravi Varma had painted several versions of 'Sakuntala', one of his most famous series of paintings. A particular one - featuring a love-lorn Sakuntala, lying on her stomach, writing a letter to her lover. With her finger tips on a lotus leaf, accompanied by her closest companions Anasooya and Priyamvada was sent for the Madras show that year. The Duke of Buckingham was impressed by this painting and it was chosen to be the frontispiece for Sir Monier William's tanslation of Abhijnana Sakuntalam.

Birth of Śakuntala (Raja Ravi Varma)

Śakuntala (Raja Ravi Varma)

Śakuntala (Raja Ravi Varma)

Śakuntala Patralekhan (Raja Ravi Varma)

Sakuntala Patralekhan (Raja Ravi Varma)

Attributed to Raja Ram Varma **Śakuntala Patralekhan**

Raja Ravi Varma **Bharata & Lion Cub**

(Raja Ravi Varma) Menaka & Śakuntala

Abanindranath Tagore (1871-1951), The leader of the New Bengal School was born in the Tagore House of Prince Dwarkanath at Jorasanko, Calcutta. Son of Gunendranath, this great painter from Bengal; soon became an institution in himself.

Abanindranath's first formal training in pastel water colour and life - study was under the private supervision of his Italian tutor Signor Gilhardi, the Vice Principal of the Govt. School of Art. He attended the studio of Charles Palmer, an English painter for instructions in oil paintings and portraiture from 1894 and continued over the next four years. His pedecessor Ravi Varma, after looking at the Abanindranath's paintings, on a visit to the Jorasanko establishment, remarked:-

"Now I am sure of the future of Indian art. It is very bright." The subject matter of the painting of Ravi Varma and Abanindra Nath Tagore (who later established himself as a progenitor of a new national vocabulary in art as well as a pioneer in regenerating the decandent art and aesthetic scene in India) was also as far apart as is commonly assumed. As the older painter lifted his subjects from Puranic and legendary lore, classical poetry and drama, and mythology, so did Abanindranath Tagore pick up subjects from the same sources in his Sakuntala, Radha Krishna Series, Shiv Parvati and Uma etc.

This artistic genius also wrote about Sakuntala that appeared in print in the year 1895 from Brahmo Samaj Press, Calcutta.

Sakuntala in hermitage

Fisherman with the signet ring

Śakuntala by Kshitin Majumdar

Of the students of Abanindranath, Kshitin Majumdar developed rich and sensuous and yet subtle combination of colours.

'Sacountala' by John Schweppe.; inspired by a sculpture by Camille Claudel

The National Museum of India has in its repository, a set of 53 paintings which it had acquired in 1989. It serialises with great artistic merit and vividness the wellknown legend of Sakuntala.

National Academy of Visual Arts (Lalit Kala Academi, New Delhi) brought out in 1991 its portfolio No. 36 eight of these paintings under the title 'Kalidasa's Sakuntalam'. In its brief introductory commentary and from its title the Lalit Kala Academy Portfolio seems to maintain as if these paintings aim at illustrating Kalidasa's masterpiece 'Abhijnanasakuntalam'.

The Folio Society, London, in its publication entitled 'Sakuntala' containing the English renderings of Kalidasa's text, i.e., Abhijnanasakuntalam, the story of Sakuntala as handed down to us through the epic Mahabharata and

Abanindranath Tagore's Sakuntala and brief article under the title 'A tale retold in Pahari miniatures' by Dr. Daljeet and twelve leaves of his painted series recognises the set of paintings as an independent attempt aiming at retelling Sakuntala - tale in its own way.

In the Holdings of the **National Museum**, there is another set of twenty one paintings illustrating a colloquial Avadhi text of Shakuntala legend. The entire story part has been covered in just ten of these twentyone folios - Instead of conveying these pictorially, the artist seems to depend more on its textual inscriptions. It is essentially a creator's approach, where the artist re-creates to his own fancy and convictions Sakuntala's story and instead of copying Kalidasa's lyricism, the artist chooses his own medium and thus Abhijnanasakuntalam has had the subtlest role here.

The Aravali Books International, New Delhi published in 1998 a book on Sakuntala that comprises of three parts, the full length legend of Sakuntala, the legend that under wentchanges through ages and in the third an elaborate study of this painted series.

Sages preventing Dushyanta from hunting in a holy place

Sakuntala and Dushyanta with their son Bharat, Maratha Style, dated : A.D. 1789, Colophon page; mentioning poet's name as Kavi Niwaz and date Samvat : (1788-89).

Sage Kanva's hermitage, Maratha style, dated : AD. 1789

The Union, Maratha style, dated : A.D. 1789

Sage Durvasa's curse, Maratha style, dated : A.D. 1789.

PART- TWO

9

Malavikagnimitra

Text

Malavikagnimitra .- Bombay : [s.n.], 1868.

EditorAnonymous.

Malavikagnimitra / by Kalıdasa; Bombay : [s.n.], 1891.

Editor 'Anonymous'.

[Ed. with the comm. by Katayavema].

Malavikagnimitra / by Kalidasa .- Calcutta : [s.n.], 1871.

Editor 'Anonymous'.

Malavikagnimitra / by Kalidasa; Madras : [s.n.], 1885.

[Ed. with a commentary by Nissanka Mrityunjaya].

Mālvikāgnimitra / by Kālidāsa .- Srirangam : Śrī Vaṇīvilās Press, 1908.

xviii, 156, [2] p.; 22 cm.

(Vānīvilās Sanskrit Series; 5)

Text contains the ancient commentaries of Nīlakaṇṭha and Kāṭayavema.

Malavikagnimitra / by Kalıdasa; Vizagapatnam : [s.n.], 1884.

Editor anonymous

[Ed. with the commentary of Kātayavena].

Mālavikāgnimitra / by Kālidāsa; ed. [with an introd., English tr. and notes] by A.S. Kṛṣṇa Rāo foreword by S. Kuppuswamy Śāstrī - 2nd ed. - Madras : V. Rāmasvāmi Śāstrulu & Sons, 1951.

lxxxii, [387] p.; 18 cm.

First published in 1930.

Includes index.

Comedy of court-life in five acts.

Malavikagnimitra / by Kalidasa; Ed. by Dadaji Davji; comm. by Katayavema. - [s.l.] : [s.n.], 1892.

Includes explanatory notes.

Mālavikāgnimitra / by Kālidāsa; ed. by F. Bollensen. - Leipzig : [s.n.], 1879.

Mālavikāgnimitra / by Kālidāsa; ed. [with a Sanskrit commentary 'Vijayā' and tr. into Bengali with notes] by Gurunāth Vidyānaidhi Bhaṭṭācārya. - Calcutta : New Sarasvatī Press, 1918.

xxii, 392 p.; 20 cm.

Malavikagnimitra / by Kālidāsa; ed. [with a commentary 'Sārārthasandipanī' by] Haridās Siddhāntavāgīś Bhaṭṭācārya. - Calcutta : New Sarasvatī Press, 1913.

xvi, 296 p.; 18 cm.

Malavikagnimitra / by Kalidasa; ed. [with Sanskrit notes and Bengali tr.] by Haridass Bhattacharya. - 2nd ed. - Nakipur : [s.n.], 1922.

Malavikagnimitra / by Kalidasa; ed. by Haripada Chattopadhyay. - Howrah : [s.n.], 1917.

Malavikagnimitra / by Kalidasa; ed. [with annotation] by Jivanand Bhattacharya .- [s.l.] : [s.n.], [18-?].

Malavikāgnimitra of Kālidasa / by Kalidasa; ed. by K.A. Subramania Iyer with introd. by S. Radhakrishnan. - New Delhi : Sahitya Akademi, 1978.
lxii, 248 p.

Malavikagnimitra / by Kalidasa; ed. [with English notes] by Kashinath Pandurang Parab; comm. by Kāṭayavema .- Bombay : [s.n.], 1890.

Malavikagnimitra / by Kālidāsa; ed. by Kāśīnāth Pāṇḍuraṅga Parab .- 3rd ed. -

Bombay : Nirnayasāgar Press, 1912.

105 p.; 22 cm.

First published in 1890.

Malavikagnimitra / by Kalidasa; ed. by Kashinath Pandurang Parab and rev. by Pansikar and W.L. Sastri. - 3rd ed. - Bombay : [s.n.], 1912.

Malavikagnimitra / by Kālidāsa; ed. [with introd., notes, various readings and English tr.] by Moreśvar Rāmacandra Kāḷe. - Bombay : Bombay Vaibhav Press, 1918.

lii, [248] p.; 22 cm.

Contain the commentary 'Kumāragirirājīya' of Kāṭayavema.

Malavikagnimitra / by Kālidāsa; ed. by Nārayan Rām Ācārya. - 9th ed. - Bombay : Nirnayasāgar Press, 1950.

vi, 96, [2] p.; 22 cm.

Includes index.

Contains Kāṭayavema's commentary 'Kumāragivirājīya'.

Mālavikāgnimitra / by Kalidasa; ed. by Narayan Ram Acharya .- Bombay : Nirnay Sagar Press, 1950.

iv, 96 p.; 21.5 cm.

Malavikagnimitra / by Kalidasa; ed. [with ancient comm.] by Nilakanth and Katyavema. *Sri Vani Vilasa* (Sanskrit); Vol. 5, No. 5.

Editor 'Anonymous'.

[Malavikagnimitra] Textum primus edidit et varietatem scripturae / ed. by O.F. Tullberg. - Bonn : [s.n.], 1840.

Vol. 1 contains 'Mālavikagnimitra'.

Malavikagnimitra / by Kalidasa; ed & [tr. into Hindi] by P.D. Shastri. - Delhi : Atmaram & Sons, 1964.

151 p.; 18.5 cm.

Includes Sanskrit text.

Mālavikāgnimitra / by Kālidāsa; ed. [with a commentary 'Sukhabodhinī' and notes] by Pratāpacandra Vedāntabhūṣaṇ Bhaṭṭacārya .- Calcutta : Metcalfe Press, 1913.

iv, 223, [11] p.; 18 cm.

Mālavikāgnimitra / by Kālidāsa; ed. [with a commentary 'Mañjubhāṣiñi] by Revatīkānta Bhaṭṭācārya. - Calcutta : Metcalfe Press, 1913.

viii, 262, [2] p.; 19 cm.

Mālavikāgnimitra / by Kālidāsa; ed. by S.P. Paṇdit with the commentary of Kāṭ ayavema. - Bombay : Bombay Sanskrit Series, 1869.

Mālavikāgnimitra / ed. [with notes and comm. 'Kumāragirirājiya of Kāṭayavema'] by Shankar Pandurang Pandit. - Bombay : [s.n.], 1869. 2nd ed. appeared in BSS; No. VI, in 1889.

Mālavikāgnimitra / by Kālidāsa; ed. [with an introd., English tr. and notes] by Śivarām Mahādev Parāñjpe. - Poona : Govardhan Press, 1918.

[315] p. : plates; 18 cm.

Mālavikānimitra / by Kālidāsa; ed. [with a Sanskrit commentary 'Saralā'] by Śrīraṅga Śarmā .- Poona : Citraśāla Press, 1918.

xxiv, [307] p.; 21 cm.

Tr. and notes by Raghunāth Dāmodar Karmārkar.

Mālavikāgnimitra / ed. [with notes] by Taranath Tarkavācaspati .- Calcutta : [s.n.], 1870.

Malavikagnimitra / by Kalidasa; ed. by Taranath Bhattacharya. - 2nd ed. - Calcutta : [s.n.], 1887.

Translations

Bengali

Malavikagnimitra / by Kalidasa; tr. into Bengali by Ashok Guha. - Calcutta : Nababharati, 1962.

viii, 86 p.; 22 cm.

Malavikagnimitra / by Kalidasa; tr. into Bengali by Gurunath Bhattacharya and Kavyavyakaranatirtha Kalipada. - Calcutta : [s.n.], 1917.

Malavikagnimitra / by Kalidasa; tr. into Bengali by [Ed. with a Sanskrit comm.

Vijaya] Gurunath Vidyanidhi. - Calcutta : [s.n.], 1918.

Malavikagnimitra / by Kalidasa; tr. into Bengali by Haridas Bhattacharya. - 2nd ed. - Nakipur : [s.n.], 1922.

[Ed. with Sanskrit notes].

Malavikagnimitra / by Kalidasa; tr. into Bengali by Jyotirindranath Tagore. - Calcutta : [s.n.], 1901.

Malavikagnimitra / by Kalidasa; tr. into Bengali by Surindramohan Thakur. - 1859.

16 July 1830 issue of '*Somprakash*' writes that the translator wrote in assistance with Shri Ramnarayan Tarkaratna.

Malavikagnimitra / by Kalidasa; tr. into Bengali by Saurindromohan Thakur. - 2nd ed. - Calcutta : [s.n.], 1877.

Malavikagnimitra / by Kalidasa; tr. into Bengali by Vimala Dasgupta. - Calcutta : [s.n.], 1910.

Malavikagnimitra / by Kalidasa; tr. into Bengali *In* Sanskrita Sahitya Sambhar / ed. by Gaurinath Sastri & et al. [Vol. 11]. - Calcutta : Navpatra Prakashan, [197 -].

Includes Bengali rendering of 'Malavikagnimitra', 'Ṛtusamhara', 'Śringarasastakam', 'Śringaratilaka' & Pushpavanavilasam'.

Bohemian

Malavika a Agnimitra / by Kalidasa; tr. into Bohemian by Josef Prelozil Zubaty. - Prague : [s.n.], 1893. - (Sbornik svetove poesie; No. 16).

Danish

Kongen og danseriden : Lystspil : fem Akler / by Kalidasa; tr. of Malavikagnimitra into Danish by Edvard Brandes. - Kobenhavn : [s.n.]. 1874.

Dutch

Danseres en Koning = Malavika en Agnimitra / by Kalidasa; tr. into Dutch from Sanskrit by J.Vliet. - Haarlem : [s.n.], 1882.

English

Malavikāgnimitra / by Kalidasa; tr. into English [with a comm. by Kāṭayavema]. - Bombay : [s.n.], 1891.

Malavikagnimitra / by Kalidasa; tr. into English *In* Annotation on Sanskrit classics. *The Sanskrit Reader* = Saṁskṛtapāṭhāvalī 1884; Vol. II, Pt. 4; Pp. 48ff.

Mālavikāgnimitra / by Kalidasa; tr. into English by A.S. Krishna Rao. - Madras : [s.n.], 1930.

Foreword by Kuppuswami Sāstri.

2nd ed. published in 1951.

Malavikagnimitra / by Kalidasa; tr. into English by Arthur W. Ryder. - London : [s.n.], 1912.

[Everyman's Library; No. 629].

Also published from New York in 1912.

Reprint appeared in 1928.

Malavikagnimitra / by Kalidasa; tr. into English by L.D. Bembalakar .- [s.l.] : [s.n.], 1956.

Story of the Malavikagnimitra in English.

Malavikagnimitra / by Kalidasa; tr. into English by Bela Bose. *In* The Dramas of Kālidāsa. - Allahabad : [s.n.], [n.d.].

— Collected works of Kalidasa. - Allahabad : [s.n.], 1946.

Malavikagnimitra / by Kalidasa; tr. into English prose by C.H. Tawney. - Calcutta: [s.n.], 1875.

— 2nd ed. - Calcutta : [s.n.], 1891.

— 3rd ed. Varanasi : [s.n.], 1964.

Rev. ed. by Rewa Prasad Dwivedi.

Mālavikāgnimitra / by Kalidasa; tr. into English by C.R. Devdhar and N.G. Suru. - Bombay : [s.n.], 1959.

— 3rd ed. - Delhi : [s.n.], 1966 ?

Ed. critically with notes and appendix.

Malavikagnimitra / by Kalidasa; tr. into English by G.R. Nandargikar. - Poona : [s.n.], 1879.

Translated in prose style.

[Malavikagnimitra] *In* Select specimen of the theatre of the Hindu. (Vol. II) / tr. into English by H.H. Wilson. - London : [s.n.], 1871.

Includes tr. of Malavikagnimitra [Pp. 345 - 354].

Malavikagnimitra / by Kalidasa; tr. into English by Haraprasad Sastri. - Calcutta: [s.n.], 1907.

Mālavikāgnimitra / by Kalidasa; tr. into English by Kailashnath Bhatnagar. - 2nd ed. - Lahore : [s.n.], 1941.

Ed. with a critical introduction.

[Malavikagnimitra] *In* Plays of Kalidasa / by Kalidasa; tr. into English by K.V.K. Sundaram. - New Delhi : Patriot Publishers, 1988.

286 p.; 22 cm.

Includes Malavika and Agnimitra; Urvashi and Pururavas and Shakuntala recognised.

Malavikagnimitra / by Kalidasa; tr. into English by M.C. Sadagopachariar. - Bombay : [s.n.], 1889.

Edited with English notes.

— Kumbhakonam : [s.n.], 1900.

Mālavikāgnimitra / by Kalidasa; tr. into English by M.R. Kale. - Bombay : [s.n.], 1918.

Ed. with introd., notes, various readings etc.

The Malavikagnimitra [of Kalidasa] / by Kalidasa; tr. into English by M.R. Kale; rev. by Jayanand Dave and S.A. Upadhyaya. - Delhi : Motilal Banarsidass, 1960.

Mālavikāgnimitra / by Kalidasa; tr. into English by P.S. Sane, G.H. Godbole and H.S. Ursekar. - 2nd ed. - Bombay : [s.n.], 1952.

Includes the comm. of Kāṭayavema and Marathi tr. by P.M. Upadhye.

Mālavikāgnimitra / by Kalidasa; tr. into English by R.B. Athavale and H.R. Nawre. - Ahmedabad : [s.n.], 1941.

Malavikagnimitra / by Kalidasa; tr. into English by R.D. Karmarkar. - 3rd ed. - Poona : [s.n.], 1937.

4th ed. appeared in 1950.

Malavikagnimitra / by Kalidasa; tr. into English by S.B. Bhagavat. - Poona : [s.n.], 1897.

Malavikagnimitra / by Kalidasa; tr. into English by S.P. Pandit.

Malavikagnimitra / by Kalidaa; tr. into English by S.S. Ayyar. - Poona : [s.n.], 1896.

Includes comm. by Kāṭayavema and others.

Mālavikāgnimitra / by Kalidasa; tr. into English by S. Rangachar. - 2nd rev. ed. - Mysore : [s.n.], 1961.

Mālavikāgnimitra / by Kalidasa; tr. into English by Shivaram Mahadev Paranjape. - Poona : [s.n.], 1960.

Ed. with an introd. & notes.

French

Agnimitra et Mālavikag : comēdie en cinq actes et un prologue, melee de prose et de vers, traduile du Sanscrit et du Prācrit / by Kalidasa; tr. into French by Victor Henry .- Paris : [s.n.], 1889.

Mālavikā et Agnimitra : traduit pour la premiēre fois en francais / by Kalidasa; tr. into French by P.E. Foucaux. - Paris : [s.n.], 1877.

[Bibliothēque orientale elzēvirienne; No. 14].

German

[Malavikagnimitra] - Malavika und Agnimitra / by Kalidasa; tr. into German [from original Sanskrit] by Albrecht Weber Berlin, 1856.

This was the first translation of the play being available to the educated Germans at that time.

[Mālavikāgnimitra] / by Kālidāsa; German tr. by L. Fritze. - Leipzig : [s.n.], 1881. Metrical rendering.

Mālavikāgnimitra / by Kalidasa; tr. into German by Leopold von. Schroeder. *Prinzen Zofe* (Munich), 1902.

Reference in *Orientalische Bibliographie.* Vol. XVI.

[Malavikagnimitra] Der Kōnig and die Tānzerin / by Kalidasa; tr. into German by Lion von Feuchtwanger. - Mūnchen : [s.n.], 1917.

This adaptation was staged in Germany.

[Malavikagninitra] Mālavikā und Agnimitra / by Kalidasa; tr. into German by Ludwig Pritze. - Leipzig : [s.n.], 1881.

Gujarati

Malavikāgnimitra / by Kalidasa; tr. into Gujarati by B.S. Vyas.

Based on M.R. Kale's edition.

Mālavikāgnimitra / by Kālidāsa; tr. into Gujarati & [ed.] by Baḷvantrāy Kalyāṇrāy Thākōr. - Baroda : The editor, 1933.

vii, 240 p.; 18.5 cm.

Includes append and index.

Mālavikāgnimitra / by Kalidasa; tr. into Gujarati by K.H. Dhruva.

[Malavikagnimitra =] Prēmnī prasādī / by Kālidāsa; tr. into Gujarati by K.K. Śāstrī. - Karachi : Nāgarik Prakāśan Mandir, 1932.

xii, 92 p.; 18 cm.

Tr. of Mālavikāgnimitra.

[Malavikagnimitra] *In* Traṇ nāṭako : [Mālavikā, Ūrvaśī anē Śakuntalā / by Kālidāsa; tr. by Kēśavrām K. Śāstrī. - Ahmedabad : Gurjar Granthratna Kāryālay, 1948.

xlviii, 291 p.; 18.5 cm.

Tr. of Mālavikāgnimitra, Vikramorvaśiya and Abhijñānaśākuntalam.

Mālavikāgnimitra / by Kalidasa; tr. into Gujarati by Ranchodbhai Udiram Dave. - Bombay : [s.n.], 1870.

Hindi

Mālavikāgnimitra / by Kālidāsa .- New Delhi : Sasta Sahitya Mandal, [n.d.].

Hindi rendering.

Mālavikāgnimitra [nāma prācīna kāvya] / by Kalidasa; tr. into Hindi by Gaurishankar Vyas. - Indragarh : [s.n.], Saṁ 1899.

Rendering in prose and verse.

Mālavikāgnimitra / by Kālidāsa; tr. into Hindi by Govindadās Śastrī. - Varanasi : [s.n.], 1944.

Mālavikāgnimitra / by Kalidasa; tr. into Hindi by Jayadev Pandey .- Arrah : [s.n.], 1925.

Mālavikāgnimitra / by Kālidāsa; tr. into Hindi by Rāmchandra Mishra. - Varanasī: Chaukhamba Vidyabhavan, 1951.

Mālavikāgnimitra / by Kalidasa; tr. into Hindi by Mohan Dev Pant. - Jullundur : [s.n.], 1963.

2nd ed. published in 1964.

Foreword by Sansar Chandra Sharma.

[Saṅkṣipta] Mālavikāgnimitra / by Kalidasa; tr. into Hindi by Niranjanadev Śāstrī.

An abridged Hindi translation.

Malavikagnimitra / by Kalidasa; tr. into Hindi by P.D. Shastri. - Delhi : Atmaram & Sons, 1964.

151 p.; 18.5 cm.

Includes Sanskrit text.

Malavikāgnimitra / by Kalidasa; tr. into Hindi by Purushottam Datta. - Lahore : [s.n.], 1942.

Mālavikāgnimitra / by Kalidasa; tr. into Hindi by Rama Shankar Jaitli.

Mālavikāgnimitra / by Kalidasa; tr. into Hindi by S.S. Pathak; ed. by M.R. Kale. - Bombay : [s.n.], 1960.

Mālavikāgnimitra / by Kālidāsa; tr. into Hindi by Sītaram Lāla. - Kanpur : The translator, 1899.

Mālavikāgnimitra / by Kālidāsa; tr. into Hindi by Sitārām Lālā. - Indragarh, Kota: Gaurīshankar Vyās, 1909.

Mālavikāgnimitra [bhāṣa] / by Kālidāsa; tr. into prose and verse by Lālā Sītārām.- Allahabad : Prācin-Natak Maṇimālā, 1913.

iv, 62 p.; 18.5 cm.

Mālavikāgnimitra / by Kālidāsa; tr. into Hindi by Sitarāma Lālā .- Babura, Agra : Jaydev Pandey, 1925.

Mālavikāgnimitra / by Kālidāsa; tr. into Hindi by Suryakumar Joshi .- New Delhi: Sasta Sahitya Mandal, [n.d.].

For children.

Mālavikāgnimitra / by Kalidasa; tr. into Hindi by Taranish Jha. - Allahabad : [s.n.], 1964.

Ed. with a comm. with notes.

[Vikramorvāsiya aur] Mālavikāgnimitra / by Kalidasa; tr. into Hindi by Viraj .- Delhi : [s.n.], 1957.

Hungarian

Mālavikāgnimitra / by Kalidasa; tr. into Hungarian by Jōzef Schmidt .- Gyoma : [s.n.], 1922.

Italian

Malavica ed Agnimitro : dramma in Cinque atti / by Kalidasa; tr. into Italian by Antonio Mirazzi. *Teatro scelto Indiano (Milan).*, 1871; Vol. 1; Pp. 301 - 417.

Mālavikāgnimitra : [drama Indiano tradotto in Italiano] / by Kalidasa; tr. into Italian by Francesco Cimmino .- Naples : [s.n.], 1897.

Mālavikāgnimitra / by Kalidasa; tr. into Italian by Michele Karbarker. *In* Selection of verses in Italian stanzas.

Reference in East & West (Rome), July 1955, Vol. VI, No. 2; Pp. 160 - 162.

Kannada

Mālavikāgnimitra / by Kalidasa; tr. into Kannada by Dhondho Narasimha Mulabagal.- Dharwar : [s.n.], 1897.

Malavikagnimitra / by Kalidasa; tr. into Kannada by Gurunath Narayana.

Malavikagnimitra / by Kalidasa; tr. into Kannada by M.S. Subrahmanya Sastri. - Bangalore : Central College, 1952.

16, 92 p.; 18 cm.

Mālavikāgnimitra / by Kalidasa; tr. into Kannada by N. Subha Śāstri.

Maithili

Mālavikāgnimitra / by Kālidāsa; tr. into Maithili by Govinda Jhā .- Darbhanga : Maithilī Sāhitya Parisad, 1947.

iv, 72 p.; 22 cm.

Tr. from original Sanskrit.

Reference in *Indian PEN.* Dec. 1946; Vol. XII; P. 180.

Malayalam

Māḷavikāgnimitram / by Kālidāsa; tr. into Malayalam by A.R. Rājarāja Varma .-

Trivandrum : B.V. Book Depot, 1949.

91 p.; 19 cm.

— Trivandrum : B.V. Book Depot, 1954.

26, 104 p.; 18 cm.

Mālavikāgnimitra / by Kalidasa; tr. into Malayalam by E. Raghava Variar, 1957.

Prose rendering.

Mālavikāgnimitra / by Kalidasa; tr. into Malayalam by Kunhaikuttan Thampuran.

Mālavikāgnimitra / by Kalidasa; tr. into Malayalam by Kuntur Narayan Menon.

Manipuri

Mālavikāgnimitra / by Kālidāsa; tr. by Aribam Brajabehārī Śarmā .- Imphal : The author, 1964.

ii, 89 p.; 18 cm.

Tr. from original Sanskrit drama.

Marathi

[Malavikagnimitra] Saṅgīta Mālavikāgnimitra nāṭaka / by Kalidasa; tr. into Marathi by B.G. Varde. - Bombay : [s.n.], 1895.

Adapted into musical verses.

Mālavikāgnimitra / by Kalidasa; tr. into Marathi by G.K. Bhatt .- Kolhapur : [s.n.], 1962.

Mālavikāgnimitra / by Kalidasa; tr. into Marathi by Ganesh Lele .- Bombay : [s.n.], 1867.

Mālavikāgnimitra / by Kalidasa; tr. into Marathi by Gopal Shrinivas Banahatti .- 2nd rev. & enl. ed. - Nagpur : [s.n.], 1962.

Ed. with explanatory notes.

Includes appendices.

Mālavikāgnimitra / by Kalidasa; tr. into Marathi by Magsulkar and others .- Poona [s.n.], 1962.

Edited with Sanskrit text, notes, critical appreciation.

Includes appendices.

Mālavikāgnimitra : [sār va vicār] / by Kālidāsa; tr. into Marathi by Mahādev Vyaṅkaṭ eś Lele. - Bombay : Vividhjñānavistār, 1904.

60 p.; 24 cm.

Abridged rendering into Marathi with occasional comments and notes.

Mālavikāgnimitra / by Kalidasa; tr. into Marathi by P.M. Upadhye. - 2nd ed. - Bombay : [s.n.], 1952.

Mālavikāgnimitra / by Kalidasa; tr. into Marathi by S.G. Desai; ed. by M.R. Kale.

Mālavikāgnimitra / by Kalidasa; tr. into Marathi by Vaman Ganesh Joshi. - 1893.

A musical translation.

Adaptation

Islāmpūrkar, Vāman Śāstrī. Raja Agnimitra / by Vāman Śāstrī Islāmpūrkar. - Bombay : Vāsudev Moreśvar Potdār, 1889.

xxiv, 204 p.; 18 cm.

Novel in Marathi based on Kālidās play 'Mālavikāgnimitra.

Nepali

Mālavikāgnimitra / by Kālidāsa. - Varanasi : Hitaiṣī Co., 1948.

178 p.; 17 cm.

Sanskrit drama rendered into Nepali.

Oriya

Malavikagnimitra / by Kalidasa; tr. into Oriya by Bhagirathi Nepak .- Cuttuck : Orissa Book Store, 1980.

Māḷavikāgnimitra / by Kālidāsa; tr. by Lakṣmīnārāyaṇa Haricandana. - Tekili : The translator, 1928.

x, 98 p.; 17 cm.

Mālvikagnimitra / by Kalidasa; tr. into Oriya by Mṛtyunjay Rath.

Pt. Mṛutyunjaya Rath
(1882-1924)

Punjabi

Mālvikāgnimitra / by Kālidāsa; tr. into Punjabi by Parmānand Behl. - [s.l.] : The translator, [n.d.].

170 p.; 23 cm.

Reference in the National Bibliography of Indian literature (Vol. 3) ed. by B.S. Keshavan. - New Delhi, 1962.

Russian

Mālavikagnimitra / by Kalidasa; tr. into Russian by K. Balmont. - Moscow : [s.n.], 1916.

Includes an introd. by S. Oldenberg.

Sindhi

Ba ratana / by Kalidasa; tr. into Sindhi by Asudomal Tekchand Gidwani. - Bombay : Lok Seva Mandal, 1964.

73 p.; 18 cm. - (Devanagari Sindhi Sahityamala; 46).

Includes portions of 'Malavikagnimitram' and 'Vikramorvasiya'.

Mālavikā ain Agnīmitra / by Kālidasa; tr. into Sindhi by Āsūdomal Ṭekchand Gidvāṇī .- Hyderabad, Sind : Blavatsky Press, 1926.

v, 60 p.; 18 cm.

Tr. of Mālavikāgnimitra.

Swedish

Mālavikā : ett indiskt skādespel / by Kalidasa; tr. into Swedish by H. Edgren. - Melmo : [s.n.], 1877.

Tamil

Mālavikagnimitra / by Kalidasa; tr. into Tamil by Natesa Sastri Sirukambar. - Madras : [s.n.], 1911.

Mālavikāgnimitram / by Kālidāsa; tr. into Tamil P. Sambandha Mutaliyār. - Madras : The translator,

1930. 68 p.; 21 cm.

Maḷavikai / by Kalidasa; tr. into Tamil by S.A. Ramaswamy. - Madras : [s.n.], 1965.

An abridged tr. into prose form.

Telugu

Mālavikāgnimitramu / by Kalidasa; tr. into Telugu by E.M. Śāstri.

Malavikagnimitramu / by Kalidasa; tr. into Telugu by Gopal Krishna Rentala. - Vijayawada : [s.n.], 1968.

Māḷavikāgnimitramu / by Kālidāsa; tr. into Telugu Kandukūri Vīrēśaliṅgamu .- Rājahmundry : Hitakāriṇī Samājam, 1950.

vi, 94 p.; 21 cm.

First published in 1885.

Māḷavikāgnimitramu / by Kālidāsa; tr. into Telugu by Mallampalli Śarabhēśvar a Śarma. - Masulipatam : Trivēṇi Publishers, 1949.

viii, 88 p.; 18 cm.

Mālavikāgnimitramu / by Kalidasa; tr. into Telugu by Panchangam Venkatanarasimhachari. - Telugu : [s.n.], 1949.

Malavikagnimitramu / by Kalidasa; tr. into Telugu by Sitaram Śāstri.

Rendering in prose form.

Malavikagnimitramu / by Kalidasa; tr. into Telugu by Subbarayudu Vaddadi.

Malavikagnimitramu / by Kalidasa; tr. into Telugu by Vatsavayi Venkata Niladriraju.

Andhra Māḷavikāgnimitramu / by Kālidāsa; tr. into Telugu by Vēdamu Vēṅkaṭ arāyaśāstri. - Madras : Vēdamu Vēṅkaṭarāyaśāstri & Bros, 1919.

vii, 64 p.; 22 cm.

Māḷavikāgnimitramu / by Kālidāsa; tr. into Telugu by Yarasūri Mallikārjunarāvu. - Rajahmundry : The translator, 1951.

iv, 96 p.; 18 cm.

Critical Studies of Malavikagnimitra

Anonymous. Malavikagnimitra sāra vīcāre. *Vividha - jñānavistara;* Jan. 1903, Vol. XXXIV; No. 1; Pp. 18 (appendix); Feb. - March 1903; Nos. 2 - 3; April 1903; No. 4, Pp. 17 - 32; May - June 1903; No. 5 - 6; Pp. 33 - 40; July 1903, No. 7; Pp. 41 - 56; Aug. - Sept., 1903, No. 8 - 9, Pp. 57 - 60.

Apte, M.V. Agnimitracen remakarana. *N.Bh.* Aug. 1962; Vol. XV, No. 11; Pp. 12 - 16.

Concept of love in the Malavikagnimitra; a discussion in Marathi.

Bhat, G.K. Malavikāgnimitra : time - analysis. *Marathwada University Journal*; Aug. 1962; Vol. III, No. 1; Pp. 59 - 68.

Bhattacharya, Pranati. Polity of the Malavikagnimitra *OH;* Jan. - June 1966; Vol. XIV, No. 1; Pp. 37 - 43.

Summary in *Pr. Jy.* Vol. V, No. 1.

Bollensen, Friedrich. Beitrage zur erklārung der Mālavikā. *Zeitschrift der Deutschen Morgenlandischen Gesellschaft,* 1859; Vol. XIII; Pp. 480 - 490.

Cappeller, Carl. Observations ad Kālidāsae Mālavikāgnimitra. - Kōnigsberg : [s.n.], [n.d.].

Cimmino, Francesco. Al Une observazioni sul dramma Malavikāgnimitra, 1904. Atti della Acc. Pontanian (Napoli); Vol. XXX IV.; Pp. 1 - 16.

Gaidhani, R.N. A Note on the Nāndī in the Mālavikāgnimitra. *All India Oriental Conference* XVII. (Summary); P. 185.

Gaidhani, R.N. A note on Nandi in the Malavikagnimitra. *SPAIOC;* (Annamalai) Vol. XVII.

Gaidhani, R.N. A note on the verse 15th in the first Act of the Mālavikāgnimitra. *All India Oriental Conference* XVII (Summary); P. 185.

Gaidhani, R.N. The nun's complicity in the plots of the Vidusaka in the Malavikagnimitra. *SPAIOC* (Annamalai); Vol. XVII.

A note on I. 15 of the Malavikagnimitra.

Ghosh, N.N. Do the references to the Yavanas invasion of India found in the Yuga Purana, Patanjali's Mahabhasya and the Malavikagnimitra form the evidence of single event? *JGJRI* No. 1946; Vol. IV; No. 1; Pp. 45 - 60.

Goodwin, Robert E Kalidasa's metadrama : Malavikagnimitra / by Rober E. Goodwin. *Journal of South Asian Literature* 1988; Vol. 23, No. 1; Pp. 119 - 136.

Haag, F. Zur textskritik und erklārung des Mālavikāgnimitra. Frauen feld, 1872.

Textual criticism of the drama.

Hiepert, N. Die Parivrājika in Kalidasa's Malavikagnimitra. *ZII;* 1925; Vol. III; Pp. 140 - 145.

Joshi, Nikanth Purushottam. Malavikagnimitra : eka adhyayan. *Tri;* April, 1957; Vol. II, No. 7; Pp. 57 - 66.

A study in Hindi.

Kunhan Raja, C. The hero in the Malavikagnimitra. *ABORI;* 1942, Vol. XXIII, Nos. 1 - IV; Pp. 369 - 379. (Silver Jubilee Issue).

Kunhan, Raja C. The interpretation of the Bharatavakya in the Mālavikagnimitra. *JGJRI;* No. 3 - 4; Pp. 211 - 216.

Kunhan Raja, C. Mālavikagnimitre Bhatarutavakyam. *Mañ.* Jan., 1955; Vol. IX, No. 5; P. 86.

Kunhan Raja, C. Notes on Kalidasa : The Bharatarakya in the Malavikagnimitra *JOR* (Madras); Vol. VI (Sanskrit section); Pp. 11 - 32.

[Malavikagnimitra] *Indian Autiquary;* Vol. IV. p. 222.

Book review of English tr. by C.H. Tawney.

Nanavati, R.I. 'Delayed entry of the heroine in the Mālavikānimitra' / by R.I. Nanavati. *Proceedings of the All India Oriental Conference,* (30th session) at Visva Bharati, Santiniketan; No. 1980. Paper presented at the Conference Pp. 273 - 276.

Negi, J.S. Date of the Pusyamitra Yavana conflict and the identity of Sindhu mentioned in the Malavikagnimitra : some Indological studies. Vol. I, 1966; Pp. 73 - 82.

Neve, Eelix. [Book - review of Malavika et Agnimitra; French tr. of P.E. Foucaux] *Le Musēon. Review Internationale;* Vol. IV; Pp. 659 - 663.

Ojha, Kailashchandra. A. historical problem connected with Malavikagnimitra. *JGJRI;* Feb. 1951; Vol. VIII, No. 2; Pp. 197 - 202.

Pandey, Gangasahai. Mālavikagnimitra ki Padmavati. *Vikrama* (Hindi); April - May 1951; Vol. V; No. 3; Pp. 20 - 21.

Parikh, J.T. Malavikagnimitra no Vidusaka *Gujaratamitra* (Annual) Saṁ, 2010.

Parikh, J.T. A popular festive element in the plot of the Mālavikāgnimitra. *BCGV;* Aug., 1956; No. 3; Pp. 13 - 18.

[Performance of Mālavikagnimitra in Germany]. *Literarisches Zentral blatt;* 17 March, 1917.

Powell - Price, J.C. Note on the river Sindhu of the Malavikagnimitra. *JUPHS;* 1941; Vol. XIV, No. II; Pp. 125 - 127.

Radicchi, Anna. Il metro e il ritmo di Mālavikagnimitra. II. 4. *Colom;* 1966, Vol. XXXI; Pp. 1 - 39.

Summary in *Pr. Jy.* Vol. IV, Part 1.

Radicchi, Anna. Introdusione allo studio di documentidel treatro Indiano - Malavikagnimitra, II - 4. *Colom;* 1966; Vol. XXXI; Pp. 1 - 25.

Summary in *Pr. Jy;* Vol. IV; Part. 1.

Radicchi, Anna. La Dansa di Malavikagnimitra. *Colom.* Vol. XXXI; Pp. 1 - 48.

Summary in *Pr. Jy.* Vol. IV, No. 1.

Radicchi, Anna. La Musica di Malavikagnimitra. II. 4. *Colom*; 1967, Vol. XXXII; Pp. 21 - 103.

Summary in *Pr. Jy;* Vol. V, No. 1.

Ranganna. S.V. Malavikagnimitra natakada vimarshe .- Mysore : Sharada Mandira, 1960.

vi., 153 p.; 18 cm.

In Kannada.

Sāstri, A.D. Pañcaratra in the Malavikagnimitra. *BCGV;* August, 1964; Vol. XI; Pp. 17 - 24.

Reproduced in *Vikrama (Kā. Vi)*, 1964; Pp. 115 - 121.

Sastri, Haraprasad. Malavikagnimitra by Kalidasa / by Haraprasad Sastri. - Calcutta : Hare Press, 1907.

ii, 17 p.; 21.5 cm.

A critical exposition of the drama.

Sastri, Shrikanta. Malavikagnimitravastughatanakausalam *Vikrama* (Kā Vi); 1964; Pp. 29 - 31.

Schuyler, Montgomery. Bibliography of Kālidāsa's Mālavikagnimitra and Vikramorvaśīya. *Journal of American Oriental Society* 1902; Vol. XXIII; Pp. 93 - 101.

Tawney, C.H. [Book - review of Malavika et Agnimitra; French tr. of P.E. Foucaux] *Indian Antiquary;* Vol. VII; P. 60.

Thakore, B.K. Kālidasa's Malavikagnimitra : a study *IHQ* (Suppliment to Vol. XI); Pt. 1; 1935; Pp. 1 - 44.

Thakore, B.K. Mālavikāgnimitra : a study. *All India Oriental Conference* VII; Pp. 85 - 89.
(Summary)

—— *Indian Historical Quarterly Supplement;* Pp. 44.

(Summary)

Thakore, B.K. Malavikagnimitra : a study. *Proceedings of AIOC;* 1935; Vol. VII; Pp. 85 - 89.

Upadhyay, B.S. On the river Sindhu or Malavikagnimitra. *JBHU;* 1941 - 42; Vol. VI; Pp. 171 - 179.

Reference in ABIHI; 1942, Vol. V.

Upadhyay, B.S. The river Sindhu of the Malavikagnimitra. *JUPHS;* 1941; Vol. XIV, No. 1; Pp. 9 - 20.

Summary in *ABIHI;* 1941; Vol. IV; P. 252.

Vanshidhar Vidyalankara. Kalidasa ki Mālavika *Vi Bh.;* March, 1934; Vol. XIII, No. 3; Pp. 278- 285.

Vanshidhar Vidyalankara. Malavika and the dance. *Triveni;* May 1938; Vol. X, No. 11, Pp. 35 - 45.

Vliet, J. van der. Malavika - Mañjulika. *Bijdrage voor de taal - land - en* Vlokenkunde van *Nederlandsch Inde;* Vol. V; Pp. 169 - 170.

A discussion on the similarities between the two characters Mālavika of Kalidasa's drama and Manjulika of Kathasarita sagara, Taranga, 14.

Weber, Albrecht. Zur esklārung der Mālavikā. *ZDMG* 1860; Vol. XIV; P. 261.

10

Vikramorvasiyam

Text

Vikramorvasiyam / by Kalidasa; ed. with a commentary and explanation, 1830.

Anonymous (edition).

Vikramorvasiyam / by Kalidasa .- Bombay, 1859.

Anonymous (editor).

Vikramorvaśīyam / by Kālidāsa . - Calcutta : [s.n.], 1830.

Anonymous (editor).

Vikramorvasiyam / by Kalidasa .- Calcutta, 1870.

Anonymous (editor).

Vikramorvasiyam / by Kalidasa .- Conjevaram, 1883.

Anonymous (editor).

Vikramorvasiyam / by Kalidasa .- Madras, 1884.

Edited with a commentary.

Anonymos (editor).

Vikramorvasiyam / by Kalidasa .- Vizagapatnam, 1883.

Anonymous (editor).

Vikramorvaśīyam / by Kālidāsa; ed. [with a Sanskrit commentary 'Candrika' and a Hindi tr.] by Cakradhar Śāstri; rev. by Parameśvarānanda Śāstrī .- Lahore : Anglo - Oriental Press, 1926.

xxii, 236, [4] p.; 21 cm.

Vikramorvaśīyam / by Kālidāsa; ed. by Cārudeva Śāstrī with commentary of Kāṭayavema. - Lahore : [s.n.], 1929.

Vikramorvaśīyam / by Kālidāsa; ed. [and tr. into German] by F. Bollensen. - St. Petersburg, 1846.

Vikramorvaśī / by Kālidāsa; ed. by G. Bh. Vaidya .- Bombay : [s.n.], 1894.

Vikramorvasiyam / by Kalidasa; ed. by H.D. Velankar. - New Delhi : Sahitya Akademi, 1961.

Vikramorvasiyam / by Kalidasa; ed. by H.R. Karnik and S.G. Desai. - Bombay : Booksellers Publishing Co., 1959.

56, 275, 251 p.; 18 cm.

Vikramorvasiyam / by Kalidasa; ed. [with the commentary of Taranath Sarma] by Jivanand Vidyasagara Bhattacharya. - Calcutta, 1873.

Vikramorvasiyam / by Kalidasa; ed. by K.B. Paranjape. - Bombay, 1898.

Vikramnorvasiyam / by Kalidasa; ed. [with a commentary of Ranganatha] by K.P. Parab and M.R. Telang. Bombay : Nirnaya Sagar Press, 1888.

—— 2nd ed. - Bombay, 1889.

Vikramorvaśīyam / by Kālidāsa; ed. by Monier - Williams .- Hertford : [n.d.], 1849.

Vikramorvaśīya / by Kālidāsa; ed. [with an English tr., notes and various readings] by Moreśvar Rāmacandra Kāḷe. -. 3rd ed. - Bombay : Sudhākar Press, 1912.

[378] p.; 22 cm.

Contains the commentary 'Arthaprakāśikā'.

Vikramorvasiyam [of Kalidas] / by Kalidasa; ed. by M.R. Kale. - Delhi : Motilal Banarsidass.

Text with English translation, notes introd. etc.

Vikramorvasiyam / by Kalidasa; ed. [with a commentary] by P.C.N. Charya. Vizagapatnam, 1883.

Vikramorvaśiyam / by Kalidasa; ed. by P.S. Sane and S.A. Upadhyaya. - Bombay: Educational Publishers, 1971.

32, 412 p.; 22 cm.

Vikramorvaśīyam / by Kālidāsa; ed & [Latin interpretation] by R. Lenz. - Berlin : [s.n.], 1833.

Vikramorvasiyam : Herausgegeben nach Dravidischen Handschriften by Kalidasa; ed. by R. Pischel. *In* Monatsb der Kōnigl. Akad. der Wiss Zu Berlin. 1875. Pp. 609 - 670.

Vikramorvaśīyam / by Kālidāsa; ed. [with an introd., prose order, tr., notes and appendices] by Raghunāth Dāmodar Karmārkar. - Poona : Citraśālā Press, 1920.

xxvii, [163] p.; 20 cm.

Vikramorvasiyam / by Kalidasa; ed. [with notes] by Ramamaya Sharma. - Calcutta, 1870.

Vikramorvaśīyam / by Kālidāsa; ed. [with Sanskrit and Hindi commentaries, notes, introd.] by Rāmacandra Miśra. - Banaras : Caukhamba Sanskrit Series Office, 1953.

xviii, 264 p.; 18 cm.

(Haridās Sanskrit Series; 242).

Includes append and index.

Vikramorvaśīyam / by Kālidāsa; ed. [with an introd., tr. and notes] by S.B. Aṭ halye and S.S. Bhāve. - Bombay : Keśav Bhikājī Ḍhavale, 1948.

xl, 338 p.; 19 cm.

Includes appendices and index.

Vikramorvaśīyam / by Kālidāsa; ed. by S.P. Paṇḍit. - Bombay : Bombay Sanskrit Series, 1879. (Bombay Sanskrit Series; No. 16).

— rev. & enl. ed. by Bhaskar Ramchandra Atre.

— 3rd ed. - Bombay : Govt. Central Book Depot, 1901.

10, 135, 177 p.

Vikramorvaśīyam / by Kālidāsa; ed. [with a commentary 'Kalpalata'] by Surendranāth Śāstrī. - Bombay : Nirṇanayasāgar Press, 1942.

xcix, 271 p.; 22 cm.

Includes index.

Includes an introduction in Sanskrit and English and discussion on the structure of Sanskrit drama.

Vikramorvasiyam / by Kalidasa; ed. by Ramnarayana Tarkaratna. - Calcutta : 1868.

Adaptation (Sanskrit)

Shukla, Rama Kant. Vikramorvaśīyasya dhvanināṭyarupantaram. - New Delhi : Devavani Parishad, 1992.

A Radio play based on the Vikramorvasiya of Kalidasa condensed to about forty five minutes to an hour play long.

Translations

Bengali

Vikramorvasiyam / by Kalidasa; tr. into Bengali. - Calcutta : [s.n.], 1868.

Anonymous (translator).

[Vikramorvasiyam] Urbashi / by Kalidasa; tr. into Bengali by Apreshchandra Mukhopadhyay. - Calcutta.

An adaptation in three act; Act one contains 5 scenes, Act Two has 3 scenes & Act three has 7 scenes.

Apareshchandra Mukhopadhyay (19-07-1875 - 15-05-1934)
(Veteran Bengali stage actor and playwright who adapted 'Vikramorvasiyam' of Kalidasa into Bengali)

Vikramorvasiyam / by Kalidasa; tr. into Bengali by Dvarkanath Gupta, 1862.

Vikramorvasiyam / by Kalidasa; tr. into Bengali by Ganendranath Thakur. - 1901.

Play was written thirty three years ago, ie., in 1869.

Vikramorvasiyam / by Kalidasa; tr. into Bengali / by Guru Bandhu Bhattacharya .- Calcutta : [s.n.], 1963.

In prose style.

— 2nd ed. - Dacca : [s.n.], 1868.

Vikramorvasiyam / by Kalidasa; tr. into Bengali by Kalikinkar Chakrabarti, 1867.

Vikramorvasiyam / by Kalidasa; tr. into Bengali by Kaliprasanna Simha .- Calcutta : [s.n.], 1857.

Play was staged in September 24, 1857 at 'Vidyotsahini' auditorium.

Kaliprasanna Sinha

Vikromorvasiyam / by Kalidasa; tr. into Bengali by Nagendranath Tagore, 1868.

[Vikromorvasi] / by Kalidasa; tr. into Bengali by Ramsaday Bhattacharya, 1859.

Vikromorvasiyam / by Kalidasa; tr. into Bengali by Tarkaratna Jadunath. - [Calcutta] : Kavyaprakash Press; [n.d.].

[Vikromorvasiyam] *In* Mahakabi Kalidaser samagra rachanabali / by Kalidasa; ed. by Dhyaneshnarayan Chakrabarti .- Calcutta : Book House, [1973].

2 Vols.,*Contents* : *Vol. 1* - Ṛtusaṃhar & Kumarasambhav.

Vol. 2 - Meghadutam & Vikramorvaśī.

Bohamian

Urvasi : drama v peti jedanich od Kalidasy / by Kalidasa; tr. by Emanuel Fait. - Prag : [Program of the Czech Realgymnasium], 1890.

Czech

Vikramorvasiyam / by Kalidasa; tr. into Czech by V.J. Novotny.

Translated for an opera.

Dutch

Urvasi : een oud Indisch Tooneelstuk van Kalidasa wit den oorspronkeliijken text vertaal, en van een inleiding voozien. N.V. Adi Poestaka. Gravenhage, 1932.

English

Vikromorvaśīyam / by Kālidāsa; tr. into English [prose from the original Sanskrit with an introd.] by Ānanda Ācharya. - London : Francis Griffiths, 1914.

xxxvi, 79 p.; 17.5 cm.

[Vikromorvasiyam] Urvasie / by Kalidasa; tr. into English [poetry] by Aurobindo Ghosh. - Bombay : [s.n.], 1899.

— Calcutta : [s.n.], 1911.

[Vikromorvasiyam] Vikramorvasie or The Hero and the nymph / by Kālidāsa; tr. from the Sanskrit by Sri Aurobindo. - 2nd ed. - Pondicherry : Sri Aurobindo Ashram, 1941.

vi, 118 p.; 21.5 cm.

3rd ed. published in 1952.

Vikromorvasiyam / by Kalidasa; tr. into English by Brajendranath De. *Calcutta Review*; October 1884; Pp. 440 - 442.

Vikromorvasiyam / by Kalidasa; tr.into English by C.R. Devadhar. - Delhi : [s.n.], 1966.

Includes the text.,Reprint.

Vikramorvaśīyam / by Kālidāsa; tr. into English [prose] by E.B. Cowell .- Hertford: [s.n.], 1851.

Vikromorvasiyam / by Kalidasa; tr. into English [& ed. with and notes] by Gajanan Bhaskar Vaidya. - Bombay : 1895.

[Vikromorvasiyam] / by Kalidasa; tr. into English by H.H. Wilson *In* Select specimens of the theatre of the HIndus / by H.H. Wilson. - London : [s.n.], 1871.

Contents : English translation of Vikramorvasiyam. Pp. 183 - 273.

— 3rd ed. - New Delhi : Asian Educational Services, 1984.

Includes Vikramorvasiyam.

Vikromorvasiyam / by Kalidasa; tr. into English by H.R. Karnik and S.G. Desai. - Bombay : [s.n.], 1959.

[Ed. with an introd.].

[Vikromorvasiyam] / by Kalidasa; tr. into English by H.W. Wells. In Sanskrit plays from epic sources / tr. into English verse by Henry W. Wells .- Baroda : Maharaja Sayajirao University, 1968.

xi, 258 p.; 22.5 cm.

Includes Vikramorvasiyam of Kalidasa.

[Vikromorvasiyam] / by Kalidasa; tr. into English by H.W. Wells. *In* Six Sanskrit plays / tr. into English by H.W. Wells. - Bombay : [s.n.], 1964.

Contains an English rendering of Vikramorvasiyam.

Vikromorvasiyam / by Kalidasa; tr. into English [& Gujarati] by J.T. Parikh. - Bombay : [s.n.], [n.d.].

Included the text.

Vikromorvasiyam / by Kalidasa; tr. into Hindi; [& ed. with introd.] by K.B. Paranjape .- Bombay : [s.n.], 1898.

Vikromorvasiyam / by Kalidasa; tr. into English by M.R. KaleBombay:[s.n.], 1898.

[ed. with a commentary in English].

2nd edn. published in 1903.

3rd edn. published in 1912.

11th edn. published from Delhi in 1967.

Vikromorvasiyam [of Kalidasa] / by Kalidasa; ed. by M.R. Kale. - Delhi : Motilal Banarsidass.

Text with English translation, notes, introd. etc.

Vikromorvasiyam / by Kalidasa; tr. into English by Monier - Williams Hertford : [s.n.], 1849.

Vikromorvasiyam / by Kalidasa; tr. into English by O.K. Ghosh *In* Tales from Indian classic Bombay : Jaico, 1961.

Contains the story of the classic.

Vikromorvasiyam / by Kalidasa; tr. into English [& ed. with notes] by R.N. Gaidhani. - [s.l.] : [s.n.], [1947 - 48 ?].

Vikromorvasiyam / by Kalidasa; ed. & tr. into English [prose, notes & etc.] by Raghunath Damodar Karmarkar. - Poona : [s.n.], 1920.

Vikramorvasiyam / by Kalidasa; tr. into English by Ramanaya Sharma. - Calcutta: [s.n.], 1870.

Vikramorvasiyam / by Kalidasa; [Ed. with an introd.] English notes etc. by S.B. Athalye and S.S. Bhawe .- Bombay [s.n.], 1948.

Vikramorvasiyam / by Kalidasa; Ed. with English notes by S.P. Pandit .- Bombay 1879.

Vikramorvasiyam : a Sanskrit play / by Kalidasa; ed. with English notes..., by Shankar Pandurang Pandit.; rev. by Bhaskar Ramchandra Atre. - 3rd ed. - Bombay : Govt. Central Book Depot, 1901.

10, 135, 177 p.

Vikramorvasiyam / by Kalidasa; Ed. with a comm. Kalpalata; an introd. in Skt. and English by Surendranath Sastri. - Bombay : [s.n.], 1942.

Vikramorvasiyam / by Kalidasa; a English summary by T.A.V. Dikshitar. *Bhavan's Journal*. June, 1956; Vol. II, No. 23; Pp. 52 - 54.

Adaptation

Ghosh, O.K. Tales from Indian classics .- Bombay : Jaico Publication, 1961.

Contains Vikramorvasiyam and Sakuntala.

French

Vikramorvasiyam = Ourvaci donnee pour prix de l'heroisme / by Kalidasa; tr. into French by P.E. Foucaux. [Paris] : [s.n.], 1861.

Also published in 1879.

German

[Vikramorvasiyam] Urwasi, der Preis der Tapferkeit : ein Indisches schauspiel / by Kalidasa; tr. into German by Albreeht Hoefer .- Berlin : [s.n.], 1841.

ALBRECHT HOEFER (1812-1883)

German Indologist Albrecht Hoefer was born on 2.10.1812 in Greifswald. He was a professor at Greifswald who had translated Kalidasa's 'Urvashi' in 1841. This linguist died on 10.1.1883.

Vikramōrvaśīyam / by Kālidāsa; tr. into Gujarati by Kēśavlāl H. Dhruv. - 2nd ed.- Ahmedabad: Satyanārayaṇ Press, 1912.

viii, 36 p.; 13 cm.

[Vikramorvasiyam] Parākramnī prasādī athvā Vikramōrvaśīya nāṭak / by Kālidāsa; tr. by Kēśavlāl Harṣadrāy Dhruv.3rd. ed.,Ahmedabad: The translator, 1912.

184 p.; plate, tables; 14.5 cm.

Tr. into Gujarati by Keshavlal Harshadrai Dhruva under the nom de plum, 'Vanamali'.

A free adaptation of the Vikramoruasiaym in Gujarati.

Vikramorvashiyam / by Kalidasa; tr. into Gujarati by Keshavram Kashiram Shastri.

Vikramorvasiyam / by Kalidasa; tr. into Gujarati [prose and verse] by Kilabhai Ghanashyam Bhatt. - Bombay : [s.n.], 1898.

Includes critical, explanatory and mythological notes.

Vikramorvasiyam / by Kalidasa; tr. into Gujarati by J.L. Dave, ed. by M.R. Kale. Bombay, 1960.

Vikramorvasiyam / by Kalidasa; tr. into Gujarati and English with edited text. by J.T. Parikh. - Bombay : [s.n.], [n.d.].

Vikramōrvaśīyam / by Kalidasa; tr. into Gujarati Ranchodbhāī Udayrām Davē .- Bombay : The translator, 1924.

ix, 152 p. : ill.; 21.5 cm.

First published in 1868.

Vikramorvasiyam / by Kalidasa; tr. into Gujarati by Sragdhara Nandi .- Ahmedabad: [s.n.], 1962.

[Vikramorvasi yam] Urwasi und der Held : Indisches melo drama aus dem Sanskrit and Prakrit metrisch ubersetzt / by Kalidasa; tr. into German by B. Hirzel .- Fraufeld: [s.n.], 1838, Metrical translation

[Vikramorvasiyam] Urvasi / by Kalidasa; tr. into German by E. Lobendanz .- Leipzig : [s.n.], 1861.

3rd ed. published in 1884.

[Vikramorvasiyam] Vikramorvaśi ist Urwasi, der preis der Tapferkeit / by Kalidasa; tr. into German by F. Bollensen .- St. Petersberg, 1846.

First German rendering.

Friedrich Bollensen was born on 12.1.1809 in Rosdorf near Goettingen. He served in the St. Petersburg University as an Assistant Professor. In the St. Petersburg Academy, he found material for a critical edition of Kalidasa's Urvashi that had been collected by a deceased scholar Robert Lenz. In 1846, Bollensen published this text in St. Petersburg. It is accompanied by an excellent German translation and numerous notes on Prakrit and Sanskrit passages and the metre. He also edited Kalidasa's Malavikagnimitra in 1879 (Leipzig) Bollenson died in Wiesbaden on 29.2.1896.

Vikramorvasiyam / by Kalidasa; [a summary of the drama being] tr. into Germany by Friedrich Rueckert. 1834.

Included a few translated verses.

[Vikramorvasiyam] Urvasi : ein Indisches schauspeil / by Kalidasa; tr. into German by Ludwig Fritze. Leipzig : [s.n.] 1880.

(Reclams Universla Bibliothek; No. 1465).

Verse rendering.

Gujarati

Vikramorvasiyam / by Kalidasa; tr. into Gujarati by B.V. Vyas; ed. by M.R. Kale .- Bombay, 1966.

Vikramorvashi yam / by Kalidasa; tr. into Gujarati by Balavantray Kalyanray Thakur.- Vadodara : Maharaja Sayajirao Vishvavidyalaya, 1958.

xii, 144 p.; 18 cm.

First published in 1953?

Hindi

Vikramorvaśīyam / by Kālidāsa; tr. into Hindi :- Allahabad : Government Press, 1873.

Vikramorvasiyam / by Kalidasa; tr. into Hindi .- Prayag : Govt. Press, 1893.

Tr. Anonymous.

Vikramorvasiyam / by Kalidasa; tr. into Hindi by Ashubodh and Nityanand .- [s.l.]: [s.n.], [n.d.].

Vikramorvasīyam : trotakam / by Kālidāsa; tr. into Hindi by Chakradhar Śāstrī .- Lahore : Lakśmaṇdas Pyarelal, 1926.

Vikramorvaśīyam / by Kālidāsa; tr. into Hindi by Chandrakant Pāṭhak .- Varanasi: Pustak Bhavan, 1936.

Vikromorvasiyam / by Kalidasa; tr. into Hindi by Gadadhar Malviya [19th cent.].

Vikromorvasiyam / by Kalidasa; tr. into Hindi by Induja Awasthi - New Delhi : National School of Drama.

Typed script.

(Induja Awasthi, translated 'Vikramorvasiyam' of Kalidasa in Hindi for the National School of Drama, New Delhi.)

[Vikromorvasiyam] Urvasī / by Kālidāsa; tr. into Hindi by Jayagopala .- Lahore : Shiromaṇi Pustakalay, 1925.

Vikramorvasiyam / by Kalidasa; tr. into Hindi. by Ramachandra Mishra. - Benaras: Chaukhamba Vidyabhavan, 1953.

(Haridas Sanskrit Series; 242).

2nd ed. published in 1963.

[Ed. with Sanskrit and Hindi Comm., notes, introd. and appendices]

[Vikramorvasiyam] Urvaśī nātak / by Kālidāsa; tr. into Hindi by Rāmlal Kuṇvar .- Almora: [s.n.], 1927.

Vikramorvasiyam / by Kalidasa;tr. into Hindi by Rashinath Dev. Aligarh:[s.n.], [n.d.].

Vikramorvasiyam / by Kalidasa; tr. into Hindi by Sharan Narayan Dutt. - Delhi : [s.n.], [n.d.].

Vikramorvaśīyam / by Kālidāsa; tr. into Hindi by Sharaṇ Sahgal .- New Delhi : Sasta Sahitya Mandal, [n.d.].

Vikramorvasiya / by Kalidasa; tr. into Hindi by S.S. Pathak; ed. by M.R. Kale. - Bombay, 1960.

Vikramorvaśīyam / by Kālidāsa; tr. into Hindi by Tarṇīś Jhā. - Allahabad : Rāmnārāyaṇ Benīmādhav, 1963.

2nd ed. published in 1965.

[Vikromorvasiyam] Vikram aur Urvaśī / by Kālidāsa; tr. into Hindi by Ṭhākurdatta Mishra .- Allahabad : Kitab Mahal, 1958.

First published in 1955?

[Vikromorvasiyam] Vikramorvashi tatha Malavikagnimitra / by Kalidasa; tr. into Hindi by Viraj .- Delhi : Rajpal & Sons, 1957.

206 p.; 18 cm., 2nd ed. published in 1962.

Vikramorvaśīyam / by Kālidāsa; tr. into Hindi by Viśṇu Prabhākar .- New Delhi : Sasta Sahitya Mandal, [n.d.].

Adaptation

Shukla, Narasimharam. Urvasi aura main. - Allahabad : [s.n.], 1952.

An adaptation of Kalidasa drama in Hindi.

Singh, Ramdhari 'Dinkar' Urvasi.

A free Hindi poetic version independently written on Urvasi theme.

Hungarian

Vikromorvasiyam / by Kalidasa; tr. into Hungarian by Pāl Pitroff. - Budapest : [s.n.], 1914.

Italian

Vikramorvasiyam / by Kalidasa; tr. into Italian by Francesco Cimino. - Turin : [s.n.], 1890.

Kannada

Vikromorvasiyam / by Kalidasa; tr. into Kannada by M. Basappa Sastri, 1883.

Vikramorvashiyam / by Kalidasa; tr. into Kannada by S.V. Parameshvara Bhatt .- Mysore : Usha Sahitya Male, 1955.,77 p.; 18 cm.

Vikramōrvaśīyam / by Kālidāsa; tr. into Kannada by Sōsale Ayyā Śāstri. - Mysore : G.T.A. Printing Press, 1911.

iv, 96 p.; 21 cm.

Latin

Urvasia / by Kalidasa; textum Sanscritum, edidit, interpretationem Latidam et notas illustrantes [by] Robertus Lenz .- Berlin : [s.n.], 1833.

Includes the text.

Maithili

Vikramorvaśīyam / by Kālidāsa; tr. into Maithili by Bhavanāth Jhā. - Patna : Āryavarta Prakāśan, 1957.

viii, 86 p.; 18 cm.

Maithili rendering from original Sanskrit.

Vikramorvasiyam / by Kalidasa; tr. into Maithili by Surendranath 'Sumana' Unpublished work.

Malayalam

Vikramōrvaśīyam / by Kālidāsa; tr. into Malayalam by K.C. Kēśava Piḷḷa .- [s.l.] : Kēraḷōdayam Press, 1910.

88 p.; 19 cm.

Vikramorvasiyam / by Kalidasa; tr. into Malayalam by K.Vasudev Moosad .- Trichur : [s.n.], 1926.

Vikromorvasiyam / by Kalidasa; tr. into Malayalam by Kodangallur Kunhikuttan Thampuran, Cranganore.

Vikromorvasiyam / by Kalidasa; tr. into Malayalam by Kunnunni Nampishan .- Ernakulam : [s.n.], 1957.

— 3rd ed. - Kottayam : [s.n.], 1966.

Vikromorvasiyam / by Kalidasa; tr. into Malayalam by Sankunni Kottanathil.

Manipuri

Vikramorbaśī / by Kālidāsa; tr. by Takhellambam Thoibī Devī .- Imphal : The author, 1962.

100 p.; 18 cm.

Marathi

Vikromorvasiyam / by Kalidasa; tr. into Marathi by B.A. Thamhankar. - Bombay: [s.n.], 1872.

Vikromorvashiyam / by Kalidasa; tr. into Marathi by Govind Ballal Deval .- 1889.

2nd ed. published in 1955.

Vikromorvasiyam / by Kalidasa; tr. into [Musical] Marathi by G.C. Deo .- Poona: [s.n.], 1887.

Vikromorvasiyam / by Kalidasa; tr. into Marathi by Keshkar. - 1889.

Vikromorvasiyam / by Kalidasa; tr. into Marathi by Krishna Sastri Rajwade .- Poona : [s.n.], 1874.

Vikramorvaśīyam : sār va vicār / by Kālidāsa; tr. into Marathi Mahādev Vyaṅkaṭ eś Lele .- Bombay : Vividhjñānavistār, 1905.

58, [2] p.; 24 cm.

Translation in abridged form with occasional comments.

Vikromorvasiyam / by Kalidasa; tr. into Marathi by S.G. Pandit; ed. by M.R.Kale.- Bombay, 1966.

Vikromorvasiyam / by Kalidasa; tr. into Marathi by Vasant V. Bapat; ed. by M.R. Kale .- Bombay, 1960.

Adaptation

Gadgil, Amarendra. Vikramorvasi .- [s.l.] : [s.n.], 1956.

A story in Marathi adapted from Kalidasa's drama.

Islāmpūrkar, Vāman Śāstrī. Vidagdhapurūravā / by Vāman Śāstrī Islāmpūrkar. - Bombay : Vāsudev Moreśvar Potder, 1889.

xx, 160 p.; 18.5 cm.

(Potdārāñcī Nītipar Aṇi Manorañjak. Pustakamala; 7). Marathi Novel based on Kālidāsas famous Sanskrit play 'Vikramorvasiya'.

Nepali

Vikramorvaśhi / by Kālidāsa .- Varanasi : Hitaiṣī Co., 1950.

180 p.; 17 cm., Reprint

Rendering from original Sanskrit.

Vikromorvashi / by Kalidasa; tr. into Nepali by Kesar Shamsher. 2nd ed. - Nepal: The author, 1846.

iv, 134, 4 p.; 18 cm.

Oriya

[Vikromorvasiyam] Sura - sundari / by Kalidasa; tr. into Oriya by Abhinna Chandra Das. - Cuttuck : [s.n.], 1956.

A liberal metrical rendering.

["] Bikramorbaśīya / by Kālidāsa; tr. into Oriya by Gopīnātha Nanda. - Cuttuck : Bikramadeba Barmā, 1908.

40 p.; 18 cm.

["] Bikramorbaśī / by Kālidāsa; tr. into Oriya by Mṛtyuñjaya Ratha.- Cuttuck : The translator, 1915.

72 p.; 18 cm.

The play was first written in 1905 and appeared in the year 1909.

Vikromorvasiyam / by Kalidasa; tr. into Oriya by Raja Birmitrodaya Simhadev - Sambalpur : [s.n.], 1910.

Persian

Vikrama - Urvashi / by Kalidasa; tr. into modern Persian by S.A.H. Abidi .- New Delhi : [s.n.], 1959.

Punjabi

Vikramorvasī nāṭak / by Kālidāsa; tr. from Sanskrit by Mān Singh .- Amritsar : Khālsā Samācar, 1927.

132 p.; 18.5 cm.

Also published in 1932, 1934, 1938, 1941, 1945, 1949.

Russian

Vikramorvasi / by Kalidasa; tr. into Russian with introd. by V. Miller .- Moscow : [s.n.], 1897.

Sindhi

Vikramorvashī / by Kālidāsa; tr. into Sindhi by Āsūdomal Ṭekcand Gidvāṇī. - Hyderabad, Sind : Blavatsky Press, [n.d.].

iii, 51 p.; 18 cm.

Vikramorvashi / by Kalidasa; tr. into Sindhi by Dayal Kotumal Dhamija 'Asha'. - Bombay : Sarasvati Sahitya Sadan, 1965.

106 p.; 18 cm.

Spanish

Vikramorvasi drama del poeta indio Kalidasa; [Spanish] version directa del Sanskrit / by F. Garcin Ayuso. - Mandrid : [s.n.], 1874.

Swedish

[Vikromorvasiyam] Vikramorvaci / by Kalidasa; tr. into Swedish by A.J. Calnin Helsingborg : [s.n.], 1866.

[Vikromorvasiyam] Vikramorvaci : ōfversatt och fōrklaradt / by Kalidasa; tr. into Swedish by C.J. Bergstedt. - Stockholm : [s.n.], 1846.

[Vikromorvasiyam] Urvasi och hennes hjälte / by Kalidasa; tr. into Swedish by Hilding Andersson. - Lund : [s.n.], 1906.

Tamil

[Vikramorvasiyam] Vikram Ūrvaśi / by Kālidāsa; tr. into Tamil by P. Sambandha Mutaliyar .- Madras : The translator, 1929.

64 p.; 21 cm.

Tr. of Vikramorvaśīyam into Tamil.

Vikromorvasiyam / Kalidasa; tr. into Tamil [prose] by S.A. Ramaswami .- Madras: [s.n.], 1965.

An abridged rendering.

Vikramorvasiyam / by Kalidasa; tr. into Tamil by S. Raja Sastri. - Madras : [s.n.], 1911.

Telugu

Vikramorvasiyam / by Kalidasa; tr. into Telugu [s.l.]: M.S.B. & V.L. Society, 1879.

Vikramorvasiyam / by Kalidasa .- Madras : Venkataraya Sastri, 1948.

36 p.; 17.5 cm.

Telugu rendering.

Vikromorvasiyam / by Kalidasa .- Vijayawada : Jayanti Publications, 1971.

88 p.; 17.5 cm.,Telugu rendering.

Vikramorvasiyam / by Kalidasa; tr. into Telugu [prose] by Gopal Krishna Rental .- Vijayawada : [s.n.], 1968.

Vikromorvasiyam / by Kalidasa; tr. into Telugu by N.V.R. Krishnamachari.

Vikromorvasiyam / by Kalidasa; tr. into Telugu by Nanduri Ramakrishnacharya .- 1955.

Vikromorvasiyam / by Kalidasa; tr. into Telugu by P. Mahadev Sharma.- Hyderabad: [s.n.], [1968?].

Vikromorvasiyam / by Kalidasa; tr. into Telugu by P. Saryanarayana.

Vikramōrvaśīyam / by Kālidāsa; tr. into Telugu Vaḍḍādi Subbārāyuḍu .- 2nd ed. - Rajahmundry : Śrīvidyānilaya Mudrākṣaraśāla, 1912.

76 p.; 18 cm.,First published in 1889.

Vikromorvasiyam / by Kalidasa; tr. into Telugu by Vatsavayi Venkataniladriraju.

Vikramōrvaśīyam / by Kālidāsa; tr. into Telugu by Vēdamu Veṅkaṭarāyaśāstri .- Madras : Vēdamu Veṅkaṭarāyaśāstri & Bros., 1948.

130, [36] p.; 19 cm.

First published in 1921?

Urdu

Vikram Urvasī / by Kālidāsa; tr. into Urdu by Aziz Mirzā, Agra: Matba Shamsī, 1907.

lxviii, 92 p.; 24 cm.

Vikram Urvasi / by Kalidasa; tr. into Urdu by Aziz Mirza. - 2nd ed. - Lucknow : [s.n.], 1924.

CRITICAL STUDIES OF VIKRAMORVAŚIYAM

Banhatti, Srinivas Narayan. Natyacharya Deval:Pune : The author, 1967.Book received the 'Sahitya Akademi Award' of 1969 in Marathi language.It contains an article entitled 'Vikrmorvashiya: Kalidas āṇī Deval'.Pp. 106 - 122.

Barnett, L.D. [Book review of Vikramorvasiyam; a critical edition of Charudev Shastri]. *JRAS,* 1930. P. 935.

Bavisatthakaha / ed. by Jacobi .- [s.l.] : [s.n.], [n.d.].

Pp. 58 ft.

Deals with the linguistic aspects of Vikramorvasiyam. (Reference in HKG).

Bedekar, V.M. [Book Review of Vikramorvasiyam; ed. by H.D. Velankar]. *ABORI;* Jan. 1963; Vol. XLII Nos. 1 - IV; Pp. 90 - 98.

Belvalkar, S.K. [Book review of Vikramorvasiyam; a critical edition of Charudev Shastri]. *ABORI,* 1931. Vol. XII, No. III; Pp. 298 - 299.

Belvalkar, S.K. The Vikramorvaśiya of Kālidasa. *Annals of the Bhandarkar Oriental Research Institute; 1930; Vol. XII, No. I.*

Book review by S.K. Belvalkar of critical edition of Charu Deva Shastri.

Bender, Ernest. [Book review of the Vikramorvasiyam; ed. by H.D. Velankar]. *Journal of American Oriental* Society; 1962; Vol LXXXII; P. 415.

Bhat, G.K. Vikramorvasiya. *Amṛta (Dipavali Suppliment);* Nov. 1960; Pp. 26 - 52,A literary study.

Bhavanagari, Nina C. Ausinari no krodha. *Svādhyaya;* Vol. VII, No. 4.

Literary study of Vikromorvasiyam.

Bhawe, S.S. Vikramorvasiyam : Act IV. *Bharatiya Vidya;* 1948; Vol. IX. K.M. Munshi Diamond Jubilee Vol. Pt. 1.; Pp. 62 - 80.

Literary study.

[Book review of Telugu translation of Vikramorvasiyam by P. Mahadev Sharma]. *Triveni;* 4 January 1969, Vol. XXXVII, No. 4; P. 90.

[Book review of 'Urvasi' a Czech rendering of Kalidasa play by V.J. Novotny] *Archiv Orientalni. - [Prague];* Vol. XIX; P. 198.

[Book review of Vikramorvasiya; critically ed. by H.D. Velankar] *Bulletin of the Institute* of Traditional Culture, Madras, 1964; Vol. VIII, No. 1.

[Book review of Vikramorvasiyam of Kalidasa] *Indian PEN* Nov. 1939; Vol. V; P. 167.

Caland, W. Eine niewe verse vande Urvasi - mythe. *Kern Fel. Vol.*; Pp. 57 ft.

Though deals not directly with the problem of the Vikramorvasiya but as a background of the problem.

Cesare, Cantu. Analysis of the Vikramorvaśīya and the Meghaduta. *In* Documenti della storia universale .- Turin, 1865.

Mentioned in the East and West Rome, July 1955, Vol. VI, No. 2. Pp. 160- 162.

Devendra Kumar. Vikramorvasiya ki apabhramsa gitiyan. *Vikrama (Vikrama University Journal) Kalidasa Viśeṣaṅka;* 1967. Pp. 45 - 47.

Dharma Rao, G. Urvasi in legend and literature. *Triveni;* July 1952; Vol. XXIII, No. 2; Pp. 109 - 116.

Covers 'Urvasi' as described in Rigveda, Kalidasa, Aurobindo and Tagore.

Foulkes, T.A. complete collection of the various readings of the Madras manuscripts. Vol. IV. Vikramorvasiya Acts I - V. Madras : [s.n.], 1907.

Ghosal, Sibendra Nath. [Book review of Vikramorvasiyam ed. by Surendranath Sastri]. *Prachya Vani;* Jan. - April 1945; Vol. II, Nos. 1 - 2; P. 60.

Ghosh, Aurobindo. The character of the hero: an essay. *In* Urvasie / by Kalidasa; tr. into English by Aurobindo Ghosh .- Bombay : [s.n.], 1899.

— Calcutta: [s.n.], 1911.

2nd ed. in 1941.

3rd ed. in 1952.

Ghosh, Aurobindo. Two essays on Vikramorvasiya. *In* Vikramorvasie. - 3rd ed. - Pandicherry : [s.n.], 1952.

Gonda, J. [Book review of 'Urvasi' in Dutech translation]. *Djawa;* 1932, Vol. XII; P. 344.

Gonda, J. [Book review of Vikramorvasiya; ed. by H.D Velankar]. *Zeitschrift der Deutschen Morgenlandishen Gesellschaft;* 1963; Vol. CXIII; Pp. 380 - 82.

Gopalacharya, A.V. Vikramorvasiya nāndislokanubhavah. *Maharaj Sanskrit Mahapathasala Patrika (Mysore);*1954; Vol. XXVII; Nos. 1-4; Pp.1 - 19.

Gorekar, N.S. [Book review of Persian rendering of Vikramorvasiyam by S.A.H. Abidi]. *Indian PEN;* May 1962; Vol. XXVIII; Pp. 123 - 124.

Hertal, Johannes. Die Geburt des Pururavas. *WZKM;* 1911; Vol. XXV; Pp. 153 - 186.

Janaki, S.S. The Vikramorvasiya of Kalidasa : a study of the poet's sources. *Sanskrit Ranga (Annual);* 1962 - 63 & 1963 - 64; Vol. IV; Pp. 12 - 34.

Traces all the sources on which Kalidasa's play is based.

Janaki, S.S. [On Vikramorvasiyam]. *Pracya Jyoti;* Vol. V, Part. 1.

Jayaswal, Sitaram. [*Book review of Vikramorvasiya in Hindi by Sitaram Jyaswal]. Indian PEN;* Sept. 1954, Vol. XXIV; Pp. 318 - 319.

Jayaswal, Sitaram. [Book review of Vikramorvasiya aur Mālavikāgnimitra; Hindi tr. of Viraj].

Indian PEN; Sept. 1958; Vol. XXIV; Pp. 318 - 319.

Kantawala, S.G. The Saṅgamaniya gem episode in the Vikramorvasiya. *JGJRI* (Umesh Mishra Comm. Vol.); 1969; Vol. XXV; Nos. I - IV; Pp. 417 - 423.

Review appeared in BITC; Jan. - June 1971; P. 181.

Konow, Sten. [Authenticity of Vikramorvasiyam]. *Gottinger Geleherte Anneigen* 1894; P. 478.

Koparkar, D.G. Time analysis of the Vikramorvasiya Act III. *Oriental Thought* April - July 1956; Vol. II, Nos. 2 - 3; Pp. 143 - 149.

Kosambi, D.D. Urvasi and Pururavas. *In* Myth and reality. - Bombay: [s.n.], 1962.

Kosambi, D.D. Urvasi and Pururavas. *ISPP;* 1959; Vol. 1; Pp. 141 - 175.

Covers both Vedic and Kālidasa's treatment of Urvasi and Pururavas.

Kosambi, D.D. Urvasi and Pururavas. *JBBRAS* (N.S.);1951; Vol. XXVII; Pp.1 - 30.

Kotnis, V.K. An introduction to the Vikramorvasiya of Kalidasa with a foreword by K. Ramaswami Sastri .- Madras: [s.n.], [1939].

A review appeared in *Indian PEN;* Nov. 1939; Vol. V; P. 167.

Kulkrani, K.A. A remarks of Vidusaka in consideration of 'Lajjakaram tu yat' on the stage. *SPAIOC* (Kurukshetra); 1974; P. 70.

Lenz, Roberts. Apparatus criticus ad Urvasiam fabulam Calodasi, quem tamquam suae eivs libri editionis appendicem londinii Conscriptis. - Berlin, 1834.

Textual criticism of Vikramorvasiyam.

Ludwig, A. Pururavah und Urvasi Zusātze und Berichtigungen. *Sitzungsberichte der Prussischen Akademie der Wissenschaften* No. IV.

Ludwig, A. Pururavah und Urvasi Zusatze und Berichtigungen. [Sitzen...No. IV].

Reference in *OB*; Vol. XII.

Ludwig, A. Pururavas and Urvasi *Sitzb. Būhm Ges. Wiss;* 1897; No. XX.

Mallikarjuna, Paraddi. Urvasi : a wife and mother. *DRMKS;* 1970; Pp. 30 - 35.

A Note on Pravesaka of the Vikramorvasiyam and the Viskambhaka of Sakuntalam Act IV. *Vidya* (JGU); Jan. 1960; Vol. III, No. 1; Pp. 21 - 24.

Padhye, D.G. Srimahakavikalidasaviracitam Vikramorvasiyam. *Tarangini (Osmania University Journal,* Hyderabad); 1964 - 65; Pp. 18 - 28.

Padhye, D.G. Vikramorvasiyam : caturthah ankah. *Tar;* 1961 - 62; Pp. 32 - 40.

On the grammer & lingusics and also a literary study of the Prakrit portions.

Paliwal, Sudha. Vikramorvashiyam ka samikshatmak adhyayan. - Delhi : Eastern Book Linkers, 1993.

xv, 132 p.; 22 cm.

Pandya, Jatin. Kalidasa's vision in the Vikramorvasiya. *Vidya (Journal of The Gujarat University);* Aug. 1966; Vol. IX, No. 2; Pp. 21 - 23.

Pandya, Jatin. Mrigalanchana Rohini conjunction in the Vikramorvasiyam. *Vikrama University Journal (Kalidasa Viśeṣaṅka);* 1964; Pp. 79 - 90.

— *BCGV;* August 1965 - 66; Vol. XII - XIII; Pp. 60 - 73.

Pandya, V.G. Vikramorvasiyanadarsana. *Vidya (Journal of Gujarata University);* August 1966. Vol. IX.

Reference in *JOIB;* 1966; Vol. XVI.

Pandhye, D.G. Srimahakavikalidasaviracitam Vikramorvasiyam. *Tar* ; 1964 - 65; Pp. 18 - 28.

Deals with the theme, characterization etc of the classic.

Padhye, D.G. Vikramorvasiyam : caturthah ankah. *Tarangini;* 1961 - 62; Pp. 32 - 40, A literary study.

Parikh, J.T. Vikramorvasiyam : an appreciation. *BCGV* Aug. 1955; No. 2; Pp. 40- 58.

Pavolini, P.E. Una nuova versione Puranica della leggenda di Urvasi *GSAI;* Vol. XXI; Pp. 291 - 298.

Reference in *OB;* Vol. XXI.

Pischel, R. Vikramorvasiyam : herausgegeben nach Dravadischen handschriften. *Menatsb der Konigl. Akad der Wiss. Zu Berlin,* 1875; Pp. 609 - 670.

Pisharoti, K. Rama. Vikramorvasiya : a study. *JGJRI;* Nov. 1943; Vol. 1; No. 1; Pp. 123 - 137.

Pisharoti, K.R. Vikramorvasiya : a study of the sources. *Maharaja College Magazine (Ernakulam);* Vol. XXII, No. 3; Pp. 206 - 212.

Ramanathan, C. The external parts of the IV Act of the Vikramorvasiyam : a study. *SPAIOC* [Ujjain]. 1972; P. 188.

Ramanujaswami, P.V. [Book review of Vikramorvasiyam; critically edited with an English tr. by R.N. Gaidhani] *Journal of Sri Venkateshwara Oriental Institute;* Jan. - June 1948; Vol. IX, No. 1; Pp. 43 - 44.

Ranganna, S.V. Vikramorvashiyanatakada vimarshe - Mysore : Sharada Mandira, 1960.

vi, 155 p.; 18 cm.

In Kannada.

Rao, G. Dharma. Urvasi in legend and literature. *Triveni;* July 1952; Vol. XXIII, No. 2; Pp. 109 - 116.

Discusses Urvasi as found in Rigveda and in the writings of Kalidasa, Tagore and Sri Aurobindo.

Rasik Vihari. Urvasi : sahitya mein eka pratika. *Sarasvati;* May 1970; Vol. LXXI, Part 1; Pp. 369 - 372.

Gives a comparative study with Aurobindo and Tagore's view of Urvasi.

Renou, L. [Book review of Vikramorvasiyam; ed. by H.D. Velankar].

Journal Asiatique; 1962, Vol. CCL; Pp. 471 - 73.

[Review of S.G. Kantawala's paper on the 'Saṅgamaniya gem episode in the Vikramorvasiya] *BITC;* Jan. - June 1971; P. 181.

Sastri, P.S. Pururavas : a vedic drama. *BUJ;* 1956 Pp. 41 - 43.

Reference in R.N. Dandekar's 'Vedic bibliography' Part II; 1961; P. 183.

Shah, U.P. [Book review of Vikramorvasiyam; ed. by H.D. Velankar]. *Journal of Oriental Institute* [Baroda], 1962; Vol. XII, No. 4; Pp. 468 - 470.

Sharma, Kundan Lal. Urvasipururavasorākhyānam. *Visva - Samskritam;* August 1966; Vol. III, No. 4.

Shesha Ayyar, K.G. Vikramorvasiyam : an appreciation. *QJMS;* Jan., 1921; Vol. XI, No. 2; Pp. 161 - 167.

Singh, Satya Prakash. An Introduction of the character of Urvasi. *Vikrama* (Kā. Vi); 1967; Pp. 89 - 96.

Sivarama Sastri, N. The soliloquy of Pururavas : a study in textual criticism. *M. Hiriyanna Comm. Volume* [Mysore], 1952; Pp. 189 - 202.

Deals with the textual criticism of the two recensions, Northern and Southern of the IV Act of the Vikramorvasiya and comes to the conclusion that inflated version is in other words the homage paid by folk drama to the genious of Kalidasa.

Tetsuo, Yamaori. The Idea in the Vikramorvasiya. (Japanese). *JIBS;* 1957; No. 9. Pp. 174 - 175.

Trivedi, Ratilal Mohanlal. Kālidāsa's Vikramorvaśīyam : a historical drama. *All*

India Oriental Conference XVII (Summary); P. 46.

Based on the history of the Gupta kings, Rāmagupta and Candragupta and queen Dhruvadevī.

Trivedi, Ratilal Mohanlal. Kalidasa's Vikramorvasiya : a historical drama. *SPAIOC;* Vol. XVII.

Upadhye, A.N. [Book review of Vikramorvasiyam; ed. by H.D. Velankar] *Bharatiya Vidya;* 1962; Vol. XXII, No. 1 - 4; Pp. 85 - 89.

Upadhye, A.N.; *Ed.* Paramatma prakasa. Bombay : [s.n.], 1934.

On Vikramorvasiya (authenticity).

Vamshidhar Vidyalankar. The Art of Kalidasa in Urvasi *JOU* (Theology and Arts); 1941 - 42; Vol. IX; Pp. 20 - 30.

Vanshidhar Vidyalankala. Kalidasa ki Urvasi. *Visāla Bharata* July 1934; Vol. XIV, No. 7; Pp. 43 - 49.

Velankar, H.D. Vikramorvasiya Konesvari : introduction on textual criticism. *ABORI;* 1958; Vol. XXXVIII; Pp. III - IV, 251 - 261, 262 - 298 (text edited).

'The Vikramorvaśīya of Kālidāsa'. *Annals of the Bhandarkar Oriental Research Institute; 1961, Vol. XLII, Nos. I - IV.*

Book review of critical edition of Prof. H.D. Velankar.

Vora, M.M. Urvasi ane Chitralekha.

A radio - talk delivered from the All India Radio, Bombay.

Wright, J.C. Pururavas and Urvasi. *BSOAS;* 1967; Vol. XXX; Pp. 526- 547.

Wright, J.C. [Book review of Vikramorvasiyam; ed. by H.D Velankar]. *Bulletin* of the school of Oriental and *African Studies,* London. 1962; Vol. XXV; P. 654.

11

Abhijñaśākuntalam

Text

Abhijñaraśākuntalam / by Kālidāsa'.- Bombay: [s.n.], [n.d.] Anonymous (Editor).

Reference in M. Schuyler's 'A bibliography of Sanskrit Drama' p. 49.

Abhijñānaśākuntalam / by Kālidāsa .- Calcutta : [s.n.], 1761.

This is the first printed edition of the Sanskrit play 'Abhijñānāśākuntalam' of Kālidāsa.

(Editor) Anonymous

Abhijñanaśākuntalam / by Kālidāsa; comm. by Premachandra .- Calcutta [s.n.], 1839.

Anonymous (Editor)

Abhijñānaśākuntalam / by Kālidāsa .- Bombay : [s.n.], 1861.

Anonymous (Editor)

Abhijñānaśākuntalam / by Kālidāsa .- Patna : [s.n.], 1907

Anonymous (Editor)

Abhijñānaśākuntalam / by Kālidāsa; commentary by Abhirāma .- Srirangam : Śrī Vāṇī Vilās Press, 1917.

iv, 332 p.; 18 cm.- (Śri Vāṇī Vilās Sanskrit Series; 13)

Includes index.

Abhijñānaśākuntalam / by Kālidāsa; commentary by Śrīnivāsācārya .- Madras : V. Rāmasvāmi Śāstrulu, 1934.

xvi, 319 p.; 20 cm.

In Telugu script.

Abhijñānaśākuntalam / by Kālidāsa [tr. into English by Sir William Jones] .- London : [s.n.], 1789.

This is the first English rendering of the play.

Includes the text.

Abhijñānaśākuntalam / by Kālidāsa; comm. by Śatavadhana Śrinivasacharya. - Madras : V. Ramasvami Śastrulu & Sons, 1950.

[536] p.; 18 cm.

Abhijñānaśākuntalam / by Kālidāsa.; ed. by A.L. Chēzy. - Paris : [s.n.], 1830.

In Bengali script?

Abhijñānaśākuntalam / BY Kālidāsa; ed. [with an introd.] by Āśubodh Vidyābhūṣaṇ and Nityabodh Vidyāratna. - Calcutta : Vācaspatya Press, 1914.

[184] p. : plates; 21 cm.

Abhijñānaśākuntalam / by Kālidāsa; ed.d [with notes in English] by Banārasī Dās Jain and Madan Gopāl Śāstrī. .- Lahore : Dās Bros, 1923.

xvi, 136 p.; 24 cm.

Includes append. & index.

Abhijñānaśākuntalam / by Kālidāsa; ed. [with a comm.] by D.V. Pant. - Calcutta: [s.n.], 1871.

Abhijñānaśākuntalam : [with commentary Nilakanthi] / by Kālidāsa; ed. by G. Gopalareddy.- Delhi : Bharatiya Vidya Corporation, 1996.

xxviii, 201 p.

Abhijñānaśākuntalam / by Kālidāsa; [commentaries by Śrīnivāsācārya and Rāghava Bhaṭṭa]; ed. by Gaṇeś Kāśīnāth Kāḷe.- Bombay : Lakṣmī Veṅkaṭeśvar Press, 1917.

xiv, 447 p.; 22 cm.

Abhijñānaśākuntalam / by Kālidāsa; ed. [with a commentary 'Abhijñānakaumudī and a Bengali tr.] by Haridās Siddhāntavāgīś Bhaṭṭācārya.- Nakipur, Khulna: The editor, 1923.

xii, 690 p.; 20 cm.

Abhijñānaśākuntalam / by Kālidāsa; ed. by Ishvarachandra Vidyasagar. - Calcutta: [s.n.], 1880.

Also published in 1887 & 1889.

Abhijñānaśākuntalam / by Kālidāsa; ed. by Jagamohan Tarkalankar and K. Tarkaratna; a preface in Bengali by V. Majumdar .- Calcutta : [s.n.], 1869.

Abhijñānaśākuntalam / by Kālidāsa; ed. by Jagan Mohan Sharma and Kedarnath.- Calcutta : [s.n.], 1869.

Abhijñānaśākuntalam / by Kālidāsa; ed. [with notes] by K.N. Nyayapañcānana .- 2d ed. - Calcutta : [s.n.], 1888.

Abhijñānaśākuntalam / by Kālidāsa; ed. by Kantannatha Śastri Telang; the commentary 'Kiśorakeli' by Navakiśora Kar Sastri. Hindi tr. by Ramateja Pandeya .- Varanasi : Chowkhamba Sanskrit Series Office, 1955.

34, 644 p.; 18 cm.

Abhijñanaśākuntalam / by Kālidāsa; ed. by Krishnanath Bhattacharya .- 3rd ed.- Calcutta :[s.n.], 1902.

Includes commentary

Abhijñanaśākuntalam / by Kālidāsā; ed. by M.R. Kale. - Delhi : Motilal Banarsidas.

Text with English translation, notes etc.

Abhijñanaśākuntalam / by Kālidāsa; ed. by M.B. Godabole and K.P. Parab, comm. '*Arthadyotanika*' by Raghavabhatta .- Bombay : [s.n.] 1883.

Also published in 1886, 1895 (3rd ed.), 1913 (6th ed.).

Abhijñanaśākuntalam / by Kālidāsa; ed. [with various readings, introd., English tr., notes and appendices] by M.R. Kale; rev. by K.M. Śembavanekar. - 7th ed. - Bombay : Gopāl Nārāyan & Co., 1934.

lxxxv, [431] p.; 22 cm.

Commentary by Rāghava Bhaṭṭa.

Abhijñanaśākuntalam / by Kālidāsa; ed. [with an English., notes and various readings] by Moreśvar Rāmacandra Kāḷe.- 3rd rev. ed.- Bombay : Śāradākridan Press, 1907.

[792] p.; 22 cm.

Commentlary 'Arthadyotanika' by Rāghava Bhaṭṭa.

Abhijñanaśākuntalam / by Kālidāsa; ed. [with an introd., glossary, English and Bengali tr., various readings and a commentary 'Sarala'] by Nabinacandra Vidyāratna. - Calcutta : Ratnā Press, 1901.

xxv, [770] p.; 21 cm.

Abhijñanaśākuntalam / by Kālidāsa; ed. [with various] readings by Narāyan Ram Acharya .- Bombay : Nirnaya Sagar Press, 1947.

iv, 264 p.; 21.5 cm.

Abhijñanaśākuntalam / by Kālidāsa; ed. by Narayan Ram Acharya .- 12th ed.- Bombay : Nirnaya Sagar Press, 1958.

12, 272 p.; 21 cm.

Abhijñanaśākuntalam / by Kālidāsa, ed. [with a commentary 'Lakshmi'] by Narayan Śastri Khiste. - 2nd ed.- Varanasi : Master Khilarilal & Sons, 1957.

32, 672 p.; 18 cm.

Abhijñanaśākuntalam / by Kālidāsa; ed. by O. Bohtling K. - Bonn: [s.n.], 1842.

Abhijñanaśākuntalam / by Kālidāsa; ed. [with an English tr., various readings, notes and appendices] by P.N. Pāṭaṇkar. - 2nd ed.- Poona : Aryabhūṣaṇ Press, 1902.

[335] p.; 21 cm.

Abhijñanaśākuntalam / by Kālidāsa; ed. [with notes] by Premchandra Bhattacharya; rev. by Ramamaya Sharma. - Calcutta : [s.n.], 1864.

Abhijñanaśākuntalam / by Kālidāsa; ed. by Richard Pischel .- Kiel : [s.n.], 1877.

The Bengali recension with critical notes.

2nd ed. published in 1886.

——— rev. ed. - Cambridge: [s.n.], 1922 (Harvard Oriental Series; no. 16).

Richard Pischel (1849-1908)

Richard Pischel was a scholar with profound knowledge of Indian Shadow Theatre, Sanskrit drama, Prakrit grammar, Buddhism and Vedic studies. Richard was born 18.1.1849 in Breslau. He held the Chair of Indology in Berlin University in1902 and was invited to give lectures at Calcutta and died in Madras on 26.12.1908, shortly after the set foot on Indian soil for the first time. Calcutta University honoured him by buying his private library. This wellknown Sanskritist obtained a Ph.D. degree in Breslau in 1870. His thesis, written under the guidance of Stenzler, was De Kālidāsae Cakuntali recensionibus ("On the recensions of Kaslidasa's Shakuntala). He compared the so called Devanagari recension and the Bengali recension which had been translated by Sir William Jones in 1790 (A year later from English into German by G. Forster). Pischel considered the Bengali version to be the older and more original one. In 1878, he published a critical edition of the Bengali recension.

Abhijñanaśākuntalam / by Kālidāsa; ed. [in the original Sanskrit and Prakrit] by Richard Pischel; rev. by Carl Cappeller. - 2nd ed. - Cambridge (Man) : Harvard University Press, 1922.

xviii, 260 p.; 26 cm.-

(Harvard Oriental Series; 16).

Abhijñanaśākuntalam of Kālidāsa / by Kālidāsa; ed. by S.K. Belvalkar. - New Delhi : Sahitya Akademi, 1965.

vi. 148 p.

Abhijñanaśākuntalam / by Kālidāsa; ed. [with a commentary 'Mitabhāṣinī and English tr.] by Śāradārañjan Rāy. - Calcutta : Navavibhākar Press, 1908.

v, 376 p.; 22 cm.

Abhijñanaśākuntalam / by Kālidāsa; ed. by Śivaraja Śastri. - 2nd ed. - Meerut : Lila-Kamal Prakashan, 1961.

56, 367 p.; 22 cm

Abhijñanaśākuntalam / by Kālidāsa; ed. [with a commentlary 'Sahṛdaya'] by T.E. Śrinivāsācārya. - Kumbakonam : Śrīvidyā Press, 1901 - 1902.

2 Vols.; 21 cm.

Acts 1 - 5 only.

Abhijñanaśākuntalam / by Kālidāsa; ed. by T. Holme .- London : [s.n.], 1902.

[De Calidasae Sacuntala] / by Kālidāsa; ed. by C. Rabe. .- Breslau : [s.n.], 1845.

Kālidāsa : complete collection of various readings of the Madras manuscripts / by Kālidāsa; comp. & ed. by T. Foulkes. - Madras : Government Press, 1904 - 07.

4 Vols.; 22 cm.

Contents : Vol.1 Meghasandeśa, Raghuvaṁśa, Kumārasambhava.

Vol. 2 Abhijñanaśākuntalam (Acts 1 to 5)

Vol. 3 Abhijñanaśākuntalam (Acts 6 & 7)

Vol. 4 Vikramorvaśīya (Act 1 to 5)

Kālidāsa Granthavali /by Kālidāsa; ed. by Rampratap Tripathi

Kālidāsa Granthavali / by Kālidāsa; ed. by Reva Prasad Dvivedi - Varanasi: Banaras Hindu Vishvavidyalaya, 1976.

xlvi, 596 p.; 22 cm.

Kālidāsa Granthāvalī / by Kālidāsa; ed. [with a Hindi tr.] by Sītārām Caturvedi. - 2nd ed. - Banaras : Akhil Bhāratīya Vikram - Pariṣad, 1950.

3 Vols in one; 25 cm.

First published in 1944.

Includes bibliography.

Contents : Vols 1 & 2 : Raghuvaṁśa, Kumārasambhava, Meghadūta, Ṛtusaṃhāra, Abhijñānaśākuntala, Vikramorvaśīya and Mālavikāgnimitra.

Vol. 2 : Articles in Hindi on Kālidāsa by diverse hands.

[Shakuntala] / by Kālidāsa *In*. Raghunatha Rao, R. The art of translation .- New Delhi : Bharatiya Anuvad Parishad 1990.

Includes excerpts from Shakutala in Sanskrit, English & Kannada version.

Works of Kālidāsa .- Calcutta : [s.n.], 1901.

2 Vols.

In English

Woks of Kālidāsa / by Kālidāsa; ed. with an exhaustive introd., translation, critical and explanatory notes in English by C.R. Devadhar. - Delhi : Motilal Banarsidas, 1981.

Various paginations; 17.5 cm.

Adaptation (In Sanskrit)

Bhatt, J.A. Mānasaśākuntalam .- Bhavnagar : Parvati J. Bhatt, 1982.

Sanskrit play in five scenes and title means the story of Śakuntala in the mind of the master poet Kālidāsa.

Read by the author in the English Session of the Gujarat Rajya Sanskrit Adhyapak Mandal, Jetalpur in April, 1982.

Bopardikar, Kumud M. Sangitasakuntalam. *Guñjaravah* May 1967; Vol. II, No. 2.

Chandrasekhar, K. Premapāśitaḥ Śārṅgaravah *Sanskrita Pratibha* (New Delhi); Oct. 1959; Vol. 1, No. 2.

A Dravidian work (Language not mentioned), rendered into Sanskrit by V.H.Subrahmanya' Śāstri that bases on an episode from Abhijñanaśākuntalam, designed as a dramatic dialogue between Śārṅgarava, a pupil of Kaṇva who had escorted the latter foster daughter Śakuntalā to Duṣyanta and Priyaṁvada, one of her two friends. Title means Śārṅgarava in the noose of love.

Desai, S.G. Svapnavilasitam *Saṁvid* (Bombay); Nov. 1966 - May 1967; Vol. III, Nos. 2-4.

It is a fantasy in two acts presenting the highlights of the plays of Kālidāsa through two sets of his characters, the jesters on one hand and the heroines of his plays on the other set, a uniquye idea of the playwright.

Jaggu Vakulabhusana. Prasannakāśyapam .- Melkote : The author, 1951.

67 p.; 18 cm.

Includes author's commentary 'Bhāvollāsini'.

Prasannakāsyapam is a play in three acts by Jaggu Vakulabhusana, it is a supplement to the Abhijñanaśakutalam of Kālidāsa. *Hindu* wrote in its issue dated 22 December, 1946 that the play purports to take the theme of Kālidāsa classic one step further than the resolution of the 7th Act, as if to satisfy the curiosity of Kālidāsa's admirers regarding what might have happened next.

Joshi, H.S. & Dave, K.D. Sakuntalānyāyaḥ .- [1966 - 67]

Review by K.H. Trivedi appeared in *Sammanasyam [Sri Bṛhad Gujarāta - Sanskrit Parisad, Ahmedabad]* & March 1967; Vol. II, No. 7; Pp. 25 - 27.

Kālidāsasamārahāvasare nibaddhānām Kālidāsīyoparūpakanām sammuccayah ed. by Umesh Mishra. - Darbhanga : [s.l.], 1963.

[Maheśaṭhakkura saṁskṛta granthamala; 2]

An adaptation of eleven short stories.

Mishra, Abhiraja Rajendra. Kāśyapābhīśāpam. *In* Rūparūdrīyan [a collection of eleven plays]. -

Allahabad : Vaijayanta Prakashan, 1986.

It is a one - act play in two scenes that seeks to give Abhijñānaśākuntalam, a new turn.

Mishra, Ramavatar. Śākuntalam., Darbhanga.

A Sanskrit play in one act, an abridgement of the Abhijñanaśākuntalam of Kālidāsa.

Pandya, Gajendrashankar Lalshankar. Śākuntala *Saṁvad (Bombay)*, August 1975.

Fourth acts play in Sanskrit based on Kālidāsa work; originally composed in Gujarati in the form of a ballet.

Parikh, J.T. Chāyaśākuntalam .- Surat : The author, 1957.

An experimental one act play in Sanskrit based on Abhijñānaśākuntalam but modelled on the third and fourth acts of the Uttaramacaritam.

Śākuntala nṛtanātika : a Sanskrit play in three acts. - Bombay : [s.n.], 1986.

Noticed earlier by S.B. Velankar. The entire story of the Abhijñanaśākuntalam is retold in the form of paraphrase of the parent play. In this way it stands unique among the adaptations of the great work. Here and there it lifts up verses from the parent work and fits them into its texture very artistically.

Vardachari, Venkatadriagaram. Sakuntalacaritam. - 1962.

A Sanskrit work, based on the classic 'Abhijñanaśākuntalam ?

Vasudeva Sarma, K.N. Antarvāhinī. *Viśvasaṁskṛtam (Hoshiarpur)*; Vol. III, nos. 1 - 4, Nov. 1973 - Feb., May, August, 1974.

A suppliment to the Abhijñanaśākuntalam in six scenes based on the purely imaginary theme. The play begins with Kaṇva feeling extremely sad after Śakuntala's departure and ends with tearful fare well of Kanva and Gautami by the ashrama girls.

TRANSLATIONS

Assamese

Sakuntalna / by Kālidāsa; tr. by Atulcandra Hājarikā .- 2nd ed. - Gauhati : Asamīyā Sāhitya Mandir, 1948.

x, 184 p.; 19 cm.

Śakuntala / by Kālidāsa; tr. [from Sanskrit] by Lambodar Barā .- Guwahati : Asam Prakashan Parishad, 1990.

xxix, 102 p.; 22 cm.

Tr. into Assamese of Abhijñān Śākuntalam.

Sākuntala / by Kālidāsa; tr. into Assemese & [ed.] by Lombodara Bara. - Nalbari: [s.n.], [n.d.].

Text is Assemese script.

Śākuntala / by Kālidāsa; tr. into Assemese by Tulasinarayan Sharma. - Jorhat : Annada Sahitya Mandir 1932.

36 p.; 17 cm. (Sishu Sahitya series; no. 5).

A summary of the play for children.

Adaptations (Assamese)

Kaviraja Chakravarti. Shakuntala kavya.

Kaviraja Chakravarti was the court - poet of both king Rudra Simha and King Siva Simha (1714 - 1744). At the behest of the king Siva Simha and his queen Phuleswari, he composed 'Shakuntalakavya'. The queen Phuleswari assumed royal powers in 1726 and in Shakuntala kavya, she has been referred to as the chief consort. In this kavya, Kaviraja narrated the familiar story of Shakuntala but to highten the romantic effect, he added to it the love episode of Chandraketu and Kāmakalā.

In order to console the love - lorn and and aggrieved king, the sage Ganga, citing the examples of Rama - Sita and Nala - Damayanti, described at length the episode of separation and reunion of Chandraketu and Kamakala. There are 1059 verses in the kavya. Although the poet says that he has been inspired by the story taken from the Adiparva of the epic Mahabharata. But the influence of Kālidāsa's Abhijñana - Śakuntala is more pronnouced in the work. Perhaps, it is the only book in Assamese which bears the stamp of Kālidāsa. The poet has also named the book 'Dushyanta charita'. Scholar Jotindra Mohan Goswami states that the characters of Dushyanta, Anusuya, Priyamvada, and the episodes of Durvasa's curse, Bharata's birth at the hermitage of Kashayapa and the reunion of Dushyanta and Shakuntala, all have been woven into the texture of the Assamese kavya. But Kaviraja Chakravarti has made certain modifications in the story. In this kavya Menaka, the celestial nymph and mother of Shakuntala, the two lovers come close to each other. Menaka's friend, Sunanda, in the guise of a deer, draws Dushyanta, who is out ahunting, to the hermitage of Kanva where the king finds her sporting in the lake. Dushyanta stays at the hermitage for a whole year, and when he leaves for his capital he gives Shakuntala a ring and she, in turn, offers him a pearl necklace as a token of her love. Again, when the king refused to accept Shakuntala, Menaka, in the Kavya, takes her to the house of the nymph Prabha. These are some of the innovations made by Kaviraja Chakravarti.

Belgian

Chokontalā / by Kālidāsa; tr. into Belgian by Gērard Cotton. - 1952.

Bengali

Abhijnana Shakuntalam / by Kalidaa; tr. into Bengali by Abanindranath Thakur .- 1894 [B. 1301].

Abhijnana Shakuntalam / by Kālidāsa; tr. into Bengali by Amulya Chandra Sen .- Calcutta : Sarasvat Library, 1968.

173 p.; 22 cm.

Reference in *'Oriental Studies and Bengal. Hand - book of the 25th Session of the AIOC, Jadavpur University.'*

Abhijñanaśākuntalam / by Kālidāsa; tr. into Bengali [& English] by B.B. Goswami .- Calcutta : [s.n.], 1895.

Includes the text.

Abhijnana Shakuntalam / by Kālidāsa; tr. into Bengali by Brajanath Chakrabarti .- 1887.

Abhijñanaśākuntalam / by Kālidāsa; tr. into Bengali by Govinda Chandra Ray .- Calcutta ; [s.n.], 1893.

Also published in 1899.

Includes the text.

Abhijñanaśākuntalam / by Kālidāsa; tr. into Bengali by Haridas Bhattacharya .- Nakipur : [s.n.], 1923.

Includes the text and commentary.

Abhijnana Shakuntalm / by Kālidāsa; tr. into Bengali by Harimohan Gupta. [1869]

Serialized in *'Sambad Prabhakar'* from 1858 - 1859.

Abhijñanaśākuntalam / by Kālidāsa; tr. into Bengali by Haripada Chaudhuri .- Hoogli : [s.n.], 1898.

Abhijnana Shakuntala / by Kālidāsa; tr. into Bengali by Ishvara Chandra Vidyasagara.

Tr. in seven chapters Calcutta : [s.n.], 1854.

Also published in 1885.

——/ed. by S. Basu .- Calcutta : [s.n.], 1907.

Also published in 1908 & 1909.

Ed. appeared in 1909 contains a short life of the author and notes by Shivaratna Mitra and Taraprasanna Ghosh.

Story of Shakuntala in prose style.

Iswar Chandra Vidyasagar

Abhijñanaśākuntalam / by Kālidāsa; tr. into Bengali by Kalikesh Bandyopadhyay.- Calcutta : [s.n.], 1923.

Includes the text.

Abhijñanaśākuntalam / by Kālidāsa; tr. into Bengali by Kapildeb Das .- Calcutta : [s.n.], 1963.

Abhijñanaśākuntalam / by Kālidāsa; tr. into Bengali by Krishnagopal Bhattacharya. [1952 ?]

Abhijnana Shakuntala / by Kālidāsa; tr. into Bengali by Kunjabihari Basu .- 1888.

Tr. for the enactment of the play in 'Bangarangamanch'.

Abhijñanaśākuntalam / by Kālidāsa; tr. into Bengali [& English] by Navinchandra Vidyaratna .- Calcutta : [s.n.], 1901.

Abhijnana Shakuntala / by Kālidāsa; tr. into Bengali by Nandakumarn Kumar Ray.- Calcutta.

Appeared in the later half of the eighteenth century.

Abhijñanaśākuntalam / by Kālidāsa; tr. into Bengali by Prafullacandra Mukhopadhyay. 1889.

Abhijñanaśākuntalam / by Kālidāsa; tr. into Bengali by Ramchandra Tarkaratna .- Calcutta : [s.n.], 1848?

Abhijñanaśākuntalam / by Kālidāsa; tr. into Bengali by Ramnarayan Tarkaratna, 1860.

Abhijñanaśākuntalam / by Kālidāsa; ed. & tr. by Ramnarayan Tarkaratna. - 2nd ed. - Calcutta : [s.n.], 1869.

Abhijñanaśākuntalam / by Kālidāsa; [ed. with Sanskrit comm.;] Bengali & Eng. tr. by Ramendramohan Basu .- 3rd ed. - Calcutta : [s.n.], 1960.

4th rev. & enl. ed. published in 1963.

5th ed. published in 1970.

Abhijñanaśākuntalam / by Kālidāsa; tr. & ed. by Saradaranjan Ray .- Calcutta : [s.n.], 1922.

Abhijñanaśākuntalam / by Kālidāsa; [ed. &] tr. into English & Bengali by Saradaranjan Ray; rev. by Kumudaranjan Ray. - Calcutta : [s.n.], 1962.

Abhijñanaśākuntalam / by Kālidāsa; tr. into Bengali by Shatrujit Dasgupta .- 1959.

Abhijñanaśākuntalam / by Kālidāsa; tr. into Bengali verses by Vidyaratna Krishnapada .- Calcutta : [s.n.], 1932.

Bharatiya sahitya ratna samkalan / com. by Dhirendranath Banerjee .- Calcutta : Sanskrit Book Depot, 1980.

Contents : 'Shakuntala pratyakhyan'; Bengali rendering of Fifth Act of 'Abhijnana Shakuntalam'.

pp. 203 - 210.

De, Sabitri. Sanskrit Sahityer anubad - dhara .- Calcutta : Chinmay Majumdar [1983].

Contents : Shakuntala.

[pp. 87 - 116]

Kālidās racana samagra / by Kalidāsa; tr. into Bengali by Sudhaṁśukumar Basu; ed. by Beṇīmādhav Rāycaudhurī .- Calcutta : Reflect Publications, 1991.

430 p.; 19 cm.

First published in 1987.

Kālidāsa Samagra / by Kālidāsa; & ed. by Jyotibhusan Chaki. - Calcutta : Nabapatra Prakashan, 1982.

Various paginations; 22 cm.

Tr. into Bengali by diverse hands.

Kalidaser granthabali / by Kalidas .- 5th ed. - Calcutta : Basumati Pvt. Ltd., [1964] 3 Vols.

Kālidāser granthābalī / ed. [with Bengali tr.] by Hiralal Gupta. - Calcutta : [s.n.], 1896.

Includes both the genuine works and works ascribed to Kālidāsa such as Nalodaya, Puṣpabāṇavilāsa, Śrutabodha, Dvāviṁatputtalika, Śṛṅgāratilaka and Śṛṅgārāṣṭaka.

Kālidāser Granthābali / ed. by Rajendranath Vidyābhūṣaṇa. - 4th ed. - Calcutta : [s.n.], 1927.

Kālidāser granthābalī / ed. by Satyacharanan Śāstrī. - Calcutta : [s.n.], 1915.

Text with Bengali translation.

Kālidāser granthābalī / ed. by Sharat Chandra Chakrabarti. - Calcutta : Kālikā Press, 1916 - 1919.

Includes Bengali tr.

[Kalidaser rachanabali] / ed. by Vidyāratna Kalipada .- Calcutta : [s.n.], 1895.

4 Vols.

Includes Bengali translation.

Kanakapadma = [Abhijñanaśākuntalam] / by Kālidāsa; tr. into Bengali by Haralal Ray. 1875.

Mahākabi Kālidāser granthābalī / ed. by Nabakumar Basu. - Calcutta : [s.n.], 1892.

In Bengali.

Mahākavi Kālidāser granthābali / ed. by Upendra Nath Mukherji .- 2nd ed. - Calcutta : [s.n.], 1896.

Text with Bengali tr.

Also appeared in 1907.

Tagore, Jyotirindranth. Jyotirindranāth granthāvalī / by Jyotindranāth Thākur. - Calcutta : Basumatī Sāhitya Mandir, 1899 ?

5 Vols.; 25 cm.

Contents : *Vol. 1* : Abhijñān Śākuntala; Vikramorvaśī, Nāgānanda; Ratnāvalī; Priyadarsikā; Mudrārakṣasa, Uttar Rama carita; etc.

Vol 3 : Mṛcchakaṭik; Mālavikāgnimitra; Prabhodhacandrodaya; Karpuramañjari etc. *Vol. 4* : Veṇīsaṃhār, Mālatīmādhav, etc.

Inspired from Ishwarchandra Vidyasagar's translation.

Jyotirindranath Tagore (1849 - 1925); translated 'Abhijñanaśākuntalam' 'Malavikagnimitra' & 'Vikramorvasiyam' into Bengali.

Adaptation

Chakrabarti, Brajananth. Sakuntala. - 1887.

Bengali adaptation of Kālidāsa's Sanskrit classic.

Mallik, Raghunātha. Kālidāser galpa / by Raghunath Mallik, 1931. Also published in 1966.

Tales from the Sanskrit dramas and poems.

Mukhopadhyay, Aparesh Chandra. Sakuntala. Calcutta, 1930.

An adaptation of Kālidāsa's Abhijñanaśākuntalam in Bengali.

Bohemian

Sakontalo : drama Indickē od Kālidāsy / tr. into Bohemian by P.C. Vyprpio.

In *Poesie Svetova*. 1873; Part 6;

Pp. 200 ff.

Chinese

Abhijñanaśākuntalam / by Kālidāsa; tr. into Chinese .- 1946.

Anonymous (translator).

Chinese title : K'ung ch 'ueh nu.

Reference in the National Union Catalogue. Library of Congress, Washington. 1958 - 1962.

Abhijñanaśākuntalam / by Kālidāsa; tr. into Chinese by Chi - Hsin - Lin.

Abhijñanaśākuntalam / by Kālidāsa; tr. into Chinese by Mandju, 1907.

Reference in *Ajanta* (Hindi), Hyderabad. Vol. III, No. 9 of Sept. 1956 issue; Pp. 75 - 76.

Czech

Abhijñanaśākuntalam / by Kālidāsa; tr. into Czech by C. Vynis .- 1873.

Reference in :-

(i) *Archiv Orientalni*, Prague, Vol. XIX; P. 198.

(ii) Biswas, S.P. *Modern Review;* April 1961, Vol. CIX, No. 4; Pp. 320 - 323.

Abhijñanaśākuntalam / by Kālidāsa; tr. into Czech by Fr. Hrubin .- 1944.

Reference in:-

(i) Archiv Orientalni, Prague; Vol. XIX; P. 198.

(ii) National library Calcutta Catalogue Card Index (European Language) cyclostyle copy.

Śakuntala opera / by J.W. Tomaschek.

This Śākuntala opera by this Czech composer (1774 - 1850) was never performed.

Danish

Sacontalā eller den uheldige Ring, et. indiansk drama of Cālidas / by Kālidāsa; tr. [from the English of William Jones] into Danish by Hans West. - Copenhagen: [s.n.], 1793.

Sakuntala : skuespel : syv Optrin oversat og forklaret / by Kālidāsa; tr. into Danish by Martin Hammerich .- Compehagen : [s.n.], 1845.

2nd ed. published in 1858.

3rd ed. published in 1879.

Dogri

Abhijnan Shakuntalam / by Kālidāsa; tr. into Dogri by Shyam Lal Sharma .- Jammu: Shripati Prakashan, 1987.

iv, 120 p.; 22 cm.

Recieved 'Sahitya Akademi Translation Prize' in the year 1991.

Dutch

Shakuntala / by Kalidaa; tr. into Dutch by Bert Voeten from the English and German translation of the Sanskrit Original, 1958.

Bert Voeten, Dutch poet and the translator of Kālidāsa's Shakuntala

Sakuntala, of de beslissennde ring / by Kālidāsa; tr. into Dutch by Forster. - Haarlem : E.M. Post., 1792.

Śākuntalā, of het Herkenning steeken / by Kālidāsa; tr. into Dutch by H. Kern. - Haarlem : [s.n.], 1862.

English

Abhijñanaśākuntalam / by Kālidāsa; tr. into English by A. B. Gajendragadkar .- 7th ed. - Surat : [s.n..], 1962.

Abhijñanaśākuntalam / by Kālidāsa; tr. into English by A.H. Edgren. *In* The Classical drama of India / ed. by Henry W. Wells .- 1963.

[Abhijñanaśākuntalam] / by Kālidāsa; [Extracts from Act IV &] tr. into English by Baldoon Dhingra. *In* Asia : through Asian eyes .- London : [s.n.], 1959.

Contents :

(i) Advice to a Bride from Sākuntala IV, p. 178.

(ii) Man and nature [Extracts from Act IV], Pp. 215 - 217.

Abhijñanaśākuntalam / by Kālidāsa; ed. & English notes by N.B. Godabole & K.P. Parab .- Bombay : [s.n.], 1883.

3rd ed. published in 1895.

Includes commentary of Rāghavabhaṭṭa.

Abhijñanaśākuntalam / by Kālidāsa; tr. into English [& Bengali] by Navinchandra Vidyaratna .- Calcutta : [s.n.], 1901.

Abhijnana Sakuntalam / by Kālidāsa; tr. into English by O.K. Ghosh *In* Tales from Indian Classics .- Bombay : Jai co, 1961.

Abhijñanaśākuntalam / by Kālidāsa; tr. into English of by P. Ghosh. *Journal of Ancient History* (University of Calcutta) 1968 - 69; Vol. II, Part - 1 - 2.

Pp. 169 - 187.

Abhijñanaśākuntalam / by Kālidāsa; tr. into English by P. Lal. *In* Great Sanskrit plays in modern translation .- [Calcutta ?] : [s.n.], 1964.

Abhijñanaśākuntalam / by Kālidāsa; tr. into English by B.B. Goswami .- Calcutta : [s.n.], 1895.

Includes the text and Bengali rendering also.

Abhijñanaśākuntalam / by Kālidāsa; tr. into English by B.V. Vyas and C.M. Mehta? Bombay : [s.n.], 1962.

Includes the Comm. of Raghavabhatta.

Abhijñanaśākuntalam / by Kālidāsa; tr. into English by C.R. Devadhar .- Delhi : [s.n.], 1966.

Reprint

[Abhijñanaśākuntalam] / by Kālidāsa; tr. into English by C. Shankarram Sastri .- 2nd ed. - Madras : [s.n.], 1958.

——. ed. by S. Vishvanathan .- 3rd ed. - (Śri Bālamanorama Series; Nos. 32 & 42).

Abhijnana Sakuntalam / by Kālidāsa; tr. into English by Chandra Rajan, 1989.

Abhijñanaśākuntalam / by Kālidāsa; tr. into English by Kalikesh Bandyopadhyay .- Calcutta : [s.n.], 1901.

Abhijñanaśākuntalam / by Kālidāsa; tr. into English by Kalipada Mukherjee. - Calcutta : [s.n.], 1895.

Abhijñanaśākuntalam / by Kālidāsa; tr. into English by Krishna Kamal Bhattacharya .- Calcutta : [s.n.], 1891.

Abhijñanaśākuntalam / by Kālidāsa; tr. into English [from Bengali recension] by M.B. Emeneau. - California : [s.n.], 1962.

Employed Pischel's text.

Abhijnana Sakuntalam / by Kālidāsa; tr. into English by M. Jaganānthan .- Pudukkottai : Poet India Publications, 1988.

87 p.; 18 cm.

Abhijñanaśākuntalam / by Kālidāsa; tr. into English by M.R. Kale .- Bombay : [s.n.], 1898.

Includes commentary by Rāghavabhaṭṭa & also edited text.

Also published in 1902.

7th ed. rev. by K.M. Shembavanekar in 1934.

8th ed. with some supplimentary notes by Suresh Upadhyay.

Abhijnana Sakuntalam / by Kālidāsa; tr. into English by M. Monier - Williams, 1867.

Abhijnana Shakuntala / by Kālidāsa; tr. into English by M. Monier - Williams. *In* Glimpses of Sanskrit literature / ed. by A.N.D. Haksar .- New Delhi : ICCR, 1995.

(Tr. of Act IV) Pp. 210 - 223.

Abhijnana Sakuntalam / by Kālidāsa; tr. into English by Michael Coulson .- 1981.

Abhijñanaśākuntalam / by Kālidāsa; tr. into English by P.N. Patankar .- Poona : [s.n.], 1889.

Also published in 1902.

Abhijñanaśākuntalam / by Kālidāsa; tr. into English by R.D. Karmarkar .- Poona : [s.n.], 1952.

Abhijñanaśākuntalam / by Kālidāsa; [Ed. with Sanskrit comm.] tr. into English by Ramendramohan Basu. - 3rd ed. - Calcutta : [s.n.], 1960.

4th rev. & enl. e. published in 1963.

5th ed. published in 1970.

Includes Bengali translation and edited text.

Abhijnana Śakuntala / by Kālidāsa; [ed. 7] tr. into English S.D. and A.B. Gajendragadkar .- Bombay : [s.n.], 1920.

Abhijñanaśākuntalam / by Kālidāsa; tr. into English by S.. Rangachar .- 2nd rev. ed. - Mysore : [s.n.], 1959.

Abhijñanaśākuntalam / by Kālidāsa; tr. into English [& Bengali] by Saradaranjan Ray; rev. by Kumudaranjan Ray .- Calcutta : [s.n.], 1962.

First published in 1908.

Abhijnana Śakuntalam / by Kālidāsa; tr. into English by Shatrujit Dasgupta. - Calcutta : [s.n.], 1959.

Abhijñanaśākuntalam / by Kālidāsa; tr. into English by T.E. Shrinivasachariar and B.V. Sankar Kamesvar Aiyar. - Kumbakonam : [s.n.], 1901.

Includes edited text.

Abhijñanaśākuntalam / by Kālidāsa; tr. into English by T.G. Jennings .- Allahabad: [s.n.], 1902.

Abhijñanaśākuntalam / by Kālidāsa; tr. into English by T.R. Ratnam Aiyar. - Madras: [s.n.], 1896.

[Abhijñanaśākuntalam] / by Kālidāsa; tr. into English by Upendranarayan Majumdar. *In* English poetry, 1932.

Abhijñanaśākuntalam / by Kālidāsa; tr. into English in abridged form by V.N. Balakrishna Kirtikar .- Bombay : [s.n.], 1885.

Abhijñanaśākuntalam / by Kālidāsa; tr. into English by William Jones .- Calcutta, 1789.

Reference in "Salus, Peter H. Sakuntalā in Europe : the first thirty years.

—. JAOS -; 1964; Vol. 84; Pp. 417 ff.

—. London, 1790.

Reference in "A classified catalogue of books on the section of India in the *Toyo Bunko* acquired during the years 1917 - 1950. Tokyo, 1950.

Reprinted in 1792.

—. Edinburg, 1796.

—. London, 1870.

—. Calcutta, 1883.

—. New York, 1885.

Also appeared in 1887, 1899 & 1901.

Sir William Jones (Fellow of University College, Oxford)

Sir William Jones (1746 - 94) was the first translator of the famous Kālidāsa play 'Sakuntala' into English that appeared in print in 1789 from Calcutta. He was a fellow of University College, Oxford and came to India in 1783 as a Puisne Judge of the Supreme Court at Fort William in Bengal and founded the famous Asiatic Society at Calcutta in 1784 and remained its President till the end of his life.

'Abhijñanaśākuntalam' / by Kālidāsa. *In* Sir William Jones : a reader / ed. by Satya S. Pachori .- Delhi : Oxford University Press, 1993.

English rendering of Kālidāsa's classic Pp. 99 - 130

Abhijñanaśākuntalam of Kālidāsa: with the commentary of Raghavabhatta / by Kālidāsa; ed. by M.R Kale .- Bombay : Booksellers Publishing Co., 1957.

217 p.; 21.5 cm.

English rendering of the drama.

Includes supplimentary notes by Suresh Upadhyaya.

The Classical drama of India / by Henry W. Wills 1963

Contains the dramas of Kālidāsa.

Classical triptych : Sakuntala, The Little clay cart, Nagananda / tr. into English verse by H.W. Wells .- Mysore : University of Mysore, 1970.

Collected works of Kālidāsa / by Bella Bose .- Allahabad : [s.n.], 1946.

Includes the dramas of Kālidāsa.

The Dramas of Kālidāsa / by Kālidāsa; tr. into English by Bela Bose .- Allahabad : Kitabistan, [1945].

232 p.; 20.5 cm.

Kālidāsa translation of Śākuntala and other works / by Arthur W. Ryder .- London: [s.n.], 1912 .- (Everyman's Library; No. 629).

Also published from New York.

Reprint appeared in 1928.

Contains all genuine works in English tr.

Kālidāsa translation of Śakuntala and other works / by Kālidāsa; tr. into English by W. Arthur Ryder .- London [s.n.] 1928.

Reprint [Preface by G.L. Anderson] New York, 1959. [A Dutton Everyman Paper back, D - 40].

The loom of time : a selection of his plays and poems / by Kālidāsa; tr. from the Sanskrit and Prakrit with an introd. by Chandra Rajan .- New Delhi : Penguin Books, 1989.

343 p.; 20 cm.

The return of Śākuntala / by Kālidāsa; story of V.M. Inamdar is tr. into English by Mastivenkatesh Iyengar. *Triveni* ; 1936; Vol. IX No. 12; Pp. 39 - 51.

[Shakuntala] / by Kālidāsa. *In* Raghunath Rao, R. The art of translation .- New Delhi : Bharatiya Anuvad Parishad, 1990.

Includes excerpts from the English version of Sir M.M. Williams [Printed in 1910], Kannada & Sanskrit text.

Sakuntala / by Kālidāsa; tr. by Laurence Binyon with an introd. essay by Rabindranath Tagore.- London : Macmillan & Co., 1920.

xxix, 149 p.; 20 cm.

The present rendering is the new version prepared for the English stage by Kedarnatnh Dasgupta.

Sakuntala and her keepsake / by Kālidāsa; tr. from Sanskrit by Roby Datta .- Calcutta : Dasgupta, 1915.

vi, 166 p.; 17.5 cm.

Tr. of 'Abhijñāna - Śākuntalam.

Śakuntala : idylls of ancient India. / by R. Vasudev Row .- Madras : [s.n.], 1903.

An English rendering in idyllic poetry.

Śakuntala of Kālidāsa / by Kālidāsa; tr. into English by T.A.V. Dikshitar. *Bhavan's Journal*; Vol. II, No. 2; Pp. 49 - 52.

A summary.

Śakuntalā or Idyl of the lost ring / by Kālidāsa; tr. into English by R. Vasudev Row.- rev. ed. - 1918.

Śakuntala or the fatal ring / by Kālidāsa; tr. into English by T. Holme. - London : [s.n.], 1902.

Śākuntala or the lost ring / by Kālidāsa, tr. into English by Monier Williams. Hertford : [s.n.], 1953.

Also published in 1855, 1856.

——. London : [s.n.], 1872.

Also appeared in 1887, 1890, 1898 (8th ed.)

——. Delhi : [s.n.], 1958.

Reprinted

——. Varanasi : Ch. S.S. Office, 1961.

——. Varanasi, 1961 (Indological Book House)

Sakuntala or the lost ring / by Kālidāsa; tr.. into English by Monier - Williams. - Delhi : Zodiac Publishing Corporation, 1958.

156 p.; 18 cm.

Śakuntala : the Bengali recension / by Kālidāsa; ed. & tr. into English by R. Pischel. - Kiel, 1877.

2nd ed. published in 1886;

——. Cambridge, 1922 (Harvard Oriental Series; No. 16).

A Sanskrit classic 'Shakuntnala' / by Kālidāsa; tr. into English by John D. Mitchell. *In* Approahces to the Oriental classics / ed. by Theodore de Bary .- New York : [s.n.], 1959. Pp. 119 - 131.

Shakuntala or the Fatal ring / by Kālidāsa; tr. by Sir William Jones .- Calcutta : Society for the Rescuscitation of Indian Literature, 1901.

xv, 215 p.; 16 cm.

Reprint of the original tr. appered in print in 1789.

Shakuntala or the recovered ring / by Kālidāsa; tr. into English by A.H. Edgren .- New York : [s.n.], 1894.

Six Sanskrit plays / ed. by Henry W. Wells. London: Asia Publishing House, 1964.

xxxi, 487 p.: plates; 21 cm.

Includes 'Shakuntala' and 'Vikramorvacie' by Kālidāsa.

Tales from Kālidāsa / by Kālidāsa; retold in English by Pranab Bandyopadhyay .- Calcutta : Book Club, 1991.

108 p.; 22 cm.

Theatre of memory plays of Kālidāsa / by Kālidāsa; ed. by Barbara Stoler Miller.- New York : Columbia University Press, 1984.

387 p.; 22.5 cm.

Includes bibliography.

Three Sanskrit plays / tr. into English by Michael Coulson .- London : Penguin Books, 1981.

430 p.; 19 cm.

Includes Kālidāsa's Śakuntala.

Translations of Shakuntala and other works / by Kālidāsa; tr. by Arthur W. Ryder.- London : J.M. Dent & Sons, [n.d.].

xxv, 216 p.; 1605 cm.

(Everyman's Library / ed. by Ernest Rhys).

Includes Shakuntala; Malavika and Agnimitra; Urvashi; Dynasty of Raghu; Birth of the war - God; Cloud - messenger; Seasons.

Works of Kālidāsa / by Kālidāsa .- Delhi : Bharatiya Publishing House, 1979. Vols.

Contents : Vol. 1 : Shakuntala or the Fatal ring / tr. from the original Sanskrit into English by William Jones; Vikrama and Urvasi or the Hero and the nymph / tr. by H.H. Wilson; Kumarasambhav [tr. not mentioned].

Works of Kālidāsa / by Kālidāsa; ed. & tr. by C.R. Devadhar .- Delhi : Motilal Banarsidass, 1972.

Vols.; 22.5 cm.

Contents : Vol. 1 : Dramas

Vol. 2 : Poetry

Works of Kālidāsa / by Kālidāsa; ed. with an exhaustive introd., translation critical and explanatory notes in English by C.R. Devadhar .- Delhi : Motilal Banarsidass, 1981.

Various paginations; 17.5 cm.

Works of Kālidāsa / by Kālidāsa; tr. from original Sanskrit into English .- Calcutta: Society for the Resuscitation of Indian Literature, 1901.

5 pts. bound in one; 16.5 cm.

Contents : Part 1 : Sakuntala the Fatal ring tr. Sir William Jones (Reprint)

Part 2 : Vikrama and Urvasi = The Hero and the nymph / tr. from the original Sanskrit by H.H. Wilson.

Part 3 : Meghaduta = Cloud messenger / tr. with annotations by H.H. Wilson.

Part 4 : Kumarsambhavam = The Birth of war-god.

Part 5 : Ritusamhara = An Account of seasons.

Adaptations (English)

Chandrashekharan, K. Sārṅgarava in love *Triveni;* 11 June 1948; Vol. XIX, No. 11; Pp 596 - 605.

A shorter fiction based on the story of Abhijñanaśākuntalam.

Daljeet. Śakuntala : a tale retold in Pahari Miniatares / by Dr. Daljeet; introd. by William Radice .- London : The Folio Society, 1992.

Ghosh, O.K. Tales from Indian classics .- Bombay : Jaico Publication, 1961.

Contains Sakuntala and Vikramorvasiyam.

Robbins, J.J. Sakuntala.

Adaptation in English from Monier William's work.

Wright, Alice Morgan Sakuntala .- 1904.

An Adaptation in English based on Monier Williams work.

French

La poēsie de l'Inde Kālidāsa / by Kālidāsa; French summary by Gerard Cotton .- Bruxelles : [s.n.], 1942.

L'anneau de Śakuntala; comdedie heroique / by Kālidāsa; tr. into French by Ferdinand Herold .- Paris : [s.n.], 1896.

L'anneau de Sakontala … d'apres Kālidāsa Reprēsenēe an Thēatre de peuple de Bussang / by Maurice Pottecher Paris : Societe d' Editions Litteraires at Artistiques, 1914.

La reconnaissance de Sacountala : drame en sept acts / by Kālidāsa; tr. into French by P.E. Foucaux .- Paris : [s.n.], 1867.

Also published in 1874, 1894.

La reconnaissance de Sacontala, drame Sanscrit et Pracrit de Cālidāsa ... / by Kālidāsa; tr. into French by A.L. Chezy .- Paris : [s.n.], 1830.

... accompagnē d'une traduction franncaise, de notes philogiques, critiques et litteraires et suive d'une appendice.

——. Paris : [s.n.], 1832.

Notes et Correction supplementaires.

Oeuvres complete's de Kālidāsa / tr. into French by Hippolyte Fauche .- Paris : [s.n.], 1859 - 60.

2 Vols.

Complete works of Kālidāsa in French translation.

Sacontala, ou l'anneau fatal, drame traduit de la langue, Sanscrit en Anglais / by Kālidāsa; tr. into French by Le Citoyen A. Bruguiere .- Paris : [s.n.], 1803.

Sakontala / by Kālidāsa; tr. into French by Georg Foster. *In* Kleine schriften zu kunst and literatur. - Berlin : [s.n.], 1963.

Sacountala : ballet pantomime en deux actes tire du drame dc Cālidāsa / by Kālidāsa; tr. into French by Theophile Gautier .- Paris : [s.n.], 1859.

Sacountala : drame en sept actes melē de prose et de vers / by Kālidāsa; tr. into French by Abet Bergaigne and P. Lehugeur. - Paris [s.n.], 1884.

Sankountala / by Kālidāsa; tr. into French [from Bengali rendering of A.N. Tagore] by Karpelis Andree, T.M. Chatterjee and Amulyachandra Chakravarty. [1937?]

Sakountala : piece lyrique en cinq actes / by Kālidāsa; tr. into French by Alfred Mortier. - Paris : [s.n.], 1919.

Śakuntala, annulo recognita / fabula scenica Calidasa; [ed. by Carolus Bukhard]

——. Breslau : [s.n.], 1872.

In usum scholarum academicarum textum recensionis Devanāgaricae recognovit atque glossario Sanscritico et Pracritico.

Śakuntala : texte traduit du Sanskrit et annotē / by Kālidāsa; tr. into French by de ville Frans. - Bruxelles : [s.n.], 1943. (Collection Lebeque - 3; Series No. 31).

Śakuntala : version Tamoule / by Kālidāsa; tr. into French by Gerard Deveze. *Revue de Linguistique*. Vol. XIX; Pp. ?; Vol. XX, Pp. 68 - 78; Vol. XXI (1888). Pp. 48 - 53.

German

Freiherrn von. Śakuntalā, schauspiel in fūnf aufzūgen frei nach Kālidāsa's altindis chem drama / by Kālidāsa; tr. into German by A. Wolzogen .- Schwering: [s.n.], 1869.

——. Leipzig : [s.n.], 1879?

Kālidāsa's Ring - Śakuntala : herausgegen, ūbersetzt und mit anmerkungen versehen / by Kālidāsa; tr. into German by Otto Bōehtlingk .- Born : [s.n.], 1842.

Also published in 1846., Devanāgari recension.

OTTO VON, BOEHTLINGK, 1815-1904

One of the greatest 19th century Indologist, Otto Von Boehtlingk was born on 11.6.1815 in St. Petersburg. A member of the Imperial Academy of Sciences in St. Petersburg, he edited and translated Kālidāsa's classic 'Ring - Cakuntala' from Bonn in 1842. He died in Leipzig on 1.4.1904.

Romantisches Mārchendrama in fūnf akten und einem verspiel, frei nach Kālidāsa fūr die deutschen būhren / by Kālidāsa; tr. into German by Leopard Von. Schreoder .- Munich : [s.n.], 1903.

Sakontala, order der Enscheidende ring : deutsche ubersetzt mit erläuterungen / by Kālidāsa; tr. into Germany by Georg Forster. - Mainz : [s.n.], 1791.

Also published from Leipzing

—— 2nd ed. - Frankfurt : [s.n.], 1803.

—— Heidelberg : [s.n.], 1820

—— Leipzig : [s.n.], 1879

Forster rendered his German version from William Jones English translation.

Sakontala, order der verhāngnissvolle ring : indisches drama des Kālidāsa in sechs aufzūgen. Metrisch fūr die Būhne bearbeitet / by Kālidāsa; tr. into German by Wilhelm Gerhard .- Leipzig : [s.n.], 1820.

Śakuntala / by Kālidāsa; tr. into German [metrisch frei bearbeitet] by Arthur .- Dresden : [s.n.], 1871.

Śakuntala / by Kālidāsa, tr. into German by F. Bodenstedt .- Leipzig : [s.n.], 1887.

[Sakuntnala] / by Kālidāsa; tr. into German by Friedrich Rueckert, 1867.

The play was rendered in 1855 and appeared in print in 1867, as translator's posthumous work.

[Sakuntala] / by Kālidāsa; tr. into German by Georg Herder. Herder, 1803.

New edition with a short dedication in which the reader finds a renewed expression of admiration for this classical Indian playwright.

Śakuntala / by Kālidāsa; tr. into German by H.C. Kellner .- Leipzig : [s.n.], 1890.

Śakuntalā / by Kālidāsa; tr. into German by Hōppl. 1854.

Sakuntala / by Kālidāsa; tr. into German by Johann Gottfried Herder.. *In* Zentreuten Blaettern, Gotha, 1793.

Original title : Ūber ein morgenlāndischen drama.

Śakuntala / by Kālidāsa; tr. into German by Max Mueller. *In* Deutscher būhrenfassugn .- Berlin : [s.n.], 1902.

Śākuntala / by Kālidāsa; into German by Rūckert. *In* Rūckert's nachlass.-. Leipzig : [s.n.], 1867.

Also published in 1876.

Sakuntala / by T.P. Scharwenka lib. Carl Wittowsky .- Berlin & Posen : Bote und Bock, 1885.

Śakuntala / by Kālidāsa; tr. into German by Wittkowsky; music by Ph. Scharwenka.- Berlin : [s.n.], 1883.

Śakuntalā : drama in sieben akten aus dem Indischen ūbertragen und eingeleitet / by Kālidāsa; tr. into German by Hans Losch .- Stuttgart : [s.n.], 1960.

Sakuntala : ein Būhrenspiel in 3 Aufzūgen; die Orchesterpartie fūr Clavier ūbertragen / by Felix Weingartner Kassel and Leipzig : Paul Voigt, 1884.

Śakuntala : ein Inndisches schauspiel / by Kālidāsa; tr. into German by Ernest Meier. *In* Die Klassischen dichtungen der Inder 2. Theil, Stuttgart, 1847 - 54.

Reprint in Bibliothek auslāndisher Klassiker, No. 58. - Hildburgshausen, 1867.

—— 2nd ed.- Leipzig : [s.n.], 1874.

Śakuntala : ein Indisches schauspiel in sieben akten : deustche ūbertragen / by Kālidāsa; tr. into German by Rolf Lauckner .- Berlin : [s.n.], 1924.

Śakuntala : fūr die deutschen būhnen bearbeitet / by Kālidāsa; tr. into German by Donsdorf .- Wien : [s.n.], 1876.

Śakuntala : Indisches schauspiel / by Kālidāsa; tr. into German by G. Schimilinsky.- Dresden : [s.n.], 1900.

Śakuntala (Kōrzere text form) mit kritischen und erklārenden Anmerkungen herangegebe / ed. by Carl Cappeller .- 1909.

CARL CAPELLER (1840-1925)

Carl Johannn Wilhelm Capeller, a German Indologist was born on 22.3.1840 in Alexkehnen in Eastern Prussia. He began his studies in 1860 in Berlin, where he read Classical languages, Indo-European linguistics, Sanskrit annd Lithuanian. He earned his doctorate in 1868 for Latin thesis Observationes ad Kālidāsae Malavikagnimitram. Several scholars were of the opinion that this drama could not be ascribed to Kālidāsa. Capeller compared a number of passages from Malavikagnimitra and other dramas of Kālidāsa's. He came to the conclusion that Kālidāsa was indeed the author and that he must have written the drama in the later part of his life.

Carl Capller specialised in Sanskrit drama. He has several critical editions to his credit.

Capeller was appointed reader of Sanskrit in the University of Jena in 1872. He became associate professor in 1875. In 1921, when he was 81 years of age, he discontinued giving lectures. He died on 17.7.1925 in Jena.

In 1909 Capeller edited and translated Kālidāsa's Shakuntala. He added Prakrit index, a list of metres, and copious notes. This translation was used by the well known producer Reinhard to stage the play in Nuernberg in 1942. He did not give preference to any one manuscript. He tried to cull the best from each tradition, a subjective method not approved by all scholars.

Śakuntala : metrisch übersetzt / by Kālidāsa; tr. into German by Edmund Lobendanz.- Leipzig : [s.n.], 1854.

Also published in 1867, 1871, 1878, 1884 (7th ed.).

Śakuntala : metrisch übersetzt / by Kālidāsa; tr. into German by Luduwig Fritze. In Indisches theater. Vol II. - Chemnitz : [s.n.], 1877 - 79.

Śakuntala, oder der erkenungring / by Kālidāsa; tr. into German by B. Hirzel .- Zūrich : [s.n.], 1833.

2nd ed. published in 1849.

Śakuntala oder der ring der wiedererkennung : drama ih sieben akten nach dem Indischen Urtext des Kālidāsa / by Kālidāsa; tr. into German by W. Kurt Riedier .- Thalwil : [s.n.], 1948.

German

Śākuntala opera (with libretto by John Philip Neuman). 1820.

Not preserved.

Śakuntalā : schauspiel in fūnf akten nanch Kālidāsa / by Kālidāsa; tr. into German by Paul Kornfield .- Berlin : [s.n.], 1925.

Scene Gesetzt / by Carl Telle *Wien;* 1884. Contains "Ballet in Zwi Akten und funf Bildren. Musik [by] S. Bachrich.

Gujarati

Abhijñan Śākuntal / by Kālidasa; tr. into Gujarati by Baḷvantray Kalyāṇrāy Ṭhākōr.- Rajkot : The translator, 1906.

159 p.; 16.5 cm.

Also published in 1931.

Abhijñana Śakuntala / by Kālidāsa; tr. into Gujarati by Chandravadan Mehta .- 3rd ed. .- Bombay : [s.n.], 1963.

Abhijñanaśākuntala / by Kālidāsa; tr. into Gujarati by D.L. Munim annd P.C. Shah .- Ahmedabad : [s.n.], 1959.

Abhijñana Śakuntala / by Kālidāsa; tr. into Gujarati by Jashwant Dayashankar Thakur - Ahmedabad : [s.n.], 1961.

Abhijñanaśākuntalam / by Kālidāsa; tr. into Gujarati by K.H. Dhruva.

Abhijñanaśākuntal / by Kālidāsa; [ed. &] tr. into Gujarati by J.M. Shukla, R.S. Betai and M.D. Bhatt. - Surat : [s.n.], 1959.

Abhijñanaśākuntal / by Kālidāsa; tr. into Gujarati by Jhaverilal Umashankar Yajnik.- Bombay : [s.n.], 1867.

Also published in 1896, 1919 (3rd ed.).

Abhijñan Śākuntal / by Kālidāsa; tr. into Gujarati by Jhāverīlāl Umyāśaṅkar Yājñik.- 3rd ed.- Bombay : Mādavlāl Jhāverīlāl Yājñik, 1919.

xx, 246, 6 p.; 16.5 cm.

Abhijñanaśākuntal / by Kālidāsa; tr. into Gujarati by Keshavram Kaṣhiram Shastri.

Abhijñan Śakuntal / by Kālidāsa; tr. into Gujarati by Maganbhāī Caturbhāī

Paṭēl.- Ahmedabad : The translator, 1915.
xxxiv, 128 p.; 22 cm.

Abhijñanaśākuntal / by Kālidāsa; tr. into Gujarati by Mansukhlal M. Jhaveri.

Mahākavi Kālidās-ni prasādi / by Kālidāsa; ed. by Nānālāl Nāthālāl Śah.- Ahmedabad : Jīvaṇlāl Amarśī Mahētā, 1932.

xxxiv, 266 p.; plates; 18.5 cm.

Mudrapratapa / by Phulchand Jhaveridas Shah. Ahmedabad : [s.n.], 1957.

Adapted and translated into Gujarati of Abhijñanaśākuntaḷam.

Shakuntal / by Kālidāsa; tr. into Gujarati by Umashankar Joshi .- Ahmedabad : Gurjar Grantharatna Karyalay, 1955.

lxxx, 368 p.; 18.5 cm.

Includes notes & bibliography.

Śākuntal / by Kālidāsa; tr. by Dalpatrām Prāṇjīvan Khakhkhar .- Bombay : M.D. Khakhkhar, 1917.

xliii, 199 p.; plates; 18.5 cm.

Tr. of 'Abhijñanaśākuntalam'.

Śakuntalā-nuṁ sambhārṇuṁ / by Kālidāsa; tr. by Kavi .- Nhānālāl Dalpatrām - Ahmedabad : The translator, 1929.

xx, 130 p.; 18.5 cm.

Tr. of Abhijñanaśākuntalam.

First published in 1926.

Shakuntala or Kanyaviday / by Kālidāsa; tr. into Gujarati by Chandravadan C. Mehta -2nd ed.- Bombay : N.M. Tripathi, 1951.

iv, 48 p.; 18.4 cm.

Tran nāṭako / by Kālidāsa; tr. into Gujarati by Sastrī K. Keshavram .- Ahmedabad : [s.n.], 1948.

Adaptations

Pandya, Gajendrashankar Lalshankar [Śākuntalanritya natika].

Gujarati play in four acts of moderate length based on Kālidāsa's classic. The Śākuntala story is told here in free verse of the playwright's own composition with only the necessary links in prose which also mostly is of the playwright himself.

Hindi

Abhijnana Śakutalam / by Kālidāsa; Bombay .- Education Society Press, 1888.

Tr. into Hindi.

Anonymous (Translator).

Abhijñanaśākuntalam / by Kālidāsa; tr. into Hindi .- Delhi : Atmaram & Sons, Anonymous (Translator).

Abhijñanaśākuntalam / by Kālidāsa; tr. into Hindi.- Delhi : [s.n.], 1955.

Anonymous (Translator).

Abhijnana Śākuntalam / by Kālidāsa; - New Delhi : Sastā Sahitya Madal.Translated into Hindi

Anonymous (Translator).

Abhijñana Śākuntalam / by Kālidāsa; - Varanasi : Bhargava Pustakalay, 1956.

Commentary by Sītarām Śastrī.

Abhijñanaśākuntalam / by Kālidāsa; [ed. by Frederic Pincott] - London : [s.n.], 1876.

2nd ed. published in 1890.

Includes Hindi translation.

[Abhijñanaśākuntalam] Sakoontala natak : being an appendix to the English and Hindustani dialogues in the universal character / ed. by J.B. Gilchrist London : [s.n.], 1826.

Abhijnan Shakuntalam / by Kālidāsa; [ed. by Rammurti Sharma]. - Delhi : Eastern Book Linkers, 1989.

viii, 344 p.; 22 cm.

Abhijnana Sakuntalam / by Kālidāsa; tr. into Hindi by Abdulla Muhammad .- Agra : [s.n.], 1886.

Abhijñanaśākuntalam / by Kalidasa; tr. into Hindi by Babu Ram Tripathy .- 2nd ed. - Agra : [s.n.], 1962.

Abhijnana Śakuntalām / by Kālidāsa; tr. into Hindi by Baldevprasad Mishra .- Delhi: [s.n.], 1949.

Abhijnana Śakuntalām / by Kālidāsa; tr. by Baldev Śāstrī .- Lahore : Meharcand Lakṣmaṇdās, 1937.

xxviii, 260 p.; 18.5 cm.

Abhijnana Śakuntalām / by Kalidasa; tr. into Hindi by Brajbhusan Pandey .- Allahabad : [s.n.], 1953.

Abhijnana Śakuntalām / by Kālidāsa; tr. into Hindi by Candraśekhar Śarmā .- Allahabad : Ramdayal Aggarwal, 1917.

Abhijnana Śakuntalām / by Kalidasa; tr. into [Brajbhasa] Hindi by Dhonkal Miśra. 1799.

Abhijnana Śakuntalām / by Kalidasa; tr. into Hindi by Devadatta Śastrī .- Varanasi: Chaukhamba Vidyabhavan, 1961.

IVth Act only.

Ed. with notes etc.

Abhijnana Śakuntalām / by Kālidāsa; tr. into Hindi by Dhruv Aggarwal .- Allahabad: Ramnarayanlal Beniprasad, 1972.

Ed. & tr. of Vth Act only.

Abhijnana Śakuntalām / by Kalidasa; tr. into Hindi by Ganesh Prasad Lal .- Fatehgarh : [s.n.], 1890.

Abhijnana Śakuntalām / by Kālidāsa; tr. into Hindi by Hardayāl Singh .- New Delhi : Sasta Sahitya Mandal, [n.d.].

Tr. for children.

Reference in Mangal Nath Singh's *'Hindi men uccatara sahitya'* .- Varanasi: [s.n.], Saṁ 2014.

Abhijnana Śakuntalām / by Kalidasa; tr. into Hindi by Hiraka .- *Vīṇā* (*Kā. Vi*); p. 185.

Hindi metrical tr. of four verses of Śākuntala.

Abhijnana Śakuntalām / by Kālidāsa; tr. by Induśekhar .- Delhi : Atmaram & Sons, 1958.

Abhijnana Śakuntalām / by Kalidasa; tr. into Hindi by Jvalaprasad Miśra. [19th cent.]

Abhijnana Śakuntalām / by Kālidāsa; tr. by Jvālā Prasād .- Bombay : Venkatesvar Press, 1949.

Abhijnana Śakuntalām / by Kalidasa; tr. into Hindi by Kapildev Dvivedi. - Allahabad: [s.n.], 1958.

Also published in 1962 (IV Act only).

Edited with notes etc.

Abhijnana Śakuntalām / by Kalidasa; tr. into Hindi by Kazim Ali Jawan .- Lucknow: [s.n.], 1875.

Abhijnana Śakuntalām / by Kālidāsa; tr. into Hindi by MohanRākesh .- Delhi : Radhakrishna Prakashan, 1965.

228 p.; 18.5 cm.

Abhijnana Śakuntalām / by Kalidasa; tr. into Hindi by Nandlal Vishvanath Dubey.- 1888.

Abhijnana Śakuntalām / by Kālidāsa; tr. into Hindi by Nārāyaṇ Śāstrī .- Varanasī: Master Kheläḍilal & Sons, 1958.

Abhijnana Śakuntalām / by Kālidāsa; tr. into Hindi by Pratap Nārāyan Miśhra .- Patna : Khadgvilas Press, [n.d.]

Abhijnana Śakuntalām / by Kālidāsa; tr. into Hindi by R. B. Joshi and Uṣmā Joshī.- Laskar, Gwalior : Sarasvatī Sadan, 1962.

Abridged rendering of the play.

— 3rd ed. - Agra : [s.n.], 1967.

Abhijnana Śakuntalām / by Kalidasa; tr. into Hindi by Raja Lakshmansingh, 1876.

This is the first modern Hindi play and also the first translated work written in 1863 and published in 1876.

Tr. into Hindi in prose verse form.

Abhijnana Śakuntalām / by Kālidāsa; tr. into Hindi by Lakshman Singh .- Bombay: Education Society Press, 1888.

Abhijnana Śakuntalām / by Kālidāsa; tr. into Hindi by Raja Lakśman Singh; ed. by Śyāmsunder .- Allahabad : Indian Press, 1913.

Abhijnana Śakuntalām/ by Kālidāsa; tr. by Raja Lakshman Singh .- 4th ed.- Agra: Sahitya Ratna Bhandar, 1923.

Abhijnana Śakuntalām / by Kālidāsa; tr. by Raja Lakśmaṇ Singh .- Allahabad : [s.n.], 1944.

Abhijnana Śakuntalām/ by Kālidāsa; tr. into Hindi by Raja Lakśman Singh .- 4th ed. - Allahabad : Indian Press, 1960.

Abhijnana Śakuntalām / by Kālidāsa; tr. into Hindi by Raja. Lakśman Singh .- 4th ed. - Lucknow : Ganga Pustakmala Karyalay, 1960.

xxxiii, 131 p.; 18.5 cm.

Abhijnana Śakuntalām / by Kalidasa; tr. into Hindi by Raja Lakshman Singh .- Agra : Hindi Sahitya Sammelan.-.

3rd ed. Prayog : [s.n.], [Saṁ 2004].

Abhijnana Śakuntalām / by Kālidāsa; tr. into Hindi by Raja Lakshman singh .- Agra : Ratnashram, [n.d.].

Abhijnana Śakuntalām / by Kālidāsa; tr. into Hindi by Raja Lakśmaṇ Singh. - Agra : Vinod Pustak Mandir, [n.d.].

Abhijnana Śakuntalām / by Kālidāsa; tr. into Hindi by Raja Lakśmansingh .- New Delhi : Sasta Sahitya Mandal, [n.d.].

Abhijnana Śakuntalā nātak / by Kālidāsa, tr. into Hindi by Rāmgulāmlāl .- Vanaras: Baijnāthprasad, 1926.

110 p.; 18.5 cm.

Abhijnana Śakuntalām / by Kālidāsa; tr. into Hindi by Rāmkṛṣṇa Ācarya .- Agra: Vinod Pustak Mandir, 1969.

Abhijnana Śakuntalām / by Kalidasa; tr. into Hindi by Ram Murti Sharma .- Meerut: [s.n.], 1969.

Also published in 1974.

Abhijnana Śakuntalām / by Kalidasa, tr. into Hindi by Ramtej Pandey, ed. with a Skt comm. Kiśorakeli by Nav Kishor Kar and Hindi comm. 'Racirā' of the editor .- Banaras: [s.n.], 1935.

[Haridas Sanskrit Series; No. 41].

—— ed by Kantanath Telang .- rev. ed. Varanasi : Ch. S.S. Office, 1960. 5th ed. published in 1964.

Abhijnana Śakuntalām / by Kalidasa; tr. into Hindi by Ramateja Pandeya. ed. by Kantanatha Śāstri Telanga; the commentary 'Kiśorakeli' by Navakiśora Kar Sastri.

Varanasi : Chowkhamba Sanskrit Series Office, 1955.

34, 644 p.; 18 cm.

Abhijñana Śakuntalām / by Kalidasa; tr. into Hindi by Ramtej Pandey .- Varanasi: [s.n.], 1961.

Includes Hindi Commentary 'Nandanā'.

Abhijnana Śakuntala / by Kalidasa; tr. into Hindi [Brajabhasa] by Nevaj,

Abhijñana Śakuntalām / by Kalidasa; tr. into Hindi by Prabhakar Shrotriya.

Viṇa (Kā. Vi); Pp. 200-201.

"Translates I . 17; II. 10; IV. 8 etc."

Abhijñana Śakuntalām / by Kalidasa; tr. into Hindi by Shrisharan .- Dehli.

Abhijñan Śakuntalām / by Kālidāsa; tr. into Hindi by Surendradev Śāstrī .- Allahabad: Ramnarayanlal Beniprasad, 1967.

Abhijñana Śakuntalām / by Kālidāsa; tr. into Hindi by Vāgiśvar Vidyālaṃkāra .- Delhi : Hind Pocket Books, 1960.

Abhijnan Śakuntalam / by Kalidasa; [tr.into Hindi ?] & ed. by Vasudevkrishan Chaturvedi .- Agra : Mahalakshmi Prakashan, 1979.

[624] p.; 21.5 cm.

Abhijñana Śakuntalām / by Kalidasa; tr. into HIndi by Vijayachandra Sharma.- Jallandhur : [s.n.], 1962.

Abhijnan Shakuntalam / by Kalidasa; tr. into Hindi by Viraj .- Delhi : Rajpal & Sons, 1962.

177 p.; 18.5 cm.

Abhijñana Śakuntalām / by Kalidasa; tr. into Hindi by Vrajanath Bhattacharya .- Bombay : [s.n.], 1916.

Edited with a Hindi Comm. 'Manoramā'.

Abhijñana Śakuntalām / by Kālidāsa; tr. into Hindi by Vrajratna Bhaṭṭa .- Bombay: Khemraj Śrikṛṣṇadās, 1933.

Kālidās granthāvalī / by Kālidāsa; tr. by Kanhaiyālal Miśra. - Moradabad : Himālay Depot, 1925.

vi, 335 p.; 22 cm.

Contains Hindi rendering of the works (in prose) attributed to Kālidāsa, viz. Nalodaya, Meghadūta, Ṛtusaṁhāra, Śṛṅgāratilaka, Puṣpa-bāṇa-vilāsa, Vikramorvaśīya, Abhijñānaśākuntala, Mālavikāgnimitra, Śruta-bodha, and Śṛṅgāraṣaṣṭaka.

Kalidas granthavali / by Kalidasa; ed. with notes & comm. in Hindi by Rama Pratap Tripathi .- Allahabad : Kitab Mahal, 1966.

various paginations.

Kālidāsa granthāvalī / by Ram Tej Pandey .- Kāśi : [s.n.], 1962.

In Hindi tr.

Kalidas granthavali / by Kalidasa; Hindi tr. by Ramateja Sastri; ed. by Brahmananda Tripathi .- Varanasi : Chaukhamba Surabharati Prakashan, 1996.

796 p.

Kālidās granthāvalī / by Kālidāsa; tr. by Sītārām Caturvedī .- 2nd ed. - Banaras : Akhil Bhāratīya Vikram Pariṣad, 1950.

925 p.; 25 cm.

First published in 1944.

Includes Sanskrit bibliography.

Parts 1 & 2 contain Raghu vaṁśa, Kumārasambhava, Meghadūta, Ṛtusaṁhāra, Abhijñanaśākuntala, Vikramorvaśīya and Mālavikāgnimitra and Part - 3 covers essays on Kalidasa by diverse hands.

Kālidās - granthāvali / by Kālidāsa; tr. into Hindi by Sītārāma Caturvedī .- 3rd ed.- Varanasi : Akhil Bhāratiya Vikram Parishad, 1947.

Kāldās granthavali / ed. by Sita Ram Chaturvedi .- 2nd ed. - Benaras : [s.n.], 1950.

3 Vols in 1.

First published in 1944.

In Hindi

—— 3rd ed. - Aligarh : [s.n.], 1962-63.

Part III Contains articles on Kālidāsa by diverse hands.

Kalidas ke natak / by Kalidasa; tr. into Hindi by Bhagavat Sharan Upadhyay .- Delhi : Kitabghar, 1980.

199 p.; 22 cm.

Adaptation

Gupta, Maithilisharan Śakuntalā .- Jhansi : [s.n.], 1971.

Hindi adaptation in poetic form.

Śakuntala ko Durvāsa kā abhiśāp. *Sarasvati.*

May 1909; Vol. X, No.5; Pp. 207-209.

Poem highlighting the curse episode of Abhijñanaśakuntalam.

Śakuntala - patra - lekhana *Sarasvati;*

Nov. 1908, Vol. IX, No. 11; Pp. 491-492.

An elaboration of the love - letter of Śakuntala in Kuṇḍalī metre (15 verses).

Joshi, Ilachandra. Śakuntala *Viśāla Bharata;* Sept. 1931; Vol. VIII, No. 3; Pp. 329-333.

A long poem based on the Abhijnanasakuntala.

Mishra, Pratap Narayan. Sangitasakuntala .- Patna : [s.n.], 1908.

Hindi adaptation of Abhijñāna Śākuntala of Kalidasa.

Mishra, Ramavatar. Śākuntalam. *KUS*; Pp. 89 - 95.

A Hindi one - act play based on the theme of Abhijñanaśākuntala.

Ojha, Prafullachandra. *'Mukta'*. Sakuntala rupaka. *Tripathagā* (*Lucknow*); Jan. 1959; Vol. IV, No. 4; Pp. 65-88.

Hindi ballet based on Sakuntala.

Sharma, Chandrashekhar. Sakuntala ki katha .- Prayag : [s.n.], 1917.

A Hindi novel based on the Sanskrit classic of Kalidasa.

Simha, Kamalananda. Dusyanta ke prati Śakuntala kā premapatra (Rolā). *Sarasvati* Dec. 1901; Vol. II, No. 12; Pp. 334 - 997.

Hindi poem in 50 verses in Rolā metre based on the love - letter of Śākuntala.

Hungarian

Śakuntala / by Kalidasa; tr. into Hungarian by Fiōk Karoly .- Budapest : [s.n.], 1887.

Selected works / tr. by Joself Vekerdi .- [s.l] : [s.n.], n.d.

Works of Kalidasa in Hungarian language.

Icelandic

Śakuntalā / by Kalidasa; tr. into Icelandic by Sleingrin Thoratainsohn.

Indonesian

Shakuntala / by Kalidasa; tr. into Indonesian by Imam Oleh Supardi .- Surabaja : [s.n.], 1962.

Reference in 'The National Union Catalogue'. Library of Congress Washington.

Italian

Adaptation of three dramas into Italian in rhythemic prose 1928-29 / by Umberto Norsa. 1928-29.

Adaptations of Kalidasa's drama into Italian.

La leggenda di Sakuntala / tr. into Italian by Alfano Franco.

Italian adaptation of the Sanskrit drama.

[Reference in the catalog of books represented by Library of Congress Printed Cards].

La Sacuntala di Calidasa / by Kalidasa; tr. into Italian by Osvaldo Perini .- Verona: [s.n.], 1873.

Reconoscimento di Śakuntalā di Kālidiāsa / by Kalidasa; tr. into Italian by R. Nobile. *Il Concilio Organo Officiate dell' instituto interuniversitari Italiano,* Foligno 1924. Anno II, No. 6, Pp. 447 - 466, 532 - 540.

Riconosciuta per mezzo dell' anelio / by Kalidasa; tr. of 'Abhijñānaśakuntalam' into Italian by Antonio Marazzi. *Teatro scelto indiano (Milan),* 1871; Vol. 1; Pp. 9 - 176.

Śacontalā / by Kalidasa; tr. into Italian by Berchet. *In Counciliatore;* March 1819; No. 4 & 11.

Translated from Forster's German rendering.

Śacontalā; Ossia L'Anello Fatale / by Kalidasa; tr. into Italian by L. Doria. - Darmstadt : [s.n.], 1815.

Dramma tradotto dalla lingua Orientale Sanskrit nell' idoma inglese dal, Sig. W. Jones, indi dall inglese in Francese dal Sig A. Bruguiere ultimamente dal Francese in italiano.

Sakuntala [: dramma lirico] / by Kalidasa; tr. into Italian by Alfredo Badcelli .- Rome : [s.n.], 1888.

Śākuntala / by Kalidasa; tr. into Italian by E. Brizio .- 1931.

Reference in 'The Fortune of Kalidasa in Italy' / by Carlo Della Casa. *East & West;* July 1995; Vol. VI, No. 2; Pp. 160 - 162.

Sakuntala / tr. into Italian by Giulio Pacuvio .- Turin : [s.n.], 1946.

Reference in the "Fortune of Kalidasa in Italy by Carlo Della Casa. Published in East and West. Vol. VI, No. 2; July 1995; Pp. 160 - 162.

Sakuntala / by Kalidasa; tr. into Italian by Michele Kerbarkar.

An unpublished work mentioned in M. Schuyler's 'Bibliography of Sanskrit Drama'. P. 53, Note 1.

Śākuntala / by Kalidasa; tr. into Italian by Pisani, according to the Mss. left by Michele Kerbarkar.

Reference in 'The Fortune of Kalidasa in Italy' / by Carlo Della Casa. *East & West;* July 1995; Vol. VI, No. 2; Pp. 160 - 162.

Tretro di cālidasa / by Antonio Marezzi; tradotto dal sanscrito in Italieno .- milano : [s.n.], 1871.

Translation from Sanskrit to Italian.

Collected dramas of Kālidāsa.

Japanese

[Kālidāsa's works] / tr. by Kimura Hideo.

In Japanese translation ?

Śākuntala / by Kalidasa; tr. into Japenese by Tsuji Naoshirō.

Javanese

Sapanti Sakoentala Een Javaansch Toonelspel voor de wajang - Koelit bewerkt / by Kalidasa; tr. of 'Śākuntala' into Javanese by Radān Marta Hardjana.

Reference in the 'Catalogue of the Library of the India Office' (London), 1938; Vol. II, Pt. 1.

Kannada

[Abhijnanasakuntalam] Karnataka Śākuntala nāṭaka by Kalidasa; tr. into Kannada by B. Shivaramamurty Sastri. *In* Sanskrit Association Kālidasa Volume (Kālidāsasampuṭaḥ) / ed. by Mallikarjuna Paraddi, Devangere : D.R.M. College, 1970. Pp. 13 - 20.

[Abhijnanasakuntalam] Karnataka Śākuntala nāṭaka / by Kalidasa; tr. into Kannada by Basavappa Sastri. - Mysore : [s.n.], 1883.

Asthana Vidwan Basavappa Sastry of Mysore was the second translator of this classic in Kannada. [1883 A.D.]. So excellent was this rendering that the author was awarded the title of "Abhinava Kalidas" by the then Maharaja of Mysore Krishnarao.

[Abhijnanasakuntalam] Karnataka Shakuntala natakam / by Kalidasa; tr. into Kannada by Basavappa sastri. - Mysore : Wesley Press and Publishing House, 1951.

116 p.; 21 cm.

Also published in 1922.

[Abhijnanasakuntalam] Gītāśakuntalā / by Kalidasa; tr. into Kannada by D.V. Gudappa .- Mysore : [s.n.], 1960.

Select stanzas in the form of songs.

[Abhijnanasakuntalam] Kalidasa kratigalu / by Kalidasa; tr. into Kannada by Devadu. - Holenarasipur : Adhyatma Prakashan, [n.d.].

82 p.; 16 cm.

Plays ?

Abhijñanāśākuntalam / by Kalidasa; tr. into Kannada by G.S. Balacharya, 1920.

Abhijñanāśākuntalam / by Kalidasa; tr. into Kannada by G. Venkatachar, 1914.

Abhijñanāśākuntalam / by Kalidasa; tr. into Kannada by J. Vaman Bhat .- Mangalore: [s.n.], 1935.

Abhijñanāśākuntalam / by Kalidasa; tr. into Kannada by M.B. Rainapur .- Belgaum: [s.n.], 1933.

Abhijñanāśākuntalam / by Kalidasa; tr. into Kannada by Masti Venkatesh Iyengar.

[Abhijnanasak untalam] Śākuntala nāṭaka navīna ṭike / by Kalidasa; tr. into Kannada by Mummudi Krishnaraj Wadyar; ed. by M.A. Ramanuja Ayyangar .- Mysore : [s.n.], 1914.

[Abhijnanasakuntalam] Śākuntalamṭakam / by Kalidasa; tr. into Kannada by Narahari Sastri Bellave. - Bangalore : [s.n.], 1926.

Abhijñanāśākuntalam / by Kalidasa; tr. into Kannada by S.N. Mallikarjunappa, 1953.

[Abhijnanasakuntalam] Śākuntala nāṭakavu / by Kalidasa; tr. into Kannada by Sheshagirirao Ramachandra Churamari, 1869.

Two centuries were to elapse, before Kannada literature could boast of its second play, ie., "Karnataka Shakuntala Natakam" by Churamani Sheshagiri Rao in 1869 A.D. The First Kannada play was "Mitravinda Govinda of Singararya" written as late as 1700 A.D.

[Abhijnanasakuntalam] Śākuntala nāṭakavu / by Kālidāsa; tr. by Śēṣagirirāv Rāmacandra Curamani; preface by Mudavīḍu Kṛṣṇa Rāy. - 4th ed. - Belgaum : Vidyāraṇya Granthamala, 1934.

xlii, 194 p.; 18 cm.

First published in 1869.

[Abhijnanasakuntalam] Shakuntal / by Kalidasa; tr. into Kannada by Churamani Sheshagiri Rao. - Bangalore : Karnatak Natak Akademi, 1989.

xvi, 224 p.

[Abhijnanasakuntalam] Śakuntale / by Kālidāsa; tr. into Kannada by Vāmana Bha- Mangalore : Bhaṭ & Co., 1935.

iii, 88 p.; 18 cm.

Tr. of Abhijñānaśākuntalam.

Kannada Kalidasa mahasamputa / by Kalidasa; tr. into Kannada by S.V.

Parameshvara Bhatta .- Kohaje : Snatakottara Kendra, 1972.

xiv, 1190 p.; 22 cm.

Kannada Kālidāsa Mahasampuṭa: Kālidāsan Kṛtigaḷu/by S.V. Parameshvarabhatta.- Mysore : [s.n.], 1962.

In the history of Indian literature, the onerous effort of rendering the entire works of Kalidasa from Sanskrit into Kannada is a memorable landmark. Well known literateur and scholar Prof. S.V. Parameshwara Bhatta's '*Kalidasa maha samputa*' is hailed as a wonder of the Kannada literary world by Rashtrakavi Kuvempu. Thirumale Tatacharya Sharma called it Bhatta's magnum opus and described the author as Kannada Kalidasa. The book is a beautifully produced translation of all the works of Kalidasa alongwith the original text in Sanskrit Bhatta has translated 'Ritusamhara', 'Meghadootam', 'Kumarasambhavam' and 'Raghuvamsham' into Kannada verse while the plays 'Malavikagnimitra' and 'Vikramorvasheeyam' have been translated in the prose form, interespersed with verse as in the original. Prof. Bhatta was not the first to translate Abhijnana Shakuntalam into the Kannada and neither does he feel he should be the last. Every generation, he says, should discover Kalidasa for itself, writes M.S. Raghunath.

The book 'Kannada Kalidasa Mahasamputa' received the Sahitya Akademi Translation Prize of 1990.

(Prof S.V. Parameshwara Bhatta)

[Shakuntala] / by Kalidasa *In* Raghunatha Rao, R. The art of translation .- New Delhi : Bharatiya Anuvad Parishad, 1990.

Includes excerpts from the Kannada version of Shakuntala alongwith M.M. Williams English rendering and original Sanskrit text.

Adaptation

Inamdar, V.M. Kalidasa Kathanakagalu .- Dharwad : R.G. Hukkeri, 1955.

165 p.; 18 cm.

In Kannada.

Subanna, K.V. Loka Shakuntala:- Sagara: Akshara Prakashana, 1990.

'Loka Shakuntala' of K.V. Subanna is an adaptation of Kalidasa's Abhijñana Shākuntalam and is one of the outstanding plays of contemporary Kannada theatre.

Latin

Abhijñanaśākuntalam / by Kalidasa; tr. into Latin, 1908.

Anonymous (Translator).

Reference in Orientalische Bibliographic (Oriental Bibliographic), Vol. XXIII - XXIV.

Śakuntalā : neue ausgabe in lateinischen typen / by Kalidasa; tr. into Latin.

Anonymous (Translator).

Reference in M. Schuyler's 'Bibliography of Sanskrit Drama'.

Maithili

Śakuntalā nāṭak / by Kālidāsa; tr. by Īśanāth Jhā .- Darbhanga : Sāhitya Patra Kāryālay, 1939.

120, 6 p.; 22 cm.

Malayalam

Abhijnana Śākuntalam / by Kalidasa; tr. into Malayalam by A.D. Harisharma .- Kottayam : [s.n.], 1965.

Abhijñānaśākuntalam / by Kālidāsa; tr. into Malayalam by A. Gōvinda Piḷḷa .- Trivandrum : Bhāskara Press, 1914.

160 p.; 22 cm.

[Abhijnanasakuntalam] Duṣyantanum Śakuntalam athavā premāṅgulīyakam / by Kalidasa; tr. into Malayalam by A. Krishna Menon .- 1936.

Also published from Trichur in 1950. A free prose translation.

[Abhijnanasakuntalam] Malayāḷa Śākuntaḷam / by Kālidāsa; tr. by A.R. Rājarāja Varma .- 5th ed. Trivandrum : Kamalālaya Book Depot, 1953.

lvi, 104 p.; 21 cm.

First published in 1913.

This rendering was in a way a protest against the highly Sanskritised version of Kerala Verma.

Also published in 1962.

A.R. Rajaraja Varma

Abhijñanaśakuntalam / by Kalidasa; tr. into Malayalam by Attukal Nilakant Pilla.

[Abhijnanasakuntalam] Kēraḷa Śākuntaḷam / by Kālidāsa; tr. by Āṭṭūr Kṛṣṇa Piṣ āraṭi .- Trichur : Maṅgaḷōdayam, 1936.

135 p.; 19 cm.

[Abhijnanasakuntalam] Kerala Sakuntalam / by Kalidasa; tr. into Malayalam by Attoor Krishna Pisharaṭi .- 4th ed. - Trichur : Mangalodayam, 1952.

125 p.; 18 cm.

Abhijnanasākuntaḷam : [Kēśavīyam] / by Kālidāsa; tr. into Malayalam by Avaṇapparampu Kēśavan Nampūtirippāṭu .- Vadakancheri : Aruṇōdayam Press, 1952.

188 p.; 19 cm.

Abhijnanasākuntaḷam / by Kālidiāsa; tr. into Malayalam by Ayilyam Tirunāḷ Rāma Varma .- Trivandrum : Śrīdhara Power Press, 1930.

137 p.; 19 cm.

Foreword by E.V. Krishna Pillai. First published in 1882.

Also published in 1961 from Kottayam.

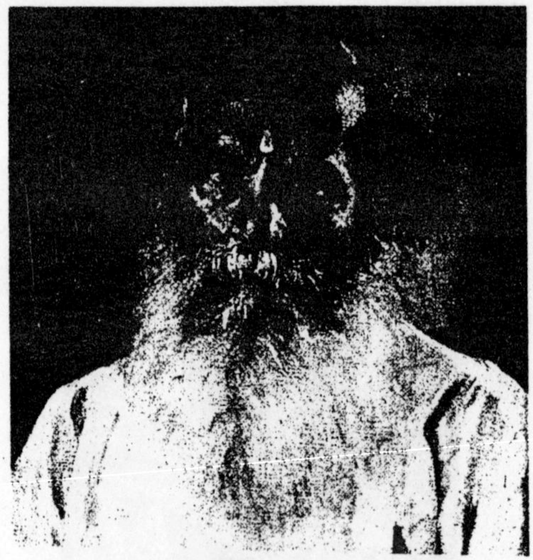

RAMA VARMA

Abhijñanaśākuntalam / by Kalidasa; tr. into Malayalam by Chattukutty Mannadiar.

Abhijnana Śākuntaḷam / by Kālidāsa; tr. by Ceruśśēri Mādhava Mēnōn; introd. by Vaṭakkuṅkūr Rājarāja Varma .- Kozhikode : Kēraḷa Press, 1949.

168 p.; 22 cm.

[Abhijnanasakuntalam] Bhāṣa Śākuntalam / by Kalidasa; tr.into Malayalam by Ceruliyil Kunnunni Nampishan .- 1949.

Also published in 1956.

7th ed. published from Kottayam in 1972.

Abhijnana Śakuntalam / by Kalidasa; tr. into Malayalam by Cheruḷiyil Kuñjuṇṇi Nampiśan .- 9th ed.- Kottayam : SPCS, 1976.

130 p.; 18 cm.

Abhijñanaśākuntalam/ by Kalidasa; tr. into Malayalam by Eruvail Chakrapani Variar.

Abhijnanasakuntalam / by Kalidasa; tr. into Malayalam by I. Nirunal [Maharaja of Tiruvankur], 1850.

This is the first Malayalam rendering, as opined by Dr. K.M. George.

Abhijnana Śākuntaḷam / by Kalidasa; tr. into Malayalam by J. Verghese. - Cochin: [s.n.], 1955.

Abhijñānaśākuntaḷam / by Kālidāsa; tr. into Malayalam by K. Mūttatu Kumāran; foreword by E.V. Kṛṣṇa Piḷla .- Trivandrum : B.V. Book Depot, 1935.

181 p.; 23 cm.

Abhijñanaśākuntalam / by Kalidasa; tr. into Malayalam by K. Nairu Nayar .- Cannore : [s.n.], 1955.

Abhijñanaśākuntalam / by Kalidasa; tr. into Malayalam by K.S. Nilakanta Nunni.- Alleppey : [s.n.], 1970.

[Abhijnanasakuntalam] Keḷīśākuntalam / by Kalidasa; tr. into Malayalam by Kaladi Raman Nampyar .- Chalakuddi : [s.n.], 1955.

[Abhijnanasakuntalam] Maṇipravāḷa Śākuntaḷam / by Kālidāsa; tr. by Kēraḷa Varma Valiya Koyittampurān; ed. by Rāma Varma Appan Tampurān .- Trivandrum: B.V. Book Depot, 1953.

xxxii, 149, [42] p.; 18 cm.

First published in 1882.Present work is the first Sanskrit drama to be translated into Malaylam.

Kerala Varma's rendering of Abhijñanaśākuntalam in Malayalam was published under the title 'Keraliya - Bhasa - Sakuntalam' in fourteen instalments in the journal Vidyavilasini during the period 1881 - 1882. The work appeared in the journal under the pseudonym "Oru Keraliyan" (a Keralite) Soon after its publication in the journal was completed, the drama was printed in the Keralavilasam Press and issued in book form in the year 1882 with slight textual variation.

Kerala Varma

Manipravala Shakuntalam

The Abhijñanashakuntala of Kalidasa translated into Malayalam by Kerala Varma Valiya Koil Tampuran (1845 - 1915) is popularly known as of Prof. S.V. Parameshwara Bhatta (Kannada)]'Manipavalashakuntalam', because of the excessive use of Sanskrit by the author. One of the first and foremost authors of Kerala to introduce a work of Kalidasa in the vernacular, Kerala Varma got the appropriate distinction of being referred to as Keralakalidasa throughout the land.

The work appeared in print in the year 1882, though it was first serialized in the journal Vidyavilasini', edited by P. Govinda Pillai, the first historian of Malayalam literature.

The text was later revised with minor variations and issued in the book form, broughout by Keralvailasam Press. The original title given to the work, was 'Keralabhashakuntalam' though the book received wider acclamation for his unique rendering of Shakuntala, but because of the preponderance of Sanskrit in this Malayalam version, he had to bow before the pressure from the world of scholars to simplify his style. So nine years later, he broughout another version under the new title 'Manipravalashakuntalam'. But the work remained inaccessible to the common reader.

If we keep aside this limitation, Kerala Varma's version remains a classic.

Abhijnanasakuntalam / by Kalidasa; tr. into Malayalam by Komittapuranam.

Abhijñānaśākuntalam / by Kalidasa; tr. into Malayalam by Kuttipuram Keshavan Nayar .- Kozhikode : [s.n.], 1956.

Abhijñanaśākuntalam / by Kalidasa; tr. [ed.] into Malayalam by M.R. Velu Pilla. - 1953.

Includes comm. 'Quilon'.

2nd ed. published in 1954.

3rd published in 1963.

Abhijñanaśākuntalam / by Kalidasa; tr. into Malayalam by P.G. Rama Ayyar.

Abhijñanaśākuntalam / by Kalidasa; tr. into Malayalam by P.K. Francis .- Trichur: [s.n.], 1954.

Abhijñanaśākuntalam / by Kalidasa; tr. into Malayalam by P.M. Parameshwaran Nambudiri. 4th ed. - Shoranur : [s.n.], 1952.

Abhijñanaśākuntalam / by Kalidasa; tr. into Malayalam by P.S. Variar.

Abhijñanaśākuntalam / by Kalidasa; tr. into Malayalam by R.C. Sharma.

Abhijñanaśākuntalam / by Kalidasa; tr. into Malayalam by Vallathol Narayan Menon, 1934.

Abhijñānaśākuntaḷam / by Kālidāsa; tr. by Vaḷḷattōḷ Nārāyaṇa Mēnōn; introd. by C.S. Nāyar. 4th ed. Trichur : Vaḷḷattōḷ Printing House, 1953.

218 p.; 23 cm.

Abhijnanasakuntalam / by Kalidasa; tr. into Malayalam by Vaḷḷattoḷ Narayaṇa Menon.- 5th ed. - Cheruthuruthy : Vaḷḷattoḷ Granthalayam, 1954.

218 p.; 21 cm.

This edition contains the comm. Priyamvada' by Kuttikrishna Marar.

[Abhijnanasakuntalam] Keralaśākuntalam / by Kalidasa; tr. into Malayalam by Veḷuttattu Narayanam Nampitri .- Trichur : [s.n.], 1954.

Abhijnanasakuntalam / by Kalidasa;a tr. into Malayalam by Venikkulam Gopal Kurup .- Ernakulam : [s.n.], 1957.

A free Malayalam Malayalam rendering.

Manipuri

Abhijñāna Śakuntalam / by Kālidāsa; tr. from Sanskrit by Aribam Brajabehārī Śarmā .- Imphal : O.K. Store, 1965.

viii, 167 p.; 18 cm. Drama.

Śakuntalā / by Kālidāsa; tr. by Phurāilatpam Bāsudev Śarmā .- Impahl : The translator, 1948.

104 p.; 18 cm.

Manipuri rendering from original Sanskrit.

Marathi

[Abhijnanasakuntalam] Śākuntalam / by Kalidasa; tr. into Marathi *In* Kāvyanāṭ akādarśa. Dharwar : [s.n.], 1881.

Anonymous (Translator).

[Abhijnanasakuntalam] Saṅgita Sākuntala nāṭaka / by Kalidasa; tr. into Marathi .- Poona : [s.n.], 1887.

Anonymous (Translator).

[Abhijnanasakuntalam] Shakuntal / by Kalidasa; tr. into Marathi by Annasaheb Kirloskar .- 1880.

Abhijñānaśākuntalam / by Kalidasa; tr. into Marathi by B.P. Kirloskar .- Poona : [s.n.], 1881.

9th ed. published from Poona in 1930.

A Musical adaptation for stage.

[Abhijnanasakuntalam] Marathi sarūpa Śākuntala / by Kalidasa; tr. into Marathi by Balkrishna Lakshman Antarakar .- Devrukh : [s.n.], 1929.

Abhijñanaśākuntalam / by Kalidasa; tr. into Marathi by D.M. Hatavalane .- Poona: [s.n.], 1956.

[Abhijnanasakuntalam] Natyarupa Śakuntala / by Kalidasa; tr. into Marathi by D.S. Ambapkar .- Kolhapur : [s.n.], 1961 - 62.

An introduction by Vasant Shantaram Desai.

Abhijñanaśākuntalam / by Kalidasa; tr. into Marathi by Govind Keshav Bhat. *In* Pāñca Saṁskṛta nāṭakeṁ .- Poona : [s.n.], 1960.

[Abhijnanasakuntalam] Mahārāṣṭra Śākuntala / by Kalidasa; tr. into Marathi by Keshav Vinayak Godbole .- Poona : The translator, 1925.

112, 6 p.; 17.5 cm.

—— 2nd ed. - Bombay : [s.n.], 1965.

Tr. into Marathi in the same metre.

Abhijñanaśākuntalam / by Kalidasa; tr. into Marathi by Krishna Śāstrī Rajvade. - Bombay : [s.n.], 1869.

Abhijñānaśakuntalam / by Kalidasa; tr. into Marathi by L.G. Lele - 1905.

Also published in 1926.

Tr. into prose & verse.

Abhijñānaśākuntalam / by Kalidasa; tr. into Marathi by M.R. Sadwilkar .- 1905.

A musical adaptation.

Abhijñānaśākuntalam / by Kalidasa; tr. into Marathi prose by Mahadev Chimanji Apte. Pt. 1 .- Poona : [s.n.], 1881.

[Abhijnanasakuntalam] Śākuntala : sār va vicār / by Kālidāsa; tr. into Marathi by Mahādev Vyaṅkateś Lele .- Bombay : Vividhjñānavistār, 1905.

vi, 110 p.; 24 cm.

Marathi rendering in abridged form with notes and occasional comments.

Abhijñānaśākuntalam / by Kalidasa; tr. into Marathi by Parasuram Pant Godbole.- Poona : [s.n.], 1861.

Abhijñanaśākuntalam / by Kalidasa; tr. into Marathi by R.B. Gunjikar .- Bombay: [s.n.], 1870.

[Abhijnanasakuntalam] Kālidāsācīṁ nāṭakeṁ / by Kalidasa; tr. into Marathi by R.P. Kangle .- Bombay : [s.l.], 1957.

Collected dramas of Kalidasa.

In Marathi.

Abhijñanaśākuntalam / by Kalidasa; tr. into Marathi by Rama V.N. Dongre - 1890.

Abhijñānaśākuntalam / by Kalidasa; tr. into Marathi by Ramchandra Shankar Valibe? .- Poona : [s.n.], 1956.

Edited with notes etc.

Abhijñanaśākuntalam / by Kalidasa, tr. into Marathi by V.G. Joshi .- 1893.

Nepali

Abhijñāna Śākuntalam / by Kalidasa .- Varanasi : Ārya Bhūṣan Press, 1976.

123 p.; 17 cm.

Nepali rendering of Sanskrit drama.

Abhijñana Śakuntalam / by Kalidasa, tr. into Nepali by Harinarayan Upadhyay.

Abhijnana Śakuntalam / by Kalidasa; tr. into Nepali by Harkabahādur Sāhi. Shillong: [s.n.], 1952.

[Abhijnanasakuntalam] Sakuntal / by Kalidasa; tr. into Nepali by Lakshmiprasad Devkota .- 1945. A poetic play.

Lakshmiprasad Devkota (b. 1909), a prolific Nepali writer had written his first epic based on Kalidasa's classic 'Sakuntal (a poetic play) in the year 1945. This literary form in Nepali was, as he said in his preface, 'like the serpent of Iceland'. He composed its 1754 stanzas in twenty different metres in three months. Such as Shardulavikridita, Mandakranta, Vasantatilaka and Drutavilambita. This adaptation of the great ancient play may not be of high literary standards owing to its lengthy dialogues and monotonous descriptions. But penned by a great romantic poet, this voluminous work in 24 contos has a historical value that remains an important contribution in the realm of poetic play for his mastery over classical Sanskrit diction, metres and figures of speech.

Critical Lakhi Devi Sundas points out that "Devkota's originality can be seen in his characterisation, dialogues and descriptions of nature which reflect Nepali character, social life and land scape. Devkota introduces among Shakunala's friends not only Priyambada and Anusuya but Charu, a third character, also. She is a very lively character who playfully teases Shakuntala for having fallen in love with Dushyanta, and comforts her when she is in a melancholy mood. Charu is an immensely realistic human character. Devkota has added a new incident also in his play. In Kalidasa's play Dushyanta does not want to go back to his capital leaving Shakuntala behind in the Ashram, because he is deeply in love with her. The Queen Mother has kept 'putra pinda upawasa' (fast for the the well - being of the son); so Dushyanta's presence is a must on the occasion. Dushyanta sends Vidushaka to the Queen Mother with the message that he (Vidushaka) be treated as son. In Devkota's Shakuntal a message comes that the enemies have attacked the kingdom, so he must return immediately to safeguard it. Dushyanta sends back the message that he has to offer protection to the rishish (sages) in their 'yajna' and he was duty - bound to stay back in the Ashram."

Abhijñānaśākuntalam / by Kalidasa; tr. into Nepali by Lekhnath .- Kathmandu : Nepal Academy, 1958.

vi, 106 p.: ill.; 24.5 cm.

Abhijñana Sakuntala / by Kalidasa; tr. into Nepali by Pahalman Singh Swar, 1959.

[Abhijnanasakuntalam] Śakuntal / by Kalidasa; tr. into Nepali by Śambhuprasad Dhuṅgel. *Gorkhali;* 1916.

[Abhijnanasakuntalam] Śakuntalā nāṭak / by Kālidāsa; tr. by Śambhuprasād Dhuṅgel.- Varanasi : Hitaiṣī Co., 1940.

220 p.; 22 cm.

First appeared serially in *Gorkhali* from Varanasi in 1916.

Rendered into Nepali from original Sanskrit drama.

Oriya

[Abhijnanasakuntalam] Śākuntala chānda / by Kalidasa; tr. into Oriya by Anant Rath .- Cuttuck : [s.n.], 1900.

Abhijnana Sakuntalam / by Kalidaa; tr. into Oriya by Baishnab Pani .- Cuttuck : [s.n.], 1955.

Abhijñanaśākuntalam / by Kalidasa; tr. into Oriya by Birmitrodaya Simhadev .- 1900.

Abhijñānaśākuntałam / by Kalidasa; tr. into Oriya by Dhaneshwar Mahapatra .- Cuttuck : [s.n.], 1961.

[Abhijnanasakuntalam] Shakuntala / by Kalidasa tr. into Oriya by Dhaneshwar Patnaik.

The Oriya version was staged in Sept. 1975 by the leading theatre of Cuttuck "Annapurva 'B' Group'.

Abhijñānaśākuntalam / by Kalidasa; tr. into Oriya by Gangadhar Meher.

In free kāvya form with additions.

Abhijnana Śakuntalam / by Kalidasa; tr. into Oriya by Gopal Krishna Panda .- Berhampur : [s.n.], 1963.

Abhijnanasakuntalam / by Kalidasa; tr. into Oriya by Gopinath Nandi.

(Gopinath Nandi, an Oriya Litterateur; remembered for his version of 'Shakuntala')

Abhijñānaśākuntalam / by Kalidasa; tr. into Oriya by Harihar Rath .- [s.l.] : [s.n.], 1898.

In prose form.

Persian

[Abhijnanasakuntalam] Aṅgushtar - i - Gumshudā / by Kalidasa; tr. into Persian by Ali Asghar Hikmat .- Delhi : University of Delhi, 1955.

Abhijñānaśākuntalam / by Kalidasa; tr. into Persian by Hadi Hasan ?

Abhijñanaśākuntalam / by Kalidasa; tr. into Persian by Indu Shekhar.

Reference in Hiralal Chopra's 'Sanskrit classics in Persia' appeared in the summary of papers of the International Sanskrit Conference of 1972.

Polish

Abhijñānaśākuntalam / by Kalidasa; tr. into Polish by S. Schayer .- 1924.

Reference in 'Indian Studies Abroad' .- Bombay : [s.n.], 1964.

Siakuntala / by Kalidasa; tr. into Polish by Przelozyl Stanislaw Schayer .- Wroclaw: [s.n.], 1954.

Opracowal Eugeniusz Sluszkeiwicz.

[Biblioteka Narodowa; Series 2, No. 111].

Reference in 'General Catalogue of printed books : ten year suppliments, 1956 - 65 .- London [s.n.], 1968.

Siakuntala / by Kalidasa; tr. into Polish by S. Schayer.- Wroclaw : Biblioteka Narodowa, 1957.

[Indian Literature] ed. by Teofil Krasnosielski. *In* World Literature (Vol. 1) .- Warsaw : [s.n.], 1880. Pp. 59 - 144.

Includes fragments of Shakuntala in Polish translation.

Siakontala Czyli pierscien prezeznaczenia / by Kalidasa; tr. into Polish by Hrabia Grabowski .- Warsaw : [s.n.], 1861.

(Wielka Biblioteka; No. 93)

Also published in 1924.

In Poland, the first attempt at translating was undertaken by H.J. Grabowski in 1861 entitled 'Siakuntala or the Ring of Destiny : an Indian drama in seven acts with a prologue.

The first translation of Shakuntala from the original appeared in Poland only in 1924. It was rendered by Stainislaw Schayer.

Redited in 1957 in the series *National Library* with the foreword of Sluszkiewicz.

Portuguese

Abhijñānaśākuntala : o reconhesimento de Chakuntalā impressao specimen do acto I do celebre drama de Kālidasa transladado litteralmente do Sanoskrit o segundo a recensao Bengali / by Kalidasa; tr. into Portuguese .- Lisbon: [s.n.] 1878.

Reference in Catalogueof the Library of the Indian Office. - London; 1938. Vol. II, Pt. 1.

Xakuntala : drama en 7 actos / by Kalidasa; tr. into Portuguese by Jośe F. Martins. - 2nd ed. - Angola : [s.n.], 1925.

Punjabi

[Abhijnanasakuntalam] Sakuntalā ate Sanskrit naṭaka diyān hora kahaniyān / by Kalidasa; tr. into Punjabi by Balwant Singh .- Amritsar : [s.n.], [n.d.].

The story of Śākuntala together with other stories of the Sanskrit plays into Punjabi.

Abhijñānaśākuntalam / by Kalidasa; tr. into Punjabi by Brijlal Sastri.

Story based on Kalidasa's magnum opus.

Abhijñānaśākuntalam / by Kalidasa; tr. into Punjabi by Charan Singh .- Amritsar : [s.n.], 1899.

[Abhijnanasakuntalam] Kalidasa de natak / by Kalidasa; tr. [from HIndi] into Punjabi by Jagadish Anand Dikshit .- Jalladhar : [s.n.], 1963.

Abridgement of Kalidasa plays in prose style.

Abhijnana Śākuntalam / by Kalidasa; tr. Punjabi by Pyara Singh Sahirai .- Delhi : [s.n.], 1962.

A metrical translation.

Rajasthani

Sakuntala / by Kalidasa; adapted into Rajasthani by Karanidan Barahath .- Phephana (Sriganganagar) : Barahath Pakashan, 1974.

100 p.; 18 cm.

Book recieved Sahitya Akademi Award.

Karnidan Barhath (b. 1925), author of Rajasthani epic 'Shakuntala'.

Russian

Kālidāsa dramii / tr. from French by K. Bel'mont with an introduction by Oldenberg. Moscow : [s.l.], 1916, In Russian.

Collected dramas of Kālidāsa.-. Moscow : [s.n.], 1955.

This edition contains an introd. and comments by I.S. Robinovich.

Śakuntala / by Kalidasa; tr. into Russian by A. Patyata. In *Russkii Vestnik* (Moscow), Aug. 1879. Vol. 142, Appendix, Pp. 1 - 48; Sept. 1879, Vol. 143; Pp. 49 - 80 & Oct. 1879; Pp. 81 - 148.

[Śakuntalā] / by Kalidasa; tr. into Russian by N. Volotsky .- Vologda : [s.n.], 1890.

Śakuntala : Indian drama in 7 acts / by Kalidasa; tr. into Russian .- St. Petersburg: [s.n.], 1868. Tr. of Act I.

Ananymous (Translator)

Scenes from Shakuntala : the Indian drama / by Kalidasa; tr. into Russian by N.M. Karamzin. *Mosk Zhurnal,* 1792. Pt. 6, bk. 2; Pp. 125 - 156; bk. 3; Pp. 294 - 323.

Act I - IV only.

Selected writings from Kālidāsa / by I.S. Robinovich .- Moscow : [s.n.], 1956.

In Russian language.

Sindhi

[Abhijnanasakuntalam] Kavi Kalidas ja amar pustak / by Kalidas; tr. into Sindhi by A.T. Gidwani .- Hyderabad : Blavatsky Press, [n.d.].

[308] p.; 18.5 cm.

[Abhijnanasakuntalam] Shakuntalā / by Kālidāsa; tr. into Sindhi (from English) by Kalyāṇ Būlcand Āḍvāṇī; foreword by Nārāiṇdās Bhaṭhījā .- Hyderabad, Sind : Candan Printing Press, 1946.

xxxvi, 154 p.; 17 cm.

Shakuntala / by Kalidasa; tr. into Sindhi by Kalyan B. Advani .- Bombay : Hindustan Ktabghar, 1955.155 p.; 18 cm.

Also published in 1962 in Devanagari / Sindhi script.

[Abhijnanasakuntalam] Shakuntala / by Kālidāsa; tr. into Sindhi by Mirza Qalich Beg .- 1896.

Spanish

Śakuntala : version directa del Sanskrit / by Kalidasa; tr. into Spanish by F. Garcia Ayuso .- Madrid : Ayuso .- Madrid : [s.n.], 1875.

(Biblioteca Sanskrita)

Swedish

Schakuntalā, eller den Fōrlorade Ringen : elt Indisk skadespel of Kalidasa, ōfversatt och fōrklaradt / by Kalidasa; tr. into Swedish by H. Edgren .- Stockholm: [s.n.], 1875.

Śakuntala / by Kalidasa; tr. into Swedish by Frans Hedberg .- Stockholm : [s.n.], 1905.

Śakuntalā : ett Indiskt dramatiskt poem af Kālidāsā; ofversatt from Sanskrit pa Engelska of W. Jones, och efter denn samt G. Forsters / by Kalidasa; tr. into Swedish by J. Ekelund .- Stockholm : [s.n.], 1821.

Tamil

[Abhijnanasakuntalam] Śākuntala nāṭakam / by Kālidāsa; tr. into Tamil by A. Kumarakurupara Ātittar .- [s.l.] : The translator, 1938.

iv, 125 p.; 19 cm.

[Abhijnanasakuntalam] Śākuntala nataka araycci / by Kalidasa; tr. into Tamil by Aṭkaḷ Maraimalai .- Madras : [s.n.], 1907.

Also published in 1934 & 1960

Author's pseudonym is N. Vedachalam.

[Abhijnanasakuntalam] Kāḷidāsa Śākuntalam / by Kālidāsa; tr. into Tamil by C.S. Saccidāṇanda Dīkṣita .- Chidambaram : Naṭanakuñcitapāda Sabhai, 1949.

xii, 126 p.; 21 cm.

Tr. of Abhijñānaśākuntalam.

[Abhijnanasakuntalam] Śākuntalam, Mēghadūta / by Kālidāsa; tr. into Tamil by K. Santāṇam .- Madras : Sundara Pracurālayam, 1953.

iii, 186 p.; ill.; 21 cm.

Abhijñānaśākuntalam / by Kalidasa; tr. into Tamil by M. Duraiswami Iyengar.

An unpublished work.

[Abhijnanasakuntalam] Cakuntalai natakam / tr. into Tamil by Naraimalai Atikal.- Pallāvaram : [The translator], 1907.

[Abhijnanasakuntalam] Śākuntala nāṭakam / by Kalidaa; tr. into Tamil by

Maraimalai Aṭikaḷ .- 2nd ed.- Pallavaram : The translator, 1933.

iv, 220 p.; 22 cm.

3rd ed. published in 1940.

Abhijnana Śākuntalam / by Kalidasa; tr. into Tamil by M.S. Natarajan .- Madras: [s.n.], 1962.

Also published in 1964.

[Abhijnanasakuntalam] Śakuntalai / by Kālidāsa; tr. by P. Sambandha Mutaliyār.- Madras : The translator, 1929.

72 p.; 21 cm.

Tr. of Abhijñānaśākuntalam.

[Abhijnanasakuntalam] Cakuntalai or lost ring / by Kalidasa; tr. into Tamil by Pavānantam Pillai.

This is infact an adaptation of the Sanskrit play.

Abhijñānaśākuntalam / by Kālidāsa; tr. into Tamil by R. Rāghava Ayyaṅkar .- Madras : The translator, 1938.

xix, 134 p. : ill.; 21 cm.

Includes index.

Title 'Apinana Cakuntala'

Abhijñānaśākuntalam / by Kalidasa; tr. into Tamil by Ramachandra. *Revue de la linguistique;* 1886 - 88; Vol. XIX - XXI.

[Abhijnanasakuntalam] Śākuntalai / by Kalidasa; tr. into Tamil by S.A. Ramaswami.- Madras : [s.n.], 1965.

An abridged prose translation.

Abhijñānaśākuntalam / by Kalidasa; tr. into Tamil by S. Bhavanandam Pillai .- Madras : [s.n.], 1912.

[Abhijnanasakuntalam] Śakuntalai / by Kālidāsa, tr. into Tamil by S. Bhavānandam Piḷḷai .- Madras : Bhavānandam Academy, 1922.

196 p.; 18 cm.

Tr. of Abhijñānaśākuntalam.

Adaptation

Ananta Palppanāpan. Sakuntalai nātakam = a tale of romance / ed. by A. Thasarathan; tr. into English by V. Gowri Shanker .- Madras : Institute of Asian Studies, 1994.

377 p. - (Folklore of Tamil Nadu Series; No. 6).

Includes Tamil Text.

This play bears the Accession number 182 in the Manuscripts Library of the Institute of Asian Studies, Madras; it is 45 centimetre long and 3.5 centimetre wide. This palm - leag manuscript was obtained by Dr. Ramachandran of S.T. Hindu College Nagar Kōil from Mr. Ku. Mumaracuvāmi, a retired Deputy Commissioner for Commercial Taxes belonging to Akastisvaram of Kanyakumari district. Coming to know of this from the newspaper, Messers. G. Stephen and N. Ramachandran Nair secured this from Dr. Ramachandran and presented to the library.

Both in literary motif and form this play deviates from Kalidasa's great master piece, a folk play based on the Mahabharatam original.

The author Ananta Palppanapan mentions his master Kamaracami Nakamani Marttanta Natar as having activated him to compose this folk play from an epic saga. The play is divided into 40 scenes and is a compound of songs, prose and verse. The invocations are made of veṇpā verse forms and songs consist of viruttams. The main play is composed of varied styles of narration such as tarus, viruttam songs and Kaṭṭ aḷaikkalilturai, a literary device much favoured by playwrights is conscpicuously present in this play. The idea conveyed ornately by the viruttam is elegantly expanded in the taru and is seen simplified in he vacanam or prose portions. This is further simplified in the prose exchanges where the patois and the peculiar idioms of the local folks crop their heads lending a quaint charm, peculiar flavour and piquancy.

Cakuntalai vilācam / by Irāmaccantira Kavirāyar.

Tamil play crafted towards the end of the 19th century, on the basis of the story 'Shakuntala'.

Telugu

Abhijñānaśākuntalam / by Kalidasa; tr. into Telugu by Ambatipudi Ramabrahman, 1912.

Abhijñānaśākuntalam / by Kalidasa; tr. into Telugu by Bangariah .- 1952.

Abhijnana Śakuntalam / by Kalidasa; retold in Telugu by Bharati .- Vijayawada : Vinoda Publications, 1956.

32 p.; 17.5 cm.

Abhijnana Śakuntalām / by Kalidasa; tr. into Telugu by Bhavanarayan Rao, 1964.

[Abhijnanasakuntalam] Śrīmadāndhrābhijñānaśākuntalamu / by Kālidāsa; tr. into Telugu by Bhuvanagiri Vijayarāmayya .- Guntur : The translator, 1949.

iii, 108 p.; 21 cm.

Abhijnana Śakuntalam / by Kalidasa; tr. into Telugu by Dasu Srimalu Pantulu .- 1883.

Also published in 1931.

Telugu prose and verse rendering.

Reference in *Orientalis che Bibliographie* 1898; Vol. XII; P. 72.

Abhijnana Śākuntalam / by Kālidasa; tr. into Telugu by Durgaraju Rangarao .- Vijayawada : [s.n.], 1965.

Abhijñānaśākuntalam / by Kalidasa; tr. into Telugu by Durlabha Subrahmanya Sarma, 1955.

[Abhijnanasakuntalam] Madhura Śākuntalamu / by Kalidasa; tr. into Telugu by Gaṇapati Śāstrī Carla .- Samisragudem : [s.n.], 1962.

Abhijñānaśākuntalam / by Kalidasa; tr. into Telugu by Guda Krishnayya .- 1912.

Abhijñānaśākuntalam / by Kalidasa; tr. into Telugu by Gurramu Venkata Subrahmanyyam, Rapalle : [s.n.], 1958.

Abhijñānaśākuntalam / by Kalidasa; tr. into Telugu by K.V.N. Appa Rao.

Abhijñānaśākuntalam / by Kālidāsa; tr. into Telugu by Kākarla Koṇḍalarāvu .- Narasapur : P Vīrarāghavasōmayājulu, 1930.

40 p.; 21 cm.

Abhijñānaśākuntalam / by Kālidāsa; tr. into Telugu by Kāñcanapalli Kanakāmba.- 2nd ed. - Vijayawada : Śrī Tirumala Śrīnivāsa Trilinga Mahāvidyāpīṭhamu, 1941.

xxx, 111 p.; 21.5 cm.- (Kavitilaka Goranthamāla; 2)

First published in 1935.

Abhijñānaśākuntalam / by Kalidasa tr. into Telugu by Kandukuri Viresalingam .- Rajahmundry : [s.n.], 1883.

Abhijnana Sakuntalam / by Kalidasa; tr. into Telugu by Kandukuri Viresalingam .- Rajahmundry : Hitakari Samaj, 1952.

135 p.; 19.5 cm.

Abhijñānaśākuntalam / by Kālidāsa; tr. into Telugu by Kandukūri Vīrēśaliṅgamu.- 7th ed. - Rajamundry : J. Jagganna, 1950.

130 p.; 21 cm.

First published in 1883.

Abhijñānaśākuntalam / by Kalidasa; tr. into Telugu by Kasi Vyasacharya with Pratipadārthatātparya (Acts I - IV) .- Guntur : [s.n.], 1928.

Abhijñānaśākuntalam / by Kalidasa; tr. into Telugu by Kavi Mudikonda Mallikarjuna.- 1908.

[Abhijnanasakuntalam] Kālidāsanāṭakamu / by Kalidasa; tr. into Telugu by Kolachalam Srinivasarao, 1925.

Abhijñānaśākuntalam / by Kalidasa; tr. into Telugu by Kotta Satyanarayana Choudhury, 1958.

Abhijñānaśākuntalam / by Kalidasa; tr. into Telugu by M. Sheshacharyulu. -1870.

Abhijnanaśakuntalam / by Kalidasa; tr. into Telugu by Mannavar Lakhnavi .- Delhi: [s.n.], 1963.

Abhijñānaśākuntalam / by Kālidāsa; tr. into Telugu by Mantripragaḍa Bhujaṅgarāvu.- Eluru : Rāma Press, 1919.

x, 104 p.; 21 cm.

Tr. of 'Abhijñānaśākuntalam'.

Abhijñānaśākuntalam / by Kalidasa; tr.into Telugu by Mocharla Ramakrishna Kavi.- Nellore : [s.n.], 1954.

Abhijñānaśākuntalam / by Kalidasa; tr. into Telugu by Narayan Śāstrī Mullapadi .- Ponnur : [s.n.], 1954.

Abhijnana Sakuntalam / by Kalidaa; tr. into Telugu by Nelatur Ramadasa Iyengar.- Madras : V. Ramasvami Sastri, 1957.

470 p.; 20.5 cm.

Abhijñānaśākuntalam / by Kālidāsa; tr. into Telugu by Panganāmāmula Rāmacandrarāvu .- Vijayawada : Dēśikavitā Maṇḍali, 1947.

iv, 114 p.; 20.5 cm.

Abhijñānaśākuntalam / by Kalidasa; tr. into Telugu by Paravastu Venkata Rangacharya .- 1872.

[Abhijnanasakuntalam] Śakuntalā nāṭakamu / by Kālidāsa; tr. into Telugu by Pēri Kāśīnāthaśāstri .- Madras : Vāviḷḷa Rāmasvami Śāstralu & Sons, 1926.

100 p.; 21 cm.

Abhijñānaśākuntalam / by Kalidasa; tr. into Telugu by Ramachandra Śastrī Korada.

Abhijñānaśākuntalam / by Kalidasa; tr. into Telugu by Ramakrishnanacharyulu Bhimaram Nanduri .- 1954 ?

Abhijñānaśākuntalam / by Kalidasa; tr. into Telugu by Ramanujatatacharya and others .- Madras : [s.n.], 1874.

Abhijñānaśākuntalam / by Kalidasa; tr. into Telugu by Rayadurgam Śāstrī Narasayya.- 1950.

Abhijñānaśākuntalam / by Kalidasa; tr. into Telugu by Shrinivasachari .- 1926.

Also published in 1934.

Abhijñānaśākuntalam / by Kālidāsa; tr. into Telugu by Vaḍḍādi Subbārāyuḍu .- Rajamahendra varam : The translator, 1906.

vi, 123 p.; 21 cm.

Abhijñānaśākuntalam / by Kālidāsa; tr. into Telugu by Vatsavāyi Veṅkaṭanīlādrirāju.- Tuni : The translator, 1933.

119 p.; 18 cm.

Abhijñānaśākuntalam / by Kalidasa; tr. into Telugu by Vedam Venkataraya Śāstri.- Madras : [s.n.], 1883.

Abhijñānaśākuntalam / by Kālidāsa; tr. by Vēdamu Vēṅkaṭarāyaśāstri .- Madras : The translator, 1896.

iii, 89, [6] p.; 18 cm.

Also published in 1955.

Vedam Venkataraya Sastry
(Translator of all the plays of Kalidasa into Telugu)

[Abhijnanasakuntalam] Śakuntala / by Kālidāsa; tr. into Telugu by Vēṅkaṭa Pārvatiśvarakavulu alias Bālāntrapu Vēṅkaṭarāvu and Ōlēṭi Pārvatīśam .- Rajahmumdry : Śrī Satyanārāyaṇa Book Depot, 1951.

118 p.; 18 cm.

This Telugu version is based on Bengali translation by Īśvaracandra Vidyāsāgar.

Adaptation

Bālakṛṣṇamūrti Paṅganāmāmula. Kālidāsa Bhavabhūti Kathalu / by Paṅganāmāmula Bālakṛṣṇamūrti .- Vijayawada : Kavitilaka Granthamala, 1947.

iv, 88 p.; 18.5 cm.

Stories in Telugu from the plays of Kālidāsa and Bhavabhuīti.

Pina Virabhadrudu. Sringāra Shakuntala / by Kalidasa; tr. into Telugu by Pinaveerabhadra. 12th century ?

Pillalamarri Pina Virana alias Pina. Virabhadrudu's Śakuntala parinayamu or Śṛngāra Śākuntalamu is a narrative in Telugu. Theme is based on the story of Sakuntala and Dushyanta from the Mahābharata alongwith certain modifications made by Kalidasa in his play Abhijñāna Śākuntalam. This was an interesting experiment by author who drew his material and mode of communication from a narrative as well as a play and combining the best of the both.

Ukranian

Śakuntalā / by Kalidasa; tr. into Ukrainian by G. Khotkevich .- Kharkov : [s.n.], 1929.

Reference in *Bibliografia Indii,* Moscow (1965).

Śākuntala / by Kalidasa; tr. into Ukrainian .- Kiev : [s.n.], 1958.

Reference in *Bibliografia Indii,* Moscow (1965).

Urdu

Abhijnana Shakuntalām / by Kālidāsa; tr. by Akhtar Husain Rāipūrī .- Delhi : Anjuman Taraqqī - I - Urdū, 1939.

128 p.; 21 cm.

Abhijnanashakuntala / by Kālidāsa; tr. into Urdu by Kishan Chand Zeba .- Delhi: Lajpat Rai & Sons, [n.d.].

112 p.; 18 cm.

Abhigyānśakuntalam / by Kalidasa; tr. into Urdu by Qudsiyah Zaidi .- Aligarh : [s.n.], 1957.

Abhijnanashakuntalam / by Kalidasa; tr. into Urdu by Saghar Nizami .- New Delhi : Adabi Markaz, 1961.

100, 256 p.; 25 cm.

Abhijñānaśākuntalam / by Kalidasa; tr. into Urdu by Sayyad Akhtar Husain Raipuri.

CRITICAL STUDIES OF ABHIJNANAŚAKUNTALAM

Acharya, P.B. 'The Denouncement and its dramatic propriety in Abhijnanaaskuntala, Uttararamacarita and Mṛcchakatika' / by P.B. Acharya. *Samskrit Ranga* (Annual Number), 1976.

Vol. 6; Pp. 38 - 58.

Adhikari, N.B. Śakuntala : an allegory. *All India Oriental Conference* I. Vol. i.li.

Adhikari, N.B. Sakuntala : an allegory. *SPAIOC* (Poona); 1920; Vol. 1; P. li.

Adhikari, N.S. Śakuntalā : an allegory / by N.S. Adhikari. *Proceedings and Transactions of the First Oriental Conference* at Poona, held on the 5th, 6th & 7th of Nov. 1919.

Adhikari, N.S. Sakuntala of Kalidasa; a new study III. *HR;* July - Dec. 1921; Vol. XLIV, No. 262; Aug. 1921, Vol. XLIV, No. 263; Pp. 76 - 88.

Agashe, Ganesh Janardan. Abhijnanasakuntalanataka *Vi. J. Vi;* March 1919; Vol. L. No. 3; Pp. 17 - 86.

An appreciation of the play.

Agrawal, V.S. Astamurti Siva. *Dr. Siddheshwar Varma Volume.*

Transaction of the Linguistic Circle of Delhi; Pp. 23 - 27.

Agrawal, V.S. Vasavadatta and the Sakuntala scenes in the Ranigumpha Cave of Orissa. *JISOA;* 1946; Vol. XIV; Pp. 102 - 109.

Ammal, K. Savitri. Anusuya and Priyamvada.

Triveni; Aug. 1948; Vol. XX, No. 1; Pp. 25 - 28.

Anonymous. Abhijnanasakuntalacarca .- Trivandrum : [s.n.], 1961.

(Anantasayanamsamskrtagranthavali; No. 191).

Anonymous. Abhijñānaśākuntalacarca / ed. by K. Raghavan Pillai .- Trivandrum: University of Kerala Sanskrit Series, 1961.
(Trivandrum Sanskrit Series).

Anonymous. Cakuntala nataka mozipeyarppum atan araicciyum. [s.l.] : [s.n.], 1934.

An article in Tamil on Sakuntala.

Reference in NLCCI.

Anonymous. Kalidasa's Sakuntala. *Aryan Path;* July 1944; Vol. XV, No. 7; Pp. 320 - 326.

Anonymous. A Note on Pravesaka of the Vikramorvasiyam and the Viṣkambhaka of Sakuntalam Act IV. *Vidya* (JGU); Jan. 1960; Vol. III, No. 1; Pp. 21 - 24.

Anonymous. Note on Sakuntala .- Calcutta : [s.n.], 1825. A literary study of the play in Bengali, English and Sanskrit.

Author could be Kalipada Mukerjee.

Anonymous. The Philosophy of Sakuntala. *Triveni;* Vol. IV, No. 5; Pp. 10 - 16.

Anonymous. Sakuntala ka naitik rahasya *Aj;* Nov. 1956; Vol. VIII, No. 11; P. 67.

A criticism of an article by Aditya Mishra.

Anonymous. Sakuntala ka Rusi bhasa men anuvad. *Aj* Sept. 1955; Vol. VII, No. 9; Pp. 77 ff.

Anonymous. Sakuntala : sar va vicara. *Vi J. Vi;* Oct. 1903; Vol. XXXIV, No. 10; Pp. 1 - 8 (Appendix); No. 11 - 12, Pp. 9 - 24; Feb. 1904, Vol. XXXV, No. 2; No. 3 - 4, Pp. 33 - 48, No. 5, Pp. 49 - 56, No. 6, Pp. 57 - 64, No. 7 - 12, Pp. 65 - 110.

An appreciation and summary of the drama in Marathi.

Anonymous. Sir William Jones edition : first book printed in Sanskrit *JAOS Proc.;* Vol. XVI; Pp. 253 ff.

Approaches to the Orient classic / ed. by Theodore de Bary .- New York : [s.n.], 1959.

Includes comments by Royal W. Weiler on the Sanskrit classic 'Shakuntala'. Pp. 132 - 136.

Atmaram Sastri. Sakuntale Kalidasasyamanovislesananaipuni. *Samvid;* Aug. - Nov. 1965; Vol. II, Nos. 1 - 2; Pp. 161 - 165.

Avanindrakumar Vidyalankara. Asramamrga aur asrama kanya. *Vikrama* (Hindi); Jul - Aug. 1952; Vol. VI, No. 4; Pp. 41 - 44.

Avasthi, Brahmamittra. Sakuntale Kalidasasya vyaktitvam. *Sag.* [Sam. 2028]; Vol. X, No. 2; Pp. 203 - 208.

Ayyangar, N. Ramdas. Some notes on Śākuntala / by N. Ramdas Ayyangar. *Annals of the Bhandarkar Oriental Research Institute;* 1973; Vol. LIV, Nos. I - IV. Pp. 24 - 214.

Bakalov, A. Shakuntala conquers Riga / by A. Bakalov. *Soviet Land;* May, 1960.

Balbir, J.K. A Suggestion for a ballet Abhijnanasakuntalam. *JGJRI;* May - Aug 1959 ?; Vol. XVI, Nos. 3 - 4; Pp. 379 - 395.

Balbir, J.K. A Suggestion for a ballet - Abhijnanasakuntala. *SPAIOC* (Annamalai) 1955; Vol. XVII.

Bangarayya, Sri Nandvri Sakuntala vimarsanan. [s.l.] : [s.n.], [n.d.].

An essay in Telugu.

Reference in *Triveni* Vol. XXIII, No. 4; Pp. 317- 319.

Bangarayya, N. Sakuntala Vimasanamu .- Rajahmudry : The author, 1952/

187 p.; 21.5 cm.

Bartval, Chandrakumvar. Kalidasa ki Priyamvada. *Sar;* April 1947; Vol. XLVIII; Pp. 344 - 345.

Basu, Chandranath. Shakuntalatattvá .- [Calcutta] : [s.n.], 1881 [B. 1288].

Study of 'Abhijñana Shākuntalam' in Bengali with chapters on (1) Shakuntala nataker samalochana (2) Abhijñana Shakuntaler nataktattva. (3) Dushyanta (4) Nataker charitra (5) Shakuntala natakercharitra (6) Dushyanta Shakuntala (7) Abhijnana Shakuntaler artha. (8) Anyanya byektigan (9) Abhijñan Shakuntaler galpa.

Review in *CR;* 1882; Vol. CXLIX; Pp. XXIX - XXXII.

Basu, Debendranath. Sakuntalayae natyakala.

An essay in Bengali.

Review appeared in *CRNS;* July - Sept. 1924; Vol. XXIV; Pp. 241 - 242.

Basu, Ramendramohan. Abhijnanasakuntala : a synthetic study. 3rd ed. - Calcutta: [s.n.], 1960.

A critical study of the play.

Includes the text and Skt. Comm., English and Bengali tr.

4th ed. published in 1963.

5th ed. published in 1970.

Beams, John. [Book review of Abhijñanaśākuntalam : critical ed. of Frederic Pincott.] *Indian Antiquary.* V; P. 327.

Belloni - Filippi, F. La Leggenda Mahabharatianna di Sakuntala nell' dizione critica di Poona. *GSAI* N.S. 1930; Pp. 135 - 140.

Belvalkar, S.K. Abhijnanasakuntala and the Bagavadgita. *K. Raja Comm. Vol.;* 1946; Pp. 48 - 54.

Belvalkar, S.K. Canons of textual and higher criticism as applied to the Sakuntala of Kalidasa. *Asia Major;* Vol. II; P. 30 ff.

Reference in S.K. Belvalkar Fel. Vol. (Benaras); 1957.

Belvalkar, S.K. Abhijñanasakunala natakaci pathaparampara *Vi. J. Vi.;* 1925; Pp. 65 - 75.

Belvalkar, S.K. Kalidasa's Abhijñanasakuntala : its dramatic setting. *Vikrama* Volume (Ujjain); 1948; Pp. 45 - 55.

Belvalkar, S.K. Notes, textual and exegetical, on a few passages from the Śākuntala. All India Oriental Conference V, Summaries. P. 215.

—— Harvard Journal of Asiatic Studies. Vol. I, Pp. 28 - 32.

Belvalkar, S.K. Notes : textual and exegetical on a few passages from Sakuntala *SPAIOC* (Lahore); 1930; Vol. 1; P. 144.

Belvalkar, S.K. The original 'Sakuntala' *Ashutosh Mookerjee Silver Jubilee Volume* (Calcutta); 1925; Vol. III : Orientalia, No. 2; Pp. 349 - 359.

Belvalkar, S.K. Sakuntala and some Shakespearian heroines. *Deccan College Quarterly*; 1922; Pt. 1; Pp. 18 - 22.

Reference in S.K. Belvalkar Fe. Vol. 1957.

Belvalkar, S.K. Srngaric elaborations in Sakuntala. *Proc. of SPAIOC* - IV (Allahabad); 1924; Vol. II (Proceedings); Pp. 157 - 164.

Belvalkar, S.K. Srngaric elaborations in Sakuntala Act III *In* Indian studies in Honour of Chales Rockwell Lanman. - Cambridge : [s.n.], 1929. Pp. 187-192.

Belvalkar, S.K. Śṛṅgāric elaboration in Sākuntala, Act III.

All India Oriental Conference IV; Vol. 2, Pp. 157 - 164.

Bendre, D.R. Abhijnanasakuntalantila vatsalyacem adhisthana. *N. Bh;* Aug. 1953; Vol. VI, No. 11; Pp. 8 - 14.

Literary study of Abhijnanasakuntalam in Marathi.

Berchet, Giovanni. Saggio sul dramma indiano la Sacontala, ossia l' Anello Fatale di Calidasa. (Milan), 1818.

Reference in *BSD*.

Betai, R.S. Atmatattva in the Sakuntalam of Kalidasa. JUB; 1957, Vol. XXVI (New Series); Pt. 2; Pp. 152 - 158.

Bhaduri, Satyendranath. The Gautami problem in Act V of the Sakuntalam. *SPAIOC;* 1972. P. 176.

Bhardwaj, Shivprasad. Abhijnanasakuntala ki natakiyata. *Visva Jyoti;* Oct. 1965; Vol. XIV, No. 8; Pp. 32 - 35.

Bhartiya, Kanti Kishore. Sanskrit natakkar. - Uttar Pradesh : Prakashan Sakha, Suchana Vibhag, 1959.

(Hindi - Samiti granthamala; 25) *Contents : Kalidasa.* Pp. 80 - 114.

Bhat, G.K. Durvasa - sapa *In* Madhudhara .- Poona [s.n.], 1953.

Article is included in this Marathi book.

Bhat, G.K. Hamsapadikece gita *Sadhana* (weekly); 14 Nov. 1953; Vol. VI, No. 14.

Bhat, G.K. The Repudiation of Sakuntala and Dusyanta's dilemma. *SPAIOC* (Bhubaneswar) 1959; Vol. XX.

— JOIB; March 1960; Vol. IX; Pp. 274 - 283.

Bhat, G.K. Shakuntla *In* Panca Samskrta natakem .- Poona : [s.n.], 1960. Pp. 55 - 92.

An article on Act IV of the classic.

Bhat, G.K. Sakuntalantila prameya. *Citra* (Divali No.); 1943; Pp. 99 - 106.

Bhat, G.K. The Song of Hamsapadika. *Proc AIOC* - XVIII (Annamalai), 1955; Pp. 165 - 171.

Bhat, G.K. The Song of Hamsapadika. *JOIB;* 1957; Vol. VII, Nos. 1 - 2; Pp. 53 - 60.

Bhat, G.K. Treatment of super-natural in Sakuntala. *JOIB;* Sept. 1952; Vol. II, No. 1; Pp. 61 - 67.

Bhatia, Prem Prakash. Abhijnanasakuntala men premabhav. *Vina* (Ka. Vi.); Sept. 1965; Vol. XXXVIII, No. 11; Pp. 501 - 502.

Summary appeared in *Pr. Jy*; Vol. III.

Bhatt, Rajeshvari. Kaldasasyabhijnanasakuntalam. *Bharati* (JP).; Nov. 1972; Vol.

XXIII, No. 1; Pp. 11 - 14.

Bhavalkar, Vanamala. Sakuntalasya natyasastriyamanusilanam *Sag.;* 1974; Vol. XIII, No. 1; Pp. 17 - 60.

Binney, E. Les Ballets de Theophile Gautier. (Paris : Nizet, 1965); P. 331.

On French ballet 'Sacountala' performed in July 1858 by Theophile Gautier.

Binyon, Lawrence. Sakuntala. London : [s.n.], 1920.

A version prepared for English stage by K.N. Dasgupta; contains an introductory essay by Rabindranath Tagore.

Other eds, 1941, 1944.

Bohtlingk, Otto. Einige nochtraga zu meiner ausgabe der Ring - Cakuntala. *Bulletin de la classe des sciences historiques, philosophiques et politiques de l' Academic de St. Petersburg.* II; P. 119.

Bollensen, Fr. Die Recensionen der Sakuntala. *NGWG;* 1880.

[Book review of Abhijñanaśākuntala; ed. by R. Pischel. The Bengali recension]. *Zeitschrift der Deutschen Morgenländischen Gesellschaft.* Vol. LXXXII; Pp. 240 - 241.

[Book review of Abhijñanaśākuntalam; Bengali translation by Krishnagopal Bhattacharya] *Mañjusha;* Sept. - Nov. 1952; Vol. VII, No. 1 - 3 P. 63.

[Book review of Abhijñanaśākuntalam in English translation by V.N. Balakrishna Kirtikar] *In. Kritisch - Bibliographisches treifen aus dem Gebiete der Indischen Philologie Von Albrecht Weber.* Pp. 172 - 175.

[Book - review of Abhijñanaśākuntalam in English translation by William Jones]. *Calcutta Review,* 1851; Vol. XV; Pp. 87 - 108.

[Book review of Shakuntala in French translation by Bergaigne and Lehugeur]. *Bibliotheque Univ. et. reveu Suisse - 3,* XXIV; P. 663.

[Book review of 'Abhijnana Sakountla', French translation by Karpelis Andree.] *Aryan Path* Nov. 1937; Vol. VIII, No. 11; Pp. 529 - 530.

[Book review of Abhijñanaśākuntalam in Malayalam tr. by Attur Krishna Pisharoti] *Indian PEN;* March 1937; Vol. III, No. 3; Pp. 21 - 22.

[Book review of Abhijñanaśākuntalam in Telugu; tr. by Gurramu Venkata

Subrahmanyamu. *Treveṇi*. Oct. 1962; Vol. XXXI, No. 3; Pp. 253 - 254.

Borooah, Anundoram. A companion to the Sanskrit reading under graduates of Calcutta University. Pt. 4.- Calcutta, 1876.

On the Abhijñanaśākuntalam of Kālidasa.

Bukhard, C. Flexiones Practriticae quas editioni suae Sacuntali pro supplemento adjecit .- Breslau : [s.n.], 1874.

Bukhard, C. Die Kacmirer Sakuntala handschrif *SWAW. Phil - hist Cl;* 1884; B.d. 107; Pp. 479 - 640.

Review appeared in LBOP; Vol. II; P. 203.

Burnell, A.C. [Book review of Abhijñanaśākuntalam, ed. by R. Pischell]. *Indian Antiquary.* Vol. VI; P. 232.

Bukhard, C. Lectiones codices cakuntali Bikanirensis *Progr. d. Franz - Joseph's Gymn* (Wien); 1883.

Review appeared in (i) *LBOP*; Vol. 1; P. 77 &

(ii) Zeitchr. f.d. osterr. Gymnasien; 1884; Vol. XXXV; P. 78 ff.

Reviewed by G. Buhler.

Byrski Christopher. Appreciation of Sanskrit drama in Kalayug / by M. Christopher Byrski. *Sangeet Natak Akademi Journal, January March Pp. 54 - 63.*

Paper submitted to the International Sanskrit conference, Delhi, March 1971 entitled "Some aspects of Sanskrit literary criticism".

Cannon, Garland. Sir Willian Jones and Sakuntala. *JAOS;* 1953; Vol. LXXIII; Pp. 198 - 202.

Cannon, Garland. Sir William Jone's Summary of Sakuntala *JAOS;* 1963; Vol. LXXXIII; Pp. 241 - 243.

Chari, V.K. The Rhythm of action in the drama of Sakuntala. *Aryan Path;* Aug. 1962; Vol. XXXIII, No. 8.

Chattopadhyay, Aparna. The Indomitable learned Shakuntala. *Bihar Information;* 1970; Vol. XVIII; Pp. 3 - 5.

Chattopadhyay, Aparna. Sakuntala of the Mahabharata : a study. *IAC;* Jan. 1969; Vol. XVIII, No. 1.

Chattopadhyay, Kshitish Chandra. Abhijnanasakuntalapathaebhdavimarsah. *Man.;* Dec. 1958; Vol. XIII; No. 4; Pp. 83 - 84.

Chattopadhyay, Kshitish Chandra. Sakuntalagatasyabhijnanasya mulam. *Man;* Oct. 1957; Vol. XII, No. 2; Pp. 40 ff.

Chattopadhyay, Kshitish Chandra. The Sakuntala problem. *Sir William Jones Bicentenary of his birth Comm. Vol.*; 1948; P. 167.

Chattopadhyay, K.C. Sakuntalasyacchaya. *Man;* Oct. 1959; Vol. XIV; No. 2; Pp. 47 - 49.

Chattopadhyay, Kshitish Chandra. Sakuntalavimarsah - 1. *Man;* Sept. 1954; Vol. IX, No. 1; Pp. 10 - 14; No. 2, Pp. 31 - 32; No. 3, Pp. 41 & 67 - 68; No. 5, Pp. 83 - 84.

Chattopadhyay, Kshitishchandra. Sakuntlaslokavimarsah. *Man;* April 1960; Vol. XIV, No. 8; P. 212.

Chattopadhya, Kshitish Chandra. Sakauntala vimarsah. *Man.;* Aug. 1955, Vol. IX, No. 12; Pp. 209 - 210.

Chattopadhyay, K.C. Sakuntalavimarsah : Bharatah. *Man;* Sept. 1969; Vol. XIV; No. 1; P. 13.

Chattopadhyay, K.C. The Story of Sakuntala in different recensions. *Journal of Sanskrit Sahitya Parisat;* Vol. XIV, No. 2.

Reference in *Man*. XVI, No. 3; Pp. 77 - 78.

Chattopadhyay, Kshitish Chandra. The Source of the Sakuntala story and its treatment by Kalidasa. *Allahabad University Magazine;* 1937; Pp. 407 ff.

Reference in JGJRI., XXVII.

Chattopadhyay, Ramanand. A University in the Shakuntala. *MR;* July - Dec. 1923; Vol. XXXIV, No. 1 - 6; P. 216.

Chattopadhyay, Ramanand. Who painted picture of Sakuntal. *MR;* July - Dec. 1919; No. 1 - 6; P. 320.

Chaturvedi, Girdhari Lal. Re-visiting Śakuntalam : a commentary on Goethe's Śakuntala - epigram .- Mathura : Brijrani Publications, 1991.

xii, 152 p.; 22.5 cm.

Includes bibliographical references.

Chaudhari, Rama Anusuya Priyamvade. *Mañ;* Feb. 1958; Vol. XII, No. 6; Pp. 172 - 176.

Chezy, A.L. Notes et. correction suplementaires pour l' edition in 4th du drame indieu de Calidasa intitute La Reconaissance de sacountala donnee en, 1830. - Paris : [s.n.], 1831.

Dandekar, R.N. [Book review of Abhijnanaśākuntalam in English translation by R.D. Karnarkar] *ABORI* ; Vol. XXXII, Pt. I - IV; Pp. 297 - 298.

Dasgupta, Shatrujit. Śakuntala.- Calcutta : [s.n.], 1959.

Includes Bengali translation of three articles on Kalidasa :

(i) Europer Germany-te Kalidas

(ii) Russia-te Kalidas

(iii) China-dese Kalidas.

Dattagupta, Akshaykumar. Sakuntala .- [s.l.] : [s.n.], [n.d.].

Reference in *ILCBL.*

Deb, Amiya Tragicomic suffering in Sakuntala, Uttararamacarita, Cymbeline and the Winter's tale / by Amiya Deb. *Journal of Comprative LIterature* (Jadavpur); 1968, Vol. 8; Pp. 50 - 84.

Deshpande, S.H. The Hunted one : reflections on Abhijnanasakuntalam / by S.H. Deshpande. *Journal of Asiatic Society* (Bombay); 1977 - 78; Vols. 52 - 53; Pp. 112 - 121.

Deshpande, Suman B. Sakuntala Kalidasaya. *GR;* June, 1971; Vol. VI, No. 1; Pp. 1 - 4.

Dikshit, Kalikaprasad. Kusumakara Kalidasa aur Vedavyas ka Sakuntala. *Vina;* Feb. 1963; Vol. XXXVI; No. 4; Pp. 175 - 179.

Dikshit, Vinod Praksh. Abhijnanasakuntala mein bharatiya samskriti ki jhatak. *Vina;* April 1966; Vol. XXXIX, No. 6; Pp. 288 - 291.

Summary published in *Pr. Jy.* Vol. V.

Durmukh. Kalidas ke do Pātra : Dusyant aur Sakuntala. *Aj*; June, 1953; Vol. V, No. 6; Pp. 29 - 32.

Dutta, Kali Kumar. The Fisherman episode in the Abhijnanasakuntalam. *Vikrama*

(Ka. Vi.); 1960; Pp. 51 - 65.

Dwivedi, Mahavir Prasad. [Book review of Abhijñanasakuntalam in Hindi, rendered by Nandlal Vishvanath Dubey. *Sarasvati* Oct. 1908; Vol. IX, No. 10; Pp. 445 - 449.

Dwivedi, Mahavir Prasad Sakuntala. *Sar;* Oct. 1908; Pp. 445 - 449.

Emeneau, M.B. Kalidasa's Sakuntala and the Mahabharata. *JAOS;* 1962; Vol. LXXXII; Pp. 41 - 44.

Figueria, Dorothy Matilda. Translating the orient : the reception of Sakuntala in nineteenth - century Europe. - New York : State University Press, 1991. 260 p.; 23 cm.

Includes bibligraphical references and index.

Gabernatis, Angelo de. Sacountala et Grisel da. *International Congress of Orientalists;* Vol. XIII; Pp. 21 - 24. Reference in OB (1903).

Gadgil, Amarendra. Sakuntala [s.l.] : [s.n.], [n.d.].

An essay on the play.

Gangooly, O.C. Nati's song in the Abhijnanasakuntala *JMA*; 1941; Vol. XII; Nos. 1-4; Pp 89-91.

Ghosh, Manmohan. On Kalidasa's texts. *SPAIOC* (Jadavpur); 1969; Vol. XXV, P. 62.

Ghosh, O.K. Tales from Indian classic. - Bombay : Jaico, 1961.

A study of Sakuntala. (The story).

Godavarma, K. Interpretations in Sakuntala. *Proceedings of AIOC* - XIII (Nagpur); 1946; Pp. 1941 - 47.

Godbole, K.V. Sakunatla natakavarila sankanna uttara. *Sah.;* Dec. 1951; Pp. 749-755.

Gopalaswami Aiyangar, T.K. Katham mrtpindabuddhih Sakuntala - Vidusakah. *Vi Saṁ;* August 1967; Vol. IV; No. 4; Pp. 322 - 326.

Goswami, Kishorilal. Abhijnanasakuntala aur Padmapurana. *NPP;* 1901; Vol. V (Old Series); Pp. 27 - 128.

Greene, Lily Dexter. Nature study in The Sanskrit drama Sakuntala. *IA* March 1930, Vol. LX; Pp. 46 - 48 and April, 1931; Pp. 64 - 66.

Gubernatis, Anglo De. Analysis of Sakuntala. *In* Letteratura Indiana. - Milan : [s.n.], 1884.

Reference in *CDCFKI*.

Hamaker, H.A. Over de Sakuntala van Kalidasa. *Mnemesyne;* 1823; Vol. II; P. 213.

Reference in BSD.

Harihar Sastri. Kalidasa's ideal of Rajarsi. *Triveni;* Dec. 1948; Vol. XX, No. 5; Pp. 257 - 259.

Hauschild, R. [Book review of Abhijñanaśākuntalam in English by MB. Emeneau]. *Orientalische Literaturzeitung* 1965; Vol. LX, No. 1 - 2; Pp. 77 - 78.

Hedrstrom, O.F. Om Sakuntal. Upsala, 1875.

Reference in BSD.

Hertel, Job [Book - review of Abhijñanaśākuntalam / ed. by Carl Cappeller]. *Zeitschrift der Deutschen Morgenländischen Gesellschaft*. 630 - 636.

Heyne [on Sakuntala] *Gottingsche Anzeigen;* July 23, 1791; Vol. 67; P. 1006.

German critic recognised the lack of action in the Śākuntala play.

Hillebrandt [Book - review of Abhijñanaśākuntalam / ed. by Carl Cappeller]. *Gōttinger Gelecherte Anzeigen* 1909; Pp. 929 - 933.

Holden, C.L. Sakuntala. *VQ;* Feb. - April, 1947; Vol. XII; Pp. 271 -276.

Inamdar, V.M. The moral problem of Sakunala *Triveni;* Sept. 1936; Vol. IX, No. 3; Pp. 60 - 67.

Index : Abhijñanaśākuntalaslokah. *In* A Descriptive Catalogue of the MSS. in Govt. Oriental Manuscript Library, Madras. [12491].

Jaidev Vidyalankar. The bindu [expansion]and arthaprakriti in the Abhijnanasakuntala of Kalidasa. *SPAIOC*. (Kurukshetra); 1974; P. 51.

Jain, Harindra Bhusan. Kalidas ke Abhijnana ki tattvika samiksha. *Vikrama* (Ka. Vi.); 1960; Pp. 67 - 82.

Jain, Harindramohan. Abhijnanasakuntalam par Valmiki Ramayan ka prabhav. *Vikrama* (Ka. Vi.); 1967; Vol. X; Pp. 63 - 68.

Jensen, Hans. Kalidasa Indiens grosster dichter und sein drama Sakuntala : ein

Vortrag. [s.l.] : [s.n.], 1959.

Jhala, Shankar Singh. Kalidasasya sarvasvamabhijnanasakuntalam. *Samm*; March 1967; Vol. II, No. 7; Pp. 17 - 18.

Jog, K.P. A Fresh revaluation of the inner meaning of the Sakuntala. *H.D. Velankar Comm. Vol.* (Bombay); 1965; Pp. 206 - 213.

Josef, T.F. Idyll and reality in the Sakuntala and the Tempēst. *Jadavpur Journal of Comparative Literature;* 1965; Vol. V; Pp. 1 - 21.

Joshi, Madanıal. Visvakavi Kalidasa aur unki Sakuntala *Vina;* Dec. 1951; Vol. XXV, No. 2; Pp. 88 - 95.

Joshi, Natvar. Abhijnanasakuntale ghatitanam ghatananam samayanirdharanam. *SPAIOC* (Ujjain); 1972; P. 470.

Kahradkar, Suhasini. Sakuntale nayakanayikayoh duhkham daivadhinameva *Sāmm;* May, 1970; Vol. V, No. 17; Pp. 26 - 27.

Kantawala, S.G. Hamsapadikagitih. *Su. Bh.;* 1972; Vol. X.

On Kalidasa's Abhijnanasakuntalam (Importance of Hamsapadikagiti).

Kanumantha Rao, R. Kalidasa's Sakuntala : a view point *Triveni;* Oct. 1967; Vol. XXXV, No. 3; Pp. 42 - 44.

Karandikar, J.S. Sakuntalantila Kamhi sanka. *Saho;* Oct. 1951; Pp. 591 - 592.

Kashyap, E.R.A. Ekam samaradhanam : Abhijnanasakuntala of Kalidasa. *BJ;* Nov. 1970; Vol. XVII, No. 7 & 1971; No. 13.

Keith, A. Berriedale Sanskrit - natak : udbhav aur vikas : siddhanta aur prayog / tr. into Hindi by Udaybhanu Singh. - Delhi : Motilal Banarsidass, 1965.

Kenghe, S.T. The Curse and hte ring episodes of the Sakuntala. *OT;* Oct. 1956; Vol. II, No. 4; Pp. 70 - 79.

Khandewal, Jaikishanprasad. Kalidas aur Abhijnanasakuntala. [s.l.] : [s.n.], 1970.

An article in Hindi.

Kshite, Mukund, Sastri. Sakuntaliyan. *SS;* (Saṃ 2007); Vol. V, No. 4; Pp. 138 - 144.

Koniyev, V. Śakuntala kā Rūsi Bhāṣa men anuvād; *Ajanta [Hyderabad];* Sept 1955; Vol. VII, No. 9, Pp. 77 ff.

Based on an article by V. Koniyev in *Tass*.

Konow, Sten. [Book review of Abhijñanaśākuntalam / ed. by Saradaranjan Ray]. *Indian Antiquary* Vol. XXXVII; P. 112.

Kothala, S.S. Sakuntala, *Bharati* (JP); March 1973; Vol. XXIII; No. 5; Pp. 121 - 122.

Krishanappa, B. Sakuntala natakada vimarse. - Mysore : [s.n.], 1922.

Kulkarni, G.R. A University in the Shakuntala. *MR*.

Kulkarni, G.V. Symbolism in Sakuntala, *SPAIOC* (Ujjain); 1972; P. 184.

Kunhan Raja, C. Kalidasa's Sakuntala : a study in contrast and harmony *Prof. M. Hiryanna Comm. Vol.* (Mysore); 1952; Pp. 75 - 81.

Kunhan Raja, C. The Sakuntalacarca. *JOR* (Madras); 1936 - 37; Vol. 1, Nos. 1 & 2; Pp. 6 - 12.

Kunhan Raja, C. Sakuntale Kasyacicchloksya aucityacarca. *Man;* April 1955, Vol. IX, No. 8; Pp. 111 - 112.

Kunhan Raja, C. Time - analysis in the Sakuntala. *JOR* (Madras).

Reference in C. Kunhan Raja Presentation Volume.

Kunhan Raja, C. Time analysis in the Sakuntala of Kalidasa. *Proc. AIOC - VII* (Baroda); 1935; Pp. 71 - 84.

Lal, P. Shakuntala. *Illustrated weekly of India*; 2 July 1967; Pp. 35 ff.

On Kalidasa's magnum opus.

Layalpurkar, Savyasachi Sakuntala - anguthi : German - Bharat Sahitya ek naya sujhav. *Dh. Y.;* 10 July 1966; Vol. XVII; No. 28; P. 16.

Leifer, W. Shakauntala : the beginning and future of a literary encounter. *Vikrama* (Ka. Vi.); 1967; Pp. 103 - 107.

Lele, Vaman Keshav. Shakuntal shailishastriya adhyas. - Thane : Itihas - Patrika Prakashan, 1997.

205 p.; 22 cm.

In Marathi.

Levi, Sylvain. [Book review of Abhijñanaśākuntalam / ed. by Saradaranjan Ray]. *Journal Asiatique Series* - X, Vol. XVI; No. 2; Pp. 395 - 398.

Levitt, Stephan Hillyer. 'Kalidasa's compounds in Abhijñanasakuntala and Vikramorvasi' / by Stephan Hillyer Levitt. *J. Orient Inst.;* March - June, 1979; Vol. 28, Nos. 3 - 4; Pp. 16 - 35 ft-n.

Limaye, K.G.G. Agabai angathi. *Sah.;* Sept. 1951; Pp. 525 - 526.

A problem of lost ring in Sakuntala.

Mahavir, Nīra. Mahabhartiy sakuntalo pakhyanat Kalidasaviracitamabhijnanasakuntalam Vaisistyam bhajate *GP;* Dec. - Jan. 1964 - 65; Vol. XVII, No. 5; Pp. 287 - 289.

Maheshchandra, *Sastri*. Kanvamuni ke asram ki yatra : Dushyant Sakuntala ki milanbhumi. *Dh.* Y.; 15 June. 1961; P. 10.

Mandal, Pareshchandra. Implications of the hermit's blessing in the first act of Kalidasa's Abhijnanasakuntala. *SPAIOC* (Kurukshetra); 1974; P. 138.

Mankad, D.R. Kalidasa Malavikagnimitra with samasloki Gujarati tr. with a Gujarati commentary named Manomika. *Indian Historical Quarterly* Sept. 1933; Vol. 9, No. 3; Pp. 817 - 820.

Man Singh. Abhijnanasakuntala men Durvasa ka Sāp. *Pracya - Prajna;* 1971; Vol. IV. Pp. 53 - 83.

Maraimalaiadigal, M.S.V. A Critical study of Sakuntala.- Madras : [s.n.], 1907.

Also published in 1933.

In Tamil.

Mathur, Vijayendra. Abhijnanasakuntala men varnit sthanon ka parichay. *Bharati* (Ng); 1950; Vol. 1, No. 4; Pp. 246 - 249.

Mathur, Vijayendra Kumar. Sakuntala ke kucha prakritika varnanon ki sarthakata. *Bharati* (Ng); Aug. 1950; Vol. 1, No. 8; Pp. 666 - 671.

Mathur, Vijayendra. Topography of Abhijnanasakuntala. *MR.;* 1950; Vol. LXXXVIII, No. 4; Pp. 319 - 320.

Mehendale, M.A. Dusyanta vartananu aucitya. *Samskriti;* 1947; Pp. 408 - 409.

Mahendale, M.A. Sakuntalatila pratika; bhramara *N. Bh.;* April 1949; Vol. II. No. 7.; Pp. 536 - 539.

Mehendale, M.A. Sakuntalatila pratika mṛga. *N. Bh.;* Sept. 1948; Vol. I, No. 12; Pp. 14 - 18.

Mehendale, M.A. Symbolism in Sakuntala. *New Democrat;* 30 Jan. 1948.

Reference in *Indian PEN;* March 1948; Vol. XIV; P. 42.

Mirashi, V.V. Sakuntala natakantila ek prasanga Nagpur : Phulora Saradamandala, 1935.

Reference in *V.V. Mirashi Fel. Vol.* 1965. (Nagpur).

Mishra, Aditya. Sakuntala ka naitik rahasya. *Aj;* Oct. 1956; Vol. VIII, No. 10; Pp. 57 - 60.

Mishra, Mohan. Influence of the Arthasastra on the Abhijnanasakuntala of Kalidasa. *SPAIOC* (Varanasi); 1961; P. 64.

Mishra, Rudrakant. A. Critical evaluation of the role of the two companions of Sakuntala. *SPAIOC* (Ujjain); 1972.

Mishra, Umesh. Dusyant kā ek aṁsik caritra. *Kishora* (Ka. Vi.).- Patna : [s.n.], 1944.

Reference in *Umesh Mishra Comm. Vol. 1970.*

Mishra, Vidyaniwas. Sakuntala aur grismagama. *Dh. Y.;* 4 April 1965; Vol. XVI, No. 14; P. 10.

Mukherjee, Kalipada. Notes on Sakuntala. - Calcutta : [s.n.], 1895.

Literary study of the play.

Muller, B. Kalidaa's Sakuntala und ihre Quelle .- Breslau : [s.n.], 1874.

Munshi, K.M. Peep into the wonder - world of beauty. *DRMKS;* Pp. 21 - 29.

On Sakuntala (Aesthetics).

Murty, Suryanarayana. Sakuntalamu. - [s.l.] : [s.n.], 1964.

Musalgarnkar, Shriram Gajanan Sastri. Kalidasasya sarvasvamabhijnana - sakuntalam. *Vina;* 1961; Vol. XXXIV, No. 9; Pp. 186 - 191.

Nagaraja Sarma, A.V. 'Theme of the Sakuntala' / by A.V. Nagaraja Sarma. *All India Oriental Conference Proceedings*, (Annamalai) 1955, 18th Session, Pp. 156 -160.

Narang, Indrachandra. Sakuntalanatakasya ramyatamah solakh. *San;* [Saṁ 2026]; Vol. V, No. 4; Pp. 36 - 41.

Neve, Felix. [Book review of French translation of Shakuntala by Bergaigne and

Lehugeur . *Le Musēon. Revue Internationale.* Vol. IV; Pp. 658 - 659.

Nissel, Karl. [Book review of Sakuntala : German rendering of Edmunds Lobendanz] *In* Blätter t. lit. Unterhaltung. 25. Sept.; p. 613 ff.

Reference in Literatur - blatt für Orientalische Philologie - II.

Palsikar, S.M. Sakuntalaca's ahava anka. *N.Bh;* Jun. 1968; Vol. XXI, No. 9; Pp. 25 - 29.

Article in Marathi.

Panchal, Goverdhan. The Curtain in Abhijnana Sakuntala / by Goverdhan Panchal. *Sangeet Natak Akademi Journal;* July - Sept. 1976; Vol. 41; Pp. 5 - 12.

Pandey, Chandrabali. Abhijnanasakuntala men isti ka mahattva. *SPAIOC* (Bombay); 1949; Vol. XV.

Pandey, Chandra Bali. Abhijñāna Śākuntala mem iṣṭikāmahattva. *All India Oriental Conference* XVI; i; P. 44.

Pandurangi, K.T. A Note on the title Abhijnasakuntalam. *Vikrama* (Ka. Vi.); 1964; Pp. 123 - 135.

Parikh, J.T. [Book review of Śakuntala : Gujarati tr. of Chandravadan Mehta] *Indian PEN* ; Feb. 1965; Vol. XXXI; Pp. 26 - 27.

Phadke, Ananta, *Sastri*. Sakuntalavisayak sanka. *VSM* (Annual); 1958; Pp. 191 - 198.

Pischel, R. De Kalidasae cakuntali recensioni bus : particula prima dissertatio inauguratis .- Breslau : [s.n.], 1870.

Prem Kishor. Sakuntala ke German anubad. *Ajanta* (Hyderabad); June 1954; Vol. VI, No. 6; Pp. 21 - 24.

Prema Nandkumar. Kalidasa's Abhijnanasakuntalam. *Indian PEN* ; Feb. 1960; Vol. XXVI; Pp. 33 - 39.

A critical insight into the play.

Raghavan, V. [Nati's song in Abhijnanasakuntala]. *JMA* ; 1941 Vol. XII, Nos. 1 - 4; P. 92.

Ramkumar. Abhijnanasakuntalasya samskriti ki pristhabhumi. *Vi. San.* May 1968; Vol. V, No. 3; Pp. 219 - 225.

Rāman Mēnōn, T.K. Kāḷidāsanum Śākuntaḷavum / by T.K. Rāman Mēnon. -

Trivandrum : B.V. Book Depot, 1940.

202 p.; 23 cm.

Critical studies.

Ramanujayangar, A. Sakuntalanatakavimarsah *MSPP;* April 1926; Vol. II, No. 2; Pp. 68 - 77.

Ramasahay, *Vedantasastri* Delineations of the characters of Sakuntala, Anusuya and Priyamvada of Kalidasa's Abhijnanasakuntala [s.l.] : [s.n.], 1925.

Ranade, G.H. The Nati's song in the prelude to the Abhijñanasakuntla of Kalidasa. *JMA;* 1940; Vol. XI, Nos. 1 - 4; Pp. 90 - 94.

Ranganna, S.V. Shakuntala natakada vimarshe .- Mysore : Sharada Mandira, 1959.

247 p.; 18 cm.

In Kannada.

Rao, Kutumba. A study of dialogues in Abhijnanasakuntala. *SPAIOC;* 1955; Vol. XVIII.

Rao, L.S. Sheshagiri? The tragic element in Sakuntala. *Triveni;* April - May 1948; Vol. XIX, No. 9 - 10; Pp. 537 - 541.

Rao, Ramachandra S. Kanva as a sthiraprajna. *JMU;* 1956 - 57; Vol. XVI; Pp. 19 - 23.

Ray, Tikaram Bhatt. Sakuntale Dusyantacariranivedanam. *Pratibha* (VSV); [Saṁ 2027]; Pp. 49 - 51.

Ŗaychaudhuri, Durgaprasanna. William Jones and his translation of Kālidāsa's Śakuntala.

Renou, L. Recensions of Sakuntala. *L. Inde Classique*. P. 276.

Ruben, Walter. Sakuntala : heute und heir. *Theater der Ziet*. (Berlin); 1957; Pp. 15 - 17.

Reference in Festschrift Walter Ruben (Berlin, 1971).

Ruckmini, M.A. Where Kalidasa excels : Sakuntala, a play of nature. *Aryan Path;* April 1943; Vol. XIV, No. 4; Pp. 156 - 160.

Sahal, Kanhaiyalal. Abhijnanasakuntala ki ek Kahavat. *So.P.;* June 1962; Vol.

XIII, No. 4; P. 78.

Sahana, Satyakinkar. Sakuntala - rahasya. - Calcutta : [s.n.], 1959.

An article in Bengali.

Salus, Peter H. Sakuntala in Europe : the first thirty years. *JAOS;* 1964; Vol. LXXXIV; Pp. 417 ff.

Sapre, Dhundiraj Gopal. Gautamim tamaveksyaiva yatha vittha tathaiva sa. *Vikrama (Ka. Vi);* 1966; Vol. IX; Pp. 29 - 30.

Sarabhai, Mrinalini. Creations. - Ahmedabad : Mapin Publishing, 1986. Pp. 58 - 60.

On Shakuntala.

Sarkar, Biharilal. Shakuntala rahasya. - 1895.

Studies an 'Abhijnana Shakuntala'.

Contents : Introduction; 'Shakuntalar tapoban tyag o nataker pusti'; Rajsabhay pratyakhyan; Birahanubhūti o nataker parinati.

Sarkar, Biharilal. Sakuntalarahasya. - Calcutta : [s.n.], 1896.

An essay in Bengali (Literary study).

Sarkar, V. Śakuntalarahasya [s.l.] : [s.n.], [n.d.].

An article on Sakuntala.

Reference in KHCSL.

Satya Vrat. A Versified adaptation of Abhijnanasakuntalam (I - IV) / by Satya Vrat. *Vishveshvaranand Indological Journal;* June - December 1981; Vol. 19, Nos. 1 - 2; Pp. 99 - 105.

Sauer, W. Sakuntala : Goethe und Schiller. *Korrespondanzbi f.d.* Gel. u. Realschulen Wrottembergs; Vol; XL. Pp. 997 - 304.

Reference in *OB*, Vol. IX.

Schyler, Montegomery. The editions and translations of Sakuntala. *JAOS* 1901; Vol. XXII, No. 2; Pp. 237 - 248.

Shah, Ramesh Chandra Ramanlal. Abhijnanasakuntalam. *Samm;* March 1967; Vol. II. No. 7; Pp. 21 - 22.

Shakuntala natak : ek adhyayan .- Darbhanga : Saphalata Prakashan, [n.d.].

72 p.; 18.5 cm. In Maithili.

Sharma, Harihar Sarup. Sakuntala men upeksa. *Sar;* Dec. 1915; Vol. XVI, No. 6; P. 2, 250 - 353.

Appreciation of the play in Hindi.

Sharma, Manohar. Mahakavi Kalidas varnita Sakuntala ki vidai aur Rajasthani lokgit. *Viś;* 1968; Vol. V; No. 1; Pp. 17 - 31.

Sharma, Mukund Madhava. Yā srsti srasturadya *Sāg.;* [Saṁ 2024]; Vol. VI, No. 2; Pp. 169 - 174.

On Shakuntala's first verse.

Sharma, P.P. Kalidasa's Shakuntala : some delights / by P.P. Sharma *Indian Literature;* May - June 1979; Vol. 22, No. 3; Pp. 75 - 85.

Sharma, Siddharameshvar. Sakuntalanatakasya ekamadhyayanam. *Bharati* (JP); Dec. 1960; Vol. XI, No. 2; Pp. 50 - 51.

Shastri, S.N. Geographical inset in Sakuntalam. *SPAIOC* (Darbhanga) 1948; Vol. XIV.

Shastri, Surendra Nath. The Geographical inset in the Abhijñāna - Śākuntalam.

All India Oriental Conference XIV (Summary); Pt. i; P. 54.

Shrinivasacharya. Sakuntalasamvidhanaramaniyakam. *Sahr* Vol. XVII.

An Essay in Sanskrit.

Simha, Kshemadhari. Abhijanasakuntala : psychological study. *JGJRI;* Feb. - May 1945; Vol. II, No. 2 - 3; Pp. 243 - 268.

Sitaramayya, K.B. The Substance of tragedy : a study in comparative literature I. Abhijnanasakuntalam. *Journal of Annamalai University;* 1964; Vol. XXV, No. A : Humanities; Pp. 19 - 29.

Summary appeared in *Pr. J.* 1964; Vol. II.

Smith, R. Morton. The Story of Sakuntala in the Mahabharata. *JBRS;* 1960; Vol. XLVI; Pp. 163 - 176.

Soper, Alexander C. [Book review of Abhijñanaśākuntalam in English by M.B. Emeneau]. *Artibus Asiae (New York)* Vol. XXV; P. 318.

Tagore, P.C. Panel representing Sir William Jones translating Sakuntala. *JASB;*

1937 [III. 132 - 133].

Reference in Sadashib Chaudhuri's INDEX. JASB.

Tagore, Rabindranath. Kumarsambhav o Shakuntala. *Banga darshan* [Paus 1308].

Tagore, Rabindranath. Shakuntala. *Bangadarshan* [Ashwin 1309].

Tagore, Rabindranath. Śakuntala. *In* Pracin Sahitya (Agrahayan 1968); P. 28.

Tagore, Rabindranath. Sakuntala : its inner meaning / tr. into Bengali by J.N. Sarkar. *MR,* Jan. - June 1911; Vol. IX, No. 1 - 6; Pp. 171 - 175.

Tagore, Rabindranath. Sakuntala : its inner meaning. *VQ;* Aug. 1940; Vol. VI, No. II; Pp. 118 - 126.

Original article in Bengali in Tagore's 'Pracina Sahitya (1907).

Temple, R.C. The lost ring of Sakuntala : it is a Greek reminiscence? *IA;* March 1924; Vol. LIII; P. 68.

Thakore, B.K. The text of the Śākuntala. *All India Oriental Conference* 1; Vol. i; Pp. lx - lxiii.
(Summary)

Thakore, B.K. The text of the Śakuntalā / by B.K. Thakore. *Proceedings & transactions of the First Oriental* Conference, Poona, held on the 5th, 6th and 7th of Nov. 1919.

Thakore, B.K. The text of Śakuntala. *SPAIOC;* 1920; Vol. 1; Pp. LX - LXIII.

It appeared in Hindustan Review.

Review in *CR* (New Series); Feb. 1927; Vol. VI, Nos. 1 - 3; Pp. 423 - 426.

Tillu, Vinayak Sastri Drstibhedena Sakuntalasya adhyayanam. *Bharati* (JP); Dec. 1960; Vol. XI, No. 2; Pp. 47 - 49 & No. 3, Pp. 71 - 72.

Tiwari, Ram Chandra. Tatrankah pancamo ramyah. *Vikrama* (Ka. Vi.); 1965 - 66; Pp. 81 - 85.

On Sakuntala.

Tripathi, G.C. On the formation of the word Sakuntala. *JOIB;* Dec. 1970; Vol. XX, No. 2; Pp. 137 - 142.

Tripathi, Krishnakant Mahakavi Kalidas aur unka Abhijnanasakuntala .- Kanpur : [s.n.], 1966.

Tripathi, Mangaram. Sakuntala darshan Jabalpur : [s.n.], [n.d.].

Tucci, Giuseppe. [Book review of Abhijñanaśākuntalam in English by M.B. Emeneau]. *East & West* (Rome) New Series; Vol. XIV.

Unni, N.P. The Trivendrum plays and the Abhijṇanasakuntala - carca. / by N.P. Unni. *Vishveshvaranand Indological Journal;* March - Sept. 1975; Vol. 13, No. 1 - 2; Pp. 376 - 384.

Upadhyay, Bhagvatsharan. Kalidas ke natak. - Delhi : Kitabghar, 1979.

199 p.; 21.5 cm.

Upadhyay, Bhagwatsharan. Sakuntala ka naitik rahasya : ek naya dristikon. *Hindustani;* 1940; Vol. X, No. 3; Pp. 227 - 236.

Upadhyay, Mahadev. Abhijnanasakuntalasamiksa. *SS;* [Saṁ 2020]; Vol. XVIII, No. 4.

Vanshidhar, *Vidyalankar* Kalidasa ki Sakuntala *Vi. Bh.;* April, 1934; Vol. XIII, No. 4; Pp. 401 - 409.

Vanshidhar Vidyalankara. Sakuntala : its tragedy. *Triveni;* April 1940; Vol. XII, No. 10; Pp. 44 - 58.

Summary published in *ABIHI,* 1940; Vol. III.

Vanshidhar Vidyalankara. Sakuntala and other essay. [s.l.] : [s.n.], [n.d.].

Varadacharya, T.A. Ramayanam Abhijnanasakuntalam *JSVOI;* July - Dec. 1941; Vol. II, No. 2; P. 303 ft.

Varma, Goda K. Interpretations in Śākuntala. *All India Oriental Conference* XIII; Pt. ii; Pp. 141 - 147.

Vasudeva Rao, R. Idllys of ancient Indian Sakuntala. - Madras : [s.n.], 1903.

Venkatachalam, V. A new approach to Kalidasa. *Vikrama* (Kā. Vi); 1960; Pp. 83-103.

Discusses poetic justice in Abhijnanasakuntala & also Sanskrit literary criticism.

Vishvanatha, Satya Narayan. Sakuṇtala yokka Abhijnanata .- Warrangal : [s.n.], 1991.

An article in Telugu.

Reprint from *Jayanti;* 1958 - 59.

Vishvanathan, K. Kalidasa's Abhijnanasakuntala. *Aryan Path;* May 1960; Vol. XXXI, No. 5; Pp. 200 - 205; July 1960, No. 6, Pp. 243 - 248; July 1960; No. 7.

Vora, Minal M. The Controversy regarding Dusyanta's appeal to his conscience in Sakuntala. *SPAIOC* - XXIV (Varanasi); 1968.

Vora, Minal M. Probable cases in Patakasthanaka in Abhijnanasakauntala *SPAIOC* (Ujjain); 1972; P. 477.

Vyas, Suryanarayan. Sakuntala ki kuch samasyaen. *Par. Pat;* April 1964; Vol. IV, No. 1; Pp. 30 - 32.

Warrier, A.G.K. Kalidasa nods. *Mysore Orientalist;* March 1967; Vol. 1, No. 1; Pp. 1 - 4.

Summary in *Pr. Jy.* Vol. V, Pt. 1.

Weber, A. De sauraseni deo Varuruci und die Recensionen der Sakuntala. *IS* (Band); 1876; Vol. XIV; Pp. 35 - 69.

Weber, A. Die recension der Sakuntala. *IS;* 1876; Vol. XIV; Pp. 161 - 311.

Wells, Henry W. Sakuntala's watering - pot / by Henry W. Wells. *Literary Half Yearly;* July 1971; Vol. 12, No. 2; Pp. 3 - 10.

Wilson, H.H. Sur un drame indien : extrait du Calcutta Annual Register, et traduit par M. Dondey Dupre fils. *JAS;* 1827; Series 1, Vol. 10; Pp. 174 - 179.

Wright, J.C. [Book review of Abhijnanaśākuntalam in English by M.B. Emeneau] *Bulletin of the School of Oriental and African Studies (London);* 1963; Vol. XXVI.

Zarrilli, B. Kalidasa's Sakuntala in performance / by Phillip B. Zarrilli. *Sangeet Natak Akademi Journal;* Jan. - March 1980; Vol. 55. Pp. 17 - 40.

12

Bio-Critical Studies : A Select Bibliography

Acharya, P.B. Tragicomedies of Shakespeare, Kalidasa and Bhavabuti .- New Delhi: Meherchand Lachhanandas, 1978.

264 p.; 22 cm.

Critical study.

Acharya, P.B. Treatment of Plot in Sanskrit drama and in Shakespeare's comedies.

Summary of Papers : International Sanskrit Conference; 1972.

Adya Rangacharya, Drama in Sanskrit Literature, Bombay : Popular Prakashan, 1967.

Pp. 13, 43, 53, 54, 57, 63, 66, 72, 78, 80, 90, 91, 95, 106, 118, 121, 128, 140, 155, 157, 152, 162m 166, 173, 175, 192, 193, 200, 204.

Adya Rangacharya, Kalidasa.

This literary criticism in Kannada received the much coveted 'Sahitya Akademic Award' of 1971 in the language.

Aggarwal, H.R. The Importance of tradition and Asvaghosa in determining the date of Kalidasa. *All India Oriental Conference* XVII; 1953 pp. 257 - 260.

—— Kalidasa *Poona Orientalist* xix; 1954; pp. 12- 16.

Aggarwal, H.R. A short history of Sanskrit literature - 2nd rev. ed. - Delhi : Munshiram Manoharlal, 1963.

Contents : Kalidasa pp. 63 - 85.

Aggarwal, Vasudeva Sarma. Jyotis ke adhar par Kalidasa ke samay ka niscay. *NPP,* [Sam. 2009]; *Vol.* LVII; pp. 367-369.

Aggarwal, Vinod. Imagery in the works of Kalidasa. Ph.D. thesis, Delhi University, 1972.

Aiyar, K. Balasuloramania, Kalidasa and nature. *Triveni*, Jan-Feb 1935, Vol. VII, Pp. 341-345.

Altekar, M.D. Aesthetics of Kalidasa, *Vikrama Vol.* (Ujjain); 1948; pp. 21 - 43. Altekar, Madav Damodar Kalidasaci srsti - Bombay : The author; 1937. xii, 276 p.; 18.5 cm.

Critical study of the world of Kalidasa. Reviews appeared in the following journals :-

(i) Indian PEN; Sept., 1939; Vol. V' P. 146 (Reviews : B.R. Deshpande)

(ii) MSP; Jan. 1938 Vol. xi No. 1. Reviewer. K.N. Vatve.

(iii) Sab; May 1938; Vol. iv, No. 5 Pp. 362 - 369; Vol. 6; Pp. 449 - 454. (Reviewer; B.K. Rajwade).

Anil Kumar Kalidasa ki Ujjaini banam Shakespeare ka Straight - Ford. *Dh. Y.*; 5th June 1964; Pp. 16 & 38.

Anonymous. Beauties of Kalidasa *Man*; January 1957; Vol. I, No. 5.

Anonymous. Bhartiya Kalayah prerakah Kalidasah. *Ma. Ma* [Karttika Sam 2017].

Anonymous. Bibliography on Kalidasa - Ujjain; Vikrama University Library, 1964. Pilot fascicule (Bibliographical Services Series; 5).

Anonymous. The heroines in Kalidasa's plays : a study *Modern Review*, Feb. 1964; Vol. cxv, No. 2; Pp. 148 - 149.

Anonymous. Kalidasa as dramatist. *Indian Review* Dec. 1926; Vol. XXVII; P. 823. Review of an article in the Quarterly Journal of Mytical Society.

Anonymous. Kalidasajanmapi-thasabhara anusthanapatra [s.l.] : [s.n.], [n.d.]. This anonymous author opined that Gadda Singru village of Murshidabad as the birth place of Kalidasa which was later repudiated by V.V. Mirashi.

Anonymous. Kalidasa Jayanti Samaroha. *Aryan Path*; Jan. 1959; Vol. XXX, No. 1; P. 46. Report on the Kalidasa festival in Ujjain.

Anonymous. Kalidasakritam nayikavarnanam. *Man*; April 1958; Vol. XII, No. 8; Pp. 215 - 216.

Anonymous. Kalidasapadyesvalankaradosavivekah *San.*; Sam 2025; Vol. IV, Nos. 1-2; Pp. 15 - 18.

Anonymous. Nicula aur Kalidas. *NPP*; [Sam 1997]; Vol. XLV; P. 173.

Anonymous. [On stanzas from Asvaghosa; Kalidasa and Sriharsa] *Man*; Nov. 1961 Vol. XI, No. 3.

Arjunwadkar, Leela Kalidasa : the loom of time by Chandra Rajan. *Annals of the Bhandarkar Oriental Research Institute*; 1990; Vol. LXXI, Nos. I - IV. Pp. 338 - 340. Book review.

Athavale, R.B. Prayoga - vijnana of Kalidasa / by R.B. Athavale. *Journal of Asiatic Society (Bombay)*; 1977 - 78; Vols. 52 - 53, Pp. 17 - 24.

Aufrecht, Theodar.; Catalogus catalogorum. - Weisbaden : Franz Steiner Verlag Gmb. H, 1962. 2 Vols.; 26 cm.

Vol. 1 - P. 23.

Vol. 2 - P. 6.

Vol. 3 - P. 6.

Bakshi, Padunlal Pannalal Meghadut : Kalidasa ka atmacarita. *Sar*; Dec. 1920; Vol. XXI, Pt. 2, No. 6; Pp. 269 - 292.

An attempt to brought the life of Kalidasa as reflected from his epic.

Balakrishnan, Purasu. Glimpses of Kalidasa - Bombay : Bhavan's Book University, [1971]. Review by Prema Nandkumar published in *Indian PEN*; Oct. 1971 Vol. XXXVII; Pp. 288 - 290.

Balakrishnan, Pursau. Kalidasa's similes. *Triveni*; June 1944; Vol. XVI, No. 2; P. 141 - 146.

Balakrishnan, S. Kalidasa : the poet. *Triveni*; Vol. IV, No. 7; Pp. 64- 73.

Balasubramia Aiyar, K. Kalidasa and Nature. *Triveni*; Jan. - Feb. 1935; Vol. VII, No. 4; Pp. 341 - 345.

Balbir, J.K. A suggestion for a ballet 'Abhijnanasakuntalam'. *All India Oriental Conference* XVII (Summary); P. 283.

Bamba, Tejkumar. Janakathaomen. Kalidasa. *Ka. Vi*; 1959; Pp. 181 - 82.

Bandyopadhyay; Dhanapathi. The Date of Kalidasa. *QJMS;* Oct. 1919; Vol. X, No. 1; Pp. 75 - 96.

Bandyopadhyay, Dhanapathi. The date of Kalidasa : a rejoinder. *QJMS*, July 1920; Vol. X, No. 4; Pp. 364 - 371.

Bandyopadhyay, Pratap. Bharatiyaikyaspa pratinidhiti Kalidasah. *Calcutta Sanskrit College Magazine*; 1958 -59. Paper read at Kalidasa Samaroha, Ujjain.

Bandyopadhyay, Pratap Chandra Kalidasa dristiya Kavyasya Svarupam. *J. Skt. Sah. Parisat (Calcutta)*, May - Aug. 1967; Vol. L, Nos. 1 - 4.

Paper read in the 8th session of World Academy of Sanskrit of Bangalore, in June, 1966.

Bandyopadhyay, Pratap Chandra Kalidasa dristiya kavyasya Svarupam. *Samvid*; Aug. - May 1967- 68; Vol. IV, Nos. 1 - 4; Pp. 48 - 53.

Bandyopadhyay, Sharadindul. Kalidasa - Calcutta : [s.n.], 1943. A Bengali drama on the life of Kalidasa.

Bandyopadhyay, Sures Chandra. A companion to Sanskrit literature - Delhi : Motilal Banarsidass, 1971.

Bandyopadhyay, Sureshchandra. Sanskrit Sahityer itihas. - Calcutta : The Dacca Students Library, [1970 ?].

Bangla granthapanji = Bibliography of Bengali books in print / ed. by Sunil Kumar Ray and [et. al] - Calcutta : State Central Library, 1980. Pp. 88 - 90, 254.

Basu, Dependranath. Shakuntalay Dnatyakala / by Dependranath Basu. - Calcutta: Sarasvati Library, [1972]

190p.

Beer, Kolad. Kalidas and Brecht / by Ronald Beer. *Sangeet Natak Journal* Oct. - Dec. 1975; Vol. 38 Pp. 11 - 20.

Bendall, Cecil. Kalidasa in Ceylon. *JRAS*; 1888; Vol. XX (New Series); P. 440.

Bendre, D.R. Kalidasacya Natakanitila nandisloka. *Navabharata*; July 1954; Vol. VII, No. 10; Pp. 27 - 30.

Betai, Ramesh Chandra. Theory of aesthetic and poetry in Kalidasa *Vikrama (Ka. Vi)*; 1964; Pp. 163 - 176.

Bhaduri, Satyendranath. Some interesting sidelight on urbain improvisation in Abhijnanasakuntala. *SPAIUC* - XX; (Jadavpur), 1969.

Bhaduri, Satyendranath. Upamas of Kalidasa: their dramatic aspects. *SPAIOC* (Ujjain); 1972. P. 468.

Bhandarkar, D.R. Can we fix the date of Kalidasa more accurately, *ABORI*; Vol. VIII, Pt. 2; Pp. 200 - 204.

Bhandarkar, D.R. Solecisms of Sankaracharya, and Kalidasa *IA*; Sept. 1912; V A XLI; P. 214.

Bharadwaj, Bhagnvan sharan Kalidasasyopama vilasah *Bharati (JP)* 1969; Vol. XIX, No. 12 Pp. 416 - 418.

Bharadwaj, S.P. Kalidasa darshan - Delhi : Ashok Prakashan 1987.

486 p.; 22 cm.

Bharadwaj, Shiv Pramod, Kalidasa ke nari - patra. *V. Jy*; July 1960; Vol IX, No.5 Pp. 30 - 33.

Bharati, Kamala. Mahakavi Kalidasa ke vidusaka. *Sarasvati*; Sept. 1964; Vol. LXV, Pt. 2, No. 3, Pp. 260 - 262.

Bhardare, L.S. Imagery of Kalidasa - Bombay : [s.n.] 1960.
Review appeared in *Indian PEN* July 1970, Vol. XXXVI; Pp. 219 - 220.

Bhat, G.K. Appointment with Kalidasa - Ahmedabad : L.D. Institue of Indology 1982.

Bhat, G.K. Sanskrit drama : problems and prospectives - Delhi : Ajanta publication, 1985.

Bhat, G.K. Some aspects of Kalidasa's writings *Patkar College Silver Jubilee No.* (Goregaon, Bombay).

Bhatnagar, Kailashnath. Kavisamrat Kalidasa; Lahore : (s.n.), [Sam. 2002].

Bhatt, Bharat Ram. Yaksha - purush Kalidasa - Delhi : Rajesh Prakashan, 1989.

192 p.; 22cm.

Bhatt, H.D. Shailesh Kalidasa's last journey : a story *MR* : Oct 1962; Vol. CXII,

No. 4, Pp. 293 - 295.

Bhatt, Janardan. Kalidasa aur Bhavabhuti. *Sar*; July 1913; Vol. XIX, Pt. 2. No. 1; Pp. 373- 378.

Bhatt, Rajeshvari, Vasantasya caturascitrakarah Kalidasa *Bharati* (JP); Vol. XXI, No. 5; Pp. 179 - 181.

Bhatt, S.C. Drama in ancient India - New Delhi : Amrit Book Co., 1961.

Bhatt, Udaysankar. Kalidasa / by Udaysankar Bhatta Delhi : Rajkamal Prakasan 1950

Viii, 120 p.; 18.5 cm.

Bhattacharya, Bhavatosh, Mahakavi Kalidasa ka pracyaprticya paddhatisamnath samalocana *KSSVP*; Jan. 1963 : Vol. 1, No. 1; Pp. 25 - 26.

Bhattacharya, Bimanchandra. Sanskrit sahityer ruprekha - 5th ed. - Calcutta : Vidyodaya Library Pvt. Ltd., 1972. contents : Kalidasa. Pp. 87 - 97.

Bhattacharya, Bishwanath. Asvaghosa - Kalidasayas - samvadah *Vikrama (Ka. Vi)*; 1964; Pp. 1 - 6.

Bhattacharya, Bishwanath, Kalidasasyopama - prakaranvaicitray - vicarah - *Jr. of Karnataka University* (Humanities) (Dharwar); 1971; Vol. XV, Pp. 1 - 7.

Bhattacharya, B. Kalidasavisayakapracya praticyasamalocana *KSSVP*; Vol. 1 No. 1; Pp. 25 - 26. Summary published in *Pr. Jy.*; Vol. I, Pt. 1.

Bhattacharya, Bishwanath. Kalidasiyam natyajagat. *Sagarika* (Sagar University); [Saṁ 2023] Vol. V, No. 1; P. 5 - 16.

Bhattacharya, Bishwanath. Kavyagaurave [sic] Kalidasa Kavyam *Sag*; Sami 2024; Vol. VI, No. 3 Pp. 267 - 282.

Bhattacharya, Biswanath. Three worlds of Kalidasa. The *Vikrama University Journal: Kalidasa Visesanka*; 1959; Pp. 39 47.

Bhattacharya, Guruprasanna Kalidasa o Vikramaditya.

Bhattacharya, Guruprasanna An introduction to the mind & art of Bhavbhuti. Contains a study of Kalidasa too.

Bhattacharya, Hillol. Tragedy : ek bicchhannatar itihas *Syas Natya Patra* - 15; 1999.

In Bengali.

Bhattacharya, Manmathanath. The Birth place of Kalidasa - 2nd ed.- [s.l.]; [s.n.], 1938.

Bhattacharya, Manmathanath. The world poet Kalidasa was, Bengali ? *Proc. AIOC* (Calcutta), 1923; P. LI.

Bhattacharya, Satipati, Mahakavi Kalidasa - [s.l.] : [s.n.], [n.d.].

An article in Bengali.

Bhattacharya, Siddheshvar Mahakavi Kalidasa *KSSVP*, 1963; Vol. 1 No. 1, Pp. 11- 15.

Bhattacharya, S.P. Kavikrlgnrormanh - siksa. *KSSVP*; Jan. 1963; Vol. 1, Pt. 1, Pp. 67 - 87. Summary appeared in *Pr. Jy*; Vol. 1.

Bhandaji, The literary remains of Bhandaji - Calcutta Pp. 49 - 51. On the basis of his identify with Matradatta thought of the kashmirian home of Kalidasa.

Bhave, S.S. Kalidasa : the national poet of India. 2nd ed. Baroda : [s.n.], 1964.

Bhide, H.B. Kalidasa and the Gupta Kings. *Proc. AIOC*, Vol. 1; P. lii.

Bhide, H.B. Kalidasacya Kalanirnayaci eka navi desa *Vi. J. V.*; Jan. : 1925; Vol. Lvi, No. 1; Pp. 1 - 8.

Bibliografia Indiyi / ed. by G.K. Kotovsky. - Moscow : [s.n.], 1965; Entries on Kalidasa.

Blouch, The odor. Die zeit Kalidasa's *ZDMG*; Vol. Lxii.

Bopardikar, M.N. Kalidasacatoryam *G.R.*; Aug. 1967; Vol. II, No. 3, Pp. 13 - 15.

Bose, Bela Collected works of Kalidasa / by Bela Bose .- Allahabad : [s.n.], 146.

Brahman K.S.N. The Date of Kalidasa *SVUOJ*; 1958; Vol. 1, Pp. 75 - 88.

Buddhaprakash. Kalidasa and the Hunas *JIH*; April 1957; Vol. XXXV, P. 1; Pp. 91 - 135.

Buhler *Festschrift Kuhn*. P. 108 Deals with the sacrifice of Samudragupta and Kalidasa.

Reference in HKG.

Buhler. Die Indias chen inschriften. Pp. 24 - 25. A comparative study of Kalidasa.

On Kalidasa and Vatsabhatti; Pp. 18 ff x 24 ff.

Reference in HKG.

The Cambridge guide to world theatre / ed. - by James R. Brandes - Cambridge : Cambridge University Press, 1993.

The Cambridge guide to world theatre / ed. by Martin Bantam .- Cambridge : Cambridge University Press, 1988.

Capturing the Kalidasa rasa. *The Sunday Observer*; 25th March, 1990.

Carlo, Della Casa. The Fortunes of Kalidasa in Italy *EW*; July 1955; Vol. VI, No. 2; Pp. 160 - 162.

Chakaldar, H.C. Social life in ancient India. [s.l.]; [s.n.], [n.d.].

Chakrabarti, Bhatt Mukunda Vikramaditya Vikramabda evam Kalidasa *Vina*; March 1944; Vol. XVII, No. 5; Pp. 237 - 242 & 246.

Chakrabarti, Manmohan A few notes and comments on the Gupta - age theory of Kalidasa. *JRAS*; 1904; Pp. 158 - 161.

Chakrabarti, Manmohan. Notes on the date of Kalidasa *JRAS*; 1903; Pp. 183 - 186.

Chakrabarti, Nagendranath. A resume of criticism in Bengali on Kalidasa's works.

Vikrama (Ka Vi); 1967; Pp. 75 - 88.

Chakrabarti, Shambhunath. Kalidas rachanasangraher bhumikaparba. - Calcutta: Nabark, 1988.

1137 p.; 22 cm.

Chakrabarti, Shyamalkanti. Epistoles in Kalidasa : study In OSB : a handbok of AIOC - XXV - Calcutta : Jadavpur University, 1969,1969, P. 82.

Chandrashekharan, K. The Indian Poet's poet. *Aryan Path*; Aug. 1942; Vol. XIII, No. 8, Pp. 340 - 342.

Chandrashekharan, K. Kalidasa: The supreme poet of love. *BJ*; Dec. 1989; Vol. V, No. 10; Pp. 35 - 38.

Chatterji, Akhil Chandra, Kalidasa: his poety and mind - [s.l.] [s.n.], [1911 ?].

Review appeared in *IR*, August 1911; Vol. XII; P. 631.

Chatterji, Khirod Bihari Kalidasa. *All India Oriental Conference* II. P. 1.

Chatterji, Kshitishchandra. Bharati Kalidasasya - III *Man*; March 1956; Vol. X,

No. 7; Pp. 178 - 180.

--------. The Date of Kalidasa. Allahabad University Studies; 1926; Vol. II; Pp. 79 - 170.

Review published in 1929 in the journal 'JAOS'; Vol. LIX; Pp. 75 - 76.

--------. Kalidas ka kaal, kriti, kala - Delhi : [s.n.], 1969.

Three lectures delivered in the Lal Bahadur Shastri Kendriya Vidyapeetha, Delhi in Nov. 1969.

--------. Kalidasa and the Hunas. JIH; 1936; Vol. XV, Pts. I to III,; Pp. 93 - 102.

Chatterji, Jayashri. Kalidasiya kavye nisargollasals. SPAIOC (Ujjain); 1972; P. 177.

Catterji, K.C. The poems of the Kalidasa Allahabad University Magazine, 1936; Pp. 34 - 51.

Reference is JGJREI 1971; Vol. XXVII; Pp. 3 - 4.

Chatterji, Tarashamkar. Kalidasa kabya - [s.l.]; [s.n.], 1956.

Chaturvedi, B.K. Kavisanrat Kalidasa aur unka kavya *Vina*; Jan. 1948; Vol. XXI, No. 3; Pp. 117, 123.

Chaturvedi, Brajakishor. Mahakavikalidasa *Vikrama* (Hindi); Dec. 1942; Vol. No. 3; Pp. 38 - 40.

Chaturvedi, Giridhar Sharma Kalidasa ki alocanaen *Sar*, Dec. 1959, Vol. LX, No. 6; Pp. 377 - 380.

Chaturvedi, Shivadatta, Kalidasasya sobdayojana *Sag* (Ka. Vi); 1974; Pp. 101 - 104.

Chaturvedi, S.P. The Immortal message of Kalidasa *Kisora* (Bamkipur special Kalidasa No.); May 1944.

Reference in NUT; 1948 - 49; No. XVI; P. 103.

Chaturvedi, Somendrachandra Kalidasasya vivaharvarnanam pratibha (*VSV*); [saṁ 2027]; Pp. 64 - 65.

Chaube, Ram Kumar The date of Kalidasa Pvuc. *AIUC - IV* (Allahabad); 1927; P. 33.

Chaube, Ram Kumar. The date of Kalidasa : a new approach Proc. *ICO* (New Delhi); 1964, Vol. 1 (1966); Pp. 108 - 109. Summary.

Chaube, Ram Kumar. The date of Kalidasa. *AIUC - XXIV* (Varanasi); Oct. 1968; P. 289.

Chaube, Ram Kumar. The date of Kalidasa: summary. *All India Oriental Conferences* IV; Vol. 1. Summaries, 38.

Chaube, Ram Kumar. The history of the word Apratiratha and its bearing on the date of Kalidasa. *All India Oriental Conference XVI*. (Summaries); P. 81.

Chaube, Ram Kumar Kalidasa ki pratistha aur unke samay tatha grantha rachana kram sambandhi vivecana par ek dristi *NPP*; [Sam. 1986] Vol. X; P. 511.

Chellappan Pillai K. Similes of Kalidasa [Upamakalidasa] - 1945 (*Vishvabharati Studies*; No. 7).

Reviews by Nagardranath Aug. - Oct. 1946; Vol. XII, Pt. 2; P. 168.

China men Kalidasa *Aj*; Sept. 1956; Vol. VIII, No. 9, Pp. 75 - 76. Editorial note based on an article in People Chira [a summary of Kalidasa tr. in chinese].

Ciechoniz, Jain the old - Indian theatre in Poland / by Jan Ciehowicz *Sangeet Natak Akademi Journal* 6 April - June 1976, Vol. 40, Pp. 23 - 40.

Comparative Indian Literature / ed. by K.M. George Trichur : Kerala Sahitya Akademi, 1994 Pp. 564 - 565.

The critique of Indian theatre / ed. by M.L. Varadpande and Sunil Subhedar - Delhi : Unique Publications, 1981.

Cultural heritages of India [Vol. V] / ed. by Suniti Kumar Chatterji - rev. ed. - Calcutta : The Ramakrishna Mission Institute of Culture, 1978. P. 242.

Dalal, Minakshi L. Conflict in Sanskrit drama - Bombay : Somaiya Publications Pvt. Ltd. 1973. Contents : Kalidasa, Pp. 37, 38, 44, 280, 297, 183 - 198, 260 - 264.

Damale, Gangadhara Govinda. Mahakavi Kalidasa va tyaci kavita. *Vi.J.V.*; Sept.- Oct. 1912; Vol. XLIII; Pp. 441 - 459.

Dange K.N. Kalidasa dirghayu rahe honge *Sar*; Dec. 1971; Vol. LXXII, No. 6; Pp. 457 - 459.

Dange, K.N. Kalidasa ki rasavatta (purvardha) - *I Sar*; August 1970; Vol. LXXI, Pt. 2, No. 2; Pp. 105 - 108.

— Kalidasa ki rasavatta - II [Second Part] *Sar*; Sept. 1970; Vol. LXXI; Pp. 231 - 234.

Dange, K.N. Mahakavi Kalidasa ka vyaktitva *Sar* May 1957; Vol. LVIII; Pp. 311 - 312.

Dange, K.N. Vrksa - mitra Kalidasa *Sar*; Feb. 1971; Vol. LXXII, No. 2; Pp. 107 - 109.

Kulamani Kalidasa sandarbha / by Kulamani Das - Cuttuck : Bisvanath Kara, 1924.

275 p.;

Critical study of Kalidasa.

Das Sarbeshwar. The comic and romantic in Sanskrit dramas with special reference to Bhisa, Kalidasa, Harsa and Bhavabhuti, Summary of papers : *All India Oriental Conference* (Bhuvaneshwar); 1959, Vol. XX.

Dasgupta, Shashi Bhushan, Upama Kalidasasya / tr. from Bengali by Vishnukant a Sastri. - Delhi : [s.n.], 1962.

Dasgupta, Shashibhushana Upama prayog men Kalidasa ke upar Valmiki ka prabhav *Bhartiya Sahitya*; Jan. 1961; Vol. VI, No. 1.

Dasgupta, Sitarath. [On Kalidasa ?]

Dasgupta, S.N. Kalidasa-*I Pr. V.;* Jan.- April 1945; Vol. II, No.1 - 2; Pp. 12 - 19.

Dasgupta, S.N. Kalidasa - II *Pr. V;* July - Oct. 1945; Vol.. II, No. 3 - 4; Pp. 100 - 110.

Dass, Krishna. The female garments of Kalidasa / by Krishna Dass. *Proceedings of the All India Oriental Conference*, 28, Seminar held at Karnataka University, Dharwar in Nov. 1976. Pooa : *BORI*, 1978. Pp. 271 - 276.

Dattaraya, Govinda. Kavikulaguru Kalidasaca astitvakal *N. Bh*; Jan. 1959; Vol. XII, No. 4; Pp. 55 - 66.

De, Sushil Kumar. Aspects of Sanskrit literature - Calcutta : Firma KLM, 1959. Pp. 104 - 220.

De, S.K. Kalidasa. *Indian Historical Quarterly*; June 1940; Vol. 16, No. 2; Pp. 385 - 422.

De. S.K. Kalidasa and Vikramaditya / by S.C. De. - Calcutta : The author, 1928. XI.

571 p.; 18 cm.

Includes index.

De, S.K. Kalidasa. *IHQ; Vol.* XVI; Pp. 384 - 422; Summary appeared in *ABIHI*; 1940; Vol. III; 1944; P. 132.

De. S.K. Kalidasa Louis de la vallee Poussin comm. Vol; Pp. 16 7 - 204.

Deb. Amiya Tragi Comic suffering in Sakuntala, Uttaracmaacarita, Cymbeline and Winter's tale / by Amiya Deb. *Jadavpur University Comparative Literature* 1968, No. 8 Pp. 50 - 84.

The Denouncement and its dramatic properties in Abhijiana Sakuntala, Uttarama carita and Mrcchakatika *Sanskrita - Ranga Annual* - 6; 1972; Pp. 38 - 58.

Deo, Surendra. Kalidasa aur Bhavbhuti ke natako ka tulanat mak adhyayan Ph.D. thesis, Agra 1963.

Dev, Gayatri. Kalidasiyarupakesu samudrachrasnmunmesah [sic] *Sagarika; Kalidasa visesanka*; Vol. XIII, No. 1; Pp. 75 - 84.

Devadatta, Sastri Kalidasa : ek anusilan. - Varanasi [s.n.]; 1962.

Devadhar, C.R. Dramas of Kalidasa - Delhi : Motilal Banarasidass, 1966 various paginations; 19 cm. Critical study.

Devasthali, G.V. Kalidasa Isvarakrsna identity tenable *V.V. Mirashi fel. Vol.* - Nagpur; [s.n.], 1965, Pp. 150 - 164.

Devendra Kumar Kavivara Kalidasa ke natakon ki mukhya samasya Nari, *Vina*; Nov. - Dec. 1957; Nos. 1 - 2, Pp. 21 - 27.

Devendra Kumar Kalidasa - Bangalore; Ananda brothers, 1952.

165 p.; 18 cm.

Dhruva, Keshalal Harshadray Kalidasaya nivassthanam *Ma Ma*; Vol. XIX, No. 8; P. 11.

Dhruva, Kesavlal Harshadray Kalidasaya vrttaprayoganam nikasopalan / tr. by Rudradeva Tripathi *Ma. Ma.*; Vol. XIX, No. 10; Pp. 5 - 7.

Dictionary of oriental literatures (Vol. II); South and South - East Asia - Delhi : Vikas Publishing, 1975.

Dikshit, Kalikaprasada Kusmakara Kalidasa ki saundaryanubhuti. Vina (Kā Vī.), 1959, Pp. 139 - 141.

Dikshit, Siddhinath Kalidasa aur unka Vikramaditya. *Sar*, 1930; Vol. XXXI, Pt. 2, No. 5; Pp. 515 - 526.

Dikshit, Surendranath. Kalidasa ke natyadarsa aur adhunika Hindi naty a parampara Summary of papers : *All India Orienal Conference* [Ujjain]; P. 478.

Dikshit, Surendranath Kalidasa ki natyakala.

Dikshit, Vinod. Kalidasa even prakriti *Vina*; Jan. 1967; Vol. XL, No. 3; Pp. 146 - 147.

Dutta, Kali Kumar. Kancukin in Kalidasa's dramas. the *Vikrama University Journal Kalidasa Visesanka*; 1959; Pp. 49- 55.

Dvivedi, Ayodhyaprasad Kalidasasyopama bimbasca. *Sag*; Saṁ 2029; Vol. X, No. 4. Pp. 517 - 528.

Dvivedi Ayodhyaprasad Kalisasya candrabimbah *Sag* Saṁ 2029; Vol. XI, No. 2; Pp. 125 - 142.

Dvivedi, Channutal Kalidasa aur Shakespeare / by Channutal Dvivedi Banaras; Jan Granthamala Karyalay, 1923.

280 p.; plate, 18.5 cm.

Dvivedi, Ganesh Prasad. Kavi Kalidaa. A Hindi play on the life of Sanskrit poet and dramatist.

Dvivedi, Hazariprasad Kalidas ki Inlitya - yojna - Varanasi : [s.n.], 1965.

Dvivedi, Keshav. Amarkavi Kalidasa *Di J*; Feb. 1958; Vol. II, Pp. 18 - 21.

Dvivedi, Mahavirprasad Hindi Kalidasa ki somalocana / by Mahavir Prasad Dvivedi - Kanpur : Merchent press, 1901.

158 p.; 522.5 cm.

Dvivedi, Mahavir Prasad Kalidasa Jabbalpur : [s.n.], 1920 Nine essays on Kalidasa.

Dvivedi, Mahavir Prasad Kalidasa aur unki Kavita - Jabalpur; [s.n.], 1920. Collected essay published in Sarasvati.

Dvivedi, Mahavir Prasad Kalidasa ka saamy *Sar*; June 1907; Vol. VIII, No. 6, Pp. 222 - 227.

Kalidasa ki nirankusta / by Mahavirprasad Dvivedi - Allahabad : Indian Press,1911.

ii, 88 p.; 16 cm.

—— Mahakavi Kalidasa aur unki kavita - Allahabad Tarun Bharat granthavali, 1920.

Dvivedi, Revaprasad Kalidasa sahitya men karura ka sthan *Vikrama* (Hindi); Aug. - Sept. 1954; Vol. VIII (1), No. 3 - 4; Pp. 17 - 24.

Dvivedi, R.C. Dhvani in Kalidasa SPAIOC (Kurukshetra); 1974; P. 52.

Dvivedi, Vijayagovinda. Kalidasa ki Kavyakala ki yupasimaen *Vina* (Ka. Vi); Pp. 113 - 120.

Encyclopaedia of Indian Literature - New Delhi : Sahitya Akademi, 1987 - 1994. Pp. 239, 570, 827, 828, 1071, 1100, 1108, 1109, 1206, 1335, 1661, 1934-36, 2175, 2433, 2499, 2558, 2646, 3280, 3281, 3494, 3679, 3699, 3789, 3965, 4576, 4660.

Folk, Masyla Kalidasa in China *Indian Historical Quarterly*; Dec. 1993, Vol. No. 4, Pp. 829 - 834.

Finot, Louis. Kalidasa in China *IHQ*; 1993, Vol. IX, Pt. 4; Pp. 829 - 834.

Fisher, Ivo. Kalidasa - nejyetsi basnik staroveke India = Kalidaa - the greatest poet of ancient India.

Reference in *Arch. Or*; 1957; Vol. XXV.

The Formative influences of Kalidasa *IR*; Nov. 1918; Vol. XIX, P. 785. A summary of the article in QJMS; Oct. 1918.

Foulkes T. A complete collection of the various reading of the Madras manuscripts Vol. IV.

Vikramorvasiya Acts I - V Madras, 1907.

Francisca, Juan R. Kalidasa : his concept of beauty in nature. *Triveni*; July 1968; Vol. XXXVII, No. 2; Pp. 18 - 21.

Francisca, Juan. R. Kalidasa : his nature beauty. *Diliman Rev.*; 1963 Vol. XI, Pp. 237 - 257.

Reference in J.As SW.; Sept. 1956; Vol. XXXV, No. 5. Pp. 273- 276.

Frazer, R.W. A literary history of India - London; T. Fishe Unwin, 1898. Pp. 5 (Kalidasa praised by Goethe) Pp. 248, 288; Malavikagnimitra, et. sq., P. 288 (Vikramorvasi).

Gaidhani, R.N. The Nun's complicity in the plots of the Vidusaka in Malavikagnimitra of Kalidasa *All India Oriental Conference XVI* (Summary); P. 185.

Gajendragadkar, S.N. Heroines in Sanskrit drama; Kalidasa plays and the mrcchakatik / by S.N. Gajendragadkar. Paper presented at *the All India Oriental Conference* (22nd Session) held at Gauhati Assam in January 1965.

Gajendragadkar, S.N. Heroines in Sanskrit drama; Kalidasa plays and Mrchakatika *Summary of papers, All India Oriental Conference; XXII* [Gauhati]; 1965; Vol. 1.

Gandhi, Shanta. Relevant Sanskrit theatre / by Shanta Gandhi *Enact* March - April 1975. Contains synopsis of Kalidasa's Vikramorvashiyam in the end.

Garg, Ganga Ram. An Encyclopaedia of Indian literature - Delhi : Mittal Publishers, 1982. Pp. 169 - 170, 232, 364 - 366, 492 - 493.

Gawronski - On the date of Kalidasa. *Roeznik Orientalistycany* - Krakau; [s.n.], 1914 - 1915. Pp. 1 - 10.
Reference in HKG.

Gera, Vimla. Mind and art of Bhavabhuti - Delhi : Meharchand Lachhanadas 1973. Contains studies on Kalidasa (Pp. 254 - 270).

Ghosh, Ajay Kumar. Kalidasa Kahini o Katha - rahasya - Cuttuck : [s.n.], 1923 - 1933 reference in NLCCI (Oriya).

Ghosh, Aurobindo. Kalidasa by / Aurobindo Ghose 2nd ed. - Pondicherry : Sri Aurobindo Ashram. Deals with Kalidasa's seasons its authenticity, the substance of the poem, its poetic value.

Ghose, Aurobindo, Kalidasa : study of Kalidaa's age & his works - Calcutta. Review published in *IR*; Nov. 1929; Vol. XXX; P. 702.

Ghospukar, Mangal. Kavikulaguruhb Kalidasah *G.R.*; Oct. 1972; Vol. VII, No. 1; Pp. 21 - 22.

Glimpses of Sanskrit literature / ed. by A.N.D. Haksar - New Delhi; Indian Council for Cultural Relations, 1995. Contents : Kalidasa Pp. 5 - 7, 16, 37, 51 - 59, 61, 73, 77, 108 - 113, 132, 136, 139, 153, 181.

Gode, P.K. Psychological study of Kalidasa's upamas *Proc. AIOC* - I; 1920. Summary Paper published in Vol. II. Pp. 205 - 226.

Gode, P.K. The word Atmabhu and the date of Kalidasa *ABORI*; January 1920; Vol. 1; P. 185.

Gopal Krishna, *Sastri* - Kalidaso pajnarasajnata (1) *MSSP* January 1929; Vol. IV, No. 1 Pp. 17 - 24; April 1928; No. 2; Pp. 39 - 46 and July 1928; No. 3. Pp. 80 - 87.

Govindacharyaswami, P. Kalidasa belongs to Andhradesha *Proc. AIOC* - VIII

(Mysore); 1935. Summary, P. 26.

Govinddas, Seth. Kalidasa Jayanti par adhyaksiya bhasan. *Vina*; Nov. - Dec. 1957; Vol. XXXI, Nos. 1 - 2; Pp. 21- 27.

Goyal, S.R. The date of Kalidasa; an old suggestion modified / by S.R. Goyal *SPAIOC*; Vol. 1. P. 72 Paper presented at the *All India Oriental Conference.* (22nd semion) held at Gauhati, Assam in January 1965.

Grierson, G.L.A. Are Kalidasa's heroes monogamists ? *JASB*; 1877; Vol. XLVI, Pt. 1; Pp. 39 - 40.

Grierson, G.A. Kalidasa and the Guptas. *JARS*; 1903, P. 363.

Grotowski and the Indian tradition. *Sangeet Natak Akadami Journal*; 1972 Vol. 23. Pp. 15 - 25.

Gupta, Atulchandra : Rabrdranath and Sanskrit literature In Rabindranath Tagore 1861 - 1961 : a centenary Volume - New Delhi : Sahitya Akademi, 1961, Pp. 133 - 139. An English article that Tagore's critical appreciation of Kalidasa.

Gupta, Jagdish Vatsalya rasa ke prathama udbhavaka Kalidasa *Sam Pat*. [Caitra - Margasirsa, Saka, 1894]; Vol. LVIII, Nos. 2 - 4. (Sahitya Sanskrita - bhasa Visesa).

Gupta, S.K. The problem of Kalidasa / by S.K. Gupta Paper presented at the *All India Oriental Conference* (22nd Session) held at Gauhati Assam in January 1965.

Gurner, C.W. Imagery of moon and ocean in Kalidasa IC Jan. 1939; Vol. V, No. 3; Pp. 337 - 338, summry in Annual bibliography of History and Indology.

Gurner, C.W. Personification of night as woman in Kalidasa. *Acarya Puspanjali Vol. In Honour of Dr. D.R. Bhandarkar* (Calcutta); 1940; Pp. 323 - 324. Summary in *ABIHI*; Vol. III for 1940; Bombay, 1944. P. 86.

Gurner, C.W. The poetry of Flight in Kalidasa *IC*, Vol. VIII,; Pp. 107 - 110.

Gurner, C.W. Psychological imagery in Kalidasa *JASB*; 1943; Pp. 191 - 199.

Guruswamy Sastrigal, V.S.V. Kalidasa : the great world poet - Madras : Abhinavi Vidyathertha Mahaswamigal, 1981, X.

166 P.; 21 cm.

Harichand, M, Sastri Kalidasa et L' art poetique de L' inde (Alankarasastra) - Paris p. [s.n.], 1917.

Review appeared in the following journals (I) *JARS*; 1918; Pp. 564 - 572 (Reviewer : A.A. Macdonell) (II) *ZDMG*; Vol. LXXIII; Pp. (Reviewer : John nobel) Pp. 189 - 126.

Harichand, M. Les citations de Kalidasa dans ke Traites d Alankara JA (Series), II, 1916; Vol. VIII, Pp. 51 - 180.

Hillebrandt, Alfred. Kalidasa : an estimate of his literary merit / by Alfred Hillebrandt, tr. from & original German by S.N. Ghosal. - Calcutta : The World Press Pvt. Ltd, 1971.

Ishadatta Sastri 'Srisa'. Kalidasa ka vyapak prabhav. *Vina;* May 1944; Vol. XVII, No. 7; Pp. 336-340.

Jha, Triloknath. The problem of Varie Lectiones of Kalidasa's works. *Calcutta* Review, Jan. 1963; Vol. 166, No. 1; Pp. 29-32.

Jhala, G.C. Kalidasa : a study. - [s.l.] : Padma Publications, 1943.

Second edition published in 1949.

Jhala, G.C. Upama Kalidasasya. *Bharatiya Vidyabhavan Bulletin; Nov.* 1953; No. 10.

Karandikar, A.J. was Kalidasa influenced by the Athenian poets.

Poona Orientatists; July - Oct. 1948; Vol. XXIII, No. 3-4; Pp. 1-11.

Karmarkar, R.D. The Chronological order of Kalidasa's works.

Proceedings of *All India Oriental Conference II.* Calcutta, 1923; Pp. 239-247.

Karmarkar, R.D. Kalidasa. - Dharwar : Karnataka University, 1960. (Karnataka University Dharwar Extention Lecture Series; 4).

Keith, A.B. The date of Kalidasa. *Journal of Royal Asiatic Society of Great Britain and Ireland.* 1901. Pp. 578 - 582.

-----. Vikramaditya and Kalidasa. *Journal of Royal* Asiatic Society of Great Britain and Ireland; 1909; Pp. 433 - 439.

Kotovsky, G.C. *Ed.* Bibliografia Indiyi. - Moscow : [s.n.] 1965.

Krishnamoorthy, Keralapura. Kalidasa. - New York : [s.n.], 1972.

Kunhan Raja, C. Kalidasa : a cultural study. - Waltair : Andhra University, 1956. (Andhra University Series; No. 57).

Lele, V.R. The Heroines of Kalidasa. *Summary of Papers, All India Oriental Conference.* (Kurukshetra); 1974; P. 71.

Mainkar, T.G. Kalidasa : his art and thought. - Poona : [s.n.], 1962.

Majumdar, B.C. The date of Kalidasa. *Journal of Royal Asiatic Society of Great Britain and Ireland;* 1909; Pp. 731 - 739.

Mirashi, V.V. Kalidasa. - Nagpur : [s.n.], 1934.

Mishra, Adyaprasad. Kalidasa sahityam. - Darbhanga " [s.n.], 1962.

(Mahesathakkur samskritagranthamala; No. 2)

Narang, Satyapal. Kalidasa bibliography. - New Delhi : Heritage Publishers, 1976.

Nehru, Jawahar Lal. Kalidasah *Sanskriti Pratibha* (Sahitya Akademi, New Delhi) Oct. 1959; Vol. 1, No. 2; P. 124.

In Sanskrit (Tr. by V. Raghavan of an Abstract of the Lecture on Kalidasa Samaroha in Ujjaini on 11-11-1959.

Ogle, K.L. Kavikulaguru Kalidasa.

Pathak, K.B. Dinnaga and Kalidasa. *Journal of Bombay Branch of Royal Asiatic Society.*

1908 - 1913; Vol. XXIII; Pp. 187 ff.

Peterson, F.G. A note on Kalidasa *Journal of Royal Asiatic Society of Great Britain and Ireland* 1926; Pp. 725 - 726.

Raghavan, V. The Universality of Kalidasa's muse. *Bulletin of the Institute of Tradition Culture* (Madras). May 1959; Vol. III; Pp. 5 - 9.

Rajendranath Vidyabhusana. Kalidasa. - Calcutta : [s.n.], 1909.

An introduction by Harinath De.

Ramachandra Rao, S. The Heroines of the plays of Kalidasa. *The Quarterly Journal of Mythical Society* July 1953; Vol. XLIV, No. 1; P. 33.

Ramaswami Sastri, K.S. Kalidasa : his genius, ideals and influence. 2 Vols.

Ray, Dvijendrala. Kalidas o Bhavabhuti. *In Dvijendra granthavali* Vol. 1. Calcutta (In Bengal).

------. tr. into Hindi by Rupnarayan Pandey. - Bombay : [s.n.], 1977.

Ray, Saradaranjan. The Age of Kalidasa. *Journal of Asiatic Society, Bengal* N.S. 1908; Vol. IV, Pp. 327 - 346.

Ruben, Walter. Kalidasa : the human meaning of his works. - Berlin : Akademie Verlag, 1957.

Sabnis, S.A. Kalidasa : his style and his times. - Bombay : N.M. Tripathi, 1966.

Sashagiri Sastri, M. On some eminent characters in Sanskrit literature. *Indian Antiquary;* Nov. 1872, Vol. 1, Pp. 340 - 343.

Scharpe, A. Kalidasa Lexicon.

Sehgal, S.R. Kalidasa's influence on the west. *Indian PEN*; January 1960; Vol. XXVI, Pp. 8 - 10.

Sharma, Devidatta. Kalidasa ke manavetara pātra. *Vikrama* (Ka. Vi); 1966; Pp. 73 - 83.

Sharma, Dinbeswar. An interpretative study of Kalidasa. - Varanasi : [s.n.], 1968.

Shukla, Yashwant. Mahakavi Kalidasa. - Ahmedabad : [s.n.], 1963.

In Gujarati.

Singh, Amaldhari. Kalidasa's concept of characterization. *Prajna;* 1966 - 1967, Vol. XII, No. 2; Pp. 279 - 291.

Srikrishna Sharma, E.R. Kalidasa samisksa. - Tirupati : Venkateswara University, 1962.

Proceedings of a Seminar on Kalidasa held in January 1962.

Tiwari, Ramashankar. Mahakavi Kalidasa. - Vaanasi : [s.n.], 1961. (Vidyabhavana Rashtrabhasa Granthamala; No. 41).

Unnikrishna Nayar, V. Kalidasahridayam. - Kozhikode : [s.n.], 1964.

Upadhyay, Bhagavat Sharan. Kalidasam namami.

Essays in Hindi.

Vyas, Suryanarayana. Visvavandy kavi Kalidasa. - *Vikrama* (Hindi), Nov. 1953, Vol. VII, No. 2; Pp. 17 - 30.

Warder, A.K. Indian kavya literature. - Delhi : Motilal Banarsidasa, 1977. (Vol. 3), Pp. 122 - 154.

Winternitz, Maurice. A History of Indian literature. - New Delhi : Oriental Books Reprint Corporation, 1972.

First published in 1927 by University of Calcutta.

13

Doctoral Thesis : A Select Bibliography

Acharya, P.B. Tragedy - Comedy in English & Sanskrit : a comparative study of the last plays of Shakespeare, Kalidas & Bhavabhuti.

Indore, 1967-69.

Acharya. Ramjiban / Women in Kalidas : a study / by Ramjiban Acharya. Ph.D. thesis in Sanskrit approved by the University of Calcutta in 1971.

Agarwal, Abha. Women in the works of Kalidas : costumes and cosmetics / by Abha Agarwal. Ph.D. thesis in Hindi approved by the Rohilkhand University in 1982.

Agarwal, Veena. Comparative studyof Aswaghosa and Kalidas with special reference to their philosophy of life / by Veena Agarwal.

Ph.D thesis in Hindi approved by the Aligarh Muslim University in 1978.

Agnihotri, Raj Kumari. Kalidasrachnas narina samajik nirupan. Sampurnanand Sanskrit Vishvavidyalaya 1967 - 1970.

Anasuya Devi. Comparative study of Valmiki and Kalidasa. D. Litt. thesis approved by the Osmania University (1973).

In English.

Ambedkar, R.R. The critical study of the Meghaduta of Kalidas in the light of Bharata's Rasasutra.

University of Bombay, Bombay, 1973 - 75.

Archana Kumari. Kalidasa's sense of beauty and his philosophy of life : a literary evaluation / by Archana Kumari Ph.D thesis approved by the Magadh University in 1981.

Ashok Kumar. Editing and studyof the Akasase in Panktika of Meghaduta by Kalidas by Ashok Kumar. Ph.D. thesis approved by the Kurukshetra University in 1985.

Awasathi, Sudha Rani. Bhas tatha Kalidas ke natya shilpa ka tulanatmak adhyayan.

Kanpur University, 1979.

(Sanskrit).

Bhuria, Kusum. Kalidas ke rupakon ka natya shastriya vivechana Ph.D. Thesis approved from Sagar University in 1978.

Bhuria Kusum. Studyof the dramas of Kalidas from the angle of Natya sastra by Kusum Bhuria. Ph.D. thesis inHindi approved by the Sangam Ch. S. Gaur University in 1978.

Budhani, Indu Psychological study of the male characters of Kalidas by Indu Budhani Ph.D. thesis approved by the Kumaun University in 1984.

Chakrabarti, Dhynesh Narayan Poetic treasure of Kalidas from the stand point of the connoisseur of literature by Dhynesh Narayan Chakrabarti. Ph.D. thesis in Hindi, approved by the Burdwan University in 1976.

Chakrabarti, Minati, Kalidas kee kirtiyon se manav vyektitv ke vikas.

Evolution of humanism in the works of Kalidas by Minati Chakrabarti. Ph.D. thesis approved by the Vikram University in 1966.

Chaturvedi, Induwani. A comparative study of the commentaries of the Abhijnanasakuntalam of Kalidas by Induwani Chaturvedi. Ph.D. thesis approved by the University of Bombay in 1978.

Chaturvedi, Mahesh Nath. Mahakavi Kalidasa ke natakon kee darshnik prishtibhoomi : em vivechana.

Philosophical background of dramas of Kalidasa an analysis by Maheshnath Chaturvedi. Ph.D. thesis in Hindi, approved by the Kanpur University in 1974.

Chatterjee, Shubhra, Techniques of songsin the drama of Kalidasa.

Ph.D. thesis approved by the Aligarh Muslim University in 1976.

Dadhichi, Purushottam. Sanskrit dramatic practice and the drama of Kalidasa / by Purushottam Dadhichi Ph.D. thesis in Hindi, approved by the Vikram Universityin 1979.

Dailele, Nirmal. Dramas of Kalidasa; female minor characters / by Nirmal Dailele Ph.D. thesis approved by the Aligarh Muselim University in 1981.

Deo, Surendra. A comparative studyof the dramas of Kalidasa and Bhavabhuti / by Surendra Deo. Ph.D. thesis approved by the Agra University in 1963.

Dhamia, Kaushal Kumar. Similes in Kalidasa with special reference to his vocabulary / by Kaushal Kumar Dhamia Ph.D. thesis in Hindi, approved by the Punjab University in 1975.

Dikshit, Sushma. Valmiki, Kalidas tatha Bhavbhuti ke samen kathanshon aur pattron kav tulanatmak tatha alochanatmak adhyayan.

Comparative estimation of parallelism in the incidents and characters of Valmiki, Kalidasa and Bhavabhuti / by Sushma Dixit Ph.D. thesis in Hindi approved by the Kurukshetra University in 1972.

Dobhal, Purushottam. Kalidas sahitya kee darshnik prishtbhoomi.

= Philosophical background of Kalidasa works / by Purushottam Dobhal.

Ph.D. thesis in Hindi, approved by the Jodhpur Universityin 1970.

Dwivedi, Ayodhya Prasad Kalidas ka bimb vidhan. Awadesh Pratap Singh University, 1971 - 78.

Dwivedi, Ayodhya Prasad. Imagery of Kalidasa / by Ayodhya Prasada Dwivedi Ph.D. thesis approved by the Avadesh Pratap Universityin 1976.

Dwivedi, Ganesh Prasad. Comparative study of the mahakavyas of Kalidasa and Kumaradasa / by Ganesh Prasad Dwivedi. Ph.D. thesis in Hindi approved by the Gorakhpur University in 1984.

Dwivedi, Jayashankar. Mahakavi Kalidasa charya Ashveghoshayo shailee shabdbhashakal vyakaranam tulanatmika samiksha. Comparative study of the style, vocabulary, grammer and alamkaras of Kalidasa and Aswaghosha / by Jayashankar Dwivedi. Ph.D. thesis in Sanskrit, approved by the Varanaseya Sanskrit Viswavidyalaya in 1966.

Dwivedi, Kailashnath, Kalidas kee kritiyon main bhaugolik sthalon ka pratyabhigyan. (Sanskrit) Agra, 1966 - 68.

Identification of geographical dates mentioned in the works of Kalidasa / by Kailash Nath Dwivedi. Ph.D. thesis in Hindi, approved by the Agra University in 1968.

Fadia, Padma. Kalidasa & Philosophy of nature / by Padma Fadia, Ph.D. thesis approved by the Sardar Patel University in 1966.

Gaur, Parmanand Sharma Developement of lyric poetry in Sanskrit literature, from Kalidas to the end of 12th century, Aligarh University 1960.

Gopal Prasad, Kalidas ke kavyon main chitra vidhan. (Sanskrit) Bhagalpur, 1968 - 71.

Gupta, Mohan Lal, Mahakavya sahitya ko Kalidas kee den (Rajasthan), 1964 - 70.

Gupta, Prem Lata. Kalidasa's vision of beauty / by Premlata Gupta Ph.D. thesis in Hindi, approved by the Rajasthan University in 1981.

Jaiswal, Manjula Kalidas ke kavyon main dhwani .... Allahabad, 1974.

Dhvani in the kavyas of Kalidas, by Majula Jaiswal, Ph.D. thesis in Hindi, approved by the Allahabad University in 1974.

Jha, Deva Kant. Critical and comparative study of Abhijnanasakuntalam and Uttararama charitam / by Deva Kant Jha. Ph.D. thesis approved by the Magadh University in 1970.

Jha, Paramanand. Mahakavi Kalidasa kavyaishri prakriti vishkeshnam. Kameshwer Singh Darbanga Sanskrit University, Darbanga.

Analysis of nature in the works of Kalidasa / by Paramananda Jha. D. Litt. thesis approved by the K.S. Darbhanga University in 1975.

Kamal Prabhu. Kalidas mein sadrisya vidhana in Kalidasa / by Kamal Prabhu. Ph.D. thesis in Hindi, approved by the Rajastan University in 1974.

Kandpal, B.D. Kalidas ke sahitya mein bimb vidhan, Kumaun University 1975 - 79.

Imagery in the works of Kalidasa / by B.D. Kandpal. Ph.D. thesis approved by the Kumaun University in 1979.

Kandpal, K.C. Indian culture as rended through the important alankars : a study from Kalidasa to Sriharha based on the mahakavya and a drama / by K.C. Kandpal. Ph.D. thesis approved by the Kumaun University in 1985.

Kumbhaj, Krishna. Psychology in the works of Kalidasa / by Krishna Kumbhaj. Ph.D. thesis in HIndi, approved by the Devi Ahilya Viswavidyalay in 1983.

Lodhi, Jai Prasad. Estimation of the worksof Kalidasa from the point of rasa / by Jai Prasad Lodhi. Ph.D. thesis in Sanskrit, approved by the Sampoornand Sanskrit Vizwa - Vidyalaya in 1978.

Madhuri, Prabha Spiritual and cultural background of the works of Kalidasa.

(Indian culture based on the works of Kalidasa). Ph.D. thesis approved by the Agra University in 1975.

Mallik. Raghunath, Kalidas pratibha. Calcutta University, 1978, (Bengali).

Mehta, Manju. Kalidas ka manvetar vilas [sic] Garhwal University.

Depiction of nature in Kalidasa's works / by Manju Mehta. Ph.D. thesis in Hindi, approved by the Garhwal University in 1979.

Mishra, Madhusudan. Metres of Kalidasa / by Madhusudan Mishra. Ph.D. thesis approved by the Patna University in 1974.

Mishra, Pashupati Nath. Kalidas ke upamaon ka vishleshatmak adhyayan.

Critical study of the similes of kalidas / by Pashupathinath Misra. Ph.D. thesis n Hindi approved by the Patna University in 1979.

Mishra. Satya Deo. Comparative study of the concept of beauty of Bana Kalidas / by Satya Deo Mishra. Ph.D. thesis in Hindi approved by the Gorakhpur University in 1987.

Mishra, Thakurprasad, Kalidas kee kavyabhasha ka adhyayan.

Poetic language of Kalidasa : a study / by Thakur Prasad Mishra. Ph.D. thesis approved by the Sampoornand Sanskrit Visva Vidyalaya in 1978.

Mishra, Vibhuthi Ranjan. Different aspects of nature in the works of Kalidasa / by Visbhuthi Ranjan Mishra. Ph.D. thesis approved by the K.S. Darbhanga University in 1985.

Mukhopadhyay, Sudhamay. Studyof the poetry of Kalidasa and Shakespeare with special reference to their recognised master pieces : the Sakuntalam. Ph.D. thesis approved by the University of Calcutta in 1977.

Murali Krishna, Dendukuri. Impact of Kalidasa on classical Telugu literature. Andhra University 1978. (Telugu)

Nagar, B.R. Alamkaras based on the similarity in the works of Kalidasa / by B.R. Nagar. Ph.D. thesis in Hindi, approved by the Udaipur University in 1971.

Nagpal, Yashoda Devi. Nature in Valmiki and Kalidas : a comparative study. Ph.D. thesis approved by the Kurukshetra University.

Narang, Brahmavati. Kalidas ke nari patra. Meerut University in 1973.

(Women characters of Kalidasa) Ph.D. thesis in HIndi, approved by the Meerut University in 1973.

Narang, Manju. Critical study of the development of stories of the dramas of Kalidasa and Bhasa / by Manju Narang. Ph.D. thesis in Hindi, approved by the Garhwal University in 1980.

Nigam, Kiran, Kalidas kee kritiyon mein shabd shaktiyon samikshatmak adhyan.

Uniqueness and speciality of the language and alamkaras in the works of Kalidas: critical study / by Kiran Nigam. Ph.D. thesis approved by the Kanpur University in 1978.

Panda, Bala Dutt. Right conduct in the works of Kalidasa / by Bala Dutt Panda. Ph.D. thesis in Hindi, approved by the Kumaun University in 1984.

Pandey, Kamla. Critical study of the social and cultural traits depicted in the dramas of Kalidas / by Kamla Pandey. Ph.D. thesis in Hindi, approved by the Agra University in 1976.

Pandey, Shyam Raman. Kalidas kee natya vikshayak dharana.

(Dramatic practices of Kalidasa) by Shyam Roman Pandey. Ph.D. thesis in Hindi, approved by the Patna University in 1976.

Pandey, Sushila. Stagecraft in the dramas of Kalidasa / by Sushila Pandey. Ph.D. thesis in Hindi, approved by the Banaras Hindu University in 1987.

Pandya, Ramchandra Narayanji. Gujarati ma Kalidas. Baroda (Gujarati), 1960 - 65.

Pathak, H.S. Comparative study of Kalidasa and Bhavabhuti / by H.S. Pathak. Ph.D. thesis in Hindi, approved by the Ravishankar University in 1983.

Prechata, Kriyanand. Similes used by Mahakavi Kalidas / by Kriyanand Prechata. Ph.D. thesis approved by the K.S. Darbhanga University in 1976.

Puri, Prabha. Ashvaghosh aur Kalidasa ke kavyon ka tulanatmak adhyayan.

Comparative study of the works of Kalidasa and Aswaghosh. Ph.D. thesis in Hindi, approved by the Kurukshetra University in 1969.

Roopmala. Flora vanaspathi in the works of Kalidasa / by Roopmala. Ph.D. thesis in Hindi, approved by the Meerut University in 1982.

Santosh Kumari. Study of Prakrit languages used in Kalidasa's dramas / by Santosh Kumari. Ph.D. thesis in Hindi, approved by the Agra University in 1956.

Saroj, Ramakrishna. Classical study of the dramas of Kalidasa / by Saroj Ramakrishna. Ph.D. thesis in Hindi, approved by the Jabalpur University in 1979.

Saxena, Gayatri, Kalidas ke granthon par aadharit tatkaleen Bharatiya sanskriti. Agra, 1956.

Sharma, Chitra. Bhasa, Kalidas, Shudrak aur Ashwaghosh ke Sanskrit natakon mein samaj chitran. Rajasthan, 1963 - 67.

Sharma, Dimbeswar. An interpretative study of Kalidasa / by Dimbeswar Sharma. Ph.D. thesis approved by the University of Calcutta in 1963.

Sharma, Jagdish. Study of the vocabulary of Kalidasa's dramas / by Jagdish Sharma. Ph.D. thesis approved by the Ravishankar University in 1981.

Sharma, Krishna Kant. Critical study of spiritual and cultural aspects of the works of Kalidasa / by Krishna Kant Sharma. Ph.D. thesis in Hindi, approved by the Punjab University in 1984.

Sharma, Nityanand. Sabdaparipaka in Kalidas's poetry / by Nityanand Sharma. Ph.D. thesis in Sanskrit, approved by the University of Delhi in 1973.

Sharma, Radha Rani. Evaluation of the principles of polity in the works of Kalidas / by Radha Rani Sharma. Ph.D. thesis approved by the Lucknow University in 1973.

Sharma, Ram Dutt. Fauna in Kalidasa and post - Kalidasa works / by Ram Dutt Sharma. Ph.D. thesis in Hindi, approved by the Rajasthan University in 1969.

Sharma, Ram Nivas. Kalidas ke grantho ke Hindi anuvad Delhi 1974 - 79. Dept. of Hindi, University of Delhi, Delhi.

Sharma, Satyavati. Sanskrit sahitya men viseshkar Kalidas ki racanaon men prakriti ka sajiv citran.

Portrayal of nature in Sanskrit literature with special reference to the works of Kalidasa / by Satyavati Devi Sharma. Ph.D. thesis approved by the Agra University in 1964.

Sharma, Shanta. Philosophical background of Kalidasa / by Shanta Sharma. Ph.D. thesis approved by the Banaras HIndu University in 1961.

Sharma, Vijendra Kumar. Legends in the works of Kalidasa : a critical study / by Vijendra Kumar Sharma. Ph.D. thesis in Hindi, approved by the Meerut University in 1982.

Shastri, Chandra Bhanu. Philosophy in Kalidasa / by Chandra Bhanu Shastri. Ph.D. thesis approved by the Banaras Hindu University in 1965.

Shastri, Diwakar Misra. Proverb and maxims of Kalidasa / by Diwakar Misra Shastri. Ph.D. thesis in Hindi, approved by the K.S. Darbhanga University in 1984.

Shukla, Mahavir Prasad. Studyof the dramas of Kalidasa from the standpoint of Saundaryasntra / by Mahavir Prasad Shukla. Ph.D. thesis approved by the Kanpur University in 1984.

Shukla, Sarla. Comparative study of the life in the dramas of Bhasa and Kalidasa / by Sarala Shukla. Ph.D. thesis approved by the Jiwaji University in 1978.

Singh, Amaldhari. World of Kalidasa / by Amaldhri Singh. Ph.D. thesis approved by the Banaras Hindu University in 1966.

Singh, Prabhat. Evaluation of canons of Sanskrit dramaturgy in Sanskrit dramas with special reference to the dramas of Kalidasa and Bhavabhuti / by Prabhat Singh. Ph.D. thesis approved by the Punjab University in 1985.

Sud, Suman. Karuna rasa : from the view point of Valmiki, Bhasa, Asvaghosa, Kalidasa and Bhavabhuti / by Suman Sud. Ph.D. thesis in Hindi, approved by the Kurukshetra University in 1969.

Thakur, Krishna Kumar, Kalidas ki kritiyon mein varnit ashram yogavastha ka punar mulyankan. Evaluation of the concept of Asrama yogavastha as depicted in the works of Kalidasa / by Krishna Kumar Thakur. Ph.D. thesis Hindi, approved by the Ranchi University in 1979.

Tripathi, Kashinath, Kalidas ke kavyon ke alankar ka parisheelan. Study of the alamkaras in the works of Kalidasa / by Kashinath Tripathi. Ph.D. thesis approved by the Gorakhpur University in 1980.

Tripathi, Mukul Rani. Kalidasa sense of beauty / by Mukul Rani Tripathi. Ph.D. thesis in Hindi, approved by the Avadh University in 1984.

Tripathi, Sripathi. Dharmasastra materials in the works of Kalidasa / by Sripathi Tripathi. Ph.D. thesis in Hindi, approved by the K.S. Darbhanga University in 1986.

Trivedi, Bhavani Shankar. Geography in the works of Klaidasa / by Bhavani Shankar Trivedi. Ph.D. thesis in Hindi approved by the Meerut University in 1980.

Trivedi, Chandra Bhusan. Gleamings from the dramas of Bhasa and Kalidasa : critical and comparative study / by Chandra Bhusan Trivedi. Ph.D. thesis approved by the Bhagalpur University in 1981.

Upadhyaya, Arpana. An etymological study of synonyms of Raghuvamsa of Kalidasa / by Arpana Upadhyaya. Ph.D. thesis approved by the Rani Durgavati Viswavidayalaya in 1983.

Vachaspati. Kalidasa kavyesu dhvamisanam daryam. = Dhvani in the works of Kalidasa / by Vachaspathi. Ph.D. thesis approved by the University of Delhi in 1975.

Varma, Tara. Critical studyof dharma in the works of Kalidasa / by Tara Varma Ph.D. thesis in Hindi, approved by the Vikram University in 1967.

Veena Rani. Comparative study of the imagery in presenting the story by Bhasa and Kalidasa / by Veena Rani. Ph.D. thesis in Hindi, approved by the Gurukul Kangri University in 1983.

Vinod Kumari. Imagery of Kalidasa / by Vinod Kumari. Ph.D. thesis aproved by the University of Delhi in 1973.

Vyas, Rashmi Kant. Mahakavi evem Ashvaghosh kee kritiyon mein prakriti chitraka tulantmak adhyayan. Comparative study of the depiction of nature in the works of Kalidasa and Asvaghosa / by Rashmi Kant Vyas. Ph.D. thesis approved by the Vikram University in 1979.

Yadav, Babu Ram. A critical studyof the sources of Kalidasa / by Babu Ram Yadav. Ph.D. thesis approved by the Kurukshetra University in 1973.

14

Appendix

(I) Kalidasa Awards

In memory of this great Sanskrit dramatist, Madhya Pradesh Government has instituted a number of awards. There are :

(i) **Kalidasa Samman :** An award of Rs. 100,000 is given to an eminent theatre personality every year. Kavalam Narayana Panikkar, noted theatre artist of Kerala received the accolade for the year 1995.

(ii) **Kalidasa Samman for Classical Music :** Also instituted by the Govt. of Madhya Pradesh in the field of Classical Music. Award of Rs. 100,000 for the period 1994 - 95 went to late Ustad Alla Rakkha Khan, table wizard who died in early 2000.

(iii) **Rashtriya Kalidas Award** : Awarded by the Madhya Pradesh Government, this prestigious prize is given to an artist. The cash prize worth Rs. 100,000.

(iv) **Kalidasa Award for Classical Dance :** Also started by the Madhya Pradesh Government. The cash prize of Rs. 100,000 is given to noted classical dancers. Sitara Devi, Kathak exponent won the award for the year 1995 - 96.

(II) Mahakavi Kalidas Janma - Bhumi Smarak Samiti

The Samati was founded in 1973 at Village Kaviltha of district Chamoli in Uttar - Pradesh. This place is said to be the birth place of great ancient poet and playwright Kalidasa. The organisation is aided by the Government of Uttar

Pradesh. The latter has built a suitable memorial at the village. The Samiti is engaged in propagation development of Sanskrit and Hindi language and literature. The Samiti has its own Library and Theatre. It conducts seminars, lectures etc. Annually it organises Kalidasa Samaroh and invites drama groups and conducts folk dances, exhibitions and poets meet.

(III) Kalidasa Jayanti Celebrations (1958)

Kalidasa Jayanti Celebrations held at Ujjain - The city with which the Poet's name is closely associated in literature and legend - were sponsored by the Kalidasa Samaroha Samiti and organised by the Madhya Pradesh Kala Parishad. The Sangeet Natak Akademi, New Delhi nominated Dr. V. Raghavan on its behalf to serve on the Samiti set up by the Madhya Pradesh. Government and gave financial assistance to the Kalidas Samaroha. Besides symposium. All - India Kalidas Art Exhibition (20 November 1958), the weeklong celebrations were marked by performances given by various troupes in the Natya Samaroha. This Samaroha proved to be a veritable feat of tributes paid to the poet in the form of dance, drama and music. Apart from dance - dramas from his epic poetry, the festival comprised of rendering in original Sanskrit (including Prakrit in the case of Shakuntala) of all the three dramas, viz., Abhijñanaśākuntalam, Malavikagnimitra and Vikramorvashiyam. These dramas were performed by the Sanskrit College, Calcutta, the Madras Natya Sangh, Madras, and the artists combined of Gwalior, respectively. Since then, the festival is celebrated with great enthusiasm by the art connoisseurs

(IV) A postage stamp was issued by the Govt. of India as reminiscence of Kalidasa, the master dramatist while honouring Raja Ravi Varma, the great painter.

■■■